GEMS OF BUDDHISM

GEMS OF BUDDHISM

Edited by

Prof Bhikshu Satyapala

MD PUBLICATIONS PVT LTD
NEW DELHI
www.mdppl.com

Published by :

MD Publications Pvt Ltd
'MD House', 11, Darya Ganj
New Delhi - 110 002
Phone : +91-11-41563325 (Customer Service)
+91-11-41562846 (Editorial)
E-mail (orders): contact@mdppl.com
Website: www.mdppl.com

ISBN : 978-81-7533-181-5

Published and Printed by Mrs. Rajni Gupta on behalf of **MD Publications Pvt Ltd** at Times Press, New Delhi.

CONTENTS

PREFACE

I am pleased to place before you the book titled "**Gems of Buddhism**". This book is the brain child of our junior colleagues, who have come forward with an idea to re-print the old research papers of the great scholars of the past who have contributed in our Departmental journal named "*Buddhist Studies*" which has been publishing since 1974. The Department has decided to publish the research papers of the former faculty members of the Department and other contributors' research papers which have been published in our journal. It has been unanimously decided to publish those articles in the shape of a book titled "*Gems of Buddhism*". Since the research articles are in huge number, we have decided to publish it in 4-5 volumes. The present book is first in this series and hope that the scholars and academicians will appreciate it and will be of great help and may be taken in good spirit. This book consists of the research papers from first five volumes of our Departmental journal.

The present book titled "*Gems of Buddhism*" has come across a state which was dark, imaginary, uncertain and doubtful. Now it has reached its culmination which is full of light, which is a reality, where there is no doubt and no uncertainty about its existence. The main idea behind bringing out this book was firstly, to make an exposition of the research works done by the scholars of this Department to the elite world; secondly, to widen one's understanding of the *Dhamma* by developing the interdisciplinary approach; thirdly, to have a better and deep understanding of oneself and others around himself; finally for paving the way for the realization of the universal and the ultimate reality i.e. enlightenment.

Researches of different nature are being conducted at different levels specifically in the field of Buddhist Studies to unearth the hidden properties of life, to scale the immense possibilities of life and to derive the maximum benefits, of the properties within one's own life and those around him. Towards this, book will make a considerable contribution by way of revealing a number of hidden treasures, lost facts and figures of the golden and glorified history of Buddhism and that of India as well, abstruse aspects of Buddhist Philosophy, micro-analysis of life made in Buddhist Psychology, the changing problems of life and the society and the contemporary issues and their solution from the Buddhist point of view. This book contains several rich and research oriented articles focusing light on some of the very important aspects of Buddhism. Hence, we cherish the hope that the readers will find this book more useful and more helpful to measure the depth and purity of each other's knowledge leading towards the gain of supreme and complete wisdom and highest bliss of salvation.

In this endeavor, I would like to thank all my senior and junior colleagues who have supported me and given the idea to publish it. I would like to express my deep gratitude to my colleagues like Prof. K. T. S. Sarao, Dr. H. P. Gangnegi, Dr. Subhra Barua Pavagadhi, Dr. R. K. Rana and Dr. I. N. Singh in general and Dr. S. M. Haldhar, Dr. L. K. Jha, Dr. Rana Purushottam Kumar Singh, Dr. Chandrashekhar Paswan, Dr. Krishna Murari and other junior colleagues in particular. Since, the work of editing, formatting, typing and finally publishing a book always needs a spirited team work which was readily provided by young ad-hoc colleague Dr. Arvind Kumar Singh. I also express my heartiest thanks to Mr. Saurabh Jha, Dilip Kumar Thakur and Ms. Shilpa for their painstaking job of typing, formatting and giving shape to this work. I would also like to thanks Mr. Balendra Singh and Mr. Radhey Shyam. I would also like to express my thanks to our staff Mr. Anmol Kumar Jha. At last but not the least, I would also like to express my deep gratitude and thanks to Mr. Pranav Gupta, Director, MD Publication, Delhi for readily accepting our idea and giving his consent to publish this invaluable treasure of Buddhism in the form of a book. Without his consent it could have been not possible for us to get it published.

It is my extreme pleasure to bring out this book which will surely present the different aspects of Buddhist learning to the fraternity of those who are in the pursuits of Buddhist Studies. I, along with my team, have tried my best to make it free from any blemishes, but if there is any, I take this responsibility. The next volume of this book will be published shortly.

Prof Bhikshu Satyapala
H.O.D. & Editor

Department of Buddhist Studies,
University of Delhi
Delhi-110007

Date 12.01.2009
Full Moon Day, Kartika

GLORIOUS HISTORY OF THE DEPARTMENT

Arvind Kumar Singh

The sixth century before Christ witnessed the appearance of a number of great men in India, the most colossal among them being the Buddha and Mahāvīra. Buddhism had its advent as a reformatory religion against the gradually deteriorating spirit of Brāhmaṇism. Its keynote was the alleviation of all worldly miseries by mental exercises which included infinite love and compassion towards all beings, irrespective of castes, creed and socio-economic status. The Four Noble Truths including the Doctrine of Dependent Origination are its greatest contributions to the world of philosophy. The ethico-humanitarian aspect of the religion appealed to the minds of ordinary people, whereas its philosophy of the impermanence of all constituted objects and the analysis of the visible world being devoid of ultimate reality fascinated the intelligentsia. This wide outlook, combined with the proselytizing zeal of the royal and ecclesiastical missionaries, soon won over the hearts of people, not only of India but of the whole length and breadth of Asia. The propagation was further encouraged by the liberal permission given by the Buddha to everybody to learn his teachings in one's own language.

By this act, not only the diffusion of Buddha's teachings was made easier, it enriched interchange of scholars with the neighboring countries like Ceylon, Burma, Siam, etc. on the one hand and China, Tibet, Japan, Korea, etc. on the other. The aim of all these cultural exchanges was the same, i.e. the dissemination of Buddhist knowledge. The foreign pilgrims who visited India, went back to their respective countries not only after acquiring religious merit by visiting sacred places, but with heavy loads of sacred texts, which they translated and explained in their own languages. Not only expositions and commentaries were written, but independent treatises on different aspects of the religion and philosophy were also composed in various languages such as Ceylonese, Burmese, Siamese, Tibetan, Chinese, Korean, Mongolian, Tokharian, Japanese, etc., in addition to the original Pāli and Prākrit ones – thus enriching the Buddhist literature of the world into vast volumes which has come down to the posterity as an invaluable legacy. This literature inspired artists who produced exquisite pieces of painting and sculpture depicting different aspects of the life and thought of the Buddha; which are the superb specimens of their kind not only of their own period, but of the ages to come. With the gradual development of the religion with its consequent growth in the pantheon, numerous images of gods and goddesses were also produced. Art and literature supplemented each other. While some texts which became very popular and gained importance, were gradually deified and the divine ideas were translated into forms which were reproduced in various materials like wood, stone, metal, canvas and so on. Buddhist iconography and sculpture gave rise to the production of scientific texts on them. Numerous *Stūpas*, temples and monasteries were constructed on land and mountains with the bounteous gifts of devotees.

At one time the whole of Asia was studded with Buddhist monuments, many of whom like the rock-cut caves of India and the colossal images at Bamiyāna in Afghanistan, have withstood the ravages of time and even the dilapidated ruins of some others attract awe and admiration of the whole world even today. The monumental discoveries of the last century have brought to light the remains of a once-thriving centre of Buddhism, buried under the sandy desert of Central Asia. Buddhism became 'very popular and practically became the life force of Asia, though it had to shed some of its pristine elements and assimilate some new traits of the native soil of the country it took roots in order to adapt itself into the lands of adoption. Even today many of those countries are branded as 'Buddhist countries.'

While in the countries outside India, Buddhism was practiced and Buddhist literature cultivated in full force, unfortunately in its homeland, it became dormant for a number of centuries, almost losing its separate entity in the vast ocean of Brāhmaṇic Hinduism. Buddhist gods and goddesses particularly the later ones remained incognito in the society of *Brāhmaṇic* gods, while the Buddha himself was incorporated into the lineage of the *Brāhmaṇic Avatāras*, Buddhist monuments like *stūpas*, temples and monasteries lay hidden under the earth, sheltered in jungles or were converted into other institutions. Earlier Buddhist texts disappeared from the country, while the later ones passed as popular folk literature belonging to minor religious cults.

This situation was continuing, when the religion not only got an escape from gradual annihilation, but was also revived to a new lease of life, with the attention of foreign scholars drawn towards it. Some chance discoveries of monuments and references to texts inspired a number of pioneers to further investigations, which unveiled before them mines of Buddhist literature and stupendous Buddhist monuments. Thus, from about the middle of the last century, there was a revival of studies and researches in everything Buddhist. Trailing the path shown by foreign scholars, there emerged a number of Indian scholars whose knowledge in Buddhist History, Philosophy, Literature, Art and Architecture, etc. spread their fame far and wide. A number of Indian Universities realized the importance of its studies and initiated the study and researches on all aspects of Buddhism in the relevant Departments. Unearthed by the archaeologists' spades, numerous Buddhist monuments started to see the light of the day after a long slumber. In fact, a major portion of the ancient monuments of India, which attract thousands of tourists and scholars, are Buddhist.

Though for want of reliable materials, the exact date of the birth or death of the Buddha is not easy to be ascertained, the consensus of opinion of scholars of different countries is, that the date of his *Mahāparinirvāṇa* i.e. the Great Demise, falls in the year 544 B.C., and it is generally recognized that the full moon day of *Vesākha*, i.e. April-May, is the thrice auspicious day being the day of his birth enlightenment and demise. Accordingly the year 1956 was considered as the 2500th year of his demise, but the whole of the Buddhist world decided to celebrate the 2500th Buddha Jayanti in that year. India, being the birthplace of Buddhism and now an independent country, did not lag behind and decided to celebrate it at a grand scale. The Government of India took keen interest as its topmost functionaries like the then President Dr. Rajendra Prasad, Vice-President Dr. Radhakrishan, the Prime Minister Mr. Jawaharlal Nehru, took personal interest in the celebrations. A celebrations committee was formed with Dr. Radhakrishnan as the chairman and the Prime Minister and other top-ranking officials as its members. An elaborate plan was prepared, which included International Exhibition of Buddhist Art; Symposium on the contribution of Buddhism to Indian literature, philosophy, art, world peace; visit of foreign delegates; performance of Tagore's play '*Natir puja*' (based on Buddhist theme); construction of a commemorative monument in Delhi (the Buddha Jayanti Park); publication of *Devanāgari* version of *Pāli Tipiṭaka* (from the Nalanda Pāli Research Institute), *Mahāyāna* Sanskrit Texts in *Devanagari* (from Mithila Institute of Post-graduate Studies and Research in Sanskrit Learning, Darbhanga); An Album of Ajanta Murals in colour; publication of a volume entitled '*2500 Years of Buddhism*'; on the edicts of Aśoka with a map showing places where Aśokan edicts are found; production of a documentary film on Buddhism; repair of Bodhgaya temple and establishing a site museum there; issuing of special postage stamps; construction of the Lumbini Naugarh Road and so on. Incidentally it may be mentioned that a number of Oriental Journals like the Indian Historical Quarterly, the Journal of the Bihar Research Society, etc. brought out special volumes of their journals containing papers from eminent scholars.

In addition to the above-mentioned activities, the Buddha Jayanti Celebrations Committee of the Government of India also decided to establish a chair for Buddhist Studies. The decision to establish the chair at the University of Delhi was publicly announced by the then President, Dr. Rajendra Prasad on the 24th May, 1956 at a public meeting in Ramlila Grounds, Delhi. Dr. G. S. Mahajani, the then Vice-Chancellor of the University in consultation with a committee consisting of Dr. P. L. Vaidya, Bhikkhu J. Kasyap, Dr. Babu Ram Saxena and Dr. Nalinaksha Dutt, all eminent scholars of Buddhism to hold the chair, Dr. Bisheshwar Prasad, Dr. N. N. Choudhuri and Dr. N. V. Banerjee, the then Heads of the Departments of History, Sanskrit and Philosophy respectively also assisted the Vice-Chancellor in the task.

At the outset, post of one Professor, two Research Fellows, one Stenographer and one office attendant were sanctioned. A reasonable amount of money was provided for the purchase of books for the library. The research activities started in collaboration with the existing Department of Philosophy, History and Sanskrit. Professor Bapat submitted, in due course, a comprehensive scheme for further expansion of the Department with full consideration of all round development of Buddhist studies. He initiated a proposal for expansion of Buddhist Learning. The U.G.C. approved the scheme and made a provision one Reader; three Lecturers, two part-time Lecturers and one Research assistant. Thus the Department emerged as a Research Center of Buddhist Learning. Apart from sanctioning the appointment of two Research Fellows, a stenographer and a peon, the U.G.C. also sanctioned a grant of Rs.1.08 Lakhs (recurring) and Rs.15,400/- (non-recurring) for the second five year plan period for the expenses and for the purchase of books, etc. Prof. Bapat joined in February, 1957 and the formal inauguration of the Buddhist Studies was held on the 21st October, 1957.

The year 1962 is a landmark in the history of the Department of Buddhist Studies when it became a full-fledged and independent Department maintaining its unique research oriented character. The same year the Department introduced a two-year M. Litt. Research oriented course. Dr. Bapat submitted a scheme for the further expansion of the Department, which had its preamble as under: "Considering the closer relations that India is having with the neighboring countries in Asia – Central, South-east and Far East – it would be desirable that the University of Delhi makes some arrangements of teaching courses, which would stimulate the public interest in these neighboring countries – their languages, art, history, philosophy and religion. The University has already planned a scheme of its organization and development which has enabled the Department to achieve in a substantial measure this aim of knowing our neighbors better. Buddhism is the prominent religion of most of these countries and therefore the Department of Buddhist Studies should be gradually expanded so as to include, in all its aspects, not only the study of Buddhism from different sources such as Pāli, Sanskrit, Tibetan, Chinese, Japanese, etc., but also allied subjects like the history of these neighboring Buddhist countries, the history of their philosophy, art and religion. It will enable us also to evaluate what changes have taken place in those fields from their original aspects as they were known to India."

The scheme included proposals for the institution of M.A. in Pāli and M.A. in Buddhist Studies (consolidated). The University Grants Commission sanctioned a post of Reader in Sanskrit and Pāli and those of three lecturers, respectively in Sanskrit and Pāli, Buddhist Studies (History, Epigraphy, etc.) and Buddhist Philosophy as also that of a Research Assistant. These posts were filled with the incoming of Miss Indumati Dike as Research Assistant (in 1958), Mr. Yagya Narayan Singh (now Dr. Sanghasen) and Miss Sudha Sengupta as Lecturers in Sanskrit and Pali and Buddhist Studies respectively (February 1959) Dr. V. V. Gokhale as Reader in Sanskrit and Pali (April 1959) and Dr. R. C. Pandeya as Lecturer in Buddhist Philosophy (September, 1959). A senior Research Fellowship for a period of two years from January 1958 to 1960 was granted to Dr. S. Dutt, a retired teacher of Ramjas College University of Delhi, to work on 'Buddhist Monks and Monasteries' (subsequently the work appeared in a book form). A part-time teacher in Chinese Mrs. Hwang (in early 1960) and later a part-time teacher in Tibetan were also appointed. One of the two part-time Lecturers of Tibetan was Mr. Tashi Ragbias, prior to the appointment of Mr. G. G. Gyatso.

A collection of books on Buddhist Studies towards the subsequent development of an independent Departmental library had already set in. Some books were obtained by Dr. Bapat from the personal assets of Mahapandita Rahul Sankrityayan. Dr. Rajendra Prasad, the then President of India, presented a set of Tibetan books including the Tibetan Tripitaka.

With this, an infra-structure for a full-fledged independent Department of Buddhist Studies had already come into existence, but not only till the retirement of Dr. Bapat in July, 1960, but also for two more years, Buddhist Studies worked as a unit of the Department of Philosophy. The teachers appointed under the unit were supposed to take classes in the Department of History, Philosophy (where they actually did) and Sanskrit. Dr. V. V. Gokhale took over as the Professor and incharge of the Buddhist Studies unit and the post of Reader in Pali and Sanskrit was filled by Dr. B. Jinananda (in September, 1960), Dr. Gokhale received the proposal of the institution of an M.A. course in Buddhist Studies. The proposal was accepted as such by the University, but the U.G.C. modified it to that for an M. Litt. (Research Degree) course, with a view to retaining and strengthening the research-oriented character of the unit.

The Buddhist Studies unit was allowed to function as an independent Department from July 1962 and the M. Litt. Course in Buddhist Studies came into operation. Of course, the Ph.D. programme of the Department has not only been going on right from the inception of the unit, but was also making desired progress.

In 1964 the Department was permitted to convert the post of a part-time lecturer in Chinese language and literature into a full-time one. Dr. Tan Chung was the incumbent on that Post. Later in 1966 the University instituted a separate Department of Chinese Studies. Consequently the Chinese Studies unit of the Department alongwith the teacher concerned was transferred to that Department.

In 1965 the Department along with the Department of Philosophy played host to the 39th Annual Session of the All India Philosophical Congress. Incidentally by the same time, Dr. Yash Pal started taking some classes in the Department.

Dr. Gokhale retired in July 1966 and Dr. B. Jinananda officiated as the Head of the Department. A move for organizing an All India Seminar on '*Buddhism through the Ages*' was made to the U.G.C. The U.G.C. accepted the proposal providing necessary fund for the purpose. Dr. R. C. Pandeya, who on account of the post of a lecturer in Buddhist Philosophy having been upgraded, had become a Reader earlier in the same year – managed to take over as the Professor and Head of the Department in October, 1966. The above-mentioned Seminar was organized by the Department in the meantime and more than 30 scholars from various Universities of India participated.

Mr. G. G. Gyatso joined the Department as a part-time Lecturer in Tibetan in January, 1967 and became whole-time Lecturer in February 1968. Miss Latika Lahiri joined the Department as a part-time Lecturer in Chinese in July, 1967 and became a whole-time Lecturer in April, 1968. The post of Research Assistant, which was held earlier by Mr. Someshwar Prasad and later on by Dr. Raghunath Pandey, was subsequently abolished.

A two-year diploma course in Pāli was started from July, 1968. In October, 1968 the Department along with the Department of Philosophy and Sanskrit played host to the Thirteenth Annual Session of the Akhil Bharatiya Darshan Pariṣad. The Department organized the second All India Seminar in November, 1968. About 40 scholars from various Indian Universities participated. The theme of the Seminar was 'Influence of Buddhism on Indian Thought'.

The post of a Reader in Buddhist Philosophy was filled up by the incoming of Dr. Kewal Krishan Mittal in July, 1969. The earlier practice of holding a series of lectures and discussions on specific research topics was replaced by the practice of weekly seminar in which papers presented by research scholars and teachers were/are discussed.

As its contribution towards the celebration of the Gandhi Centenary year, the Department organized the third All India Seminar on the theme of '*Ahiṁsā* and *Prākrita* Studies.' About 50 eminent scholars from as many universities and institutions participated. The local Jain community took a keen interest in the Seminar.

With the joining of L. Jamspal (March, 1973) as a Lecturer in Tibetan language and literature, the Department had come to acquire the capacity to start the Diploma course in Tibetan language and literature. Consequently a proposal to that effect was made. In October, 1973, Dr. R. C. Pandeya went over to the Department of Philosophy and Dr. B. Jinananda started officiating as the Head of the Department.

In due course of time, the Department made considerable development and rapid progress keeping in view the central mission with which it had begun. It came a long way since its inception in 1957. Beginning as a very small Department with only two (2) rooms, a small library and an enrolment of two (2) research fellows, it has now grown into a big Department of with an enrolment of more than 500 students to various courses.

In order to train scholars in Pāli and Theravada Learning, a certificate and Diploma Course in Pāli Language and Literature of the duration of one year each were introduced in the year 1967 and 1968. Likewise Certificate and Diploma Course in Tibetan Language and Literature of one year each were introduced in 1968 and 1969.

In course of planning all round development of the Department and accelerating research activities it was unanimously felt that preparation of sound base in the subject by utilizing the materials preserved in original source was the most essential. With this idea in view, the proposal in instituting M.A. course in Buddhist Studies was moved in the Committees of the university in 1975. Two Research Fellowships were offered to Mr. Jivach Chandra Roy and Mr. N. H. Samtani in the month of July, 1975.

In 1981, Dr. Bhikshu Satyapala has joined the Department in the capacity of Lecturer. He is specialized in Pāli Language and Literature along with Abhidhamma Philosophy. He was awarded doctoral degree from the Delhi University. In the same year, Dr. H. P. Gangnegi also joined as Lecturer in Department who is specialized in Tibetan Language and Literature and Tibetan Buddhism. He was also awarded doctoral degree from the Delhi University. Dr. R. K. Rana has joined the Department in 1990 as an Ad-hoc Lecturer. He was also awarded Doctoral degree from the Department. In 1996, he was finally appointed full time Lecturer. He is an expert of Chinese Language and Literature and Chinese Buddhism.

In 1993, the post of the Reader was fulfilled by the appointment of Prof. K. T. S. Sarao as Reader who has before joining the Department served the Kirori Mal College as Lecturer of History from 1981 to 1993 and later in 1996 he was appointed Professor in the Department. Prof. Sarao has got two Ph.D. Degrees, one from the Delhi University and another from Cambridge University, UK. He is credited to have more than a dozen of books on Buddhism and published more than 50 research papers in refereed journals and peer reviewed journals of India and abroad. He is associated with many International Universities in all over the world and participated in many seminars and conferences at National and International repute. In 1996 Dr. I. N. Singh joined the Department in the capacity of Lecturer who has also served as Research Associate in the Department earlier. Since than no permanent post has been filled up by the University but in the year 2006 Prof. K.T.S. Sarao got three Ad-hoc Lecturers post sanctioned from the University which has been duly filled and next year he again got three Guest Faculty posts other than the Ad-hoc Lecturers. In 1993, Dr. Subhra Barua Pavagadhi has joined the Department as Lecturer and she is specializes in Pāli Language and Literature. She has also completed her Ph. D. from the Delhi University. At present, Department has six permanent faculty members out of which Prof. Sarao and Prof. Satyapala are in the rank of Professors and Dr. H. P. Gangnegi, Dr. Subhra Barua Pavagadhi and Dr. R. K. Rana are working as Readers and Dr. I. N. Singh as Senior Lecturer.

Most important development that has taken place in the Department was in 2006 when Prof. K.T.S. Sarao and other faculty members of the Department have been able to get the approval of the University to introduce a new syllabus for the M. A. Course in Buddhist Studies which consists of 43 Papers with Six specializations. In the same year by his efforts, he has been able to get three ad-hoc lecturers post in the Department and gain got another three Guest lecturers post for the Department during the academic session 2006-2007. Again in the same year with the efforts of Prof. Sarao, the Department has been awarded with the ASIHSS programme of the UGC for a period of five years i.e. 1st April, 2006 to 31st March, 2011.

At the initial stage, the work – mainly research – was started in collaboration with the existing Departments of History, Sanskrit and Philosophy. A paper on the Rise and Decline of Buddhism in the M.A. History course, a paper on readings from Buddhist literature in the M.A. Sanskrit course and a paper on the Buddhist Philosophical texts in the M.A. Philosophy course were introduced. Out of them only the first and the last could become effective. The

Department of Buddhist Studies was not an independent one at the time of its inception. It was assigned to the Department of Philosophy, though the Professor of Buddhist Studies was the de facto incharge of the studies.

The Department has been able to develop a good library of the subject containing the Pāli *Tipiṭaka* in Nāgari, Roman, Sinhalese, Burmese and Cambodian scripts, complete set of Zylograph of Tibetan *Tipiṭaka*, the Taisho edition of Chinese *Tripiṭaka*, Peking edition of Chinese *Tripiṭaka* and the standard books of research value of History, Philosophy, Art, Architecture, Religious tradition and languages. The Library of the Department was preserved in the main central Library of the University.

The Department has made a significant stride towards its further development in the year 1988-1989 when the U.G.C. grants the Department, the status of D.S.A. Under the scheme the provision of one Professorship, one photocopier, one part-time Office Assistant, etc. was made available to the Department. The Department was fortunate to fill up the post of Readership and utilized the fund granted for Photocopier etc. One significant development in this context was the establishment of one **Departmental Library** afresh located in room F-30 of Tutorial Building. At present it was situated at Room No. 304 of the Extension Building of the Faculty of Arts because Department has shifted to the above said building of the University. Late Prof. Dr. D. S. Kothari was kind enough to inaugurate and blessed the library. It is a matter of satisfaction that the fund for library was well utilized and our library is well equipped and is being utilized accordingly. The Department has another library which consists of the books donated to the Department by the relatives of our late Prof. Mahesh Tiwary which is named after his and his wife's name i.e. Lalmani-Mahesh Tiwary Library. The provision made by the U.G.C. under the DSA Programme for a separate Building for Buddhist Studies could not take off due to some unavoidable reasons which are not known to us. The U.G.C. has again extended the DSA status to the Department and it has granted an adequate financial assistant to our Department.

The Department has the tradition of organizing seminars on different fields of Buddhism from the very inception of the Department. We have organized many national and international seminars. Our scholars have also participated in many national and international seminars in India and abroad.

The Journal of the Department named '***Buddhist Studies***' was published by the Department for the first time in 1974 and an attempt has been made to bring it out every year. Thirty Four volumes of the journal have been brought out so far till 2006. The teachers and research students (including the ex-student) and renowned scholars from outside the Department have also contributed to the journal of the Department. Due to financial crisis the publication of the journal stopped for a few years. The Department was fortunate to be assigned DSA status under SAP Programme from 01-04-2004 to 31-03-2009 by the UGC. Under this programme, the Department has once again started to publish its Departmental journal which had been halted due to unavailability of funds. During this phase the Department has published Journals (Volume Numbers XXII-XXXV) except Volume XXX of the journal which was published with the help of U.G.C. grant under ASIHSS programme in 2006 which was awarded to the Department for five years i.e. from 1st April, 2006 to 31st March, 2011. Here it is imperative to mention that next two volumes of the Departmental journals are about to publish which are Volume XXXVI and XXXVII. In the meantime, the Department has decided to publish the invaluable research papers of our faculty members and other Buddhist luminaries in the form of book named "Gems of Buddhism" in three or four volumes and this one is the first outing in this line. This book has papers reprinted from first five volumes of the journal. Other volumes of the book will be published in a very short period of time. Hope this book will be appreciated by the academicians who are indulging in researches in Buddhism. This will definitely prove to be landmark in the field of Buddhist Studies.

This is the brief history of the Department which I am able to extract from the little sources available to us at present.

1

RELATION BETWEEN REASON AND AUTHORITY

B. Jinananda

Authority

The word, 'authority' is used in ordinary language to mean something akin to coerciveness or force. Commonly it implies a short of power to enforce obedience, that means that it is something which is different from freedom. But the sense varies according to the sphere in which the authoritative power is exercised, which is a process of winning obedience. In the intellectual sphere like those of religion and philosophy, it takes the form of authoritative opinion; the view of a man who has the expert knowledge, which few others have at command. Thus it takes the form of testimony '*śabda*' as to the matters of fact of which he is or has been the only witness. However, the outcome to authority or authoritative opinion is to win assent or constrain belief; without these elements authority would cease to be an authority.

Reason

The term 'reason' in most generalized sense can be defined as rational element in human intelligence as distinguished from sensual or emotional element. Etymologically it is rooted in the term 'ratio' and has sometimes the meaning of relation. However, it is said that it is the faculty specially bestowed upon human beings and it generally implies argumentative power as against instinctive or impulsive behaviour. So it does imply freedom against obedience to a particular idea or law.

There has thus been a familiar antithesis of authority and reason with which the field of philosophy and literature are so well acquainted. In drawing out the contrast between authority and reason, some thinkers hold that authority is that which produces its results through psychic processes, i.e. other than reasoning, since it demands a sort of obedience and implies force or coerciveness. And reasoning means argument and therefore freedom of thinking and acting. But this contrast is only apparent and verbal. Even in the processes of obedience or coercion, reason is at all events implicit. The extremist would hold that no authority would favour reason nor would reason allow authority. But a moderate or rather a reasonable view is that authority does not fear argument, when it insists on its legitimate influence on coercing men. The claim of all authority must submit to criticism and argument, or in other words implicitly contain freedom. Therefore, one cannot uphold that authority should be grouped in non-relational causes. "The sanction of any authority may be vindicated to the satisfaction of reason."[1]

With these preliminary remarks, we can now proceed with our subject of authority and reason in the *Pāli Tipiṭaka*. There is no sufficient scope to deal with such an extensive subject as the *Pāli Tipiṭaka*, within such a short paper. We, therefore, propose to touch the subject only by connecting it with some important topics dealt in within the *Pāli* Canon.

The authority and reason in the *Pāli* sources may be taken only at different stages in the process of thought, not as contradictory elements in them. Nor it is possible and reasonable to hold that in the *Tipiṭaka* either there is only authority or there is only reason. Both these processes are seen to be working simultaneously. When the Buddha started the propagation of his *dhamma* (doctrine), he started with reason only, he revolted against the prevalent system of thought, though in between he accepted some of the current pieces of thinking too, but that too he did out of reason only and not out of authority or supremacy of the predominant views. He refused the supremacy of contemporary religious authority because that did not appeal to his reason. But, then, for the later followers of the Buddha his teaching became the authority in the sense of testimony, only because that had reasonable, not dogmatic, faith in the Buddha's doctrine. Not only this, the Buddha himself had said to his disciples. "After my death my teachings will be your guide", that is an example of authority, that the Buddha had left behind. He had straightforwardly announced that his disciples are not supposed to follows him blindly, whatever they do, they must justify it with the touchstone of reasoning.

Sutta-piṭaka

We find a measured application of Authority and Reason in the *Sutta Piṭaka*. It is, of course, impossible to separate one *Piṭaka* or a portion of the *Dhamma* from the other. All the three *Piṭakas* are complimentary or rather interdependent. There is no doubt that all the main teachings of the Buddha, such as the Four Noble Truths (*Cattāri Ariya-saccāni*), the Eightfold Noble Path (*Ariya Aṭṭhaṅgika Magga*), the Dependent Origination (*Paṭiccasamuppāda*), etc. are the same in all the sources.

It is of course, true that they are presented in the *Dhamma-saṅgaṇī* with slight variations, as they are known the *Sutta-bhājani* and the *Abhidhamma-bhājanī*.

Whatever differences between the socalled *Hīnayāna* and *Mahāyāna*; or Southern and Northern, or even the *Pāli* and Sanskrit Buddhism, there cannot be a cogent reason to doubt the sincerity of purpose. The Buddha is venerated and followed as the Great Teacher and Spiritual Master by all Buddhists. Buddha is not a personal name. His personal name is Gautama after his lineage. Buddha means an Enlightened One. To a Buddhist the Buddha is nothing but a guide who shows him the way of Deliverance. He is neither God not an incarnation of God. The Buddha had never asked his followers to accept his views without critical enquiry. Either prayers to him or performing rituals before him were never encouraged. The Buddha always tried to impress upon his disciples that emotional devotion to him will not help one in developing one's character and may even be an obstacle in the path of salvation (Mukti).

Just before attaining the *Mahāparinibbāna* the Buddha said, "If a monk or nun, a man devotee or a woman devotee, lives in accordance with the teaching – it is he who rightly honours, reverences, venerates, holds sacred and reveres the Perfect One (*Tathāgata*) with worthiest homage". In this context a story may be mentioned in which it is stated that a monk named Vakkali,[2] out of devotion and love for the Buddha constantly used to stare at his body. To him the Buddha said, "What shall you gain by seeing this impure body of mine? Who sees the *Dhamma* sees me." In course of his search for truth it is supposed that the Buddha studied all systems of Indian Philosophy extant during his time. In the *Brahamajāla-sutta* sixty two views are dıscussed. On the basis of his previous experience the Buddha promulgated his own philosophy. Buddha's constant warning to his disciples was, not to follow him blindly. In this connection the *Kālāma-sutta* of the *Aṅguttara-nikāya* may be quoted:

"Once a group of persons named *Kālāmas* called on the Buddha to get their doubts dispelled. The Buddha said, "It is proper for you, *Kālāmas*, to doubt, to be uncertain; uncertainty has risen in you about a thing that is doubtful. Do not believe in, *Kālāmas*, what you have heard; do not believe in traditions because they have been handed down for many generations; do not believe in anything merely because the written statement of some old sages are produced; do not believe in conjectures; do not believe in that as truth to which you have become attached by habit; do not believe merely on the authority of your teachers and elders; after observations and analysis when it agrees with reason and is conducive to the good and gain of one and all, then accept it and live up to it."

But if Buddhism is considered to be based purely on reason devoid of faith it will be just to cut at the very root of the Buddha's teachings. It is not possible to proceed towards the Salvation without certain amount of faith in the Teachings. In this connection, we may again quote the same *Aṅguttara-nikāya* (4 No. 34) in which it is said that nobler the object of reverence or devotion, the highest is the blessing bestowed by it. "Those who have joyous confidence in the highest, the highest fruit will be theirs." The highest objects of faith or confidence to a Buddhist are, of course, Three Jewels: the Buddha, the *Dhamma* and the *Saṅgha*.

Confidence in all its aspects is required for resolving any stagnation and other shortcomings resulting from one-sided development of intellectual faculties (*Paññā* or reason) which often tend to turn around in circles endlessly without being able to break-through. Here, confidence or faith along with reason may be able to give quick help.

Vinaya-piṭaka

Unlike the other two *Piṭakas*, the *Vinaya Piṭaka* apparently presents itself as a case for Authority. In the *Vinaya* actually the Code of Conduct for *bhikkhu* and *bhikkhuni* are compiled.

They are told by the Buddha every now and then what they should or should not do. The rules were compulsory for the members of the *Saṅgha* and the *Saṅgha* accepted this obligation with open eyes, as they were, the Buddha said in the *Sutta vibhaṅga*, for the following tenfold benefit of the *Saṅgha*–

They were, "for the excellence of the Order, for the comfort of the Order, for the restraint of evil-minded men, for the ease of well-behaved monks, for the restraint of cankers belonging to other worlds, for the benefit of believers, for the increase in the number of believers, for establishing the *Dhamma* indeed (i.e. *Saddhamma*) and for following the rules of restraint."

When the Buddha was on his last bed just before his attainment of the *Mahāparinibbāna*, on being asked as to who would be the guide to lead the *Saṅgha*, "In future the *Dhamma* and the Law (*Vinaya*) will be your guide (*Satthā*)."[3]

This pronouncement of Buddha, of course, had not been for happy consequences. In the absence of a generally accepted supreme spiritual head the result was that immediately after his demise, dissensions arose over the interpretation of controversial points in the doctrine or individual cases of *Vinaya* rules. The result was that again and again there appeared new schools and sects.

The *Saṅgha* accepted this state of affairs without reservation, 'for the right of self-determination of the individual and of the local congregation represented by the monastic Chapter, have always seemed to it outweigh these disadvantages.' How far-reaching this right of self-determination is can be seen from the fact that it not only was, and is open to the laymen, under certain conditions, to enter at anytime into the circle of devotees of the Exalted One, and leave it again, the monk also was always free to leave the Order, and often it happened that people repeatedly during the lives became monks and returned to the world again.[4]

The question is now, where the lay scope of reason for the *bhikkhus* themselves, since they followed the Blessed One thoroughly, or if they did not follow his instructions they were accused of an offence followed by a punishment according to the *Vinaya* Code. Of course, it is true that there did not lie much scope for reason. But no judiciary can apply open reason in that sense. Reason can be applied only in forming the laws as it has been done in the case of *Sutta* and the *Abhidhamma*. When they are implemented or applied they work only as authority to action in the self-same manner, the *Vinaya* is a sort of judiciary for *bhikkhu* and *bhikkhuni*, yet it is based on the *Dhamma* or reason. Hence the authority is only secondary.

Abhidhamma piṭaka

The Buddha suggested "*Ehi Passa*" (come and see) as the motto for the doctrine promulgated by him. If, like a scientist he had not demonstrable truth to offer, he could not have this as the motto of his doctrine. But what was it? In the *Abhidhamma pitaka* he has given a complete chart or manual exhibiting the whole mechanism of mind and its operation. The level of consciousness (citta) and the plains of experience have been defined and graded.

The '*Hetus*', meaning the springs of actions or motives have been classified and grouped as: *Kusala, Akusala* and *Abyākata*, meaning wholesome, unwholesome and undefined for all moral, immoral and indeterminate. A system of relations (*Paccayas*) has been developed in the book. *Paṭṭhāna* and its (various) Commentaries. This is intended to guide the learner in understanding the different relations in which mind and body, or body and mind; mind and mental states, mental states and mental states stand. It enables him to understand how a certain mental state counteracts or strengthens other mental states, where one succeeds another or where one precedes another; where one is present and the other is absent; and how the mental complexes are coloured by the understanding motives. Having the chart or manual before him he can ascertain the level of consciousness on which he stands, the plain of experience and the result of introspections and psychological analysis are laid on the table for testing and verification. There is no hide and seek policy, no trade secret, or no '*Ācariya-muṭṭhi*'. In *Abhidhamma* is laid a sound psychological foundation of ethics and morality, nay of their entire religious life. The *Abhidhamma* standpoint of Buddhist philosophy is pre-eminently pscho-ethical. Thus we find that this part of the Buddhist philosophy is based more on reason than faith, i.e. Authority.

Endnotes

1. *Encyclopaedia of Religion and Ethics*, Vol. 2, pp. 1-8.
2. *Vakkalisutta : Saṃyutta-nikāya*, III.119 ff.
3. *Dīgha-nikāya*, II, 154 - *Yo kho Ānanda, mayā Dhammo ca Vinayo ca desito paññatto so mamaccayena satthā.*
4. Horner – *Book of Discipline*, I. p. 38.

2

THE PRATĪTYASAMUTPĀDA-HṚDAYA-KĀRIKĀ-VYĀKHYĀNA OF NĀGĀRJUNA

Reconstruction and Translation into English from the Tibetan

L. Jamspal and Peter Della Santina

Introduction

All Buddhist schools have denied the existence of the self as the identical, permanent and immutable substance which experiences the results of former actions. They have also universally rejected the notion of a Supreme God. They have, however, accepted the relative reality of pre-existence and subsequent rebirth, as well as the efficacy of *Karma*. Those who adhere to the doctrine of an identical, permanent and immutable self have opposed this view, because, as the contend, denial of an identical, permanent and immutable self controverts the efficacy of *Karma*, as well as the doctrine of rebirth. The Buddhist schools have replied to this objection with the doctrine of dependent origination. One might also add that belief in the efficacy of Karma is hardly rendered more tenable by positing the existence of a permanent and immutable self, for how can such an entity be any the better or worse for good and evil actions performed?

The doctrine of dependent origination has been expounded at length by the Buddha in numerous Sūtras, most notably the *Śālistambasūtra*, to which commentaries were composed by Buddhist masters, such as Nāgārjuna and Kamalaśīla. As the *Mādhyamika* system is founded upon interpretation of dependent origination, this doctrine has been central to its inception and development. Ācārya Nāgārjuna, the foremost exponent of the *Mādhyamika*, has written voluminously on dependent origination. Among his works are counted the *Āryaśālistambakārikā Nāma Mahāyānasūtraṭikā* and the *Dvādaśāṅgaparikṣā Nāma Ṣaḍvimśatiprakaraṇa* of the *Mūlamādhyamikakārikā*, as well as *Pratītyasamutpāda-Hṛdaya-kārikā* and commentary which is the subject of this present article. The text, although not extant in Sanskrit.[1] It is available in Tibetan translation. At present the text includes seven *Kārikās*; however, the penultimate and final *Kārikās* are certainly later additions, for the former is also found in the *Yuktiṣaṣṭikā* of Nāgārjuna and the latter in the *Abhisamayālaṅkāra* of Ārya Maitreyanātha. That these two *Kārikās* are subsequent accretions is further indicated by the fact that the commentary to the work composed by the author considers only the first five *Kārikās*.

The doctrine of dependent origination has, from the very first been of paramount for votaries of Buddhism. In the *Śālistambasūtra* the Lord has said, "The monk who sees dependent origination, sees the *Dharma*; he who sees the *Dharma*, sees the origination, sees the Buddha". While all the schools of Buddhism have, without exception, accepted the doctrine of dependent origination, it has been interpreted characteristically by the various schools. The *Mahāyāna* Buddhists adhere to the doctrine of dependent origination as expounded by Ācārya Nāgārjuna and Ārya Asaṅga, the foremost exponents of the *Mādhyamika* and *Yogācāra* schools respectively. According to the *Mādhyamika* interpretation, the two extremes of eternalism, on the one hand, and nihilism or the denial of continuity, on the other, are successfully avoided through the doctrine of dependent origination. Although the investigation of this topic lies outside the scope of this article, it may also be noted that the *Mādhyamika* interpretation of dependent origination differs characteristically from those of the pre-*Mādhyamika* schools of Buddhism, the *Vaibhāṣika* and the *Sautrāntika*. While the latter affirm the ultimate existence of the discrete constituents of dependent origination, the *Mādhyamika* declared their very dependence to constitute their voidness. Thus the doctrine of dependent origination is at the very heart of the conception of *Śūnyatā*.

Ordinary people have circled, without rest, in the three realms of desire, form and the formless (realm) from the beginningless time through the efficiency of dependent origination. However, through understanding dependent origination correctly, liberation is achieved as T.R.V. Murti aptly remarks, "The knowledge of necessity is freedom".

The constituents of dependent origination are twelve in number. Ignorance, the first of the twelve is lack of knowledge which obscures the real. He whose understanding is obscured by ignorance performs actions of three kinds conducive to rebirth; that is, virtuous, non-virtuous and meditative,[2] which constitute mental formations resulting in subsequent consciousness. Consciousness in the mother's womb in turn, gives rise to name and form; that is, the five aggregates (form, perception, feeling, impulse, consciousness) and the six sense-organs. The conjunction of consciousness and the sense-organs with their objects produces contact. From contact feelings of three varieties (pleasant, unpleasant and indifferent) are produced. Craving which arises from feeling in turn produces grasping at objects of pleasure and aversion to unpleasant ones. Moreover, when craving is present four varieties of grasping ensue; that is, grasping at sensual desires, dogma, mere moral observances and at the doctrine of substance or self. Grasping engenders becoming which implies the five aggregates. The term 'becoming' is employed, because actions performed through body, voice and mind result in rebirth. The subsequent aggregates having arisen through becoming, birth occurs. Old age, which is the maturing of the aggregates, and death, which is their destruction, inexorably follow birth. Attendant upon old age and death are grief, lamentation and sorrow, but through understanding dependent origination one is freed from *Saṃsāra*, and the city of bliss is attained.

The Heart of Dependent Origination of Ācārya Nāgārjuna

Obeisance to Mañjuśrī, the Youthfully Transformed.

(1) The twelve discrete constituents of dependent origination which were taught by the Sage are wholly included in three: afflictions, deeds and sufferings.

(2) The first, eighth and ninth are afflictions, the second and tenth are deeds, while the remaining seven are sufferings. Thus the twelve elements are included in three.

(3) From the three two originate, from the two originate seven, and from these seven, in turn, originate the three; thus the wheel of existence revolves again and again.

(4) The whole world is cause and effect, excluding this, there is no Sentient Being. From elements (which are) only empty, empty elements originate.

(5) Through the examples of oral instruction, a lamp, a mirror, a seal, a sun-crystal, a seed, sourness, and sound, the wise should understand the non-transmigration, as well as the re-emergence of the aggregates.

(6) The unwise who conceive even very subtle entities nihilistically, fail to see an object which originates from conditions.

(7) Hence, there is nothing denied or affirmed. See reality rightly, (for) one who sees reality is released (from bondage).

The Heart of Dependent Origination of

Ācārya Nāgārjuna is herein complete.

The Commentary to the Heart of Dependent Origination by Ācārya Nāgārjuna

Obeisance to Mañjuśrī, the Youthfully Transformed.[3]

The disciple possessed of renunciation, desirous of hearing, attentive, retentive, appreciative and able to dispel thought construction having drawn near to the Master, asks thus about the doctrine of the *Tathāgata*. In what are "*The twelve discrete constituents of dependent origination which were taught by the Blessed Sage*" included, for I beg to see and study (them). The Master having understood him to ask about the essence of those (twelve) elements, thus spoke these lucid words from the verse, "(*These twelve*) *are wholly included in three: afflictions, deeds and sufferings*". Thus twelve is ten plus two. Constituents alone are discrete as the constituents of a chariot have been shown to be, therefore, discrete constituents. "The *Sage*" because mighty[4] of body, voice and mind, (while) *"Taught by the Sage"* is synonymous with demonstrated and elucidated. The twelve constituents do not originate from causes (like) god, nature, necessity, spirit, nor through dependence on others, time, intrinsic character[5], chance[6], circumstances, nor free will, etc. they are dependently originated. As the roof beams of a house depend one upon another, these twelve discrete constituents *"Are wholly included in three: afflictions, deeds and sufferings". "Wholly"* means all without remainder.

Question: Which are afflictions, which deeds, and which sufferings? How and in what are these constituents of dependent origination included?

Answer: *"The first, eighth and ninth are afflictions"*. Of the twelve constituents, the first is ignorance, the eighth craving and the ninth grasping. Know these three to be afflictions. If it is asked which are deeds, (then) *"The second and tenth are deeds"*. The second is mental formations and the tenth becoming. Know these two elements to be included in deeds. *"The remaining seven are also sufferings"*. (Five) constituents are included in afflictions and deeds. Know the seven which remain to be included in sufferings. Thus, consciousness, name and form, the six sense-organs, contact, feeling, birth and old age and death. The word *"also"* (serves) to include (sufferings which are not among the seven constituents), i.e. the sufferings of separation from the beloved, meeting with the despised and of frustrated desires. Thus *"The twelve elements are included in three"*. Therefore, know these twelve elements are afflictions, deeds and sufferings. The Tibetan particle 'ni' Sanskrit 'tu', which occurs in the text after the word 'chos', rendered as *"elements"*, and the phrase 'gsum-du-dus', given as (*"are included in three"*), thus indicates (that there) remains part of a sentence (which is wanting); that is, the constituents demonstrated in the *sūtra* are herein complete. Thus it has been determined that there are none apart from these.

Question: Just so, but please demonstrate what these afflictions, deeds and sufferings originate from?

Answer: *"From the three two originate". "From the three"* which are afflictions (ignorance, craving and grasping) *"two"* which are deeds (mental formations and becoming) *"originate"*. *"From the two"* (which are deeds) *"originate seven"*. Thus (those seven) sufferings demonstrated above (i.e., consciousness, name and form, the six sense-organs, contact, feeling, birth, and old age and death). *"From the seven, in turn, originate the three"* which are afflictions. Thus again from the three (which are) afflictions originate two (which are) afflictions originate two (which are) deeds: *"Thus the wheel of existence revolves again and again"*. (In the world of) becoming there are three (realms): (that of) desire, form and the formless (realm). Ordinary people have become like a wheel which revolves without rest. The (Tibetan) particle 'ni'

(Sanskrit 'tu' which occurs between the phrase 'khor-lo-de-nid', rendered as *"the wheel of existence"*, and the phrase "yan-dan-yan-du-khor", given as *revolves again and again*") thus indicates a sense of uncertainity. That is, while a wheel revolves successively (each point following upon the preceding one), in the three realms it (does) not happen thus. (Therefore) uncertainity is indicated.

Question: Who is called the Sentient Being[7], the Supreme Lord of all individuals? How is his creation?

Answer: *"The whole world is cause and effect"*, excluding false imputation, *"There is no Sentient Being"*. That which is falsely imputed does not exist when analysed, so it is not fitting that what is just falsely imputed[8] should exist substantially.

Question: If so, then who transmigrates from this world to the next?

Answer: From this to the next world not so much as an atom transmigrates, however, *"From elements (which are) only empty, empty elements originate"*. Entities are devoid of self and selfhood[9], thus afflictions and deeds have become the causes. From these five (i.e. ignorance, craving, grasping, mental formations and becoming) (which are) empty originate sufferings devoid of self and selfhood. The seven empty elements (i.e., consciousness, name and form, the six sense-organs, contact, feeling, birth, and old age and death) are imputed to be effect. Such is the purport. Thus what is devoid of self and selfhood is neither self nor selfhood. However, from elements devoid of self originate elements in (their) own-being devoid of self. Thus understand it, as it has been demonstrated.

Question: From elements in their own-being devoid of self originate only elements in their own-being devoid of self. What are examples of this?

Answer: *"Through"* examining the Example of *"oral instruction, a lamp, a mirror, a seal, a sun-crystal, a seed, sourness and sound"* also know (what is in its) own-being devoid of self, as well as the subsequent existence. For instance, if there were transference of the instructions from the Master's mouth to the disciple, then the Master (would) become devoid of the instructions. Therefore, there is no transference. Nor are the instructions of the disciple from any other (source) because, if so, they would be without cause. As with the instructions from the Master's mouth, so in a like manner at the point of death the mind does not transmigrate to the subsequent existence, because this would result in the error of eternalism. Nor does the subsequent existence originate from any other (source), for this would result in the error of nihilism. As the Master's instructions are the cause of those of the disciple, (yet whether) those (of the disciple) be identical with those (of the Master) or different, is inexpressible. So in a like manner, (whether) the mind at the point of death and the mind which belongs to (the subsequent) birth be identical or different is inexpressible. Similarly, from a flame an oil lamp (is kindled), from a form an image is produced in a mirror, from a seal an impression, from a sun-crystal fire, from a seed a sprout, from the juice of a sour fruit saliva is *engendered,* or yet again from a sound an echo is produced. Thus *"The wise should understand the non-transmigration, as well as the re-emergence of the aggregates".* There are aggregates of form, feeling, perception, impulse and consciousness. Their re-emergence means that from an extinguished cause another effect (immediately) originates, (but) from this world to the next not so much as an atom transmigrates. Therefore the wheel of becoming is produced through the propensity for erroneous conceptualization. The particle *"as well"* indicates opposition. (That is), the opposite of the re-emergence of aggregates should (also) be understood. One who understands entities as impermanent, full of suffering, empty and 'insubstantial, will not be deluded in regard to entities. Free from delusion, attachment will not originate, free from attachment, malevolence will not originate; free from malevolence, actions will not be performed; free from actions, grasping at entities, becoming will not be engendered; free from becoming, rebirth will not occur; and free from rebirth, suffering of the body and mind will not originate. Thus the erroneous views, the extremes of eternalism and nihilism, etc., are dispelled. (In this regard) there are two verses. *The "unwise who conceive even very subtle entities nihilistically, fail to see an object which originates from conditions. Hence there is nothing denied or affirmed. See reality rightly, (for) one who sees reality is released (from bondage)."*

The commentary to the Heart of Dependent Origination, composed by Ācārya Nāgārjuna, is herein complete. Translated and corrected by the Indian Masters Jinamitra, Dānaśila, Śīlendra Bodhi and (Tibetan translators Vande Ye-ses-sde (Jñānasena), etc.

Endnotes

1. That is, with the exception of half of the fourth *kārikā,* which is found in Prajñākaramati's commentary to the *Bodhicaryāvavatāra,* and the fifth *Kārikā* which is preserved in Candrakīrti's commentary to the *Mūlamādhyamikakārikā* where it is attributed by the author to Ācārya Nāgārjuna.
2. Actions of this kind result in rebirth in the realms of form and the formless (realm).
3. In accordance with the tradition adhered to by the Tibetan translators, the object of invocation, i.e. Mañjuśrī, indicates that the text in question belongs to the *Abhidharmapiṭaka.* Had the invocation mentioned either "All Buddhas and *Bodhisattvas*" or "The Ominiscient One", it would have indicated that the text belonged to the *Sūtrapiṭaka* or *Vinayapiṭaka* respectively.
4. Tibetan: sku-dan-gsun-dan-thugs-thub-pas-na-thubpa'o, Sanskrit: *Kāyavāṅmanomaunānmuniḥ.* The Sanskrit terms '*mauna*' and '*muniḥ*' have been consistently rendered in Tibetan as 'thub-pas-na' "because mighty", and 'thub-pa' "mighty one". The Sanskrit terms do not ordinarily indicate such a meaning and are usually defined as "silence", "sage" or "one who has taken a vow of

silence". We have chosen to follow the interpretation of the Tibetan translators and have found support for our choice in *Prajñākaramati's* commentary to the *Bodhicaryāvatāra* where the terms, '*mauna*' and '*muni*' are defined in two ways thus: *sarvakalpanāvirahāt samāropapavadantadvaya-maunād asaikṣyanvāṅmanaḥkar-malakṣanamauntrayayogādvā munirbuddho bhagavān.*

5. Tibetan: no-bo-nid, Sanskrit: *svabhāva*, is here distinguished from Tibetan: ran-bzin, Sanskrit: *prakṛti*. Although the term, '*ran-bzin*' can also be rendered as '*svabhāva*', we have chosen the present arrangement on the hypothesis that 'ran-bzin' is a reference to the '*prakṛti*' of *Sāṅkhya* school, while 'no-bo-nid' may possibly correspond to the doctrine of *svabhāvavāda* adhered to by one school of the *Cārvākas*.
6. Tibetan: '*dod-rgyal*', Sanskrit: *yadṛcchā*. The etymology of the Tibetan term, '*dod-rgyal*', literally 'power to wish' seems to favour an interpretation along the lines of will or volition. However, the Sanskrit term, '*yadṛccha*', is most commonly used in the sense of accident, spontaneity or chance. We have chosen to translate '*dod-rgyal*' as chance, principally in view of the fact that the term (Tibetan) '*gyi-na*', (Sanskrit) '*svecchā*', which is clearly employed in the sense of free will as in *Bodhicaryāvatāra* VI, 24 occurs later in the list of erroneous causes. Hence, the translation of '*dod-rgyal*' (*yadṛcchā*) as "will" would result in redundancy.
7. Tibetan: *sems-can*, Sanskrit: *sattva*, literally menas 'one endowed with consciousness' is used here in the sense of 'self' or "supreme self".
8. Brtags-pa 'analysed' is given in the Tibetan text. However, we have made the amendation to *btags-pa*, "imputed", on the grounds of context and sense.
9. Tibetan: *bdag-gi-ba*, Sanskrit: *ātmīya*, is the genitive case of 'self' in Tibetan. Thus it might be rendered as 'mine' or 'is pertaining to a self'. In translating it as 'selfhood', we have followed the usage of Kenneth K. Inada in his translation of the *Mūlamādhyamikakārikā*.

Glossary of English Terms with Tibetan and Sanskrit Equivalents

English	**Tibetan**	**Sanskrit**
affirmed	bzag-par-bya-ba	prakṣiptavya
affliction	non-mons	kleśa
aggregate	phun-po	skandha
becoming	srid-po	bhava
birth	skye-ba	jāti
cause	rgyu	kāraṇa, hetu
conceive	rnam-brtags-pa	*vikalpa*
condition	rkyen	pratyaya
consciousness	rnom-par-ses-pa	vijñāna
constituent	yan-lag	aṅga
contact	reg-pa	sparśa

craving	sred-pa	tṛṣṇā
deed	las	karma
denied	bsal-bya	apaneya
desire	'dod-pa	kāma
discrete	bye-brag	bheda
dispelled	bsal-ba	nivāraṇa
effect	'bras-bu	phala, *kārya*
empty	ston-pa	śūnya
eternalism	rtag-pa	śāśvata
feeling	tshor-ba	vedanā
form	gzugs	rūpa
formless	gzugs-med	ārūpya
grasping	len-pa	upādāna
ignorance	ma-rig-pa	avidyā
imputed	yan-dag-par-btags-pa	samāropita
dependent origination	rten-'byun	pratītyasamutpāda
lamp	mar-me	dīpa
mirror	me-lon	darpaṇa
mental formation	'du-byed	saṃskāra
(the) mind at the point of death	'ehi-gar-sems	maraṇāntikacitta citta
(the) mind which belongs to (subsequent) birth	skye-bar-gtogs-pai-sems	aupapatyaṃsikacitta
name and form	min-dan-gzugs	nāmarūpa
nihilism	chad-pa	uccheda
object	don	artha
old age and death	rga-si	jarā-maraṇa
oral instruction	kha-ton	svādhyāya
own-being	ran-bzin	*svabhāva*
reality	yan-dag	bhūtataḥ
re-emergence	nin-mtshams sbyor-ba	pratisandhi
sage	thub-pa	muni
seal	rgya	mudrā
seed	sa-bon	bīja

self and selfhood	bdag-dan-bdag-gi	ātmāmīya
sentient being	sems-can	sattva
six sense-organs	skye-mched-drug	ṣaḍāyatana
sour fruit	skyur-poi-bras	āmla phala
subsequent existence, next world	'Jig-rten-pha-rol	para loka
subtle	phra-ba	sūkṣma
suffering	sdug-bsnai	duḥkha
sun-crystal	me-sel	arkakānta
Supreme Lord	dban-phyug	īśvara
this world	jig-rten-'di	aihika loka
unwise	rnam-par-mi-mkh-as	avica*kṣana*
wheel of existence	srid-pai-khor-lo	bhavacakrakam
world	'gro	jagat

प्रतीत्यसमुत्पादहृदयकारिका*

नमो मञ्जुश्रिये कुमारभूताय

ये द्वादशाङ्गभेदाः मुनिनोदिताः ते प्रतीत्योत्पन्नाः ।
क्लेशकर्मदुःखेषु च कृत्स्नतया त्रिषु संगृहीताः ॥1॥
नवाद्याष्टमाः क्लेशाः, द्वितीयो दशमश्च स्तः कर्माणि ।
शेषाश्च सप्त दुःखं, त्रिष्वाप्ताः द्वादश धर्मास्तु ॥2॥
त्रिभ्यौ द्वौ सम्भवतः, द्वाभ्यां प्रभवन्ति सप्त, सप्तभ्यः ।
त्रयश्च, भवचक्रकं हि तत्तु परिभ्रमति पुनः पुनः ॥3॥
सर्वजगद्धेतुफले, अतो नास्ति सत्त्वः कश्चनापरः ।
शून्येभ्य एव धर्माः शून्याः, प्रभवन्ति धर्मेभ्यः ॥4॥
स्वाध्यायदीपमुद्रादर्पणघोषार्ककान्तबीजाम्लैः ।
स्कन्धप्रतिसन्धि संक्रमश्च विद्वद्भिरुपधार्यौ ॥5॥
सुसूक्ष्मेष्वपि भावेषु येषामुच्छेदकल्पना ।
तदविचक्षणैरर्थो नेक्ष्यते प्रत्ययोद्भवः ॥6॥
नापनेयमतः किञ्चित् प्रक्षेप्तव्यं न किञ्चन ।
द्रष्टव्यं भूततो भूतं भूतदर्शी विमुच्यते ॥7॥
॥ आचार्यनागार्जुनेन विरचिता प्रतीत्यसमुत्पादहृदयकारिका समाप्ता ॥

* These *Kārikās* and the Commentary are reconstructed from the Tibetan translation.

प्रतीत्यसमुत्पादहृदयव्याख्यानम्

नमो मञ्जुश्रिये कुमारभूताय

अत्र श्रामण्य-शुश्रूषा-श्रवण-धारण-अवगमन-कल्पनाऽपोहानां शक्तिमान् कश्चिदेकः शिष्यः आचार्यस्य अन्तिके समागत्य तथागतशासनमारभ्येत्थं पृच्छति स्म। अत्र भगवता

ये द्वादशाङ्गभेदाः मुनिनोदिताः ते प्रतीत्योत्पन्नाः ।

केषु संगृहीताः? तान् द्रष्टुं श्रोतुञ्चेच्छामि। स तेषां धर्माणां तत्त्वं पृच्छतीति वेदित्वा आचार्यः पुत्र,

क्लेशकर्मदुःखेषु च कृत्स्नतया त्रिषु संगृहीताः ॥1॥

इत्यंशगतपद्येनाह। तत्र द्वौ च दश चेति द्वादश। अङ्गान्येव भेदा इत्यङ्गभेदाः। रथस्याङ्गवदङ्गभूताः प्रदर्शिताः। कायवाङ्मनोमौनान्मुनिः। तेन मुनिना उदिताः प्रदर्शिताः व्याख्याता इति पर्यायान्तर्गतम्। ते च (द्वादशाङ्गभेदाः) प्रकृति-नियम-पुरुष-अपराधोनत्व-ईश्वर-काल-स्वभाव-यदृच्छा-स्थानभाग स्वेच्छादिभ्यो हेतु-भ्यो नोत्पद्यन्ते। अमी तु प्रतीत्यसमुत्पन्नाः। एते च द्वादशाङ्गभेदाः क्लेशकर्मदुःखेषु चान्योन्ये समाश्रित्य नडकलापन्यायेन त्रिष्वेव कृत्स्नतया संगृहीताः भवन्ति। कृत्स्नतया अशेषतयेत्यर्थः।

प्रश्नः। कतमे क्लेशाः? कतमानि कर्माणि? कतमानि च दुःखानि? ते च प्रतीत्यसमुत्पादभेदाः केषु कथं संगृह्यन्ते? उत्तरम्।

नवाद्याष्टमाः क्लेशाः

द्वादशानामाद्योऽविद्या, अष्टमः तृष्णा, नवमश्च उपादानमिति अमी त्रयः क्लेशेषु वेदितव्याः।

कतमानि तानि कर्माणि?

द्वितीयो दशमश्च स्तः कर्माणि ।

द्वितीयः संस्कारः। दशमश्च भवोऽमू द्वौ घर्मौ कर्मसु संगृहीतौ वेदितब्यौ ।

शेषाश्च सप्त दुःखं, त्रिर्ष्वाप्ताः द्वादश धर्मास्तु ॥2॥

क्लेशे कर्माणि च संगृहीतानां (भेदानां) ये च शेषाः सप्त भेदाः, ते दुःखे संगृहीताः वेदितव्या।। तद्यथा विज्ञान-नामरूप-षडायतन-स्पर्श-वेदना-जाति-जरामरणानि। चशब्दः समुच्चयार्थः। प्रियवियोग-अप्रियसंयोग-इच्छन्नप्यलाभानां दुःखानि समुच्चीयन्ते। अत एवेमे द्वादशाङ्गधर्माः क्लेशकर्मदुःखेषु वेदितव्याः। तुशब्दः वाक्यशेषार्थः। सूत्रे प्रदर्शितधर्माः एतेष्वेव परिसमाप्ताः। अतोऽन्यः कोऽपि न वर्त्तत इति व्यवच्छेदः।

प्रश्नः। तेऽवगताः। क्लेशकर्मदुःखेषु कतमेभ्यः (धर्मेभ्यः) कतमे (धर्माः) उत्पद्यन्त इति प्रदर्शयेत्। उत्तरम् ।

त्रिभ्यो द्वौ सम्भवतः

(अविद्यातृष्णोपादानेभ्यः) त्रिभ्यः क्लेशेभ्यः (संस्कारो भवश्च; कर्म नाम द्वौ (धर्मौ) प्रभवतः।

द्वाभ्यां प्रभवन्ति सप्त

उपरि च निर्दिष्टानि (विज्ञाननामरूपषडायतनवेदनास्पर्शजातिजरामरणानि) दुःखानि।

सप्तभ्यः।

त्रयश्च

विज्ञाननामरूपषडायतनवेदनास्पर्शजातिजरामरणेभ्योऽविद्यातृष्णोपादानानीति क्लेशाः प्रभवन्ति। पुनश्च तेभ्यस्त्रिभ्यः क्लेशेभ्यो द्वे कर्मणी प्रभवतः।

भवचक्रकं हि तत्तु परिभ्रमति पुनः पुनः ॥3॥

भवस्त्रयम्, कामरूपारूप्याणि। एतेषु न तिष्ठतः संसारचक्रभूतस्यास्य पृथग्जनस्य जगत् सर्वथा स्वात्मना भ्रमति। तुशब्दोऽनियमितताया: प्रद्योतकार्थ। यथा चक्रं क्रमशः भ्रमति तथैव (पृथग्जनरूपी जगत्) भवेषु न वर्त्तत इत्यनियमितताया: प्रद्योतकः।

प्रश्न। तर्हि सर्वेषां कायानामीश्वर इतिह सत्त्वः कतमः? कतमा चास्य सृष्टिः? उत्तरम्।

सर्वजगद्धेतुफले

समारोपविनिर्मुक्तं

अतो नास्ति सत्त्वः कश्चनापरः।

अयन्तु समारोपति एव। परीक्षितत्वन्यायेन न भवति। यत् प्रज्ञप्तिसत् न च तद् द्रव्यसत्त्ववेन भवितुमर्हति।

प्रश्नः। यदि एवं, तर्हि अस्मात् लोकात् परलोके कः (पुद्गलो) गच्छति? उत्तरम्। अस्मात् (लोकात्) परलोकेऽणुमात्रोऽपि न संक्रामति। अपि तु

शून्येभ्य एव शून्याः धर्मा प्रभवन्ति धर्मेभ्यः ॥4॥

आत्मात्मीयतारहितधर्मक्लेशकर्माख्येभ्यो हेतुभूतेभ्यः शून्येभ्य एव पञ्चधर्मेभ्यः आत्मात्मीयतारहितदुःखानीति फलारोपिताः सप्त शून्याः धर्माः प्रभवन्तीत्यर्थः। तद्यथा आत्मात्मीयतारहिता एते अन्योन्ये नात्मा न चात्मीयता, परन्तु स्वभावेनात्मना रहितेभ्यो धर्मेभ्यः स्वभावेनात्मना रहिता एव धर्माः प्रभवन्ति। एवमेव अवगन्तव्यमिति प्रदर्श्यते।

प्रश्नः। स्वभावेनात्मना रहितेभ्यो धर्मेभ्यः स्वभावेनात्मना रहिताः धर्माः प्रभवन्तीत्यत्र के दृष्टान्ताः? उत्तरम्।

स्वाध्यायदीपमुद्रादर्पणघोषर्ककान्तबीजाम्लैः ।

एतेषां दृष्टान्तानां परीक्षयाऽपि स्वभावेनात्मनोऽभावः परलोकश्च वेदितव्यौ। तद्यथा गुरुमुखात् शिष्यमुखे आख्यानानि न संक्रामन्ति गुरोराख्यानाभाव-प्रसंगात्। शिष्यस्याख्यानमपि नान्यस्मात् सम्भवति हेतोरभावप्रसंगात्। गुरुमुखाख्यानवद् मारणान्तिकचित्तमपि परलाके न गच्छति, शाश्वतदोषप्रसंगात्। परलोकेऽपि नान्यस्मात् प्रभवति, अहेतुकदोषप्रसंगात्। यथा गुर्वाख्यानहेतोः प्रभावितः शिष्यः तदेव, ततो भिन्नश्चेति अभिधातुं न शक्यते तथेव मारणान्तिकचित्ते समाश्रितमौपपत्यशिकचित्तमपि तदेव, ततो भिन्नञ्चेत्यभिधातुं न शक्यते। एवमेव वह्नेः प्रदीपः। रूपाद्दर्पणे प्रतिबिम्बः। मुद्रायाः प्रतिमुद्रा। अर्ककान्तादग्निः। बीजादङ्कुर। अम्लफलपिण्डाद् लालायते। घोषात् प्रतिध्वनिश्च प्रादुर्भवति। एते च तदेव, ततो भिन्नश्चेति न सुबोधाः। तथेव

स्कन्धप्रतिसन्धिरसंक्रमश्च विद्वद्भिरुपधार्यौ ॥5॥

तत्र स्कन्धः इति रूपवेदनासंज्ञासंस्कारविज्ञानस्कन्धाः। तेषां प्रतिसन्धिरितिनिरुध्य तस्मादेव हेतोरपरस्य फलस्योत्पत्तिः। अस्मात् लोकात् परलोके अणुमात्रमपि वस्तु न संक्रामति। तथापि संसारचक्रं विभ्रान्तविकल्पवासनया उत्पद्यते। चशब्दो विपरीतः। भावानामनित्यतादुःखताशून्यताऽनात्मतानामधिगतौ भावेषु न मुह्यते। अमोहे न रज्यते। अरागे न द्विष्यते। अद्वेषे न कर्म संस्क्रियते। अकर्मणि भावो नोपादीयते। अनुपादाने भवो न अभिसंस्क्रियते। अभवे न जायते। अजातौ कायिकं मानसिकं च दुःखं न प्रभवति। एवमेवात्रैषां पञ्चानां हेतूनामनुपचयितत्वे परत्र फलं न भविष्यति। इदमेव मोक्ष इत्यभिधीयते। ततश्च शाश्वतोच्छेदानीनां कुदृष्टीनां निवारणं भवति। अत्र द्वे कारिके

सुसूक्ष्मेष्वपि भावेषु येषामुच्छेदकल्पना ।
तदविचद्वाणैरर्थो नेक्ष्यते प्रत्ययोद्भवः ॥6॥
नापनेयमतः किञ्चित् प्रक्षेप्तव्यं न किञ्चन ।
द्रष्टव्यं भूततो भूतं भूतदर्शी विमुच्यते ॥7॥

॥ आचार्यनागार्जुनेन विरचित प्रतीत्यसमुत्पादहृदयव्याख्यानं समाप्तम् ॥

आर्यदेशीयोपाध्यायजिनमित्रेण, दानशीलेन, शीलेन्द्रबोधिना
(भोटदेशीयेन) वन्दे ये-शेस्-स्दे (ज्ञानसेन) आदिभिश्च
(भोटभाषया) अनूद्य सम्पादितम्।

3

BUDDHIST AND NYĀYA METHODS OF VYĀPTIGRAHA

S. R. Bhatt

Anumāna is a process of the knowledge of an object (*artha*) on the basis of the cognition of its mark (*liṅga* or *hetu*). This knowledge is made possible through the relation of *vyāpti*. For any *anumāna* the necessary condition is some kind of *vyāpti*, a specific type of relation between *liṅga* and *sādhya* (*artha*). The systems of Buddhist and *Nyāya* logic agree with respect to the definition of *anumāna* and its minimum necessary condition in the form of *vyāpti*. But they differ with regard to the nature of *vyāpti* and accordingly also in the mode of apprehending it (*vyāptigraha*).

The Buddhist conception of *vyāpti* represents an invariable and necessary relation based on some a priori principles.[1] According to Buddhism no relation is ever cognized through the senses (*na sambandha indriyena gṛhyate, Pramāṇa Samuccaya* II. 28) and therefore its basic can never be found in experience. In this respect be traced to some a priori source, and *vyāpti* also is no exception to this. Not only are all relations a priori in origin, the idea of necessity also is never supplied to us empirically. All experiences are contingent and conditional and can never yield the knowledge of necessity. Thus all relations and for that matter all necessary relations have an a priori basis.

According to Buddhist logic *vyāpti* is the relation of the necessary absence of one when the other is not present (*avinābhāva* or *nāntarīyakatva*). There is therefore in every necessary relation a dependent part and another upon which it depends. Now there seem to be two and only two ways in which one fact can be dependent upon another fact. First, it can be a dependence which obtains between cause and effect. We can, for instance, connect smoke always with fire. If any one questions the correctness of this necessary relation it can be pointed out that no effect can come into being without its cause. Secondly, it can be a dependence which obtains a genus and its species or between a whole and its parts. From the fact of an object being a *siṁśupa*, for instance, we can legitimately infer that is a tree. Here the predicate (i.e. tree) is obtained by analyzing the subject (i.e. *siṁśupa*) and the conclusion, though trivial, is necessarily true.

Accordingly to the Buddhists then, amongst the relation of succession it is only that of cause and effect (*tadutpatti*) and among that of coexistence it is only the identity of essence (*tadātmya*) that provide the basis for necessary relationship. Thus the two a priori principles upon which *vyāpti* is based are always *tadātmya* and *tadutpatti*.

The *Naiyāyikas*, on the other hand, regard *vyāpti* as a relation of invariable concomitance (*sāhacaryaniyama-vyāptiḥ*). They do not talk of any necessity but only of uncontradictedness (*avyabicāritva*). It is an invariable and unconditional relation (*niyata-anupadhika sambandha*) of concomitance, which does not admit of any exception. There is a reason why the *Naiyāyikas* do not talk of the element of necessity in *vyāpti*. They are thorough empiricists and therefore do not accept anything a priori. So the only basis *vyāpti* can be provided with is experience. But no experience can ever give us necessity. We can at the most talk of invariable concomitance on the basis of repeated observations (*bhūyodarśana*) of positive (*anvaya*) and negative (*vyatireka*) instances.

Though the *Naiyāyikas* are thorough empiricists they are saved from the traditional redical empiricism of the *Cārvākas* and the consequent rejection of *anumāna* by their acceptance of *sāmānya-lakṣaṇa pratyakṣa*. In fact, they resorted to this type of extraordinary perception simply to account for the origin of *vyāpti*. The Buddhists were not required to invent any such device because they traced *vyāpti* to a priori source.

Both the Buddhists and the *Naiyāyikas* take *anumāna* as not only formally valid, but also materially true.[2] And hence the question arises as to how *vyāpti*, the very basis of *anumāna*, is established and ascertained. The divergence of views with regards to the nature of *vyāpti* has led them to propound two different modes of establishing and ascertaining it.

The Buddhists derive the knowledge of *vyāpti* from the a priori principles of *tadātmya* and *tadutpatti*. They agree that we have so stipulated the connotation of these terms that to talk of them as non-necessary or contingent relations involves a self-contradiction. Though the origin of *vyāpti* (*utpatti*) is thus non-empirical, its ascertainment when we experience two different entities co-existing in the same locus. For the ascertainment of the relation of *tadutpatti* the Buddhists put forth the rest of *pañcakaraṇī* which is an explication of their fundamental principles of *trairūpya*. The *pañcakaraṇī* can be defined as "If all other conditions remaining the same, the appearance of one phenomenon is immediately followed by that of another, and its disappearance is immediately followed by disappearance of the other, then the two are related as cause and effect." If X is taken for cause and Y for an effect, it can be formulated as under,

i. – X – Y ii. – X iii. – Y iv. – Y v. – Y

Contrary to the Buddhists the *Naiyāyikas* start with experience and reach a priori reasoning. This is to say, according to them the origin of *vyāpti* is in experience but its final ascertainment is in a priori reasoning. *Vyāpti* is based on repeated uncontradicted observation of agreement in presence and also in absence between two phenomena, which is ultimately ratified by *tarka*. When we find two phenomena having positive (*anvaya*) and negative (*vyatireka*) coincidence (*sahacāra*), between them, of which no contrary instance is ever observed (*vyabhicāragraha*) we can presume that there must be natural relation of invariable concomitance between them. To ward of the possibility of such a relation being based on any condition (*upadhi*) repeated observation (*bhūyodarśana*) is needed. If even after repeated observation there is any doubt about its being a *vyāpti*, *tarka* or indirect proof is resorted to end the doubt. Thus the tentative *vyāpti* that "all cases of smoke are cases of fire" can be proved indirectly by disproving its contradictory. If this be false then its contradictory "some cases of smoke are not cases of fire" must be true. But such a supposition involves practical contradiction (*vyāghāta*) as it implies the occurance of the effect without its cause, thus its falsity establishes the truth of the original hypothesis.

Endnotes

1. There are two marks of *vyāpti* relation viz., invariable concomitance and an inner necessity connecting the two terms of the relation, of these two it is the inner necessity which is primary and the invariable concomitance is just its consequence.
2. When the Buddhist talks of material truth, it is with reference to phenomenal reality (*sāṃvṛtika satya*) and not with reference to the ultimate reality (*pāramārthika satya*).

4

THE PHILOSOPHICAL POSITIONS OF DIGNĀGA AND ŚAṄKARA

Chandra Kanta Datta

The conception of the immediate object is different in the Buddhist and the *Advaita Vedāntin* schools, and hence they believe in two different theories of *Pramāṇa-vyavasthā* and *Pramāṇa-samplava*, respectively. In the school of Dīgnāga, two different kinds of object are cognized by the two *Pramāṇas*, i.e. Perception and Inference, which lead to his conception of *Svalakṣana* and *Sāmānya-lakṣana*. On the other hand, the school of Śaṅkara admits static objects and one object can be cognized by any of the sources of knowledge or *Pramāṇas*.

The conception of object in the Dīgnāga school rules out the possibility of objectivity in knowledge; whereas in the school of Śaṅkara, there is every possibility of objectivity in the sphere of knowledge. The function of knowledge also varies in both the schools. In the Dīgnāga school the knower and the known are not independent of each other, but both conjoin to form the 'real'. In other words, the cognizer and the content must synchronize to get at the real, i.e. the '*kṣana*' or the moment of reality. Therefore, the function of knowledge is only the epistemic confirmation of reality. A theory of knowledge always follows a theory of reality. In the school of Śaṅkara, the objects of the external world have an existence independently of their knowledge by the subject or the perceiver. The origin of knowledge is from the soul. Thus, the function of knowledge is to discover reality, the realm of reality is exclusive and objective. The purpose of a theory of knowledge is only to discover what there is.

Dīgnāga's Realistic Ontology

Dīgnāga conceives ultimate reality in the form of *Svalakṣana*, or the thing-in-itself which is known through perception. According to him, "It is through perception itself that perception devoid of thought determinations is proved."[1] Perception has sensation at its basis. The sensation lasts for a moment, therefore, the ultimate reality is also momentary. Explaining the moment, it is said, "That form of a thing which does not persist after is production is, what is called *Kṣana*, 'Moment'; and that, which has this form is held to be '*Kṣanika*', 'Momentary'[2]. The moments are the disconnected bits of reality, which constantly follow one another. The perception is that of a bare particular or a moment only. There is a flow of innumerable particulars. The perception is non-synthetic and non-ideal process of cognition of the moments. The reality is also described as practical efficiency or *Artha-Kriyā-Kāritva*, which means that the existence always does something. A permanent thing can do nothing because causality is not consistent with the idea of permanence. Thus the conception of non-permanence and momentariness shows that the Buddhists conform to the dynamic view of reality.

The right cognition based on perception explains what is existent. Perception is a part of ontology and in perception there is no distinction between the subject and the object. The perception originates because of the chance encounter between a moment of consciousness and a moment of an object. This chance encounter is the real perception. Subsequent moments in the series are governed by the impression of the first moment and they follow their own law. Hence the subsequent moments are included in '*kalpanā*'. Thus '*kalpanā*' has a vital role to play in our knowledge of the external world.

In the school of Dīgnāga, cognition and error do not belong to two different levels. Knowledge belongs to the level of '*kalpanā*' and erroneous cognition is also a matter of '*kalpanā*'. The distinction between the validity and the invalidity of knowledge is a distinction between two sub-classes and not a distinction between two species, as it is in the non-Buddhist schools of thought. Therefore, validity of knowledge is also within itself.

Dharmottara[3] says that the object of cognition is double. The first moment refers to the direct apprehension of the object of reality. In the second moment the form of the object appears which is a construction. The directly perceived and the distinctly conceived are indeed two different things. A moment is that of sensation and a chain of moments forms the object of construction. The construction is always on the basis of some sensation. Moreover, all construction, knowledge, language, names and namable things are refuted by arguments and their existence proved imaginary by the Buddhists. The notion of 'Universal' is also criticized by the Buddhists.[4]

The ideal of pure sensation is given by Dīgnāga, but it has its origin in the works of *Sarvāstivādins.* The *Sarvāstivādins* admit that natural construction is present in every sensation and on its basis a thing is perceived as an object of the phenomenal world.[5] the conception of ultimate reality, open to perception and based on sensation, shows the realistic tendency of Dīgnāga's ontology. Dīgnāga constructs a system which in spirit is closer to the *Sautrāntika* position. In fact, he tries to establish some kind of compromise between the extreme idealism of *Yogācāra* and the staunch realism of *Sautrāntika.* He takes a clue from idealism when he analyses knowledge and tries to show that the object of knowledge can be reduced to certain basic sensations. But Dīgnāga, and following him *Dharma*kīrti, refuse to stop at the level of sensation as the *Yogācāras* do. They go a step further and argue, contrary to the spirit of the *Yogācāra*, regarding the source of sensation. They question, why is it that perception is made possible only when something is present before our eyes. But it ceases as soon as that thing is removed. Dharmakīrti shows by his experiment that the origin of sensation does not lie in the mind. It is because of the presence of something external to it. This goes against the philosophy of *Yogācāra*.

In any idealistic system there can be no talk of things-in-themselves, as it is in the system of Dīgnāga. In idealism the variegated nature of knowledge can be explained in only such terms as *Vāsanā* and *Ālaya-vijñāna*. In order to explain the existence of matter apart from ideas, the notion of different levels of truth is also found in the idealism. All these idealistic featues are conspicuously missing in the system of Dīgnāga and an object is ontologically independent of the ideas. Therefore, it can be safely that Dīgnāga is a realist in ontology.

Dīgnāga's Idealistic Theory of Knowledge

Dīgnāga's conception of *Sāmānyalakṣana* or construction refers to the negative aspect of his epistemological theory. This also indicates the possibility of the indirect reality or the reality of the phenomenal world. The reality of the phenomenal world is known by the indirect source of knowledge or inference. Dīgnāga's philosophy is based on the basic difference between the two sources of knowledge, viz. perception and inference.

In ordinary life the two sources of knowledge are not found in their pure form. One has to go beyond the actual experience and presuppose a transcendental difference. In perception the image is vivid and in inference the image is vague.[6] The experience leads us to infer on the basis of relations of identity, causality and non-perception. Inference is a process of thought. It is a synthetic operation of thought which helps in the construction of an object. Inference has a double function. It is a process of thought as well as a mode of communicating thought. Inference represents the spontaneous, synthetic, certain and conscious element in cognition. Through a logical mark it leads to a conclusion, when a thing is certainly cognized.

According to Dīgnāga, the object of knowledge is a construction out of the sense-data. It is a construction of the mind. Any substance or matter is just the result of our imagination. There is no extention of sensation in reality. The imagination constructs the images of the objects, whenever there is a sensation to stimulate it. Memory is also the result of construction and not a direct reflex of reality. The external objects only appear to be real. In fact they have only a borrowed reality. The construction of an object is ideal from the empirical point of view. It is based on experience.

The object of perceptual knowledge is a moment. When series of moments combine a thing becomes a construction and an object of non-perceptual knowledge. Non-perceptual knowledge is the knowledge of generalization of the unique moments. There is no relation between any two moments. In cognition, the two types of moments just get synchronized and get merged into each other. The cognition is the result of clash between these two types of moments. The object of non-perceptual knowledge is non-momentary aided by imagination. Imagination or *Kalpanā* for them is not a creation of experience but in every experience *Kalpanā* plays a role. In inference *Kalpanā* plays a role, but it is not empirical; it is a priori.

Perceptual knowledge has no concern with the concepts and words, but non-perceptual knowledge becomes functionless without concepts and words. Non-perceptual knowledge is valid and definite because it is determined by the conscious moments. Therefore, it points to the possibility of a valid system of concepts. This system is called inference. Inferential knowledge leads to the knowledge of the phenomenal world. This means that the phenomenon has its roots only in ideas. The epistemological idealism shows that the objects as they are known to us, are not the objects as they are in themselves. This position leaves the ultimate nature of reality out of consideration. Besides, this also shows that the things as they are, are not known in moral perception. What we get in normal perception is only our idea of what is. This conception of *Sāmānya-lakṣana* shows that Dīgnāga is an idealist in epistemology.

PART II

The purpose of the *Vedānta* texts is to give knowledge, and knowledge is the means to discover what is real. For the discovery of the real, there should be valid means of knowledge can only be considered valid if there is an existent object as its content. The notion of an existent object is the ground for one's belief in the independent existence of objects of the external world. The external objects only appear to be real and are not real ultimately. Still the existence of the external world is given in experience as a positive reality. The soul is the subject in all the cases.

The analysis of the status of the subject and object reveals the philosophical standpoint of Śaṅkara – where his ontology is separated from epistemology.

Śaṅkara's Idealistic Ontology

Brahman in *Advaita Vedānta* is Absolute in itself and it is beyond relation. As a result of the combination of Absolute with *Māyā*, it becomes the cause of the world. All changes take place only in the sphere of *Māyā*. Brahman is constant and changeless. *Māyā* is responsible for all change. Time is presupposed in the very concept of *Māyā*. *Māyā* is the *Kāla-śakti* (time-power) of Brahman.[7] It is an instrument for creation. Through the power of *Māyā*, the Absolute appears potential and creative. *Māyā* is eternal and has no beginning.[8] *Māyā* is the superimposition and confined to the realm of non-self. Underlying the superimposition of the world, is the ultimate reality, i.e. self of *Ātman*. This self is identical with Brahman.

A thing is produced in the world only when its cause is there. The appearance is there, which is the effect, because Brahman, which is the cause, is there. Brahman is the cause and it is the ultimate reality. In our ordinary life, the world does not appear to be false; it appears to be real. To account for the appearance of something which is not there, is not possible, except in an illusion. *Advaita Vedānta* conforms to the fact that the world is an illusion. In every illusion there is an underlying reality and in this case, it is the self or Brahman.

An important issue emerges regarding illusion, i.e. who is illuded? Śaṅkara would agree to the view that illusion is of the subject or the self. The purpose of *Vedānta* philosophy is to show the way for achieving liberation and it is possible by an intuitive knowledge of Brahman as being one with the self. Till that knowledge is not there, the subject is in illusion.

Śaṅkara believes ultimately in the complete identity of self with the Brahmana. His idea of Brahman is that of pure consciousness. The importance attached to the concept of pure consciousness brings Śaṅkara in the category of an idealist in ontology.

Śaṅkara's Realistic Epistemology

Śaṅkara is a realist in epistemology because he starts with the assumption that both the subject and the object must exist as distinct from each other and this is also the final conclusion of his system.[9] There is a fundamental distinction between the subject and the object and the objects of the world, which is, the non-self are completely independent of the subject or the self. The basis for the objects of external world is *Māyā*. The projective power of *Māyā* superimposes the non-real on the real due to ignorance. The body which is non-real is identified with the self, which is real due to some innate illusion. The entire empirical life depends on this illusion or the wrong identification of the body with the self. The identification is illusory, still it underlies all the activities of the empirical life. The acceptance of illusion affirms the existence of *Māyā*. *Māyā* is not a separate entity. It seems always present, and thus, it has no beginning. This idea may appear to show that it is a part of Brahman. But this is logically irreconciliable because the nature of *Māyā* is totally different from that of Brahman. If *Māyā* is located in the *Jīva* like *Avidyā*, then Śaṅkara can no longer be considered a monist and his system becomes dualistic. Rejecting both the alternatives, it has to be accepted that it forms the basis for the objects of knowledge and it is the power of *Māyā* by which the appearance of the world is possible.

Thus *Avidyā* from the side of the *Jīva* or soul, and *Māyā* from the side of the Brahman or Absolute create the appearance of the world full of objects of the empirical life. These objects form the realm of the non-self. As long as Śaṅkara accepts this distinction between the self and non-self or the subject and the object, he is a realist in epistemology.

The above analysis reveals the difference in ontology and epistemology of Dīgnāga and Śaṅkara. Both start with a common aim i.e. to know the reality, but the difference in their approach regarding the status of the object in the external world leads to different conclusions. Their philosophical position becomes a contrast, because the immediate object is conceived differently. In Dīgnāga's school, the question of objectivity in knowledge is ruled out, whereas in the *Advaita Vedāntin* school of Śaṅkara, objectivity is possible in the sphere of knowledge. The function of knowledge in both the schools also varies. In the system of Dīgnāga, it is to confirm the reality epistemically, while in the Śaṅkara's, it is to discover what there is. In the former, a theory of knowledge follows from a theory of reality and thus ontology in inseparable from epistemology. In the latter, a theory of knowledge is distinct from the theory of reality and ontology is separable from epistemology.

The purpose of this paper is to draw the attention to the contrast in the philosophical position of Dīgnāga and Śaṅkara, who are the representatives of the two main traditions in Indian philosophy, namely, the Buddhists and the *Advaita Vedāntins.*

Endnotes

1. Randle, *Fragments From Dīgnāga* pp. 9-10.
2. Śāntarakṣita, *Tattva-Saṅgraham,* Vol. 1, Transl. G. N. Jha (Baroda Oriental Instt., 1973) p. 246.
3. *Nyāya-bindu of* Dharmakīrti *with a Sanskrit commentary by Dharmottarāchārya,* Ed. Acharaya Chandrasekhara Sastry, Kashi Sanskrit Series 22, The Chowkhamba Sanskrit Series, Banaras, 1954, p. 8.
4. *Sarva-Darśana-Saṅgraham by Mādhva,* The Chowkhamba Sanskrit Series, Vol. X. Cowell and Gough, Varanasi, 1961,p. 21.
5. *Abhidharma kośabhāṣya of Vasubandhu,* Ed. P. Pradhan, Tibetan Sanskrit Works Series, Vol. VIII, K.P.J. Research Instt. Patna, 1967, pp. 72-3.
6. *Nyāya-bindu Tikā* (op. cit.) p. 15.
7. *Vākya-padīya of Bhartṛhari,* Kāṇḍa I, Ed. K. A. Subramanian Iyer, Deccan College, Poona, 1966, p. 3.
8. *Śaṅkara-bhāṣya on the Vedānta-Sūtras,* Transl. George Thihbaut, Motilal Banarasidass, II, i, 36.
9. *ibid.,* I, i.

5

PATH TO SECURE HAPPINESS

G. G. Gyatso

I bow down before the Omniscient One. This is the tenth semi-chiliod (500 years period) of the fourth Buddha, the period of moral discipline. The 20th century is the beginning of the era of weapons.

We have witnessed remarkable progress in material attainments. But no matter what advances as made in this sphere, there is a proportionate increase in unhappiness, not in happiness. For example, the poor may think that they will be happy if they acquire a little wealth: those with no social position may think that they will be happy if they acquire some higher status. If such people get what they want, they may indeed be happy for a short time, but before long their elation will revert to unhappiness – to unhappiness of even greater depth.

Whatever comforts there are in this life, e.g. delicious food, they can be enjoyed only as long as they last. The taste itself is never long-lasting. Similarly all worldly comforts can last for us only until we die, that is, for a hundred years or so at the most. The next life is longer and of more significance. Those who attempt to make themselves happy by amassing wealth incur further worries and problems, viz., the economy and hardship involved in saving, protection of the wealth against theft, and anxiety and concern lest the wealth be wasted. At the end of this life, each individual has to leave all of his wealth behind. He, therefore, clearly derives no ultimate benefit from it. One should, therefore, concern oneself with one's next life, and equip oneself with some knowledge of proceedings relevant to the next life. Certain people argue that there is no other life purely because they have no visible evidence of it. The idea, however, that a thing cannot exist unless one has visible evidence of it is clearly fallacious. There definitely is another life.

One can remember an action performed last year. One can even remember incidents of one's childhood. As one grows up there is obviously a continuous connection between one's childhood experiences and one's adult perception. It follows that one's earliest thoughts and experiences must also be connected to some previous cause.

Each 'seed' produces its own kind. The faculty of perception, therefore, must have the cause of the same nature as itself, which must originate in a previous life.

The body is not the 'cause' of the mind, because a dead body does not contain a mind. If the body were the 'cause' of the mind then a well-developed body should imply a well-developed mind, which it clearly does not do. The 'elements' are important for the maintenance of the body, but they are certainly not the seed. Inanimate things cannot produce animate results. In the same way empty space cannot change into any material object. Our bodies derive from our parents' reproductive cells, therefore, we have a physical resemblance to them. Our minds, however, may be different from theirs, for the 'seeds' of our minds do not derive from theirs. Intelligent parents may produce singularly dull child. The 'body' seeds of the parents cannot produce the 'mind' seeds of the offspring's. Therefore, the seeds of the child's mind must lie in some earlier life. The body and mind are united due to 'Karma' or deeds which produce result.

A newborn one has inherent desires and instinctive knowledge of how to satisfy them. For example, the newborn baby instinctively knows how to suck the mother's milk without having to be taught how to do so. This knowledge must have its origins in a previous life.

We know that our forefathers never saw or believed in modern knowledge, equipment or achievements. Being 'perceivable' is, therefore, clearly not a prerequisite for existence. One can perceive the past and the future through the power of meditation. Many people can remember their previous lives.

If one does not believe in another life, it is unlikely that he will become religious. If one knows religion and practices it, he can remove sorrow. One who practices religion learns to be satisfied with what one has, and develops a personal and civic consciousness which makes him shy away from evil actions. Hence, one lives peacefully. The learning and practicing religion are, therefore, the best method to derive maximum satisfaction by a person who wants happiness.

6

THE RELIZATON OF ŚŪNYATĀ AS AN INDETERMINATE MEDITATION

Ha-U-Kim

When we consider a substantial view, the concept of 'existent' or 'non-existent' can be confirmed through speculative determination for there are speculative modes, i.e. the concepts of time, space, quality, quantity, intentional relation, etc. in that view. Contrarily, in the consideration of the meaning of '*anātman*' as something devoid of speculative determination (i.e. indetemination; *śūnyatā*), there will be no more intentional graspings such as "this is mind, I am this, this is myself". In this case, we need not confirm the '*ātman*' as non-existent, but it should be understood as the unreality (*śūnyatā*) of the existent, that is to say, it is to be negligible. Because it is like a stolen thing.[1]

Since the self-existent is untrue (*mṛsā*), we need not confirm it as the concept of 'non-existent'. But one may concern with the concept of 'non-existent' as referred to reality through a speculative determination. Therefore, we need not "affirm" it whether it is 'existent' or 'non-existent'. In the *Mādhyamika*, what is called 'unreality' (*śūnyatā*) or 'untrue' (*mṛṣā*) does not mean to confirm it in terms of metaphysical, or any other logical cognition, but it is clarified by an indeterminate meditation. When we understand the following instruction, that is to say, "in this situation there is neither to be true nor untrue,"[2] we are free from the intentional determination of both concepts of existent and non-existent as referred to reality. After having freed ourselves from any intentional determination (on account of the quiescence of all viewings) there is no more remainder to be captivated. The indeterminate meditation does not mean a passive cognition; but it is a dynamic or transcendental intuition (*prajñā* or *śūnyatā*), i.e. it is continuously "going beyond" all knowledge situations. Therefore, it is not captivated by 'stolen things' (*moṣadharma*). Candrakīrti has brought out clearly the meaning of the verse by Nāgārjuna that "If stolen things are untrue, no one should be captivated by them"[3] as follows:

"When we say that they are untrue and stolen things, no one should be captivated by them. Does their non-existence (*abhāva*) exist? If any meaning of a word, whatsoever, exists, there is wrong view by seeing (i.e. viewing) *abhāva* after blaming it. But since we never view any meaning of a word, we will never be captivated by them. And since *abhāva* does not exist at all, your abuse is unreasonable."[4]

The opponent does not understand "*upādāya-prajñapti*" (a description without real reference) in the manner of indeterminate meditation. Therefore he holds on to the 'meaning of a word' (*padārtha*) in as much as he is forced to fabricate its concept as referring to reality. Here the opponent easily confuses the level of *prapañca* (conceptual fiction) with that of a substantial reference.

When the *Mādhyamika* declares that "we never view any meaning of a word" in the sense of indeterminate meditation, he realizes the level of *prapañca* so that he purifies the unreality of all views in the way of "going beyond" and he has no point of view. We may label two different kinds of *prapañca*; one is to say the level of "*upādāya-prajñapti*" in the manner of indeterminate meditation, and the other is the intentional description with a substantial reference. The former is the meditative observation of *prapañca* as it is, which is not associated with synthetic function, whereas the latter ensues from the intentional fabrication associated with thought (*vikalpa*) the is untrue (*mṛṣā*). As for as we are under untrue knowledge-situation, we need not confirm it as existent or non-existent. The only way to deliver ourselves from it is "going beyond" the realm of delusive attempt in other words, we have to transform the level of *prapañca* into a mark (*upāya*) of awakening level i.e. indeterminate realization in a whole instead of committing ourselves to substantial confirmation with the help of propositional function.

When we consider about the realization of the level of *prapañca* in the sense of *svabhāva-śūnyatā* (i.e. *niḥsvabhāvatva*) towards that of *prapañca-śūnya*, we may understand that the level of *prapañca* is no more the function of growth, but a mark towards indeterminate realization for reality.

The contextual meaning may correspond with the meaning when Chi-tsang says that "there are two kinds of *pratītya-samutpāda*; one is correct one, whereas the other is a wrong one" in his Commentary on the Madhyamaka-śāstra, Part I as regards the *Mādhyamika's* point, the level of *prapañca, upādāya prajñapti* and *pratītya samutpāda* are devoid of growth and diminution which are affected by imaginative construction and discrimination. This is due to realization of the unreality (*śūnyatā*) of all appearances and the relativity (*śūnyatā*) of conceptual operations.

As for the truth or correct knowledge, it can not be understood with the help of a substantial concept, because it only commits ourselves to the realm of objectification by "grasping" instead of realizing a wholeness in the indeterminate observation. In fact, truth does not exist for our "grasping", but a term for our realization of a whole. Therefore, it does not mean a term for substantial statement. This non-committed or indeterminate attitude does not commit ourselves to reality with any determinate standpoint, but means an indeterminate meditation.

Since the awareness of relativity (*śūnyatā*) leaves aside relational knowledge, viz., logical, dialectical, causal efficiency and psychological knowledge, the meditative awareness points to the open field or wholeness that goes beyond the question of inclusion and exclusion of phenomenal world or the horizon of Reason's devices.

As for the Buddhist doctrine, "this being, that arises" (*asmiṁ sati idaṁ bhavati*) the same is not to be explained with the help of the objective knowledge of causality, but is initiated to observe the wholeness in the light of relativity, i.e. the awareness of the wholeness of mutual dependence in the indeterminate (*śūnyatā*) or non-committed (*anabhiniveśa*) manner. Here, '*idaṁ*' is not referred to as a substantial term but a nominal one in the awareness of the relativity of mutual dependence. So far as we understood *pratītya-samutpāda*, it is free from any logical concept as involved in the identity or indifference of relationship between cause and effect. When we are concerned with the logical confirmation of '*idaṁ*' as a substantial term, there is not only an attribute of the subject but also it having 'invariable concomitance' (*vyāpti*).

For the *Mādhyamika* the subject is regarded as what is not produced by its own nature (*svabhāva-anutpāda*). When Nāgārjuna equates *śūnyatā* with the middle path, the middle path is in accordance with non-committed attitude which need not define any intentional knowledge such as the affirmation of 'existent' or of 'non-existent' but the clarification or "illumination" (*paridīpakam*) of *śūnyatā*.

The *Mādhyamika's* declaration that "we have no view of our own", is the indeterminate or meditative attitude which has a correspondent context with the manner of 'illumination of *śūnyatā*' (*śūnyatā paridīpakā*)[5] by the Lord. Nāgārjuna declares in his *Madhyamaka-kārikā*, XIII 2b, that "saying by the Lord that stolen things are unreal, reveals *śūnyatā*". On this Candrakīrti comments as follows:

"In saying so the Lord does not intent to clarify 'non-existence of things', but to clarify *śūnyatā*, and it means to clarify 'non-production of them through their own nature."[6]

Considering the above instruction by the Lord, the unreality of all appearances (*dharamāṇāṁ śūnyatā*) can not be defined as the view of 'non-existence of things', but it affords to transform its means (*upāya*) into awakening – understanding (*prajñā*). Here, both *upāya* and *prajñā* can not be classified into two different concepts in terms of conceptual confirmation, but they can be said to be two levels in the light of all comprehensible meditation, which, in other words, they are one and the same thing because they are not separated from each other in terms of indeterminate meditation as like "*rūpa eva śūnyatā* as well as *śūnyatā eva rūpa*". In the consideration of *śūnyatā*, we may regard two aspects for its function; one is the unreality of all appearances in the sense of means (*upāya*), whereas the other is the realization of the former in the manner of *prajñā*. But both can not be regarded as two separated concepts in the intentional cognition. At the time of all comprehensible meditation, *upāya* and *prajñā* are "co-illuminating" in the sense of 'indeterminate' relativity (*eva*). In such a case, it is "going beyond" the concepts of both identity and difference.

Endnotes

1. See *Madhyamaka-kārikā*, XIII, 1.
2. *Madhyamaka-vṛtti*, pp. 237-8.
3. Op. cit., XIII, 2a.
4. Op. cit., p. 239. See MV, p. 246.
5. Op. cit., XIII, 2b.
6. Op. cit., p. 239.

7

BUDDHIST EPISTEMOLOGY
The Number of Pramāṇas

Kewal Krishan Mittal

It hardly needs to be state that the question of *Pramāṇa*, i.e., the source and proof of knowledge-in all its four aspects of Number (*Saṅkhyā*). Nature (*Svarūpa*), object (*Arth* or *Viṣaya*) and the Result (phala); constitutes the heart and soul of Epistemology as we have it in various systems of Indian philosophy.[1] I intend drawing through this short paper, the attention of the scholars to the question of the number of *Pramāṇas* as pertains to the Buddhist Epistemology. While doing so I am fully conscious of the first reaction, they may well evince. It is likely to be said. "What is there in this question? It is already settled. The Buddhist accept two *Pramāṇas Pratyakṣa* (perception) and *Anumāna* (inference) and the fact is testified not only by the modern historians of Indian Philosophy"[2] but also by such well-known authors of compendia on Indian Thought as Mādhavācārya[3] and Haribhadra Sūri."[4]

I dare challenge the view, throwing thus overboard the heavy burden of tradition, emboldened by an oft-quoted advice of the Buddha, as we find it recorded in *Aṅguttara-nikāya*. "Believe nothing", the *Tathāgata* is attributed to have said, "because a so called wise man said it. Believe nothing because, the belief is generally held. Believe nothing because it is written in ancient books. Believe nothing because it is said to be of a divine origin. Believe nothing because someone else believes it. But believe only what you yourself judge to be true".

Contrary to the general belief, what I judge to be true is that Buddhist Epistemology, in general, does not accept *Anumāna* (Inference) as an independent source and proof of knowledge and the only school of Buddhist Philosophy that seem to do so fails to show it as such and succeeds merely in depicting *Anumāna* to be an instrument dealing with connected, directed and reflective but abstract thought, at best.

I, for one, am not able to understand as to why should not we check our tendency to lamp together schools of thought that differ widely. Covered, as they are, by the general name of Buddhist Philosophy, it is alright for us, to seek in them the common and essential. But, in the process, we must not gloss over the important differences and distinctions. Because, if we do so, we are likely to confuse issues. To me, it seems an all the more unpardonable a mistake when knowing fully well the various distinctions and differences among various schools of thought one attributes something to the totality of them what may legitimately or illegitimately belong to only one of them.

To my mind, Mādhavācārya, as also all those who seem to follow him in this, appears to commit precisely this serious mistake. For, he is not only aware of the division of Buddhist Philosophy into four important points of departure with the names *Vaibhāṣika*, etc.[5] but also takes note of their epistemological differences.[6] Further, he does indicate very clearly that only one of the schools, namely, the *Sautrāntika* alone could, if at all, accept '*Anumāna*' as an additional *Pramāṇa* to *Pratyakṣa* to gain knowledge of the external objects, in particular, and that too by implication as his actual words are : "According to the *Sautrāntikas* the external objects are not graspable by *Pratyakṣa* (*Sautrāntikena pratyakṣagrāhyortho na bahirmataḥ*)."[7] In the light of this, one is left wondering as to what makes Mādhavācārya attribute the view to the Buddhists, in general, that they accept two *pramāṇas.*

It is true; the *Sautrāntika* school is distinguished from the *Vaibhāṣika* in being the upholder of *Bāhyānumeyavāda* as against the *Bāhyapratyakṣavāda* view of the latter. But that is all that we have of the *Sautrāntika* position. I am unaware if there is any detailed treatment of *Anumāna* in all its (already mentioned) aspects by any thinker claiming to be a *Sautrāntika.* Scholars are yet not sure to which of the four well-known schools of Buddhism, namely, *Vaibhāṣika, Sautrāntika, Yogācāra* and *Mādhyamika* do Dharmakīrti, the celebrated author of the well-known epistemological treatise '*Nyāyabindu*' and Dharmottara, the accredited commentator of the work belong.[8]

May be, they, along with Dīgnāga, the author of such important works on Buddhist Epistemology as *Pramāṇasamuccaya, Nyāyapraveśa* and *Ālambanaparīkṣā.* etc. subscribe to a school independent of all the four. Their school is known, roughly, by the name of the school of Buddhist logic. It is to this school that Śāntarakṣita, the author of *Tattvasaṅgrahaṃ* and Kamalaśila, the commentator of the work also seem to belong. Despite having a common bond, pressed by their metaphysical considerations, the great logicians seem to pull in different directions. If Dīgnāga is keen to take a neutral stand and wants his logic to be an instrument for the use of both Realists and Idealists and is ready to drop the character 'non-illusiveness (*abhrāntaṃ*)' from his definition of *pratyakṣa* to that effect, [9] then Śāntarakṣita and Kamalaśīla do lean towards the *Yogācāra* position and Dharmakīrti and Dharmottara towards a position somewhat between the *Sautrāntika* and the *Vaibhāṣika.*[10] T. R.V. Murti's remark seems to be apt in this context when he observes, "there is no such a thing as a neutral logic which every philosopher accepts or has to accept."[11]

No doubt, they (the Buddhist Logicians) all, apparently accept both *Pratyakṣa* and *Anumāna* as *Pramāṇas.* But, somehow, caught in the web of their own reasoning, guided or misguided by the consequences of accepting a certain definition of *Pratyakṣa* (*Pratyakṣaṃ Kalpanāpoḍhaṃ*), they find it extremely difficult to maintain even *Savikalpa pratyakṣa* (determinate Perception) to be an instrument of knowledge what to say of the *Anumāna* "which is" in the words of Satkari Mookerjee, "invariably associated with ideal construction (*Kalpanā*)."[12]

It is hard for me to agree with Mookerjee when he suggests that Dīgnāga's omission to put *pratyakṣa* under the rubric of "valid knowledge" (*Samyagjñāna*) was a trifling matter unduly made capital of by Uddyotkara[13] and so was the fact of not caring to supply the word *Jñāna* in his definition of *Pratyakṣa* on the part of Śāntarakṣita.[14] For, the explanation of Kamalasīla on Śāntaraksita's behalf and declaring not only *Pratyakṣa* but also *Anumāna* to be 'valid knowledge'- *dvividhaṁ Samyagjñānaṃ*[15] and *Pratyakṣamanumānañca* on the part of Dharmakīrti[16] by way of amending the view of Dīgnāga are of little avail when, despite Dharmottara's clever logical tight-rope-walking the School of Buddhist Logicians is unable to come out of Logical difficulties of its own making.

The significance of Dīgnāga's omission and Śāntarakṣita's lapse. I am sure, could not have been lost to Mookerjee and he should not have ridiculed the Brāhmaṇical critics on the point had it been kept by him in his mind that *nirvikalpa pratyakṣa*-which alone is revelatory of knowledge-was of little practical use and *Savikalpa* was invalid because of *Vikalpa.* More so, when he is not only aware of the situation but also takes not of it elsewhere in his brilliant work on Buddhist Philosophy.[17] "Unless and until it is determined" he observes about *nirvikalpa pratyakṣa* "as such the experience is as good as non-existent (*Asatkalpa*), because it can not lead to any activity and so there is no acquision of anything."[18] Despite referring to distinction drawn by Dharmottara between *Vikalpa* (reflective thought) that arises in the trail of perception and generated under its influence (*Pratyakṣabalotpanna*) and that represents pure imagination without any touch with external reality and mentioning the same to be of vital importance according to him (Dharmottara). Mookerjee could not avoid the inescapable conclusion about Sa*vikalpa-Pratyakṣa* as je states. "the contention that perceptual knowledge together with *Vikalpa* should be held as valid testimony therefore falls to the ground"[19] 'therefore' in the statement refers to his argument a part of which runs thus, "the purely subjective character of this reflective process, which is necessary for the interpretation of Perception, does not in any way detract from or add to the evidentiary value of perceptual knowledge."[20]

Dharmottara is blowing hot and cold when he asserts that there is a distinction of vital importance between two varieties of *Vikalpa* and also insists at the same time that 'both the varieties are equally unreliable and invalid by their very constitution'.[21] This alone is enough to reach the conclusion drawn by Mookerjee in some-what round-about manner.

Summing up, I may say that as far as I am concerned I do not think it can be validly affirmed that the Buddhists accept *Anumāna* as a source and proof of knowledge. This, however, does not mean that the way *Anumāna* has been conceived by the Buddhists has no utility of its own. *Anumāna*, understood the Buddhists way has immense value as an instrument of purely formal logic.

Endnotes

1. Cf. *Nyāyabindu Ṭikā* (Biblotheca Indica edition) p. 7; *Prakaraṇapañcaka* p. 38; *Parīkṣāmukhasūtra Ṭikā* 1-as quoted and referred to by T.R.V. Murti, *The Central Philosophy of Buddhism*, p.151, fn. 2.
2. See, e.g., S. Radhakrishnan, *Indian Philosophy*, Vol, I, pp. 462-469; M. Hiriyanna, *Outlies of Indian Philosophy*, p. 188 ff; Chandradhara Sharma, *A Critical Survey of Indian Philosophy*, pp. 131-132; Sinha, J.N., *A History of Indian Philosophy*, vol, II, p.414ff.
3. *Sarvadarśanasaṅgraha*, Ch.II, verse 36 (edited by U.S. Sharma Rishi), p.102.
4. *Saḍdarsanasamuccaya*, verse 9.
5. The same as supra note 3 (2nd line of the verse).
6. Ibid verses 37, 38, pp. 102 - 103.
7. Ibid verse 37, second line.
8. See Introduction (in Hindi) by one Chandrashekhar Shastri to the Kashi Sanskrit Series (No. 22) edition of the *Nyāyabindu*.
9. Cf. Th. Stcherbatsky, *Buddhist Logic*, Volume I, pp. 155 ff.
10. Ibid.
11. T.R.V. Murti, *The Central Philosophy of Buddhism*, p. 152.
12. See, *The Buddhist Philosophy of Universal Flux* (Calcutta 1935), p. 275.
13. Ibid, p.274 (See fn. 2 for Uddyotkara's criticism).
14. Ibid.
15. *Tattvasaṅgraham Pañjikā* (Gaikwad's Oriental Series edition), p.367.
16. *Nyāyabindu* (supra note 8), pp. 7, 8.
17. Op, cit, (Supra note 12), pp. 343-345.
18. Ibid, p. 343.
19. Ibid, p.344.
20. Ibid.
21. Ibid. p. 343.

8

A NOTE ON TIBETAN BUDDHIST ICONOGRAPHY

Krishna Ghosh

Shortly after the death of the Buddha, differences of opinion arose in the matter of discipline and thought. These differences necessitated convening at least four councils which in due course resulted in permanent schism in the *Saṅgha* (Buddhist Church). Finally out of this cross current two main schools, *Hīnayāna* (Southern) and *Mahāyāna* (Northern) were established.

The *Hīnayānists* followed the primitive Buddhism. The worship of deities was secondary for them, while the *Mahāyānists* formulated new ideas and started worshipping the Supreme Being and other divinities chiefly the *Bodhisattvas.* The *Yoga* doctrine of ecstatic union and the *Mantrayāna* doctrine of spell and charms were added in the early centuries of Christian era, to *Mahāyāna.* A step further developed with the worship of female energies of the gods in conjuction with male energy. This form of Tantric Buddhism, widely known as *Vajrayāna,* was introduced into Tibet along with its full-fledged pantheon in the seventh century A.D. during the reign of king Sron-btsan-Sgam-po.

Buddhism could not take a firm footing in the foreign soil due to the strong hold of *Bon,* the indigenous cult of Tibet. It was Padmasambhava (called Guru Rinpoche by Tibetans) the Indian Teacher of the *Yogācāra* school, who visited Tibet on the invitation of King Khri-Sron-Ide-bstsan in the eighth century A.D. He made a compromise with the native cult *Bon* in order to make *Mahāyāna* Buddhism acceptable and popular among the common people. He freely admitted the rites and demonical deities of *Bon* into the Buddhist pantheon. Thus Tibetan Buddhist pantheon is a mixture of Buddhist and *Bon* deities.

The study of Tibetan Buddhist iconography is both fascinating and bewildering. The number of deities in Tibetan pantheon seems to be unlimited with a host of gods, goddesses, demons and spirits. Deniker[1] gives the number as five hundred or more than that.

Some of these divinities are in human form and have their origins in myth, legend, history or pure imagination. The forces of nature and doctrinal system also have been deified in human or Tantric forms. Further variety of forms of certain individual divinities make the Tibetan Buddhist pantheon really huge.

Tibetan iconographical researches have been done extensively by scholars like P.H. Pott,[2] E. Pander[3], G. Tucci[4], W.E. Clark[5], A. Gordon[6], A. Getly[7] and others.

This apart, secondary sources, texts like *Sādhanamālā*[8], *Niṣpanna Yogāvalī*[9] and a few Tibetan Pantheons[10] are valuable for the study of Tibetan Buddhist iconography.

Tibetan Buddhist deities are divided into several groups like the Buddhas, the *Bodhisattvas*, the feminine deities, the tutelarly or protectors (*yi-dam*), the protectors of the religious law (*chos-skyong*), the eight terrible ones (*drag-ched*), the non-Buddhist spirits (*dam-can*) and other minor divinities, *Genii*, Guardians of the four cardinal points, etc.

Tibetan Buddhist images either sculptural or pictorial are highly decorative. The statues whose dimensions vary from the length of half an inch to several feet in height, are made of wood, ivory, stone, copper, iron, silver, gold and especially bronze. The monasteries of Tibet contain stucco figures, wood carvings and *tanka* paintings illustrating belief in transmigration, magic circles and astrological diagrams as also gods and goddesses of the pantheon. The statues usually represent a single divinity, but often groups of three, five of eight statues are made, all having the same character and the same dimensions, so that they compose groups. For instance, the Buddha triad, the eight *Bodhisattvas*, the eight terrible ones and so on.

In Tantric Buddhism, the most striking aspect is the richness in its symbolism. The fondness of symbolization is very extensive in Tibetan iconography. Every image is a symbolic of something and every part of a particular image has a meaning. For instance, the close embrace of the male and female energies symbolizes the fusion of *upāya* (action) and *prajñā* (intelligence). The Knower becomes one with his knowledge and this oneness is mahā*sukha* (highest happiness). The *Dhyānī Buddhas* and *Dhyānī Bodhisattvas* as embodiments of active urge of enlightenment which finds its expression in *upāya*, the all embracing love and compassion are therefore represented in the embrace of their *prajñā*, the embodiment of highest knowledge symbolized by a female deity. When the union of *upāya* and *prajñā* i.e. the synthesis of heart and head, feeling and intellect, highest love and deepest knowledge have taken place, their completeness is established, perfect enlightenment is achieved.

The colours, symbols and postures (sitting and standing) all have their estoric significance. Dark blue colour signifies destruction and is the colour of the ferocious aspects of the deities who protect Buddhist law and destroy the enemies of the faith. In the same way some of the *āsanas* (sitting postures) and the *mudrās* (hand gestures) have esoteric meanings and have been used only by the Tantric deities in order to inspire fear.

Symbols, apart from symbolizing something hidden or deep, serve a great role in iconography as far as the identification of images are concerned. The identification of deities is made by the differences in ornaments[11], garments[12], *mudrās*, *āsanas*, *vāhana*[13] (the mount) on which they sit and by various symbols[14] they hold. In paintings, colours are also a point of identification.

Another feature, however, deserves mention, i.e. with regard to the pre-dominance of the wrathful forms in Tibetan Buddhist iconography. They (wrathful forms) are not restricted to the Srung-ma, the protectors and various *yi-dam* such as *Hevajra*. *Cakrasaṃvara*, *Vajrabhairava* and others, but also in the case of various peaceful deities. This can be due to the influence of *Bon* pantheon which is full of demonical deities.

The wrathful deities mostly possess stout bodies. Many of them have several heads and a number of hands. The colour of their bodies and faces is frequently compared with hue of cloud, of poison and of precious stones. The *Sādhanas* often mention that the body of a ferocious deity is smeared with ashes taken from a funeral pyre or the body is covered with blood spots and shining speaks of human fat. They are mostly adorned with the garland of freshly cut heads and hold the skull of blood. The faces of many possess a typical wrathfull expression with the yellowish brown hair standing on its end and the mouth is contorted to an angry smile, from its corners protrude long fangs. A mist of illness comes forth from the mouth and a terrific storm is supposed to be blowing from the nostrils (of the nose). The protruding, bloodshot eyes have an angry and staring expression and usually a third eye is visible in the middle of the forehead.

It would not be out of place here to mention that in Tibetan pantheon most of the gods and goddesses are fierce looking, though they are really benevolent in nature. The reason may be that the Tibetans used to live in constant fear of ghosts and demons in whose existence they had firm belief and that is why they depicted their benevolent gods and goddesses fierce so that they can drive away evil spirits.

Thus the images of divinities either painted on scrolls or made of different metals found rather a different expression in Tibetan pantheon. Tibet produced magnificent wealth of sculpture which includes many unique specimens.

Through Tibetan Buddhist iconography one can penetrate into the most mysterious religion and understand the mystery of Tibetan Buddhism. This apart, one may get insight into the Tibetan culture as well.

References

1. Lama Anagarika Govinda: *Foundation of Tibetan Mysticism*.
2. L.a. Waddell: *Lamaism*.

3. E. Schlaginweit: *Buddhism in Tibet.*
4. Thubten Jigme Norbu and Golin Turnbull: *Tibet.*
5. A. Getty: *Gods of Northern Buddhism.*
6. A.K.Gordon: *The Iconography of Tibetan Lamaism.*
7. Benoytosh Bhattacharya: *Indian Buddhist Iconography.*

Endnotes

1. Getty A., *The Gods of Northern Buddhism* (Introduction).
2. Pott. P.H., *Introduction to the Tibetan Collection of the Museum of Ethnology*, Leiden, 1951.
3. Pander, Eugen, Das Pantheon des-Tsechangtscha Hutuku; ed. by Grunwedel (A), Berlin, 1890.
4. Tucci G., *Indo-Tibetika*, I-iv, Roma, 1932-1941. Tibetan Painted Scrolls, Rama, 1949.
5. Clark, W.E., *Two Lamaistic Pantheon*, Cambridge, 1937.
6. Gordon, A.K., *The Iconography of Tibetan Lamaism*, Japan, 1960.
7. Getty A., *The Gods of Northern Buddhism*, Japan, 1962.
8. *Sādhanamālā* (ed.) Benoytosh Bhattacharya, Baroda, 1968.
9. *Niṣpanna Yogāvali* (ed.) ibid, Baroda, 1949.
10. Raghuvira and Lokesh Chandra, *A New Tibeto-Mongol Pantheon*, Vol. 3, New Delhi, 1961.
11. *Ornaments* of gold, silver, gems, turquoise, conch-shell and also of human bones are worn by Tibetan deities.
12. *Garments of* silk, wool, human and animal skins.
13. *Vāhana* : The variety of animals on which the Tibetan deities are supposed to ride are horse, yak (animal of Tibet), elephant, lion, tiger, bear, stag, buffaloes, camel, monkey, dog, sheep, pig, hare, snake, scorpion, rat, fish and so on. Also the typical animals belonging to the *Bon* mythology are the red tiger with nine heads, the dog possessing nine tongues, black snakes of blood.
14. The attributes which the Tibetan deities carry are arms to destroy the enemies of Buddhist creed, the swords, the knife, the dagger, the chopper, the club, the hammer, the lance and bow and arrow. Different types of flowers, gems, mirror, banner of victory, magic sticks, skull cup, thunderbolt, musical instruments are other important Buddhist emblems.

9

INTERPRETATION OF BUDDHIST TERMINOLOGY AT THE BACKGROUND OF CHINESE TRADITIONAL THOUGHTS

Latika Lahiri

After the introduction of Buddhism in China in A.D. 65-67, the most stupendous task was lying before a highly religious community with a team of translators from Parthia, Indo-Scythia, India and Central Asia to render the Sanskrit Buddhist texts into Chinese. This difficult task spread over several centuries after the inception of Buddhism. With Buddhism we reach a world of ideas very different from Chinese traditional thoughts and ideas. Besides this, the Indian language through which the great treasure of her religion would reveal, was completely different from Chinese. Sanskrit with its highly developed and intricate system of grammar was different from Chinese that had no systematic grammar. In the earliest period, the translators faced a serious problem to given phonetic transcription of Indian proper names specially to render the abstract notion and concrete ideas of the Buddhist expression by Chinese character which is pictographic in form and ideographic in nature. The Chinese characters are monosyllabic in sound and unifletional in form. On the contrary, Sanskrit is alphabetic, polosyllabic and highly infective. Arther F. Wright says, "the Chinese had shown little disposition to analyse the personality in its components, while India had a highly developed science of psychological analysis. In concept of time and space, there were also striking differences. The Chinese tended to think of both as finite and to reckon time in life span, generation to political eras. The Indians, on the other hand, conceived of time and space as infinite and tended to think of cosmic cons rather than of limits of terrestrial life."[1] The social and political values of the two ancient civilizations also differed. The society according to Confucius was an ordinance of heaven and based upon five relations between ruler and subjects, father and son, husband and wife, elder and younger brothers and friends. Confucian idea of filial peity was equated with worship of heaven and he regarded that for the people, it would suffice as a religion. Buddhism, on the other hand, professes the ideal of wandering ascetic who goes forth to homeless state to eliminate the sorrows of birth and diseases, old age and death. With such alien background, the task of finding out suitable comprehensive equivalents for highly technical Buddhist terminology was a formidable one. The phonetic transcription was undoubtedly a very difficult task to be performed with the help of ideographic

Chinese character which was less suited for that purpose. This would not have been that difficult in any alphabetical writing system. Moreover, with the exception of a very few Chinese monks of the team belonging to highly organised Church of Lo-yang and Ch'ang-an, others had very little knowledge of Sanskrit and in the archaic period the Central Asian and Indian monks had also scanty knowledge of literary Chinese.

In the earliest period, translation of Buddhist terminology and text was very vague and confusing. Amid evergrowing confusion caused by various forms of Buddhism introduced in China from outside, by importation of missionaries from various countries belonging to multi-farious schools and by translations of some of the *Māhāyanist* and *Hīnayānist* texts, the Chinese Buddhists were groping in darkness. Later on, they successfully evolved a chinese doctrinal system.

Throughout the history of translation of Buddhist texts into Chinese, the transcribers had followed certain rules and regulations. They had used those characters which were not commonly used in written Chinese, e.g. a, yi, ke, ge, lo, sa, fu, mi, etc. the words *Maitreya* and *Bodhisattvas* had been rendered with such sounds as Mi-lo, Fu-sa. But we find a number of common signs as shan, she shih, men were frequently used for Buddhist transcription. The Sanskrit word *Śramaṇa* had been rendered with such phonetical sound as she-men.

One Chinese syllable may be written in various ways as Chinese characters are homophonous, e.g. *shan* (to write out), *shan* (good, benevolent), *shan* (mountain). These syllabies may stand for various foreign sounds. Generally, we see the characters like *p'o, (ke or ge) chia, (ke or ge) chia* are used for transliteration. The character (*chia*) stands for Sanskrit sound *ke or ge.* Thus *Bhāgavat* had been rendered *p'o-ge-p'o.* The first syllabus *p'o* had been employed for Sanskrit sounds like *va, pa, pha, bha, vat.* A Japanese book called *Siddhakośa* has mentioned about a Record of I-chig which contains Chinese equivalent characters for Sanskrit alphabets.[2] In early period, transcription of individual words and proper names were not standardised. It went through many changes. The word '*Buddha*' had been rendered into Chinese as *Fo-t'u, Fo-t'ou.* The original word '*Buddha*' was greatly distorted. Later on, the character Fo was used for the Buddha. It may be an abbreviation of *Fo-t'ou.* Sir Charles Eliot says that these two syllables *Fo-t'ou* once pronounced like *vut-tha.*[3]

During the transitional period from ancient phonetic renderings to the time of highly developed transcription system, the same norm of using restricted characters and conventional set of signs had always been adopted for the purpose of transcription. We must note that the system of transcription is not a new innovation. During the glorious reign of the Former and Later Hans when they had close political and trade relation with the West, they had to transcribe the geographical names of those often-frequented countries. The Records of the Former and Later Hans mentioned about two hundred[4] (mostly geographical) foreign word in transcription.

The Buddhist transcribers must have made full use of this rudimentary system for rendering foreign sounds.

The Buddhist literary activity had an interesting method of transliterating Indian words. Indian proper names, specially with obvious meaning were translated, e.g. Divākara, Aśvaghoṣa, Devadatta, Aśoka and *Tathāgata* as *Jih-mu-ang* (the rays of the Sun), *Ma-ming* (neighing of a horse), *T'ien-shou* (gift of Devas), *Wu-yu* (not mournful), *Ju-lai* (one whose incoming into the world is like the coming of his predecessors), respectively. This translation of Indian proper names gives correct comprehension of their meaning. The transliterated word A-mi-ta-p'o *Amitābha* was also rendered as *Wu-liang-kuang*, boundless light. There are many such proper names which could be easily rendered into Chinese phonetic sound but it is difficult sometime to say where and when they had been transliterated or translated. But many proper names did not tend themselves to such renderings and it was a pretty difficult task to translate the Buddhistic theological terms like *Nirvāṇa* and *Samādhi*, etc.

The *Siddhakośa* (880 A.D.) a Japanese book says in *Nan-hai-kuei-chuan.* (The Record sent home by I-Ching) in Chapter XXXIV under the title Si t'an-Chang[5], he had mentioned about 49 Sanskrit letters of the alphabet which are in perfect accord with corresponding Chinese characters with a very few exceptions.[6]

A system known as Fan-ch'ieh[7] or Fan-yin was devised by Indian Buddhist monks to render approximately in Chinese the Pāli or Sanskrit syllables. Fan-ch'ieh is a system of spelling in Chinese Dictionaries.[8]It was a favourite style with the Emperor K'ang-his (A.D. 1662-1723) of the Manchu Dynasty. According to this system which is similar to Indian *Sandhi Prakaraṇa*, a syllable phonetically of two characters will be combined by dropping the final of the first and the initial of the second to produce a new sound and tone e.g. Fu-wan (to begin late evening) Fan (to respect, to turn over), Chu Yung Chung.

Hsuan Chuang and I-Ching, the noted and profound Sanskrit scholars introduced certain reforms in renderings Sanskrit equivalents for Buddhist terms in Chinese and probably after them, the rendering of Sanskrit terms was more accurate and more precise. Hsuan-chuang preferred to transliterate the Buddhist terminology rather than translating them.

In the early period of translation, most of the Buddhist terminologies were translated through Taoist terms but it was soon found that these terms did not convey the subtle meanings. The translators preferred to keep the foreign words and then transcribe them into Chinese. Consequently, we find *Prajñāpāramitā, Nirvāṇa* etc. have been transcribed as *Pan-jo-pa-lo-mi-to, Nieh p'an*, etc. Towards the end of the 4th century, Tao-an[9], one of the greatest Chinese monks, a bibliographer and collector of sacred texts, gave some practical suggestions to the members of the bureau of translators. He as a 'general manager' of the team, was always aware of the problems the transcribers often confronted with. The questions before them were whether the translation should be done to cater to the popular need of the people, so as to make it short in form, free and polished which would be welcome by the Chinese people in general or whether the translation should be faithful, literal or repetitious which would be disliked by them. In his preface to *Prajñāpāramitā-sūtra* Tao-an had given some practical suggestions to the transcribers requesting them on what points they should deviate from the original, and also mentioned three points where they should make faithful translation of Sanskrit texts.[10] Hsuan-chuang similarly formulated certain rules for the translators. He had insight in selecting words and as a translator he created marvel in using the choicest Chinese words to translate the Buddhist terms.

Through the combined efforts of both foreign missionaries and Chinese monks, enormous body of the Buddhist *Sūtras* was translated which constitutes the bulk of the Canon and with it thousands of new terms were assimilated into Chinese Buddhism. Among the foreign missionaries who made a greatest contribution in translation were An Shih-kao from Parthia, *Dharma*rakṣa from Tukhara, Kumārajīva from Kucha.

Buddhism grew and developed with two indigenous religions – Confucianism and Taoism. Taoism is a mystic philosophy which was directly opposed to Confucianism. Taoism is ascetic and pantheistic. Buddhist philosophy is also regarded as a philosophy of asceticism which emphasizes the withdrawal from the world. Here, we, in fact, find some similar ideas with Taoism and in the Taoist circle Buddhism made its headway. Buddhism entered into China as a foreign religion but soon found expression in Taoist mystic words "The Chinese who became interested in the foreign religion were attracted by its novel formulae for attainment of supernatural power, immortality or Salvation and not by its idea. This early Buddhism (in China) was generally regarded as a sect of Taoism".[11] The defenders and propagators had to find some arguments to reconcile the Buddhist ideas with traditional Chinese thoughts. Thus Tao (The Way, The Truth, A Principle) was the expression used for *Dharma* or *Bodhi*, Ying-jen for *Arhat*, Wu for *Nirvāṇa*, Hsiao-hsun filial submission and obedience for *Śīla*.

It is of utmost importance to have correct evaluation of Chinese comprehension of Buddhist terms. Both the Indian and Chinese *Mādhyamika* texts have sizeable technical vocabularies. The question whether a Chinese term conveys the meaning of Indian equivalent depends on whether the translation keeps the formal system of the original and whether it is understood by the Chinese. If this is fulfilled, then the technical meaning of the term is understood.

In the middle of the Later Han Dynasty (1st Century B.C. to 1st Century A.D.) there was a revival of Taoism. In order to differentiate the original from the revived Taoism, the name Hsuan-hsueh, Dark Learning was known to the contemporary Chinese and Neo-Taoism to the West. Hsuan means dark, profound, metaphysics. This term originated in the first chapter of Lao-tze's The Book of Tao:

> "They may both be called the Cosmic Mystery
>
> Reaching from the Mystery into the deeper Mystery
>
> Is the Gate to the secret of all Life".[12]

The Neo-Taoists took delight in contemplating mystery behind all mysteries – the ultimate behind the phenomenal world. They speculated that there must be some absolute Principle at the origin of all phenomena, and some ultimate reality that brings forth universal harmony. The idea of Wu or Non-being is the basis of all things. "Though Heaven and Earth in their greatness are richly endowed with the myriad things: though their thunder moves and their winds circulate, through their revolving operations the myriad transformations came to be – Yet it is the Silent and Supreme non-being that is their origin."[13]

The Chinese literary society during the 4th century A.D. was greatly dominated by Neo-Taoism, at the same time the *Prajñā* School was gaining supremacy among the Buddhist Circle. Both the Schools were influenced by similar philosophy. According to the Buddhist all things by nature are empty or *śūnya* and the Neo-Taoist held that everything had their origin in non-being (Wu wei). Liu-chin (A.D. 438-495) made this statement, "from the K'un-lun Mountain eastward the term 'Great Oneness' is used and from Kashmir westward the word *Sambodhi* Cheng chueh (Buddhist expression) is used". In the Record of the Later Han Dynasty Fan-yeh (A.D. 398-445) says about Buddhism, "If we examine closely, its teaching about purifying the mind and gaining release from the ties of life and its casting aside both 'emptiness' and 'being' we see that it belongs to the same current as do the Taoist writings."[14] So we feel that the Buddhist and Taoist scholars belonged to the same intellectual trend. An interesting incident I am quoting from the biography of Hui-yuan[15] (A.D. 334-416). One day while the monk Hui-yuan was discussing in the assembly, the audience who gathered there became restless, confused and bewildered about the exposition of the Buddhist theory of reality. The monk immediately quoted the idea of reality of Lao-tze and Chuan-tze and then only the audience became satisfied and pacified.

Many scholars used Lao-tze's and Chuang-tze's ideas and thoughts to expound Buddhist ideas. Such use of Taoist terminology to explain Buddhist concept was known as Ke-yi[16] method of analogy. This method was a specialized system of teaching Buddhism to the literary and gentry class who were well versed in Confucius and Taoist classes. In the beginning of the 4th Century A.D. Tao-an (A.D. 312-385) who came from an eminent Confucian family evolved this system. This method of Ke-yi was employed for those who were well-equipped with the doctrinal terminologies of Taoism and Confucianism but were ignorant of Buddhist terminology. But Tao-an himself had to give up Ke-yi when he found this method of instruction useless. Later on, Hui-yu, the disciple of Kumārajīva condemned this system. Tao-an in the early stage always taught Buddhism with the help of "Three Mysteries" Lao-tze, Chuang-tze and I-Ching (The book of Change).

So we find that the Buddhist ideas and concepts were equated with Chinese ideas and thoughts. Thus the five important cardinal virtues of Confucianism Wu-ch'ang were equated with the five Buddhist *Śīlas* and the four Buddhist *Mahābhūtas* with the Chinese five Elements Wu-hsing.

During the period of disunity lasting from the disintegration of the Han in 220 A.D. till the Sui (A.D. 590-617) and the T'ang (A.D. 618-907), Taoism became increasingly important. The Buddhist antithesis of *Bhūta-tathatā* or Absolute Chen-ju and the temporal, permanent and change, *Nirvāṇa* and cycle of life and death found their equivalents in the Taoist ideas of non-being and being. Wu and yu, the *Mahāyānist* concept of *Prajñā* (Chih-hui), the void *Śūnyatā* (K'ung) Stillness (*Śānti*, Chi), expediency (*Upāya*, Feng-shih), amalgamated with their counterparts in Hsuan-hseuh of Saintliness (Sang), Emptiness (hsu)[17], Non-being (Wu-wei), etc.

In course of discussion between *Tathāgata* and Subhūti in the *Vajracchedikā Prajñāpāramitā Sūtra*[18], Subhūti concluded saying, Yi-ch'ieh hsien-Shang Chieh-yi wu-wei fu-erh-yu-Cha'pie. The sages and wisemen all adopted diffusive doctrine that admits of no particular distinction (Wu-wei) has been interpreted in many ways. It means non-activity, passive, spontaneous, trascendal, non-phenomenal noumenal interpreted as *Nirvāṇa*, etc.[19] "The famous Taoist doctrine of Wu-wei is no less than the practical application of this philosophy of the infinite to our daily life."[20]

Among hundred of *Sūtras* translated into Chinese a sizeable number comprises *Dhāraṇī*. These texts show that these are the works of transcription rather than that of translation. The transcription of *Dhāraṇī* does not confront with major obstacles. It does neither require thorough knowledge of intricacies of Sanskrit grammar, nor it requires knowledge of literary Sanskrit. For transcribing *Dhāranī*, a knowledge of Indian script was sufficient.

The Indian script in a variety of *Brāhmī* called *Siddhaṃ*[21] became very popular and played an important part in Chinese Buddhism ever since it was introduced in China and Japan in the 8th century with spread of *Mantrayāna*, the esoteric school of true word. *Siddhaṃ* script was specially employed to transcribe *Dhāraṇī*s, *Mantras* and *Vijākṣaras* or germ letters. An attempt was made in early period to transcribe the Indian formulae phonetically syllable by syllable with corresponding Chinese sound but before long it proved to be inefficacious. With the advent of the 8th century the transcribers mostly used *Siddhaṃ* letters. The prolific translator Hsuan-chuang made certain reforms in the method of translation. The terms regarding esoterism like *Dhāraṇīs* or *Maṇḍalas* were left untranslated by him.

Long before the spread of Buddhism the Chinese were familiar with Taoist spells, magic charms and sorcery. Therefore, they became very much interested in Buddhist *Mantras* and *Dhāraṇīs.* The first foreign monk who arrived at Ch'ang-an in 625 A.D. with the text of thousand of *Dhāraṇīs* and *Sādhana*, was a native of Central India. These texts were translated under the name of T'o-lo-ni-chi-ching *Dhāraṇī* Saṅgraham. The original is lost, the translations exist.

The following centuries saw a galaxy of *Tāntrik* adepts who brought many more *Mantrayānic* texts. Among the foreign monks special mention may be made of Subhakara Siṁha, Vajrabodhi and Amoghavajra, all from India, Subhakara Siṁha translated *Mahāvairocana*, the basic text of *Tantrayāna.*

Under the imperial patronage, by the pious devotion of selfless painstaking and preserving monks, by their loyal supporters and by private contribution the translation work continued unceasingly, unabated throughout the long period of Buddhism in China. The latest Japanese editions of the Catalogue of Chinese *Tripiṭaka* contains 85 volumes and 3053 items. It is a rare wonder in the history of human civilization, so far its amount and perfection are concerned. It is matchless and cannot be compared with the translation work carried on by the team of modern world. Indian philosophical ideas and thoughts, political and social systems were opened to the Chinese which had lasting cultural impact on Chinese mind.

Living in the highly advanced scientific world we really wonder how could it be possible to produce such bulk of Buddhist Canon in Chinese by simple human endeavour.

References

1. Arthur F. Wright: *Buddhism in Chinese History.*
2. Sir Charles Eliot: Hinduism and Buddhism.
3. *The Catalogue of Chinese Tripiṭaka*, Taisho Edition, Vols. 18, 50.
4. James Legge: *The Tao.*
5. Fung Yu-lan: *The History of Chinese Philosophy* (Translation from Chinese to English).
6. Fung Yu-lan: *Chung-kuo-che-hsueh-shih* (in Chinese).
7. Lin Yu-tang: *Wisdom of China and India.*
8. K.K.S. Ch'en: *Buddhism in China.*
9. R.H.Van Gullik: *Siddhaṃ.*
10. E. Zurcher: *The Buddhist Conquest of China.*
11. Soothhill: *Dictionary of Chinese Buddhist Terms.*

Endnotes

1. Arthur F. Wright: '*Buddhism in Chinese History*', pp. 33-34.
2. J. Takakusu : *A Record of Buddhist Religion as Practised in India and Malaya Archipelago*, P. Ix, Ixi.
3. Sir Charles : Eliot *Hinduism and Buddhism*, Vol. III, p. 30.
4. E. Zurcher: *The Buddhist Conquest of China*, p. 40.
5. J. Takakusu : *A Record of Buddhist Religion as Practised in India and Malaya Archipelago*, pp. 170-171.
6. Ibid, pp. Ix, Ixi. T. Watters: *On Yuang Chwang's Travels in India*, Vol. II, pp. 152-56.
7. Dr. L. Wieger: *Chinese Characters*, Ed. Henri Vetch, Peking, pp. 17-18.
8. Vide Preface to *K'ang-his Dictionary*.
9. Taisho Ed. *Tripiṭaka*, Vol. 50, No. 2059, p. 351.
10. E. Zurcher: *The Buddhist Conquest of China*, p. 203. Kenneth K.S. Ch'en: *Buddhism in China*, p. 369-370.
11. Arthur F. Wright: *Buddhism in Chinese History*, pp. 32-33.
12. Lin Yu-tang: *The Wisdom of China and India*, p. 583 (Modern Library, New York).
13. Fung Yu-lan: *The History of Chinese Philosophy* (Princeton, 1953) Vol. 2, p. 2181.
14. Ibid, p. 2240.
15. C. *Tripiṭaka*, Taisho Ed. Vol. 50 *Kao-Seng-chuan* 6, p. 357.
16. Ibid, No. 2059, p. 355, E. Zurcher : *Buddhist Conquest of China*, pp. 12, 184, 187, App. IV 18.
17. Fung Yu-lan: *The History of Chinese Philosophy*, Vol. 11 E. Zurcher: *Buddhist Conquest of China*, pp. 73-74.
18. *Chinese Tripiṭaka*, Vol. 8, No. 235, p. 749, 2nd folio 1.17.
19. Soothhill : *Dictionary of Chinese Buddhist Terms*, p. 380.
20. D.T. Suzuki: *The Tao*, James Legge, *Introduction* p. 22.
21. H.R. Van Gullik: *Siddhaṃ* (Saraswati Vihar Series) Ed. by Raghuvira.

10

A NOTE ON UṢṆĪṢA-SITĀTAPATRA PRYATYAṂGIRA... DHĀRAṆĪ

Sudha Sengupta

The *Dhāraṇīs* are mystic formulae or protective spells – sometimes very short, sometimes comparatively longer – which are believed to possess immense power to bring happiness, and ward off evils, to the reciter or his client, if pronounced properly. Use of magic and spells was prevalent in India and the outside world from time immemorial. Belief in supernatural is a very old trait of human nature. In the whole of Vedic literature – not to speak of the *Atharva Veda* only – we find a number of litanies or *mantras*, that were used on different occasions.

Buddhism, in its earlier stage, was against all ritualism. But their existence in early Buddhist literature is also to be traced. The *Parittas* – more popular in Ceylon, and the verse recommended to be recited as protection against śnake-bite in *Vinaya, Cullavagga*[1] - may be cited as examples, out of a number of them. Though the exact date of these pieces are not known, still there is no doubt that they belong to the early days of Buddhism.

With the gradual development of *Mahāyāna* and its culmination into *Tantrayāna* or *Mantrayāna*, more and more rituals and mantras were introduced into it and along with the prevalence of the worship of numerous deities and innovation of different mantras, the *Dhāraṇīs* became very popular. But the *Dhāraṇīs*, though used as protective spells and even sometimes used in amulets to be tied to the body in order to protect the wearer from all kinds of evils, are somewhat different from the *Atharvavedic mantras* in that, these are quite often shortened forms of longer *Mahāyānic* texts, which are otherwise difficult to read due to their length and the recitation or reading of these *Dhāraṇīs* is supposed to bring the same merit as reading the whole text. Of course, there is no death of independent *Dhāraṇīs* in the name of different deities.

The nomenclature of '*Dhāraṇī*' is of comparatively recent origin. Though the name 'Dhāraṇī' occurs in the texts belonging to earlier period, like the *Lalitavistara* and *Sandhi-nirmocana-sūtra*[2], which are ascribed to about the 2nd century A.D., its precise use as a *mantra* did not seems to occur prior to the 4th century, when, in texts like *Kāraṇḍavyūha*[3], we find one of the typical sets of mantras as occur in different *Dhāraṇīs*, which apparently seem to be a jargon of meaningless syllables, but which, to the devotees, are laden with immense potentiality and are able to perform miracles, if used properly. From this period onwards, a bulk of *Dhāraṇī* literature grew up in India and abroad.

The full name of the *Dhāraṇī* to be discussed below is '*Āryasarvatathāgatoṣṇīṣa-sitātapatrāparājitā pratyaṁgira* (or *mahā-pratyaṁgira*) *mahāvidyā rājñī*' or '*Pratyaṁgira dhāraṇī*' or ' – *kalpa*', or a variation of the same name.

Though this *Dhāraṇī* does not hold any prominent position in the recent discussion on *Mahāyāna Buddhist Sūtras*, in other words to say, that sufficient research has not been done on this text – there is ample proof that it was very popular at one time, say from the 5-6th to the 18th century A.D. – not only in India, but more in the outside world. Numerous copies of this text have been discovered from different places – from Central Asia to Nepal, it has also a place in the Chinese and Tibetan texts. The earliest manuscript of this text seems to be those found from Eastern Turkestan which are written in 'upright' and 'cursive' Gupta scripts and as such, seems to belong to about the 7th century A.D. Excavations carried out by a number of archaeologists like Sir A. Stein, in the deserts of Central Asia have brought to light a considerable number of Buddhist texts on various objects which include a number of *Dhāraṇīs* also and our text also forms a part of them, at least two copies of which are there. One of them – a fragmentary one – has been noticed by R. Hoernle in his book entitled '*Manuscript Remains of Buddhist Literature Found in Easter Turkestan*'.[4] (It is a small complete folio, measuring 245 X 46 mm and contains four lines in each side. These eight lines contain mainly the epithets of the goddess Tārā, in verses in more or less corrupt Sanskrit and having the Khotanese peculiarity of using 'rr' in place of single 'r' after consonants, in many places).

In course of his explorations in Eastern Turkestan, Sir Aurel Stein discovered a treasurehouse of manuscripts from the 'immured Temple Library of Tun-huang' – among which there were a number of rolls made of tough paper, of varying length- from two to twenty-three feet, and one at least is as long as more than seventy feet and as such is called the gigantic roll – the width generally being ten to twelve inches. These rolls contain writings on one side in Chinese and on the other in Tokharian or 'cursive Gupta' characters.[5]

Among these rolls there is one no. 0041, which measures 10'10" X 10.1/2", contain 151 lines of writing in cursive Gupta characters at the back side. This writing comprises two *Dhāraṇīs*, one, a short one of less than ten lines, which has been identified with the *Uṣṇiṣa-Vijaya Dhāraṇī* and the other – a longer one, starting from the middle of the tenth line and continuing upto the 151st line, is a Tokharian version of the one that we are discussing here, as is evident from the name mentioned in the body of the text. Incidentally, it may be mentioned that there is no fundamental difference between Sanskrit and the language in which these texts are written (we are not sure whether they are the real languages used by the people of

Eastern Turkestan), except a few minor ones like the absence of *Visarga*, the use of 'nd' in places of simple cerebral 'd' or denial 'ta' and the like.

The 'gigantic roll' mentioned above, contains 1108 lines of writing on its inner side, most of which is in clear 'upright Gupta' script with the exceptions of a few interspersion which are in 'cursive Gupta' script. Of these, the first 197 lines constitute the *Dhāraṇī* of our discussion, in Sanskrit, which, of course, is not very correct, as is usual with other texts of the same type.[6] The composers did not care much about the grammatical correctness but their attention was engaged more to express the idea by any means. It corresponds to the previous one, i.e., the one at the back of the roll no. 0041, only the top portion, i.e. from the beginning to the middle of line,[7] is torn off.

In the Mss. collection of the Asiatic Society, Calcutta, a copy of the same *Dhāraṇī* is mentioned as no. 846 in the catalogue of Sanskrit Mss. by R.L. Mitra, as brought from Nepal. It has 18 folia of Nepalese paper 7.1/2" X 3" in size, with five lines in each page. The colour of the papers in black with the lines alternately in a gold and silver. On the front page there is a painting of the goddess. It is dated in Newari Samvat 886, i.e., 1756 A.D.[8] Another similar copy is mentioned in the catalogue by Mm. H.P. Sastri in the same collection, which has 22 folia and is dated Newari Samvat 993. The former manuscript is not traceable, while the latter is available in the collection.[9]

Notices of other copies of this text are to be found in the catalogue of Buddhist Sanskrit Manuscripts, Cambridge, by Bendall.[10] The catalogue of the Royal Asiatic Society by Hodgson[11] also records two manuscripts of the same text.[12]

The whole of the Sanskrit text of the *Mahāpratyaṁgira dhāraṇī* was transcribed into Chinese characters by the famous mystic teacher Amoghavajra (A.D. 704-774, cf. Nanjio cat. no. 155, col. 444).[13] In the Taisho Ed. of Chinese *Tripiṭaka*, there are altogether five copies of the same text of which one, no. 9443, is written in *Siddhaṃ* characters which were used to write ancient Sanskrit *mantra* texts, and the other four are either translations or transliterations of the same.[14]

It seems that most of the manuscripts mentioned above and those which will be discussed below, had been taken away from Nepal, as Nepal was one of the last resorts of later Buddhism and a flourishing centre of Buddhist learning and text of this type of literature were available in plenty. Even now the Bir Library of Kathmandu, Nepal, which is a treasure house of innumerable of valuable manuscripts, possesses a number of copies of this text.[15]

The Tokyo University Mss. Library has got not less than ten copies of the same text with slight variations. One of them resembles the one at the Calcutta Asiatic Society, being written alternately in gold and silver on black paper and having the image of the goddess painted on the first page in colour. In addition, it has got a panel of gods and goddesses painted on both the sides of its wooden cover.[16] The Tohoku and the Otani Universities of Japan also have two copies each of the same text.

In the Tibetan Buddhist canons, in both *Kanjur* and *Tanjur*, there are a number of the same text composed and translated by various scholars. The name of Chandragomin as author of a number of them is found to be mentioned.[17]

The goddess sitātapatra, in whose name the *Dhāraṇī* is composed, is a form of the goddess Tārā. She belongs to the *Kula* or group of the *Bodhisattva Vairocana*, and the *Dhāraṇī* itself also speaks of the same. There is only one Sādhanā of the goddess *Sitātapatra Aparājitā* in the *Sādhanamālā* in which she is described as 'of white colour' six arms and three faces with three eyes in each face, carrying different things in her hands, but there is no mention of her carrying the white parasol in any of her hands, which should have been there as her distinctive mark. 'She is said to have angry looks...and is led by *Variocana*'.[18]

Of the manuscripts mentioned above, there are quite a few which bear the figure of the goddess painted on the first page as has already been mentioned above. I could not have access to all of them, excepting two. But none of these two, i.e., the one in the Asiatic Society, Calcutta, and the other in the Tokyo University Collection, does agree with the description. In both of them, the goddess has one face with two hands, the left one carrying the umbrella, while the right one in a pose in between *Abhaya* and *Varada mudrā*. The picture on the Asiatic Society manuscript, of course, has got angry looks, but the one on the Tokyo University manuscript, has a sweet expression and in place of the image of *Vairocana* on her head, as in the former one, the halo behind her head is in the shape of a *Caitya*. These pictures rather conform to the description given by Gordon[19] and Getty.[20]

As the *Mahāyāna Sūtras*, particularly the *Dhāraṇīs* are given in the mouth of the Buddha himself or one of his eminent disciples, it is very difficult to have some knowledge of their real author. This is true in the case of this *Dhāraṇī* also. Nowhere do be and mention of the name of its author or the translator, not even in the Tokharian version of it, excepting in the Tibetan canons. As is under various names like '*Uṣṇīṣa sitātapatra pratyaṁgira*', *sitātapatra aparājitā*' and the like. Some of them are *Dhāraṇīs*, while some are *sādhanās, stotras* or *upadeśas*. The author of quite a few of them is mentioned to be Chandragomin.[21] Whether this Chandragomin is the same person as the grammarian, the author of *Chāndravyākaraṇa*, is a matter of dispute. But the illustrious Buddhist monk, Chandragomin, who is supposed to belong to a *kṣatriya* family of Vārendra in Bengal, is credited not only with writing the grammar, but also – as a devout worshipper of *Tārā* - to have composed Stotras and *Dhāraṇīs* of *Tārā*, including those of *Sitātapatra*.[22]

The aim of the *Dhāraṇī*: This 'invincible white-umbrella one' goddess, having been attributed lots of qualities, is described as the destroyer of all evils and endowed with all powers to do good to the devotees. She is invoked and prayed to protect the devotees and 'all living beings' from all kinds of danger – from kings (i.e., kings' wrath), thieves, fire, water, poisonous weapons, enemies, conspiracy, famine, lightning, earthquake, untimely death, mateor, royal punishment, wild animals, snakes, hot sand, birds, planets, *Yakṣas Rākṣasas, Asura, Kinnara*, and such others. The list of dangers sought to be protected from, is a long one and covers all conceivable things, and they are supposed to be destroyed by the mantra 'phat'. In conclusion, the text mentions that, "whoever, having written this overpowering queen of magic spells (*vidyā-rājñī*) named the white umbrella one, …on birch bark, cloth or tree bark, and fixes it on the body or neck, or causes it to be read, (then) throughout his whole life he shall not be harmed by (any of above mentioned dangers)"[23]. From the contents we can have an idea about the materials on which the *dhāraṇīs* are supposed to be written and used as amulets, which seems to have been widely prevalent during its high popularity.

Endnotes

1. *Vinaya (Cullavagga)*, V. 6.
2. *Lalitavistara* 2; *Sandhinirmocana sūtra* 124 (cf. *Age of Imperial Kanauj*, p. 360-6).
3. *Kāraṇḍavyūha*, ch. Vii.
4. Hoernle, *Manuscript Remains of Buddhist Literature Found in Eastern Turkestan*, Vol. 1, p. 52 ff. ms. No. 150 vii 5, pl. II.
5. J.R.A.S., 1911, p. 447 ff.
6. Ibid.
7. Ibid, p. 469.
8. *Asiatic Society*, Calcutta, *Catalogue of Sanskrit* Mss. by R. L. Mitra, no. B. 46, 227.
9. Do. Catalogue by Mm. H. P. Sastri, no. 46, p. 46.
10. *Catalogue of Buddhist Sanskrit Mss.*, Cambridge by C. Bendall, addl. No. 1348, p. 63 & addl. No. 1358, p. 68.
11. Royal Asiatic Society Catalogue by Hodgson, nos. 77, 61.
12. Ibid. A pencil note on the cover by Dr. Write describes the contents as 'Prayers or Mantras against sickness, witches, etc.' 15.
13. Nanjio, Catalogue…no. 155, coll 444; Tokyo xxv-50a.
14. Nos. 943 A; 976,977 and 945, in addition to no.944B which is in Siddham characters.
15. Catalogue of the Bir Library, Nepal, published by the Sanskrit seminar of the Tahoku University, Japan, Nos. 226, 782/2, 140/1, 230/2 and 641/6. The first two give the full name, (*Āryaśrī*) *sarvatathāgatoṣṇīṣa sitātapatra*………..'while the last three give the name as either '*mahāpratyaṁgira dhāraṇī* ' or 'm.p. *vidyārājñī*'.

16. Tokyo Univ. Library, Ms. no. 237-6, pp. 16-31.
17. Catalogue of Tibetan Buddhist Canons; Tohoku University, Sendai, Japan, 1934.
18. B. Bhattacharya, *Sādhanamālā* (O.S. no. 26) p. 395.
19. A.K.Gordon, *The Iconography of Tibetan Lamaism* (C.E. Tuttle & Co. Tokyo), p. 72
20. A. Getty, *Gods of Northern Buddhism* (Tuttle), p. 136.
21. cf. F. N. no. 17.
22. *Banglaya Bauddha Dharma* (in Bengali), N. Dasgupta, p. 160.
23. cf. the Text, also cf. Ind. Ant. 1914, p. 37ff.

11

THE PROBLEM OF LEADERSHIP IN EARLY BUDDHISM

Sanghasen Singh

The general belief is that the Buddha was the founder and the supreme leader of the Order which is known to us as the *Saṅgha*. While it may be true that he was the founder, but as regards his leadership in the *Saṅgha,* there are evidences to prove that he was not at all supreme. The *Saṅgha* was a faction-ridden organization. The *Tipiṭaka* is full of instances to show that, many a time, the Buddha had to bow before the majority opinion and had to take pains to unite the warning factions. He was compelled, at least once, to stop all efforts at reconciliation in the Order when, while staying at Kosambi, he tried to bring about concord between two groups of monks. One of the monks actually asked him to leave them to settle their differences without his interference. The Buddha left Kosambī out of disgust and frustration, and retired alone to keep retreat in the Pārileyyaka forest.[1] In fact, the Buddhist Order had also to undergo the same dialectical process, which does not leave untouched any phenomenon in this universe. The study of the origin and growth of the Buddhist Order provides us with an example to show that though basically a religious organization, it could never be immune of the process.

The last moments of the Buddha before his passing away at Kusīnārā at the age of eighty, which is euphemistically called *Mahāparinibbāna* or the Great Demise, reveal to us that the Buddha was faced with a very serious problem of succession. Some of his chief disciples like Sāriputta, Moggallāna had already passed away, and the Order was not having leaders of their caliber. Even after the exit of Devadatta, the monks loyal to his line of thinking were still their in the Order. This was probably the reason which forestalled the imposition of Mahākassapa or any other person who was closer to Sāriputta, Moggallāna, etc. as the leader of the Order, although, probably, he was the only senior monk who was alive. *Ānanda* was too junior in the Order, and had not even achieved *Arhathood.* Upāli, a past master of *Vinaya* was not likely to be picked up by the Buddha for obvious reasons. He happened to be a low-born (son of a barber of Kapilavatthu) and the Buddha was quite aware of the consequences which were likely to follow, if he had been installed as successor to the Buddha. Although it is true that the Buddha was sympathetic to the cause of upliftment of the lower castes, but he was equally handicapped in the matter, because the sons of the *Khattiyas Brāhmaṇas* and

Gahapatis were in majority in the Order. He was conscious of the fact that the installation of a low-born to his exalted position might lead to widespread repulsion in the minds of devotees scattered all over the *Majjhima Desa*. Hence his predicament. But as an able tactician, he immediately found out the solution. He summoned *Ānanda* and made a proclamation that, henceforth, the *Dhamma* or the Doctrine, would be their *Sāstā* or the teacher-leader. The significance of this event is very clear. The Buddha had no option but to make this arrangement for the sake of unity and cohesion in the Order. The students of *Tipiṭaka* find many occasions where the Buddha had left no opportunity in exhorting his followers to remain united and to avoid disputes and dissensions. This reason is not for to seek. The danger of split in the Order was always there, and he had to exert himself time and again to keep his disciples within his control.

During his life time, the Buddha was made the target of many wild attacks. There were powerful plotters within the ranks of the Order, who were not alone but were in sizable groups. The 'misdeeds' of *Chabbaggiyā Bhikkhus* (a set of six monks taken as exemplification of trespassing the rules of *Vinaya*), *Sattarasa-vaggiyā Bhikkhus* (a group of seventeen monks), etc. are quite known to the students of *Tipiṭaka*. They used to create problems for the Buddha. Sometimes, even the smaller events of misdeeds used to rock the whole organization. Above all was Devadatta, the Buddha's own cousin, who plotted against him many times, but could not succeed in dislodging him. He (Devadatta) had the patronage of a powerful king. Ajātasattu, the ruler of Magadha with his capital at Rājagaha. The early *Pāli* texts depict him to be a villain in the Order, but a close study of those texts make it clear that he was not an individual who was against the Buddha or his leadership, but represented a powerful section in the Order, who had a distinct ideology and policy of their own. They wanted to push through their line of thinking, which the Buddha did not totally approve of. The texts suggest that love of gain, favours and flattery were responsible for Devadatta's undoing. But this might be a partisan view. It is likely that the drift between Devadatta and the Buddha would have widened through the passage of time, and a moment came when they were face to face with each other. The confrontation turned into enemity, and hence, Devadatta's efforts, first, to dislodge the Buddha from his position, and then to do away with him, and ultimately, a schism. The texts suggest that for a pretty long time, Devadatta enjoyed prestige and honour in the Order. Some *Suttas* (discourses) are even ascribed to him. This was really a great honour to him and a proof of his intellectual capacity. Devadatta and the like might have felt the necessity of the change in leadership of the Order, when they found that their line of thinking could gain ascendancy only when the Buddha was removed from leadership. The *Vinaya Piṭaka* says that he went to the Buddha and suggested that the leadership of the Order should be handed over to him in view of the Buddha's approaching old age. The Buddha scorned the suggestion, saying, "Not even to Sāriputta or Moggallāna would I hand over the

Order, and would I then the, vile one, to be vomited like spittle?"[2] Devadatta showed resentment and probably vowed vengeance. This might have created bitterness in the Order. Thereupon, at the Buddha's suggestion, a proclamation was issued to the *Saṅgha* that in anything done by Devadatta in the name of the *Buddha*, the *Dhamma* and the *Saṅgha*, none but Devadatta was to be recognized. In simple words, this means Devadatta's expulsion, if not formal at least informal. This might have infuriated Devadatta and he would have sought the help of his friend Ajātasattu. The *Vinaya-Piṭaka* says that Ajātasattu agreed and provided Devadatta with royal archers to shoot at the Buddha. The plan failed. He is said to have further tried himself to kill the Buddha by hurling on him a great rock, while the Buddha was walking on the slopes of Gijjhakūṭa. Devadatta's next attempt on the Buddha's life was to persuade elephant-keepers to let loose a road by which the Buddha would pass. This plan too failed. There upon, Devadatta decided, with the help of Kokālika and several others to bring about a schism in the Order. They went, accordingly, to the Buddha and asked for the imposition of a set of five rules on all members of the *Saṅgha* : (1) that monks should dwell all their lives in the forest, (2) that they should accept no invitations to meals, but live entirely on alms obtained by begging, (3) that they should wear only robes made of discarded rags and no robes from the laity, (4) that they should dwell at the foot of a tree and not under a roof, (5) that they should abstain completely from fish and flesh. These Buddha's reply was that those who felt so inclined could follow these rules – except that of sleeping under a tree during the rainy season – but he refused to make the rules obligatory. This refusal delighted Devadatta, who went about with his party declaring that the Buddha was prone to luxury and abundance. He held an *Uposatha* meeting without the Buddha, and was successful in persuading five hundred newly ordained monks from Vesālī to join him and accompany him to Gayāsīsa. The Buddha sent Sāriputta and Moggallāna to bring back the deluded ones. Devadatta believing that they had come to join him, rejoiced, and, in spite of Kokālika's warning, welcomed them. That night he preached late to the monks, and wishing for rest, asked Sāriputta to address the assembly. Sāriputta and Moggallāna preached to such effects that they persuaded the five hundred monks to return with then Shorn of distortion, which is quite possible under such circumstances, the above description of the *Vinaya Piṭaka* suggests that Devadatta tried his best to establish a rival Order. Probably he succeeded doing so. The *Vinaya Piṭaka* description mentions the route figure of five hundred monks who joined and then desert Devadatta. But what about others who had soft corner for Devadatta, and who had joined him. Among them were many nuns and some *Sākyans* as well. It might be possible that the story of desertion was concocted for the use as a propaganda measure against Devadatta faction in the Order. This fact is corroborated by the travel accounts of Yuan Chwang.[3] According to him, a sect bearing the name of Devadatta, was quite flourishing in Bengal at that time. It may be just possible that the followers of Devadatta might have migrated from Magadha to Gauda, finding that place to be more congenial for their survival than other places. But the fact remains that a rival Order did exist and develop so as to survive till the time of Yuan Chwang and after.

One event in *Majjhima Nikāya* suggests to us the attitude of some of the chief disciples of the Buddha towards him. The Buddha was no doubt their leader, but some of them had reservations about him and his method of functioning. Once, while the Buddha was staying in the village Cātumā with some of his disciples, some new members of the Order went there at the instance of Sāriputta and Moggallāna. These persons, dwelling near the Buddha, made so much noise that they were summoned and asked to leave the place at once. But the Sākyans of the village and Brahmā Sahampati interceded on their behalf, and they were allowed to return. This event clearly shows the difference in attitudes of Sāriputta and Moggallāna towards the Buddha and the Buddhist Order. It seems, Moggallāna would have rebelled, if the villagers had not intervened and restored normalcy.

The history of early Buddhism makes it clear that many a powerful personalities had joined hands with the Buddha for the speedy expansion of the Order and the doctrines it stood for. Sāriputta, Moggallāna, Devadatta, Mahākassapa, *Ānanda*, etc. were very much equal to the Buddha in intellectual and the so-called spiritual attainments. In certain respects, it is said, they even excelled him. The early Buddhist tradition has admitted this fact. *Milindapañha,* for instance, provides very sound evidence to this effect. One of the Milinda dilemmas is as follows: "Why should Devadatta who was so wicked have been, time after time, superior in power to the *Bodhisatta*?" *The Jātaka* commentary contains numerous stories which show that, though, sometimes Devadatta was failed in his attempts to harm the *Bodhisatta*, in many cases, he succeeded in working his will. When such powerful personalities were at the helm of affairs of the *Saṅgha,* could the question of leadership be settled in the most docile and hackneyed manner, as the early Buddhist text suggest? In fact, the attempts of the compilers of these texts had been to show the Buddha as the most superior , standing head and shoulders above them, whereas to belittle the personalities of the rest. The pre-eminence which the Buddha had attained was due to the fact he continued to be the leader of the Organization. He was conscious of this truth, even when Devadatta had formally requested him to step down. The Buddha enjoyed the confidence of the majority at the times of crisis, because he happened to be the centrist in the *Saṅgha*. The fear of split always haunted the elders, and, hence, there was a forced unity. Whatever differences, dissensions, rifts and schisms which occurred in the Order are depicted to have been engineered by certain individuals for purely personal considerations. All the Buddhist text do so invariably. But for a student of history, these were the signs of internal struggles which were the reflections of socio-economic forces working in the given society. The social phenomena had got a direct bearing upon the events as mentioned above. Devadatta was not an individual, but represented a powerful faction in the Order, which was under the direct influence of the people. This history of the eastern U.P. and Bihar of the sixth and fifth centuries B.C. shows that many religious leaders were contending for supremacy. The pace of Āryanization was being challenged stoutly. The *Brāhmaṇas* who happened to be intellectually more superior were busy at work to push through the Vedic influence, particularly the belief in Vedic rituals. As a result, the performance of grand *yojanas* (sacrificial ceremonies) by feudal chiefs and their associates became the order of the day. It entailed huge expenses. Besides, the pastoral and village economy of the day was getting jeopardized due to the loss of cattle who were the main source of production. As usual, this was not to the linking of the peasantry, artisans, labourers, etc. attached to the fields and cattle-breeding farms. Under these circumstances many *Khattiyas* and their castemen mobilized public opinion against the sacrificial ceremonies, and in course of time became their spokesmen. The leaders among them went about declaring themselves to be the saviour of the people against the tyranny of the protagonists of the sacrificial culture. But the motivation seems to have been the ouster of the *Brāhmaṇas* from their exalted position as the administrators and religious leaders. That was, in fact, the root cause of the rivalry between the *Brāhmaṇa* priests and *Khattiya* leaders. The seers of the major *Upaniṣads,* the Buddha, Mahāvīra, etc. were all the product of this process. They all put up strong resistance to the supremacy of the Brāhmaṇas. Their attack was two-pronged. They established their own orders and worked day and night to corrode the religious base of the *Brāhmaṇa* priests, and, on the other hand, they moved about in the society to teach the people that everybody was born equal. The former task was performed by them openly, whereas the latter in a subtle manner. The Buddha's advocacy for *Cātuvaṇṇa-pārisuddhi* (the emancipation of the persons belonging to all the four *varṇas*), the establishment of the Order which served as an example of commune life, his disregard for riches of any sort, his help for the liberation of the woman folk, etc. are some of the factors which made him very popular with the people in general.

The Buddha's efforts were directed, to some extent, towards arousing a sense of self-confidence among the *Khattiyas.* Although they too belonged to the ruling class of those days, but they could not assert successfully in the face of *Brāhmaṇa* superiority which was established due to their being the real administrators and intellectually more sound. The *Khattiyas,* on the other hand, were less equipped with above-mentioned two pre-requisites for supremacy in the society. In course of debates with *Brāhmaṇa* priests on the question of birth superiority, the Buddha always deprecated the idea and talked of equality of human beings. He left the doors of the *Saṅgha* open to all, irrespective of caste, community or region. But at times, while discussing the relative superiority of *Brāhmaṇas* and *Khattiyas* he always asserted that the *Khattiyas* were superior to the *Brāhmaṇas* (*Khattiyo seṭṭho jane tasmim you gotta-paṭīsāriṇo*). While talking of the *varṇas* in the society, the early Buddhist texts mention the list as follows: *Khattiya, Brāhmaṇa, Vessa* and *Sudda.* In order to explain the evil aspect of the society, the instances had invariably been picked up from amongst the *Brāhmaṇa* families. As a master tactician, the Buddha made several gestures and alliances with non-*Brāhmaṇa* caste leaders and created an atmosphere where they could join hands with him and work for putting up a powerful challenge to the *Brāhmaṇical* hierarchy. The declaration of the establishment of the Order at Vārāṇasī (Isipatana Migadāva, now Sarnath) which was one of the chief centres of trade and commerce in those days, with the *dhammacakkappavattana sutta* as its manifesto, was probably with the purpose of seeking alliance with the powerful trading community. The quick admission of Yasa and his fifty-four associates of Vārāṇasī to the Order,[4] speaks volumes about this fact. In fact, many traders and bankers of those days loosened the strings of their money bags in order to help the Buddha for the expansion of his Order. How could it happen? There seem to have been a calculated move from both sides. The Jaina texts too are full of references of rich traders patronizing the Jaina Order as well. (But it does not mean that all the rich traders were inclined towards these religious movements. They patronized the *Brāhmaṇa* priests as well). There can be two explanations for this phenomenon. The burden of sacrificial expenses was too heavy and unbearable for this section of the people, and hence, they too started disapproving the performance of the sacrifices. Secondly, they were denied political and administrative share in the state machinery to the extent they were economically powerful and helpful to it. There was bound to be resentment among them. The *Khattiyas* might have made some allowances, and hence, an alliance with them.

As mentioned earlier, Devadatta represented a powerful faction in the Order, which stood for *Pan-Khattiyism.*[5] This section of the monks wanted rigorous asceticism to be compulsorily practiced by all the members of the Order. Almost all the religious Orders in those days, which emphasized upon the practice of asceticism of this or that sort, were under the leadership of the non-*Brāhmaṇas*. The *Brāhmaṇas* wre normally known to be prone to comfortable life. The basic concept of Vedic teaching being their guide in their day-to-day affairs. On the other hand, the practice of asceticism, which originated from non-Āryan beliefs and practices, was the prerogative of the non- *Brāhmaṇas.* As the Āryan settlers were much less in number than the non-*Āryans*, the advocacy of such a cause was more popular with the people in general. Devadatta was planning in two ways. The emphasis on the practice of asceticism was bound to create repulsion in the minds of the *Brāhmaṇas*. Under the circumstances, the insiders would desert the Order, and the probable new entrants would not be attracted. Secondly, through the espousal of such a cause, the non-*Brāhmaṇa* majority would flock towards him, and, hence, the actual control of the Order. Thus, it seems, Devadatta was more faithful and consistent to the cause he was assigned, when he was encouraged to join the Order. Being a practical man the Buddha could not subscribe to Devadatta's way of thinking lest he might lost his popularity among the *Brāhmaṇas* who were very helpful for the expansion of his

Order and the fulfillment of his mission. He needed powerful debaters who could face the challenges from the *Brāhmaṇas* priests. These practical considerations prevailed upon him to be so guarded in his attitude and behaviour that hundreds of learned *Brāhmaṇas* were attracted towards him and his Order. On the other hand, this advocacy for rigorous ascetic practices had made Devadatta a friend of even non-Buddhist religious leaders. *Nigantha Nātaputta* (Lord Mahāvīra) and his disciples had probably developed some link or understanding with him. In this respect, it is significant to note that those who played an active role, when he created the grand schism, were the monks from Veśālī, the birth-place of Lord Mahāvira himself.

Devadatta was not favorably disposed to Sāriputta, Moggallāna, etc. who represented the rival faction in the Order. The leadership of this faction was in the hands of those monks who had come from the *Brāhmaṇa* stock. *Ānanda*, though a *Khattiya* by birth, belonged to this faction. The Buddha's success was probably due to his capacity to provide a balance between these two factions of the Order.

After the schism created by Devadatta, the position of Sāriputta-Moggallāna faction became comparatively stronger. That is why after the death of the Buddha, when the First Council met at Rājagaha, it was this faction which provided the forum for the recitation and compilation of the Buddha's words. But it does not mean that other factions ceased to exist. The episode of Subhadda is very significant. He expressed delight over the passing away of the Buddha.[6] The *Cullavagga* account of the First Council depicts him to be a representative of those monks who were slack in religious practices. But there is every likelihood that the predominant section of the Order might have distorted Subhadda's role for their partisan considerations. There might have been yet another faction in the Order, which did not see eye to eye with this predominant faction, and expressed its reservations about the recited and compiled version of the words of the Master. The *Cullavagga* records that Purāṇa Thera and his disciples expressed their disapproval in clear-cut words. Thus the position in the Order was such that nobody could command the respect of all the factions in the Order. Hence, the Buddha's reluctance to name anybody as his successor. But on the other hand, the leadership which emerged after his death was capable enough to silence and liquidate all the rest. But the problem remained, and, in course of time, it appeared in much graver form. The Second Council was the culmination of the same. Confusion prevailed. The so-called faithful and orthodox monks of the Order were standing face to face with those who wanted to revise the principles and practices according to convenience. The socio-economic and political conditions had changed. These gave rise to new interpretations of the words of the Master, and new *Vinayic* practices in the Order, and thereby new methods of checks and balances. This led to a split and the monolith was completely shattered.

Endnotes

1. *Vinaya Piṭaka* (PTS edition), 1, 337-57.
2. Ibid, 11, 188.
3. *On Yuang Chwang's Travels in India* (Tr.) Watters.
4. *Mahāvagga, Vinaya Piṭaka.*
5. A parallel can be drawn with the Pan-Jatism movement of Haryana, Punjab, Rajasthan, Delhi and Western U.P.
6. *Mahāparinibbāna Sutta.*

12

AVADĀNAS ON THE POLITICAL ROLE OF THE TRADERS

G. B. Upreti

Sixth century B.C. witnessed the emergence of Magadha as the centre of political activity in Northern India. It was not a coincidence that the nucleus of the political power of a burgeoning state was also the stronghold of the *Gahapatis,* the *Seṭṭhis* and the *Satthavāhas.* The problem how the new developments in the fields of economy, social structure, religion and politics were interrelated has recently been discussed by many scholars. The most prominent among these scholars are D. D. Kosambi[1], R. S. Sharma[2] and Romila Thapar.[3] Original sources reveal to us that the new ideology vouchsafed for a king who could break the barriers of tribalism and bring the whole of India under one umbrella.[4] This was an ideal solution for the problems faced by the trading and mercantile class. The new ideology also emphasized the point that the king should give necessary capital to those who lived by trade.[5] As a consequence we observe close cooperation between the traders and the ruling power.

The traders arranged feast in the honour of the king,[6] and gave him money to maintain a large powerful army.[7] On his part, the king offered them financial and moral help when required.[8] He maintained friendly relations with them[9] and gave due consideration to their suggestions.[10] This, however, does not mean that the contradictions between the two sides died out. The state furnished the trader with capital but in return took away a large amount in the form of interest to fill the coffers of royal treasury.[11] Evasion of taxes was not tolerated and evading the custom duties was a very serious crime.[12] Caravans intending to evade custom duties were intercepted and ransacked by the royal officers.[13] The monks who helped the traders in such illegal activities were treated as thieves and punished accordingly.[14] But the state interfered in the activities of the trading class only when its interest suffered. Normally the state adopted the policy of *laissez faire* in the matters relating to trade and mercantile activities. The vast wealth of the Nandas can be accounted for only in this light. The traders, in their part, did not participate in politics.

This state of affairs, however, did not last long, and in the Mauryan period a violent confrontation took place between the state and the mercantile class. With the emergence of a large empire, the state needed more financial resources. A larger army and bureaucracy and spies had to be maintained for the expansion and consolidation of the empire. The state could get additional revenue from two sources, viz. (a) consolidation and expansion of rural economy, (b) state control and supervision of trade and industry. The State took both the measures together and the harm caused to the traders was double-edged. Naturally, the merchants and traders might have vehemently opposed such measures. This resulted in an ideological fight in which the state not only imposed strict restrictions on their movements, economic activities, etc., but also tried to degrade them socially.[15] A full section of the 4th book of the *Arthaśāstra* of Kauṭilya entitled *Vaidehaka-rakṣaṇa* is devoted to the problem of safeguarding the interests of the people from the deceit and exploitation by the traders and merchants.[16] The *Arthaśāstra* places them in the category of artisans, musicians, story-tellers and prostitutes, and declares that such elements are unwanted and do not deserve the patronage of an alert ruler.[17] In the concluding verse of the first chapter of the 4th book it is clearly stated that traders, artisans, musicians, beggars, buffoons and other idlers, who are thieves in effect though not in name, should be restrained from oppressing the country.[18] The religion of their choice was ridiculed and repressed.[19]

These contradictions were resolved in the time of Aśoka when a perfect understanding was reached between the traders and the state.[20] The ideal of *Dharmānuvartī Cakravartī rājā* put forward by the early *Pāli* texts was realized in practice.[21] Kosambi aptly remarked, "With Aśoka, the social philosophy expressed in the 6th century Magadhan religions had at last penetrated the state mechanism."[22] The close relations which developed between Aśoka and the Buddhists on the one hand, and the trading and mercantile class on the other, are amptly attested by epigraphic and literary sources.[23] The inscriptions of Aśoka do not refer to the economic policies followed by him, but it is rightly assumed that some of the public works undertaken by the Emperor were godsend of the traders.[24] The trading and mercantile class became a class with high status and the mainstay of the Mauryan state.[25]

The *Avadāna* literatuare which was composed in the 3rd or 4th centuries of Christian era throws very important light on the changed status of the traders and merchants. From these sources we know that they had accumulated mythical wealth and their status in society was second to none.[26] They were the urban elite class (*Śreṣṭhīva Paurajana-parivṛtaḥ*)[27] and consumed a major part of social production.[28] Their indulgence in luxuries and comforts was fantastic.[29] The king, the ministers and the town councilors respected them alike.[30] The heroes and heroines of the *Avadāna* stories mainly come from their class. They were the foremost and the most-trusted supporters of Buddhism. Other religious communities such as the *Brāhmaṇas* and the *Jainas* also sought and valued their patronage and support.

However, the most important development which took place during this period was the involvement of the traders in politics. The *Avadānaśataka* relates a story where a defeated king is financed by a rich *Śreṣthi* for reorganizing his army and taking revenge from his adversary.[31] Significantly enough the account of war between king Ajātaśatru of Magadha and Prasenjit of Kosala is also narrated in the two *Saṅgamā suttas* of *Saṁyutta-nikāya*, but the *Śreṣṭhī* does not figure there in any form. The addition of *Śreṣṭhī* in the *Avadānasataka* shows his changed position. Incidentally this story also relates that after winning the war king Prasenjit bestowed royal authority on the trader for seven days, as a token of gratitude.[32] This description need not be taken literally, but it certainly shows the elevated position of the *Śreṣthīs*. We have at least two instances in the *Avadāna* literature where the traders were elevated to the highest political position. According to the *Dharmalabdha-jātaka* of the *Mahāvastu, Sārthavāha Dharmalabdha* was elected the king of Benares when the king Brahmadatta along with the whole royal household was destroyed by an ogress and the kingdom was left defenceless.[33] To quote the original, "The Counsellors, town councilors and the country people assembled to deliberate. They consulted among themselves, saying 'friends, who of us in Benares, can become a king fit to protect this kingdom righteously?' And they all, counsellors, town councilors and country people reflected thus 'There is no fitting king for Benares other than Dharmalabdha, the merchant leader. He is virtuous and vigilant. Not even *Yakṣas* and *Rākṣasas* can succeed in tempting them. For thrice has he crossed the great ocean, and every time he has had a prosperous voyage and returned in safety.' So they set *Dharma*labdha on the golden throne and anointed him King."[34] Now to come to the *Supriyāvadāna*: In this instance, *Supriya* was anointed King of Kāśī taking into consideration his intelligence, diligence, compassion and skill in warfare.[35]

The political ambition of the trading and mercantile class brought them in direct confrontation with the ruling aristocracy. One such instance is related in the *Mūlasarvāstivāda-Vinaya-vastu.* According to this work, Viśākhā was an adopted sister of King Prasenjit, and her father-in-law Mṛgāra was his chief minister. Viśākhā had thirty-two sons who helped the king in suppressing a serious revolt. All of them were of very strong will and were offered the command of four winged army, by the king. The latter became suspicious when his *Purohita* warned him about their strength and aspirations. He was so much alarmed that he ordered them to be killed by a conspiracy, their chopped heads were sent to their unfortunate mother.[36] In the *Jyotiṣkāvadāna* it is stated that Jyotiṣka *Gṛhapati* of Champā, though supported by all the sections of society, had to renounce the world lest he should be murdered by the King.[37] Sometimes, the King and the traders came into conflict because of the reversal of the guild ruling by the former. Such a situation is related in the *Pūrṇāvadāna.*[38] The King could ask the traders to procure any commodity which he needed even if they had to procure such a commodity at a very high price.[39] He could also prohibit the sale of any particular commodity within his kingdom, and those who defied the order were banished.[40] Even after all these contradictions, the merchants and traders were considered an asset to the kingdom and the King was expected to establish merchant guilds and to look after their interests.[41]

Sometimes, they were given high posts in the government. According to the *Mūlasarvāstivādaka-Viṇaya-vastu* Mṛgāra, a reputed *Śreṣthī* of Śrāvasti was the chief minister of king Prasenjit, although such a possibility is refuted by the early *Pāli* texts. The story was thus clearly invented to suit new development which had taken place during this period. A passage of the *Mahāvastu* also informs us that a *Śreṣthī* was closely connected with the State business and the king could call him any time to perform urgent state business.[42] On the basis of epigraphic evidence, R. S. Sharma thinks that possibly the *Sātavāhanas* gave high Government posts to merchants.[43] He also accepts the fact that the merchant and traders, who headed corporate bodies and had large fortune were included in important political bodies.[44]

The importance of the merchants and traders in town and city administration is well attested by seals[45] and inscriptions.[46] The *Avadānas* declare them foremost among the townspeople (*Śreṣṭhīva Purajana-Parivṛtaḥ*). The king rarely interfered in the matters of *Gaṇas.*[47] But some influential members had already started challenging the authority of *Gaṇas*, which presages the consequent disintegration of the merchant guilds.

The *Avadāna* literature, thus, exposes the myth of political apathy and passivity of the merchants and trades and an ideal society based on *guṇa-karma-vibhāgaśaḥ*. At the same time, it helps us in establishing the historical fact that the roles of different classes in a particular society are determined by the existing means and relations of production.

Endnotes

1. *Ancient Kosala and Magadha*, Journal of the Bombay Branch of the Royal Asiatic Soceity, 27, 1960.

   The basis of Ancient Indian History, Annals of the Bhandarkar Oriental Research Institute, 75, 1955.

   Introduction to the Study of Indian History, Bombay, 1956.

   The Culture and Civilization of Ancient India, Delhi, 1972.

2. *Aspects of Political Ideas and Institutions in Ancient India*, Delhi, 1968.

   Light on Early Indian Society and Economy, Bombay, 1966.

   "*Material Milieu of the Birth of Buddhism*", Paper read at the International Congress of Orientalists, Paris, 1973.

3. *A History of India*, Part I, Penguin Books, 1968.
4. The concepts *Cakkavattī* and *Mahāsammata* can be explained only in this light. For a different interpretation of the concept of *Mahāsammata* see R. S. Sharma, Political Ideas, etc. pp. 65-69.
5. *Dīghanikāya*, (Nalanda Edition) ii, 116.
6. *The Vinaya*, (Nalanda Edition), II, 249.

7. Ibid, ii, 254-56.
8. Ibid, II, 252.
9. Such friendly gestures included receiving them in the court (*Khuddaka Nikāya*, I, N. 286) to offer them services of physicians (Vinaya, I, 291-93), etc.
10. Ibid, pp. 286-87.
11. *Dīghanikāya*, I, 116.
12. Malalsekera, *Dictionary of Pāli Proper Names*, II, 901. (N. 4), *Vinaya*, III, 58, 63, etc.
13. Ibid, IV, 176-77.
14. Ibid, III, 58, 63, etc.
15. These conclusions are based on the *Arthaśāstra* of Kauṭilya. The date and authenticity of this work is much debated among the scholars, but so for no unanimous conclusion has been reached.
16. *Arthaśāstra*, IV, 2.
17. Ibid, XIII, 3.
18. *Arthaśāstra*, IV, 1.
19. Ibid. 11, 1, 4, 36; III, 16, 20, etc. of Kosambi, "Finally, instead of the national debt and state loans, the *Arthaśāstra* recommended special measures against merchants. Spies in the proper guise would get a rich trader drunk, rob him, falsely accuse him of crime, or even murder him; the merchant confiscated goods and money would go to the state treasury (The culture, etc. pp. 164-165).
20. Kosambi, *The Culture*, etc. p. 165.
21. Ibid, p. 159 ff.
22. Ibid, p. 159.
23. Epigraphic sources include some of the minor rock and pillar inscriptions of Aśoka and the Girnār rock inscription of Rudradāmana. Under literary sources we may mention works like the *Mahāvaṃsa* and the *Divyāvadāna*.
24. Kosambi, *The Culture and Civilization of Ancient India*, etc. p. 161.
25. Ibid, p. 165.
26. The stock phrase used to describe their wealth reads: *Ādhyo mahādhano mahābhogo vistīrṇa-viśāla-parigraho Vaiśravaṇa-dhana-pratispardhi*. This huge wealth (*Prabhūta-vittopakaraṇa prabhūta-sattvasvapteyaḥ*) was counted in gold, silver, luxuries, elephants, horses, cattle, sheep, slaves, female slaves and workers besides food grain (*Mahāvastu*-TR SBB, Vol. 1, p. 31), whereas Kauṭilya had categorized them among with musicians, prostitutes, etc. as idlers and rogues by nature. The *Avadānas* place them along with the *Pārthivas, Rāṣṭrikas, Nītijñas* and *Maulidharas*.
27. A stock phrase in the *Avadāna* literature.
28. *Divyāvadāna* (ed. P. L. Vaidya), p. 172; cf. *Milindapañha* (ed. Wadekar), p. 179; also *Uvāsagadasāo* where it is mentioned that most of the *Gahavais* kept back 4 crores of *Hiraṇṇas* for managing household affairs.
29. *Avadānaśataka* (ed. P. L. Vaidya) pp. 14, 89 etc. *Divyāvadāna*, pp. 2, 16, 63, 219, etc.; Mahāvastu, (tr.), Vol. III, pp. 405, 408. A *Gahapati* named *Jyotiṣka* could buy a piece of cloth for 1000 *Kārṣāpaṇas* (*Divyā*, p. 172).
30. *Divyāvadana*, p. 112.
31. *Avadāna*, p. 27.

32. Ibid. p. 28.
33. *Mahāvastu,* III, 285.
34. Ibid.
35. *Divyāvadāna,* p. 35.
36. *Mūlasarvāstivāda-vinaya-vastu* (ed. S. Bagchi), I, 198-200.
37. *Divyāvadāna,* p. 168.
38. Ibid, p. 20 ff.
39. Ibid.
40. Ibid, p. 176.
41. Ibid, p. 350-52.
42. Mūlasarvāstivāda, I, 198.
43. II, p. 406.
44. R. S. Sharma, *Aspects of Political Ideas and Institutions of Ancient India,* etc. p. 205.
45. Ibid.
46. Such seals referred to by K. K. Thapalyal are following Nos. 55, 56 of Lucknow Museum (Mauryan), No. J 452 of Lucknow Museum (2nd century B.C.), B.H.U. No. 668 (1st century Nos. 57-60 in Marshall's list and also seals with the *Sahajātīya Nigama* and *Makkutali-Nigama* (*Journal of Numismatic Society of India,* xxv, 1968, pp. 133-34).
47. *Divyāvadāna,* pp. 19-20, 80.

13

संस्कृत व्याकरण को बौद्ध वैयाकरण चन्दगोमी की देन

हर्षनाथ मिश्र

प्राय: ऐसा माना जाता है कि किसी गम्भीर विश्लेषण के लिए पारिभाषिक शब्दावली का प्रयोग अनिवार्य होता है; परन्तु बौद्ध वैयाकरण चन्द्रगोमी ने असंज्ञक व्याकरण का निर्माण करके यह सिद्ध कर दिया कि साधारण किन्तु सशक्त शब्दावली के द्वारा भी किसी गम्भीर शास्त्र का निर्माण किया जा सकता है। उन्होंने व्याकरण की संज्ञाओं (पारिभाषिक शब्दावली) का प्रयोग किये बिना ही पाणिनि, कात्यायन और पतंजलि से भी अदृष्ट शब्दों का विश्लेषण किया, फिर भी उनका व्याकरण शास्त्र लघु, पाणिनीय व्याकरण से भी अधिक स्पष्ट और सर्वांगपूर्ण रहा। उनके इस अद्‌भुत प्रयोग को विद्वानों ने मुक्त कण्ठ से सराहा और कहा ''चन्द्रोपज्ञमसंज्ञकं व्याकरणम्'' अर्थात् संज्ञाओं के बिना व्याकरण-निर्माण के आदिकर्ता चन्द्रगोमी है। संज्ञाओं के प्रयोग ने व्याकरण को गहन बना दिया था। इसलिए व्याकरण को सरल बनाने के लिए कृतसंकल्प चन्द्राचार्य के लिये संज्ञाओं से पीछा छुड़ाना अनिवार्य था। संज्ञाओं के कुछ दोष यहाँ दिये जाते हैं, जिन्हें चन्द्रगोमी ने देखा होगा-

1. एक विधिसूत्र के अर्थबोध के लिए कई संज्ञा सूत्रों के बोझ को स्मृति में उठाना पड़ता है। जैसे ''पुगन्तलघूपधस्य च'' का अर्थबोध अङ्गसंज्ञा, उपधासंज्ञा, लघु और गुणसंज्ञा के ज्ञान के बिना असम्भव है।

2. बहुत सी संज्ञाओं का शरीर संज्ञी के शरीर से स्थूल है। इसलिए प्रयोग में गौरव होता है। जैसे सर्वनामस्थान, प्रातिपदिक आदि संज्ञाएं। यदि सर्वनाम स्थान के चन्द्राचार्य की तरह 'शिसुटि' का प्रयोग किया जाय, तो लाघव हो। प्रातिपदिक के स्थान में 'नाम' शब्द का प्रयोग लघु था। ''संज्ञा-शब्दानामर्धमात्रिकत्वम्'' यह मानना न केवल अनुभव विरुद्ध है, प्रत्युत वह 'ओर्गुण:' में गुण-ग्रहण को ज्ञापक मानने के भी विरुद्ध है। सर्वनाम में 'नाम' का प्रयोग और वृक्षादि नाम के लिए 'प्रातिपदिक' का प्रयोग करना एकरूपता में बाधक है।

3. 'वृद्धिरादैच्' 'अदेङ्गुण:' इत्यादि सूत्रों ने आत् और ऐच् शब्दों को तथा अत् एङ् शब्दों को वृद्धि गुण संज्ञा की है; किन्तु 'नवेति विभाषा' और 'अदर्शनं लोत:' से इन शब्दों के अर्थ को संज्ञा की जाती है। इस तरह कहीं शाब्दी और कहीं आर्थी संज्ञा बिना संदर्भ के स्वीकार करने में क्लेश होता है।

4. संज्ञा सूत्रों के निर्माण के पहले प्रकरण निर्देश के लिए जिस संज्ञाधिकार की आवश्यकता थी, वह नहीं किया गया है। इसलिए ये सूत्र क्या विधि सूत्र हैं या और कुछ हैं, इसके निर्णय में कठिनाई आती है। दूसरी बात यह है कि क्या संज्ञा है और संज्ञी क्या है इसका ज्ञान भी बड़ी

कठिनाई से होता है। यदि पाणिनि अपने सूत्रों में पहले संज्ञी का और बाद में संज्ञा का उल्लेख करते, तो एक व्यवस्था रहती है और उसके आधार पर कुछ समझ में आता; परन्तु पाणिनि 'अदेङ्गुण:' 'तिङ् शित् सार्वधातुकम्', इत्यादि में जिस उचित क्रम को अपनाया था उस क्रम का पालन 'वृद्धिरादैच्', 'अपृक्त एकाल् प्रत्यय:', 'आर्धधातुकं शेष्ज्ञ:', 'उपपदमतिङ्' इत्यादि सूत्रों में नहीं किया है। भाष्यकार पतञ्जलि ने कहा है कि यद्यपि संज्ञी का उल्लेख पहले और संज्ञा का उल्लेख बाद में होना चाहिए परन्तु पाणिनि को ''वृद्धिरादैच्'' सूत्र में क्षमा किया जा सकता है; क्योंकि यहाँ प्रारम्भ में वृद्धि शब्द का प्रयोग मङ्गलार्थ करना था। ''ऐतदेकमाचार्यस्य मङ्गलार्थ मृष्यताम्'' (महाभाष्य वृद्धिरादैच् सूत्र)। कैय्यट ने महाभाष्य की उस पंक्ति का अर्थ कुछ और समझ लिया और सोचा ऐसी गलती एक वृद्धिरादैच् में ही नहीं है, किन्तु 'अपृक्त एकाल् प्रत्यय:'' में भी है, तो उसने महाभाष्य में प्रयुक्त ''एकम्'' पद की रक्षा के लिए उस सूत्र को संज्ञा सूत्र की श्रेणी से निकाल कर परिभाषा सूत्र की श्रेणी में लाकर खड़ा कर दिया। नागेश ने एक अजीब अटकल लगाई और लिखा कि यद्यपि ''अपृक्त एकाल् प्रत्यय:'' संज्ञा सूत्र ही है और वहाँ भी 'वृद्धिरादैच्' की तरह संज्ञी और संज्ञा के उल्लेख में उचित पौर्वाप्पर्य का जो त्याग हुआ है; परन्तु उसके द्वारा पाणिनि यह संकेत करते हैं कि विधेय विमर्श असाधु नहीं हैं विधेय विमर्श और च्युत संस्कृति दोनों दोषों को पृथक् पृथक् गिनने से ही स्पष्ट है कि विधेया विमर्श को पण्डित-मण्डली असाधु नहीं मानती। अत: उसके लिए किसी ज्ञापक की आवश्यकता नहीं थी। वस्तुत: भाष्यकार ने 'एतदेकम्' पद के द्वारा यही संकेत किया है कि एक जगह संज्ञा के पूर्वोच्चारण को मङ्गलार्थ मानकर क्षन्तव्य मानने पर भी सर्वत्र ऐसा मानना संभव नहीं है। अत: यह दोष पाणिनि के सिर पर रहेगा ही।

5. एक संज्ञा के ज्ञान के लिए दूसरी संज्ञा के ज्ञान की आवश्यकता को देखकर ''गुणनां च परार्थत्वादसम्बन्ध: समत्वात्'' इस सर्वसम्मत सिद्धान्त की रक्षा कैसे की जा सकेगी?

6. पारिभाषिक शब्दावली जब अपने लौकिक अर्थ में भी प्रयुक्त होती है, तब और अधिक क्लिष्टता आती है। उचित तो यह था कि जो संज्ञा जिस अर्थ विशेष के प्रतिपादन के लिए की गई है; उनका उसी अर्थ में प्रयोग होता किन्तु पाणिनि ने संज्ञा शब्द का प्रयोग न केवल स्वसंकेतित संज्ञी विशेष के लिए किया है किन्तु लोक-प्रचलित अर्थ में भी किया है। 'अदेङ् गुण:'' का ज्ञाता विद्यार्थी जब ''वीतो गुणवचनात्'', ''पूर्णगुणसहितार्थ'' आदि सूत्रों में गुण शब्द का वह अर्थ नहीं पाता जो ''अद्गुण:' में है तो वह चक्कर में पड़ जाता है। ''पूस्त्र्याख्यौ नदी'' आदि संज्ञा सूत्रों के द्वारा 'नदी' शब्द का शास्त्रकार ने अपने शास्त्र में जिस अर्थ विशेष में प्रयोग करने का संकेत किया है। ''नदीभिश्च'', ''नदी पूर्णमास्याग्राहायणीभ्य:'' आदि में वह अर्थ न देखकर अध्येता को संज्ञासूत्रबोध अर्थ में आस्था न रहना स्वाभाविक ही है।

7. ''बहुगुणवतुडति संख्या'' सूत्र बनाने के बाद एक, द्वि, त्रि आदि शब्दों की संख्यावाचकता को बरकरार रखने के लिए 'उभयगतिरिह भवति'' का आश्रय लेना स्वयं पारिभाषिक शब्दावली के महत्व को कम करना है।

8. कोई संज्ञा तद्भावित को की गयी है और तद्भावित और अतद्भावित दोनों को। यह अनिश्चितता भी दोष है।

9. संज्ञा सूत्र का निर्माण बाद में किया गया है; परन्तु उस संज्ञा का जिस विधिसूत्र में उपयोग किया गया है, वह सूत्र पहले लिखा गया है जैसे आम्रेडित संज्ञा विधायक सूत्र अष्टम अध्याय में आता है, पर ''नाम्रेडितस्यान्तस्य तु वा' सूत्र छठे अध्याय में आ गया है। इसी तरह 'अनुदात्तङित आत्मनेपदम्'', ''अनुपराभ्यां कृञः'' इत्यादि सूत्र जो तङ् और तिबादि का विधान करते हैं, प्रथम अध्याय के तृतीय पाद में आ जाते हैं किन्तु तङ् को आत्मनेपद और तङ् भिन्न तिङ् को परस्मैपद की संज्ञा देने वाले सूत्र ''लः परस्मैपदम्'' और 'तङानावात्मनेपदम्' बाद में प्रथमाध्याय के चतुर्थ पाद में रचे गए हैं। इससे संज्ञा सूत्रों के निर्माण में वैज्ञानिक योजना-बद्धता का प्रभाव चन्द्राचार्य को अवश्य खटका होगा।

10. कहीं महासंज्ञा करने के कारण विशेष अर्थ लिया गया है, परन्तु कहीं उसकी अन्वर्थता नहीं मानी गई है। जैसे सर्वनाम यह महासंज्ञा अन्वर्थ है; परन्तु सर्वनामस्थान और अधिकरण आदि महासंज्ञाएं निरर्थक हैं।

11. बहुत सी संज्ञाएं ऐसी है, जो अपनी अन्वर्थता की मृगतृष्णा में छात्रों को भ्रान्त कर देती हैं, जैसे अव्यय, परस्मैपद, आत्मनेपद आदि संज्ञाएं। 'यन्न व्येति तदव्ययम्'' यह व्याख्या अव्वय के लिए जिस विकार-हीनता की सूचना देती है, वह प्रत्येक उप-कृष्ण आदि अव्वयीभाववाले अव्यय शब्दों में खरी नहीं उतरती, क्योंकि इन शब्दों का रूप 'प्रत्येकं' 'प्रत्येकस्मिन्' 'प्रत्येकस्मात्' 'प्रत्येकस्याम्', आदि रूपों में बदलता भी है। चिरं, चिराय, चिरात्!, चिरेण आदि अव्वय शब्द भी विकृति को अपनाते हैं। ''शिश्ये'', ''वृत्यते'' आदि भाव वाच्य के क्रिया रूप भी अविकृत दिखाई देते हैं। तो क्या ये भी अव्यय हैं?

    यदि परस्मैपद सर्वत्र परगामी क्रिया फल में होता और आत्मनेपद कर्तृगामी क्रिया फल में, जैसा कि 'पचति' 'पचते' 'करोति' 'कुरुते' इत्यादि स्वरितेत् अकारेत् धातुओं से होता है; तो विद्यार्थी इन संज्ञाओं की नाम-रचना ये लाभ उठाता और कृतकृत्य होता, परन्तु ऐसा नहीं होता। अनदात्तेत् और ङित् धातु हर हालत में आत्मनेपद में ही प्रयुक्त होते हैं। अनुदात्तेत् ङ्ति और स्वरितेत् धातुओं को छोड़कर शेष धातु सर्वदा परस्मैपद में ही होते हैं। उपसर्ग विशेष के लगने पर यहाँ आत्मनेपद या परस्मैपद का नियत प्रयोग बिना क्रिया-फल की परगामिता या कर्तृगामिता की परवाह के हुआ करता है। भाववाच्य और कर्मवाच्य को भी आत्मनेपद की अन्वर्थता की चिन्ता नहीं करनी पड़ती। इस प्रकार के वैचित्र्य को देखकर विद्यार्थी पूछता है ''क्या मैंने जो इन संज्ञाओं को 'यथा नाम तथा गुणः' समझा था, वह सब गलत था; केवल मृगतृष्णा थी? यदि गलत था तो ऐसे नामकरण की क्या आवश्यकता थी? तङ् और शानच्, तिस् और शतृ शब्द का प्रयोग क्या बुरा था?''

12. निष्ठा सत् आदि संज्ञाओं के निर्माण से अनुबन्ध की इत् संज्ञा में भी बाधा आती है। विधिसूत्र में इनका द्वितीय उच्चारण हो जाता है। इसलिए आद्योच्चारण रूप उपदेश का अभाव होने से उपदेश पदार्थ को बदलना पड़ता है, और वह परिवर्तन 'आदेच उपदेशेऽशिति' आदि सूत्रों में प्रयुक्त उपदेश पदार्थ से मेल नहीं खाता।

13. (क) संज्ञाओं का वैज्ञानिक वर्गीकरण भी अष्टाध्यायी में नहीं मिलता वहाँ संज्ञाओं का कोई प्रकरण नहीं है। इसीलिए भाष्यकार ने कहा है ''अष्टमेऽपि हि संज्ञा क्रियते''। शाब्दी या आर्थी उद्देश्यसंज्ञा या विधेयसंज्ञा के रूप में उनका वर्गीकरण किया जा सकता था और उन्हें किसी एक प्रकरण में लिखा जा सकता था। परन्तु ऐसा नहीं किया गया है। 'वृद्धिरादैच्' 'अदेङ् गुण:' इन संज्ञा सूत्रों के बाद ''इको गुणवृद्धी'' 'न धातुलोप.' आदि परिभाषा और निषेध सूत्रों का आना प्रकरण को खण्डित कर देता है' इस तरह अष्टाध्यायी के सभी अध्यायों में मिलने वाले संज्ञा सूत्रों के निर्माण में कोई पूर्वनियोजित योजना नहीं दिखाई पड़ती।

(ख) प्रत्याहार को महेश्वर या पाणिनि की उद्भावना मानने वालों की भ्रान्त धारणाओं का निराकरण भी चन्द्राचार्य की अनुपम देन हैं। 'हल्' सूत्र की वृत्ति में गोमी ने बताया कि 'एष प्रत्याहार: पूर्वव्याकरणेष्वपि स्थित एव। अयं तु विशेष: 'ऐऔष्' इति यादासीत् तद् 'ऐऔच्' इति कृतम्। तथाहि लधावन्ते द्वयोश्च बह्वषो गुरु: (फिट्सूत्र 2/19) तृण-धान्यानाञ्चद्व्षयाम् (फिटसूत्र 2/4) चन्द्र के इस संकेत को आधार बनाकर देखने पर फिट् सूत्र में कुछ और प्रत्याहार दिखाई पड़े, जैसे हयादीनामसंयुक्तलान्तानामन्त: (फि. 2/25) में हय्, इगन्तानां द्वयषाम् 2/26 में इक्, 'ईषान्तस्य हसादि र्वा', में हस्। इस तरह शैवागम की दीक्षा में दीक्षित नन्दिकेश्वर की काशिका में प्रतिपादित वह कल्पना बालू की दीक्षा से दीक्षित नन्दिकेश्वर की काशिका में प्रतिपादित वह कल्पना बालू की दीवार की तरह धराशायी हो गयी, जिसमें तपस्या करते हुए पाणिनि को प्रत्याहार सूत्र की उपलब्धि महेश्वर शिव का ढक्का-निनाद से हुई बताई गयी थी। चन्द्रगोमी के पूर्वोक्त उद्धरण में बहुवचन का प्रयोग यह संकेत करता है कि न केवल शान्तनव व्याकरण में अपितु अन्य पूर्ववर्त्ती व्याकरणों में भी प्रत्याहार की सत्ता थी। चन्द्राचार्य के इस संकेत सूत्र को पकड़ कर पीछे मुड़ने पर हमने पाया कि पाणिनि के पूर्ववर्त्ती आपिशल व्याकरण में भी प्रत्याहार थे, जैसा कि 'अमन्ताहु:'' और सृष्टिधराचार्य के द्वारा प्रस्तुत ''दन्त्योष्ठ्यत्वात् वकारस्य वद् व्यध वृधां न भष्'' इस उद्धरण तथा उज्ज्वलदत्त के उद्धरण ''अपिशलिस्तु न्यङ्को नैज्भावं शास्ति' में आए हुए अम् भष् ऐच् प्रत्याहार के उल्लेख से प्रतीत होता है। आपिशल व्याकरण से पूर्ववर्ती काशकृत्स्न व्याकरण में प्रत्याहार नहीं उपलब्ध होते हैं। इसलिए जब तक कोई और प्रमाण नहीं मिलता, तब तक यह मानने में कोई आपत्ति नहीं होनी चाहिए कि प्रत्याहार का प्रारम्भ व्याकरण जगत् में काशकृत्स्न व्याकरण के बाद हुआ। उदाहरण के लिये काशकृत्स्न का एक सूत्र देखिए ''यजां यवराणां य्वृत: सम्प्रसारणं कानुबन्धे''। ''यावराणाम्'' की जगह यण: का ''काशकृत्स्नं गुरुलाघवम्'' के रूप में अपनी लाघव सम्पत्ति के लिए प्रख्यात काशकृत्स्न व्याकरण के इस सूत्र

में अप्रयोग यही सिद्ध करता है कि तब तक प्रत्याहार का उद्‌भव नहीं हुआ था। इस तरह चन्द्रगोमी के अध्ययन से प्रत्याहार प्रथा पर जो प्रकाश पड़ा है; वह भी उसी की देन है।

(ग) चन्द्राचार्य ने संस्कृत-व्याकरण को सरल बनाने का स्तुत्य प्रयास किया। व्याकरण विद्या की जटिलताओं के मूल कारणों का अध्ययन तथा उनके निराकरण के द्वारा उन्होंने अपने व्याकरण शास्त्र को सरल लघु अत्यन्त स्पष्ट और सर्वाङ्गपूर्ण बनाया। अष्टाध्यायी में कात्यायन के द्वारा जिस उक्तानुक्त और द्विरुक्त की चिन्ता की गयी थी उनका, तथा पतञ्जलि के द्वारा दिए गए सुझावों का समावेश तो उन्होंने अपने सूत्रों में किया ही, साथ-साथ उन्होंने धातुपाठ गणपाठ तथा शिक्षासूत्र आदि उपकरणों को एकत्र करके व्याकरण को सर्वाङ्गपूर्ण बनाया।

अष्टाध्यायी के अनेक दोषों को दूर किया। पाणिनि सूत्र में दिखाई पड़ने वाले विधेयाविमर्श को हटाया। पाणिनि का "आद्यन्तौ टकितौ" यहाँ 'टकिता वाद्यन्तौ' बनकर शीघ्र अर्थबोध कराने लगा। यदि "रामः स्थूलः" के स्थान में "स्थूलः रामः" कहे तो अर्थ का अनर्थ हो जाएगा। "राम मोटा है" इस अर्थ के स्थान में "जो मोटा है वह राम है" इस अनभीष्ट अर्थ की प्रतीति होने लगेगी।

वचन दोष के कारण भी पाणिनि के सूत्र क्लिष्ट हो गए थे। जैसे "लुटः प्रथमस्य डारौरसः" में उद्देश्य में एक वचन और विधेय में बहुवचन के प्रयोग से ऐसा लगता था कि जैसे लुट् के "ति" को तीनों आदेश होते हों। चन्द्राचार्य ने "लुट अद्यानां डारौरस" ऐसा सूत्र करके सूत्र में तिस् और तङ् की अनुवृत्ति करके सत्र को अधिक स्पष्टता प्रदान की।

पाणिनि के "प्रहसन", 'सुहितार्थ' आदि शब्दों का शक्ति और तृप्ति आदि अर्थ प्रचलित अर्थ नहीं रह गया था। इसलिए उनके स्थान में शक्ति आदि शब्दों का प्रयोग शीघ्रबोधगम्यता के लिए आवश्यक हो गया था। इसलिए चन्द्राचार्य ने "अधः प्रहसने" इत्यादि के स्थान में "अधः शक्तौ" सूत्र किया।

'कारण' सीवन ष्ठीवन विश्राम आदि प्रचलित शब्दों की सिद्धि पाणिनि व्याकरण से नहीं हो रही थी, उनकी सिद्धि का उपाय भी चन्द्र ने दिखाया। पूर्व निर्दिष्ट दोषों के अतिरिक्त कई अन्य दोषों को भी उन्होंने दूर किया।

इस तरह चन्द्राचार्य ने व्याकरण को बोझिल बनाने वाले, व्युत्पत्ति प्रक्रिया को क्लिष्ट करने वाले तथा किसी तथ्य को समझने में सहायता न करने वाले संज्ञा सूत्रादि तत्त्वों को हटाकर सशक्त लौकिक संस्कृत भाषा में सरल स्पष्ट और लघु व्याकरण लिखने का सफल प्रयास किया।

14

'सिरिघन'-सद्द-वीमंसा

सङ्घसेनो

सक्कत-भासाय सिरिघनसद्दस्स बहू अत्था होन्ति। तत्थ एकोव सद्दो परियायमुखेन बहूनं सद्दानं ठाने पयुज्जति। एसो सिरिघनसद्दो ब्राह्मणसत्थेसु सोगतगन्थेसु च बहुधा पयुत्तो ति मयं जानाम।

अमरकोसोव पाचीनतरो सद्दकोसो, यस्मिं अस्स सद्दस्स उद्देसो लब्भति। अस्मिं कोसे देवतावग्गे कोसकारेण बुद्धस्स बहूनि नामानि उद्दिट्ठानि। 'मुनीन्द्रः श्रीघनः शास्ता' ति तत्थ लिखितं। तस्मा, अमरकोसकारस्स काले सिरिघनसद्दो बुद्धस्स नामत्थं येव पयोगं आपज्जीति अनेन वचनेन सम्मा फुटं होति। अथवा अस्स सद्दस्स अयमेव अत्थो कोसकारेन ञातो ति कथितुं सक्का।

महापण्डितेन मोनियर विलियम्सेन अत्तनो सक्कत-आंगल-भासा-सद्दकोसे एसो सिरिघनसद्दो 1099 पिट्ठङ्के1 व्याकतो होति। तत्थ अस्स सद्दस्स द्वे अत्था लिखिता - (i) coagulated milk of sour curds (ii) a Buddha or name of a Buddha. कोसकारमतेन पठमो अत्थो सद्दकोसेसु येव लब्भति, दुतियो पन पञ्चरात्रनामके गन्थे। अयं दुतियोव अत्थो अमरकोसकारेनापि मतो ति उपरि लिखितं येव।

अस्स सद्दस्स सच्छरियो अत्थो पयोगो च स्फुटार्था श्रीघनाचारसंग्रहटीका ति अमुद्दापिते गन्थे लब्भति। तत्थ एसो सद्दो सामणेरसद्दस्स अत्थे पयुत्तो। तस्स गन्थस्स संसोधनकाले मया एसो अत्थो आविकतो। सद्दस्स एसो अत्थो पयोगो च बी. एस. आपटे-महोदयानं सक्कत-आंगल-भासा-सद्दकोसे उद्दिट्ठेन अस्स अत्थेन उपत्थम्भितो होति। तत्थ a Buddhist saint ति अस्स सद्दस्स अधिप्पायो लिखितो। परं न कस्सचि सद्दकोसस्स गन्थस्स वा नाम लिखितं, येसु अयं सद्दो अनेन अत्थेन पयुत्तो होति। विगते अखिल-जम्बूदीप-प्राच्यविज्जा-सम्मेलने (भुवनिस्सिरे नगरे) श्रीघनाचार-संग्रह-टीका ति विसयं निस्साय मया एको निबन्धो पठितो। तदा मया मतं - ''सिरिघनो ति तस्सेव श्रीघनाचारसंग्रह इति मूलगन्थस्स लेखको, यं (गन्थं) निस्साय अयं श्रीघनाचारसंग्रहटीका ति गन्थो लिखितो होति। ह्योतु, एत्थ अस्मिं गन्थे सिरिघनसद्दो सामणेरसद्दस्स ठाने पयुत्तो होति, न पन गन्थकारस्स नामत्थं ति दानि इदं सम्मा पाकटं।

अस्स सद्दस्स अनेन अधिप्पायेन पयोगो न बहु पाचीनतरो। यतो तेपिटके अस्स सद्दस्स पयोगो न दिस्सति। उत्तरेसु पालिगन्थेसु अपि न लब्भतीति कथितुं सक्का। अमरकोसो व पाचीनतरो गन्थो, यत्थ अयं सद्दो उद्दिट्ठो ति मया पुब्बं येव कथितं होति। अमरकोसकारस्स कालो पन ईसातो पच्छा येव मतो, न पुब्बं। अस्स नवीनतरो पयोगो पन स्फुटार्था श्रीघनाचारसंग्रहटीका ति गन्थे पटिभाति। ये केचि पयोगा अञ्ञेसु गन्थेसु मोनियर-विलियम्सेन उद्दिट्ठा, ते सब्बे तु अमरकोसकालतो पच्छा अम्हा गन्था पन पुब्बं येव भविंसूति

मञ्ञामि। पमाणं पि विज्जति। अयं टीका-गन्थो ईसातो छट्ठसतद्दिया याव द्वादससतद्दियं कदाचि पि काले लिखितो होतीति कथितुं सक्का।

(1) अस्मिं गन्थे जातकमालाय कंसवधस्स च नाम लिखितं होति। अयं जातकमाला, यस्सा उद्देसो एत्थ कतो, अरियसूरेन ईसातो पच्छा चतुत्थसतद्दियं लिखिता।[2]

(2) अस्मिं गन्थे अलंकारिकी सद्दजालमयी जटिला भासा पयुत्ता। ईदिसाय पन भासाय कालो ईसातो छट्ठसतद्दिया याव अट्ठसतद्दियं विज्जति। यस्मिं काले बाणो, सुबन्धु, अञ्ञे च कथाकारा उप्पज्जिंसु। तस्मा, अयं गन्थो छट्ठसतद्दिया पुब्बं न लिखितो अहोसि।

(3) या लिपि अस्मिं गन्थे पयुत्ता (अम्हेहि छाया, photograph येव पत्ता), तस्सा कालो एकादस-द्वादस-सतदीसु मतो होति।

एत्थ इदं पि कथितुं भवति। विगते सम्मेलने पठिते निबन्धे मया अस्स गन्थस्स कालो ओं-सद्द-पयोगं निस्साय नवीनतरो मतो। न इदं समुचितं। यतो अस्मिं गन्थे ओं-सद्द-पयोगो न लब्भति। गन्थस्स छायायं ओं-सद्दो न बिज्जति। अयं तु अनुलेखकारस्य पमादो येव। तेन पण्डित-पटिञ्ञेन (अनुलेखकारेन) अत्तजिव्हाठितो ओं-सद्दो तत्थ अनुलेखे पि अङ्कितो।

एत्थ पञ्हो पटिभाति। बुद्ध-वन्दनागाथायं श्रीघनाचारसंग्रहकारो 'श्रामणेरा-णामाचारः संग्रहीष्यते' ति क्रियाकारं करोति, गन्थे च सब्बत्थ सामणेरानं (सिरिघन-सद्दस्स पयोगो पि दिस्सति) आचारं वण्णेति। एवं कत्वा पि गन्थकारेन गन्थस्स नाम श्रीघनाचार-संग्रहो ति किं नाम कतं ति पञ्हो चिन्तनीयो।

अयं सद्दो स्फुटार्था श्रीघनाचारसंग्रहटीका ति गन्थे सामणेर-सद्दस्स ठाने पयुत्तो ति पठममेव कथितं होति। परं एकस्मिं ठाने सिरिघनसद्दस्स सम-अत्थ-वाचि-सद्दं लिखितुकामेन टीकाकारेन 'भिक्षारिति' पदं पयुत्तं।

गन्थकारेन सामणेरभावो सामणेरानं आचारो च वित्थारेन वण्णितो। रतनत्तये सरणं गन्त्वा पञ्चसिक्खापदानि पगण्हित्वा बुद्धं भगवन्तं पब्बजितमनुपब्बज्जामीति वाचमुदीरेत्वा पाणातिपाता विरतो याव जातरूपजतपरिग्गहा स एसो सामणेरो मुनिस्स मतो।

अयं गन्थो महासंघिकानं होतीति पटिभाति। सिरिघनसद्दो न सब्बेसु निकायेसु मतो अहोसीति मञ्ञितुं सक्का। यतो अयं सद्दो अनेन अधिप्पायेन पालि-भासाय पि न दिस्सति। तस्मा, अयं सद्दो कस्मिंचि विसेसे काले ठाने च पयुत्तो अहोसि, यत्थ महासंघिका विरुल्हिं वेपुल्लं च गता अहेसु।

Endnotes

1. Monier Williams, Sanskrit-English, Dictionary, p. 1099.
2. M. Winternitz, History of Indian Literature, Vol. II. p. 276

15

SIṀHANĀDA-TĀRĀ
An Iconographic Study

Mallar Ghose *

A. K. Gordon in his book entitled Iconography of Tibetan *Lamaism*[1] has noticed a special form of *Tārā* called *Siṁhanāda.* Green in colour, *Tārā* in this aspect is endowed with a single head and two arms and is seated in *lalitāsana* on a iotus-throne supported by a roaring lion. Her *mudrās* are *vara* and *vitarka,* while the symbol is an *utpala* at left shoulder or at both shoulders.

Allice Getty also refers to this form of *Tārā*[2] and has published a Tibetan image[3] of lacquered agglomerated material. In this image we find the two-armed bejeweled goddess with a placid facial expression seated in *lalitāsana* on a lotus on the back of a standing roaring lion. With the stalk of an *utpala* in her left palm placed near the chest, she displays *vara-mudrā*[4] with her right palm resting on the knee.

However, the published *Sādhanamālā* does not contain any *sādhana* devoted to this form of *Tārā.* Nor does this form find mention in this text even as a companion goddess. The *Niṣpannayogāvalī* is also silent about this aspect. The attributes – *vara-mudrā* and *utpala* – are no doubt enjoined in most of the other forms of *Tārā.* But the lion is not associated with her.

However, it is very likely that there is a *sādhana,* though not published, conceiving this form of *Tārā,* a counterpart of *Siṁhanāda,* a popular form of *Avalokiteśvara.* We are led to presume this form a stone image (no. 337E) of *Tārā* unearthed at Sarnath. A product of ninth century A.D., its semicircular backslab is inscribed with the Buddhist creed, and the base with a short dedicatory record. Of fine modeling, the image is elegantly bejeweled. With a placid and benign facial expression and half-closed eyes, the goddess is seated in *lalitāsana* on a *viśvak-padma,* her pendant left foot lightly touching a kneeling lion; the latter with a roaring face is looking up towards the goddess. Her right palm, exhibiting *vara-mudrā* is placed against the knee, while the left palm raised to the level of the chest, holds the stalk of an *utpala.* The bun-shaped coiffure of the goddess and the short crown do not bear the figure of any *Dhyānī-Buddha.* However, on the dexter of the head is a figure of *Amitābha* in *Dhyāna-mudrā* *vajraparyaṅkāsana* on a lotus. As the figure is neither on the crown nor even above the head of the goddess, *Amitābha* cannot be regarded as the parental *Tathāgata* of this form of *Tārā.*

The image is interesting for two reasons. First, it indicates the existence of a *sādhana* hitherto unpublished. Secondly, it illustrates a rare form of *Tārā* with the lion as a mount. This animal, as is well-known, is *vāhana* of *Durgā* from very early times.

Another likely image of this form of *Tārā* lies at Bhuinpara, near Shergarh (District Balasore). The bejeweled goddess is seated in *lalitāsana* on a *viśva-padma* with her left hand carrying the stalk of an *utpala*. The right palm is raised to the level of the chest. As it is somewhat indistinct in the photograph it has not been possible to determine if it holds a rosary or displays *dhyāna-mudrā*. Below the lotus seat is a lion. The back side of the image is inscribed with Buddhist creed in characters of the tenth-eleventh century A.D. Incidentally, it points out the utility of studying the images (even late) of Northern Buddhist countries for identifying several obscure forms in the Indian images, for which the relevant *sādhanas* are not readily available.

Endnotes

1. A. K. Gordon, *Iconography of Tibetan Lamaism*, New York, 1967, p. 75.
2. Alice Getty, *The Gods of Northern Buddhism*, Tokyo, 1962, p. 123.
3. Ibid, XXXVII b.
4. An. Rep Arch. Surv. Ind., 1914-15, p. 102, LXIV B.

* Dr. (Mrs.) Mallar Ghose is a senior research scholar in the Department of Buddhist Studies, University of Delhi, Delhi.

16

A STUDY OF THE NON-SOUL DOCTRINE

G. G. Gyatso *

There are many types of *duḥkha* or sorrow in this world and the only root of all these is *avidyā* or ignorance. It is only after a thorough understanding of *avidyā,* that one can understand *nairātmya-prajñā* or non-soul wisdom. This *prajñā* is that specific knowledge through which the *kuśala* and *akuśala dharmas* (moral and immoral objects) are investigated. The gradual excellence (*uttarottara utkarṣa*) in the *prajñā* is brought by constant practice of *bhāvanā* or meditation. After its full development, the *prajñā* is transformed into *prajñāpāramitā* or transcendental wisdom.

Prajñā is of three kinds: (1) *Paramārtha-parichhedaka-prajñā* or the highest truth discriminating wisdom. At first, through it there is an indirect knowledge of the *nairātmya-tattva* or the non-soul element and later when it is perfected, the knowledge is direct, (2) *Saṁvṛti-paricchedaka-prajñā* or the manifestation discriminating wisdom, through which the five stages of knowledge are investigated into. (3) *Satvārtha-paricchedaka-prajñā* or the desires of beings discriminating wisdom, through which the worldly and heavenly desires and purposes of all beings are accomplished. Under this wisdom one knows the *Kalyāṇa-kāraka-dharmas* or the meritorious objects and is enabled to accomplish them in their unsullied form.

The *Paramārtah-paricchedaka-prajñā,* that accomplishes the knowledge of *nairātmya,* is the foremost among these *prajñās.* One should therefore exert the utmost in order to attain it.

The doctrine of *nairātmya* is equally accepted by different schools of Buddhism. However, each school propounds it in its own way. These different ways are simply the highest attainment of the same. This highest excellence of *prajñā* makes for an understanding of the *niḥsvabhāvatā* or the essenceless. As the teachers of *Prāsaṅgika* school have made a concerted effort to make us understand this truth, it is proposed to follow them in our present study.

The *ātmadṛṣṭi* or the notion of self is the root cause of all our sorrows. The understanding of things as existing in their own natural way is in fact *avidyā.* This itself is the *ātmadṛṣṭi.* It is because of this that the beings continue to wander through various mundane existences. This again is the cause of all sorrows of the world and it is because of this that *ātmadṛṣṭi* is called the root of the phenomenal world.

In *Arhat's* stage the *ātmadṛṣṭi* disappears leaving behind only the *vāsanās* or the impressions of this notion. It is because of these *vāsanās* that the *Arhat* is not able to know all the *dharmas.* As a result, he does not become omniscient (*Sarvajña*) and remains immersed in *nirvāṇa* or emancipation for many lives. He is unable to do complete good to all living beings and he himself is bereft of the highest achievement. These are thus called the sorrows of tranquility (*Śama*). The root cause of this too are the same *vāsanās* of the *ātmadṛṣṭi.* This state is called the *jñeyāvaraṇa* or the concealment of the knowledge. One can transcend this state only through the knowledge of the *nairātmya.* Therefore, it is essential that one should practice the highest form of *vipaśyanā* or meditation in order to achieve the knowledge of *nairātmya.*

Nairātmya is of two types: (1) *Pudgala-nairātmya* means the realization of the essenceless of all composite beings *(pudgala-niḥsvabhāvatā)* or individual self (*jīvātma-niḥsvabhāvatā*) (2) The second is *dharma-nairātmya* or essenceless of external objects. There are many devices *(yuktis)* to have a proper understanding of *pudgala-nairātmya.* Out of them, the *ekānekaviyuk-tatva* or the argument that distinguishes between the oneness and non-oneness, is the most important one. According to this argument *ātman* or self is neither identical *(abhiñña)* nor different *(bhiñña)* from the *skandhas* or the aggregates. The reason i.e. *hetu* here is the distinction between identity and non-identity of the self with *skandhas* through which the essenceless of the soul is established. We cannot accomplish *nairātmya* without knowing the hidden points of this *hetu* or reason. There are four such points *(maramasthāna).* These are: (1) *niśedhya-viniścaya-marma* or the point determining that which is to be denied. That which is to be denied by the said *hetu* or reason, is *ātman* which is of two kinds – *sthūla* or gross and *sūkṣma* or subtle. Merely by denying the gross, we cannot escape *ātmadṛṣṭi* which will then lead us to the existence of the *pudgala-śaśvatatva* or the permanence of the individuality. This can also lead us to the other extreme of *pudgala-uccheda* or the annihilation of the individuality, that which we deny happens to be the sense and their objects and this cuts ourselves from the mundane practice *(loka-vyavahāra).* It is therefore essential, in order to avoid both these extremes, to understand the *sūkṣma ātmadṛṣṭi* or the subtle notion of self. The *sūkṣma ātmadṛṣṭi* is of two kinds. The *parikalpita-ātmadṛṣṭi* or the imaginary notion of self is generated by the thought of various philosophical schools upholding the concept of self *(ātmavādin)* and the *Sahaja-ātmadṛṣṭi* or natural notion of self is that which happens to be the result of '*ahaṁ svabhāva-sattā*, or the existence of soul. The former is restricted in its application to human beings only whereas the latter is to be found among all living beings.

To treat *atman* or soul as unrelated to and yet having its locus in the *pañca-skandhas* or five aggregates is what this *ātmadṛṣṭi* turns out to be after examination. Since it is a sort of imposition of *ahaṁ* or ego on the *skandhas* or aggregates, it is known as *āropita-buddhi* or an imposed comprehension. To understand all this is to grasp the *niśedhya-viniścaya marma* or the point determining that which is to be denied.

(2) *Vyāpti-viniścaya-marma* or the point that determines the inevitable concomitance. That is to say that the pervading of the reason with its object to be established in the argument *ekāneka-viyuktatava* or the argument that distinguishes between the oneness and non-oneness. To see the irrationality of the concomitance between the identity or non-identity of the *ātman* with the *skandhas* is to grasp this *Vyāpti-viniścaya-marma.*

(3) *Ekatva-viyukta-viniścaya-marma* or the point that determines the distinguished identity of the *atman* with the *skandhas.* If there is oneness of nature between the *atman* and the *skandhas,* then they would be absolutely identical, but they are not, because ordinarily they are deemed to be separate. Of course, such a situation obtains only in the manifested world (*saṁvṛtika kṣetra*) and not in the ultimate one *(paramārthika kṣetra).* On considering the *atman* and the *skandhas* to be one, the problems such as the following arise. As there is one *atman* for the composed individual, so also one has to admit that there is only one *skandha.* As the *skandhas* are subject to origin and decay, so also one shall have to regard the *atman* or soul. After examining all such arguments, we come to the conclusion that the *atman* and the *skandhas* are not identical in nature. Such a realization stands for the *ekatva-viyukta-viniścaya-marma.*

(4) *Anekatva-viyukta-viniścaya-marma* or the point determining the non-oneness of the *atman* and the *skandhas.* As the natural oneness of the *atman* and the *skandhas* has been denied, so also one should deny their absolute non-oneness. If they are in nature and substance different and unrelated, then they should not matter to each other, but actually they do. It is not possible to show their separate identity. Therefore, one should realize that the *atman* and the *skandhas* are not non-identical. Such a realization is *anekatva-viyukta-viniścaya-marma.*

Summing up the points of the arguments, we may say that the independent existence of the *atman* cannot be established, because in order that it be there, we should be able to show it to be either identical or non-identical with the *skandhas.* These being the only alternatives available, one can assert that there is no *atman* on the basis of its non-availability (*anupalabdhi*). We also establish through this argument that the extremes are to be avoided and the *Madhyamaka-dṛṣṭi* or the point of view of the Middle is to be grasped.

Having established the non-existence of the individual self *(pudgala-nairātmya),* one can turn to the establishment of *dharma-nairātmya* or the non-existence of the external objects as well. As we see on the basis of the above discussion that there is no 'being of its own' in the case of a *jīvātman* or soul, so also there is no 'being of its own' in the case of any external object such as a pot and the like. There is no independent and unrelated existence of a pot apart from the earth, the water, the potter's wheel, etc., in the same way all the external objects are dependent on the conditions and materials of their being *(hetu-pratyaya-sāmagrī).* But in our intellectual grasp we take them to be independently existing. Such a view is called the *dharmātmadṛṣṭi.* The *dharmātmadṛṣṭi* should be examined in the same way, as we have done in the case of *pudgalātmadṛṣṭi*. It is only after that we would realize that the natural existence of the external objects is merely imaginary. Ultimately there is only *śūnyatā*, i.e. *paramārtha-śūnyatā*. The whole of the external world exists only in name, in formality, which is not true, but relative and interdependent. We realize that the phenomena of cause and effect, doings and their results which mark the practical existence, are born of imagination. It is the realization of the *svabhāva-śūnyatā* that makes us understand the *pratītyasamutpannatā* or interdependence of all *dharmas* or the external objects. The *pratītyasamutpannatā* and the *svabhāvaśūnyatā* are thus interchangeable terms. This is the beginning of that higher knowledge which is called the *abhiprāyika Jñāna* or the purposeful comprehension and the *anuttarā dṛṣṭi* or the unsurpassable point of view. For the device analysed above, i.e. *ekāneka-viyuktatva yukti* is alone not enough, but one may profitably utilize arguments such as *vajrakaṇayukti, sadasadanupapattiyukti, catuṣkoti-utpādānupapattiyukti, pratītyasamutpannat-vayukti,* etc. But all these will give only an intellectual comprehension of *nairātmya* and *śūnyatā*. To have a deeper understanding of them, one must enter into *savitaraka* and *avitarka* meditations that fall under the learning, that is called *adhiprajñā sikṣā*.

* Mr. Gyatso, G. G. is a Lecturer in the Department of Buddhist Studies, University of Delhi, Delhi.

17

CHINESE BUDDHIST SECTS

B. Jinananda *

The people of China are generally tolerant of all religious faiths and metaphysical systems. Among the religions of China, the one that has produced profound influence on the lives of the people is the 'worship of ancestors'. Although Confucianism has a great hold in China, still it can hardly be called a religion. It may be defined or rather analysed as a system of ethics for the proper guidance of conduct in this world; it does not concern itself with a future world. Buddhism and Taoism, both of these religions are finally established in China.

An average Chinese is a rigid believer in ancestral worship, whether he is a Buddhist or a Taoist or a Confucianist. Worship of ancestors is given the foremost place in the Chinese religious and national life. It is to be seen in nearly every phase of Chinese civilization. "It is commonly said that the Chinese belong to three religions: Confucianism, Buddhism and Taoism, and the saying is not altogether inaccurate. Popular language speaks of three creeds and an ordinary person in the course of his life may take part in rites which imply a belief in them all". Emperor Wan-li (157-162) defines Confucianism and Buddhism as two wings of a bird.

Confucianism means the teachings, precepts and philosophy of the great Chinese sage Confucius. It lays stress on leading a pious, peaceful and virtuous life. This is an ethical code of the highest morality. In addition to his moral code, Confucius taught an elaborate system of ceremonial observances which are of great importance. For more than two thousand years Confucianism has maintained its great influence in China. It has all along been a very powerful faith.

To the stricter Confucian formalist the Buddhist life has always seemed an evasion and denial of these social duties, of that filial service of the living and the dead which is his notion of morality. To him the nature of man is radically good; to the Buddhist the whole world of human activity is a scene of evil from which he seeks salvation (in fight). Indeed all that is distinctive of Buddhism was repugnant to the Confucian mind. The tonsure of the priests was a defacement of the body inherited from our ancestors; for ages the commonest form of persecution was to compel monks and nuns to return to the world and Jet their half grow. Vegetarianism involved not only a flagrant defiance of national customs but impugned the animal sacrifices prescribed in Confucian books; celibacy was denial of filial gratitude and social offence to people so proud of their native language and literature as Chinese. Yet Buddhism triumphed over all these obstacles and attained to a degree of influence and popularity, which Confucianism never reached, in the common religious atmosphere of the masses of the Chinese people.

The date of formal introduction of Buddhism in China is 67 A.D., but the Buddhist missionaries from India are said to have gone to that country two centuries prior to that date.

Buddhism as we know is divided into two great schools, viz., the Greater vehicle or *Mahāyāna* and the lesser vehicle or the *Hīnayāna*. Both the *Hīnayāna* and the *Mahāyāna* doctrines were introduced into China, but the former never gained popularity in the country. The character of Buddhist religion has been almost absolutely determined by *Mahāyānism*, again, is subdivided into partially developed *Mahāyānism* and fully developed *Mahāyānism. Mādhyamikas* and *Vijñānavādins* belong to the domain of partially developed *Mahāyānism*, while the *Avataṁśaka* School, the *Dhyāna* School, the *Mantra* School as well as the Great Chinese School of Buddhism known as the Tien-Tai School belong to the sphere of fully developed Mahāyānism.

Chinese Buddhism is not only a religion and a philosophy, but embraces many religions and many philosophies and they are not always compatible with themselves or with one another.

Buddhism was widely propagated for several centuries in China before anything was heard of Schools. But gradually the Chinese Buddhists became aware of the various Buddhistic Schools that were preached in China alongwith their sects and subdivisions.

During the rule of the kings of the Wei dynasty, Lo-yang and Ch'angnang became the great centres of Buddhism in China. The great Chinese scholar Tao-ngan created a deep interest in Buddhist literature. The disciples of Tao-ngan rendered still more valuable services which led Buddhism to flourish in China.

Lu-shan School - The first school of Buddhism founded in China was Lu-shan School. The monastery at Lu-shan was established by Hui-Yuan who was a disciple of Tao-ngan. Hui-yuan belonged to modern Tao-chou in North Shansi. He was born in 334 A.D. at Lou-fan and lived up to 418 A.D. He, in a sense, created a Brotherhood or a Corporation. In the early part of his life, he was a Taoist, but afterwards he became a Buddhist. He is said to have utilized the writings of Chuang-Tzu to explain his new faith. He settled in Hupeh in the Lu-feng Monastery which was well known for its ponds full of White Lotus. For a certain period of time this school flourished under the name of Pai-lien or White Lotus creed.

Amitābha School – Hui-Yuan's School led to the spread of *Amitābha* cult in China, which, up to this day exercises considerable influence among the various branches of

Buddhism of the Far East. It was at the instance of Hui-yuan that the complete works of the *Sarvāstivada-vinaya* were rendered into Chinese. He sent his disciples of *Kumārajīva* and got them trained by him. Moreover he sent some scholars like Fatsing, Fa-ling and others to places, far and abroad, in quest of authentic Sanskrit works. The above-mentioned scholars translated some Sanskrit books on Buddhism into Chinese.

The *Amidist* or the *Amitābha* School which was introduced into China by the Lu-shan School, founded by Hui-yuan, deserves our special attention, because of the fact that it plays not only an important role in the religious systems of both China and Japan, but also owing to the fact that it introduced a new form of Buddhism which is very appealing to Buddhist (Laymen) masses. *Amidist* and *Amidism* are the convenient terms which are adopted from the Japanese forms of the name *Amitābha,* who finds a very high place among the benevolent deities of China, Tibet and other countries of the Far East. The history of the *Amitābha* worship centres round the names of its seven patriarchs among whom two are Indians, *Nāgārjuna* and *Vasubandhu*; three Chinese, Tan-Luna, Tao-Cho'o and Shan-Tao and two Japanese, Geushin and Honen.

The cult of *Amitābha* has been current in India since the beginning of the Christian era or even earlier. It is surmised by some scholars that it was not an original Indian cult, but was rather introduced into India from Iran. But this fact should be borne in mind that two of the earliest scriptures of the *Amitābha* School, namely *Sukhāvativyūhas* are totally Indian as it is evident from their outlook and subject-matter.

The *Amitābha* School is known in China as Ching-tu (Pure Land) School. It is also known as Lotus School which teaches the attainment of salvation through faith in the God-Buddha, *Amitābha,* who gives the promise and assurance to the faithful of a life of supreme joy and happiness in the Pure Land or Western Paradise where *Amitābha* reigns in perpetual glory.

This School is totally different from other great schools of Buddhist thought. A Chinese writer has made a true and just remarks that followers of the 'Pure Land' doctrines do not belong either to the Ch'an or to Lun. But, now-a-days nearly every Ch'an monk puts his faith in the 'Pure Land' School. Many well educated Chinese Buddhists says that the Ch'an and Ching-Su teachings are not really compatible with one another, but that Ch'an doctrines are meant for the educated Buddhist, whereas *Amitābha* doctrines are fit for the unintellectual people.

The Pure Land or the *Amidist* branch of the *Mahāyāna* Buddhist sect has elevated the glory of *Amitābha* to such a pitch in large parts of the Buddhist world that it can be said that he enjoys a position of unrivalled glory and majesty. Theoretically the historical Buddha is mystically associated with the *Amitābha-Buddha.* The worshippers of *Amitābha* Buddha declare that the *Amitābha* doctrines of the "Pure Land" were actually delivered to the world by the Buddha *Śākyamuni* himself. But in the opinion of the Buddhist scholars of both the East and the West, the *Sukhāvatī* and the *Amitāyurdhyāna-Sūtras* which contain the doctrines of the "Pure Land" school are not the creation of early Buddhism and they look upon them as more or less apocryphal works.

Amitābha is unknown in the earlier Indian art and literature. Some of the obscure Buddha figures of Gåndhåra sculpture may be supposed to represent him, but according to Greunwedel and Foucher the images of *Amitābha* Buddha are late and not numerous in comparison with *Avalokita* and *Tārā.* He finds nc important place in the earlier part of the Lotus. He is mentioned in the Awakening of Faith attributed to *Aśvaghoṣa* towards the end of that work. In the *Mahāyāna-sūtrālaṅkāra* (also called *Sūtrālaṅkāra Śāstra*) of Asaṅga, there is also a mention of his heaven, but nothing more.

But the worship of *Amitābha* undoubtedly flourished in Central Asia in hoary antiquity as it is evident from the fact that the two principal scriptures of the Pure Land or the *Amitābha* School were rendered into Chinese in the second century A.D. by the natives of Central Asia and four scriptures were translated in the third century A.D. by the travelers of the same region.

We are told of *Amitābha* that many years ago he was a rich and powerful king. Imbued with a great deal of religious enthusiasm and also filled with deep love and pity for his fellow brethren, he relinquished his throne and royal insignia and became an ascetic under the name of Fa-tsane or Fa-hsiang which corresponds to Sanskrit *Dharmakara,* which means 'the mine of true religion or the divine essence'. He became a *Bodhisattva* under the guidance and influence of the Buddha of a very remote age, Shihtzu-tsai-wang or *Lokeśvaraja.* In the presence of the same Buddha, he, made a series of vow of prayers be which he took upon himself the difficult task of becoming another Buddha, for the peace and happiness of all living creatures by establishing a paradise on earth. The vows taken by *Amitābha* or Fa-tsang are forty-six in number in original Sanskrit works, but in the Chinese works 'Wu-liang shou-ching 'the vows are forty-eight in number. The vows speak of the glories and the joyful and blissful atmosphere of the paradise to which Fatsang took the vow to lead all creatures.

The Chinese names for the regions of Supreme Blessedness and Loveliness are Ching-t'u Pure Land, Hsi-t'ien western heaven and Chi-lo-shih-chieh, which is the same as the Sanskrit *Sukhāvatī* the Land of Supreme happiness. Each of the five Buddhas is supposed to preside over one of the parts of the universe as for example *Akṣobhya* rules in the eastern region whereas the *Amitābha* rules in the western part. The five Buddhas each have a 'Heaven' under their jurisdiction and all the heaven are presumed to be situated at an infinite distance from the world of mankind. Those who have attained a high degree of enlightenment, for them all the heavens are the same and all the Buddhas who rule over the innumerable heavens are the manifestations of one supreme truth.

The eighteenth of the forty-eight vows mentioned in the Wu-liang-shou-ching is responsible for the belief that mere faith in *Amitābha* and the invocations of his name will enable a man to have his rebirth in the Western Paradise. The Chinese commentators are emphatic enough to state that no amount of virtue will ensure a man to have his rebirth in Western Heaven if it is without the invocation of the name of *Amitābha.* The *Sūtra* says that a man, who sincerely invokes the name of *Amitābha* for at least a week or even for a single day, many face death with the perfect peace of mind; for *Amitābha* accompanied by a band of divine *Bodhisattvas* will surely appear before him and take him over to the Pure Land to have his rebirth in which there is neither sigh nor sorrow.

Among the attendant *Bodhisattvas* of *Amitābha* the most prominent are *Avalokiteśvara* (Chinese, Kuang-yin) and *Mahāsthāma* (Chinese, Ta-Shih-chih), Avalokiteśvara is represented to be standing on the left and *Mahāsthāma* on the right. These *Bodhisattvas* are no inferior in any way to the glory and greatness of *Amitābha* himself. Both of these attendants of *Amitābha* act as the protectors and guides of men in their dangerous journey of life and death.

"The essential features of *Amidist* doctrine are that there is a paradise of light belonging to a benevolent deity and that the man who invokes his name will be led thither. Both features are found in Zeroastrian writings. The highest heaven (following after the paradise of good thoughts, good words and good deeds) is called Boundless light or Endless light. Both this region and its master, *Ahuramazda*, are habitually spoken of in terms implying radiance and glory. Also it is a land of song just as *Amitābha's* paradise; it re-echoes with music and pleasant sounds. Prayers can win this paradise and Ahuramazda and Arch angels will come and show the way thither to the pious. Further whoever recites the *Ahuna-varya* formula, *Ahuramazda* will bring his soul to the lights of heaven, and although, so far as I know it is not expressly stated that the repetition of *Ahrumazada's* name leads to paradise; yet the general efficacy of his names as invocations is clearly affirmed."

We have already mentioned that there are three Chinese Patriarchs of the *Amitābha* School, namely, Tan-luan,Tao-cho and Shan-Tao. These patriarchs did not follow one another in quick succession.

Tan-luan belonged to the Shansi province and lived from 476 to 542 A.D. He was a great scholar and he engaged himself in writing a commentary on the *Mahāsannipāta-sūtra* which had been translated into Chinese. But he fell sick, and his illness made him feel this fact that a scholar could not render any valuable service without having a long life. With this end in view, Tan-luan went to a celebrated Taoist hermit at Nanking, While coming, he met the Indian monk *Bodhiruci,* who told him that the advice of the hermit was good for nothing and he handed over to him a copy of the *Amitāyurdhyāna-sūtra*, through which he would be able to obtain eternal life there. Tan-luan accepted his advice and threw himself heart and soul in preaching the power of *Amitābha* and the benefits derived from repetitions of the name. He lived at Fe-chou in Shansi and wrote a commentary on *Vasubandhu's* treatise on Paradise.

The second patriarch, Tao-ch'o lived from 562-645 A.D. He was born near Tao-yuan-fu. At first he went through the *Nirvāṇa-sūtra*, but at the age of forty-five he completely gave it up and took up the vow before the memorial to Tan-luan erected at Fenchu that he would preach nothing save and except the doctrine of salvation through unflinching faith in *Amitābha*. He collected the passages of scriptures relating to the Happy Land, through which he laid stress on the doctrine that ordinary mortals can be born in the Happy Land only, if they repeat his holy name. He himself is said to have repeated the holy name of *Amitābha* 70,000 times a day. He is perhaps the first person to use the terms Holy Path and the Pure Land which were only the two modes of leading a truly religious life.

The third greatest patriarch was called Shan-tao who lived from 613 to 681 A.D. He was supposed to be the incarnation of *Amitābha* and his writings were accepted as scripture. Shan-tao was born in Shanthung. He was at first a student of the Samon School, but, by chance, he came across the *Amitāyurdhyāna-sūtra* and soon he became a follower of the *Amitābha* School. He wrote a commentary on the *Amitāyurdhyāna-sūtra*. According to one story he committed suicide, which seems impossible as it was against his own teaching.

The fourth patriarch was Hui-ken. His date is not exactly known. He wrote a book (called Gunjion) in which he solved some difficult points of the doctrine.

Shao-k'ang was the fifth and the last patriarch. He was born in Chekiang.

---

* Dr. B. Jinananda is a lecturer in the Department of Buddhist Studies, University of Delhi, Delhi.

18

A STUDY OF THE LUNG-MEN CAVE INSCRIPTIONS

Latika Lahiri *

Throughout the fourth century, North China was perpetually invaded by successive hordes of Turko-Mongolian tribes following a long period of disunity, chaos and confusion. They constantly attacked and destroyed each other. But out of this utter destruction emerged a new power, a more stable and permanent government that of To-ba (Tobahach) from northernmost part of Shansi province. Thereafter, followed a period of consolidation and of political and cultural achievement of immense assurance.

The To-ba Turks, who had pastoral life, were greatly impressed by Chinese ways of life and their culture. Gradually they were completely Sinicised and merged with the main stream of Chinese civilization and culture. They established their ascendancy over North China with their capital at Ta-t'ung in Shansi as the Northern Wei Dynasty. Their rulers embraced Buddhism with great enthusiasm like the Kusanas who were foreigners in India.[1] They played a very significant role in the history of Buddhism in China (A.D. 386-543).

In the seventeenth year of the T'ai-he period (A.D. 494), the Emperor Hsiao Wen-ti shifted his capital to the south of Lo-yang in Ho-nan, which was a remarkable event. Emperors of the Northern Wei Dynasty undertook a magnificent project of constructing the caves of Lung-men near Lo-yang which continued throughout the rest of the Dynasty. With the advent of the Sui and the T'ang Dynasties, the work continued unabated on a large scale. The grottoes of Lung-men (Dragon Gate) are the greatest contribution of the To-ba Wei to China. "Epoch of great religious art is rare. The Wei period is one of them."[2]

The river I flowing through Lung-men bisects a range of small mountains into Eastern and Western groups. In comparison with the Western hill which comprises 28 cave temples (1-28), the Eastern hill comprises a far smaller number. The important caves are Ku-Yang-t'ung, P'in-Yang-t'ung and Lien-hua-t'ung. Numerous Buddhist niches were curved inside and outside the cave of the Western hills and colossal Buddhist images are to be seen everywhere in the Lung-men.

The Lung-men caves bear innumerable votive *stūpas*, episodes from the story of Buddha's life, of his previous births or *Jātakas*, images of the Buddha and a number of different

Bodhisattvas, most valuable and dedicatory inscriptions. These inscriptions are indispensable materials to evaluate the prosperity and decline of Buddhism there, desire and aspiration of the people irrespective of Imperial family, monks, nuns and laities, their superstitions and beliefs. These donatory or dedicatory inscriptions which have come down to us show not only the trend of Buddhism but also the socio-religious and socio-economic conditions that prevailed during the period.

So far, very little work has been done on these caves and very few visitors and scholars go there to investigate and study the world famous movements. Therefore, it is really difficult to assess the actual number of images and inscriptions. According to the report of an officer in 1916, the Lung-men caves possessed about 3,680 inscriptions.[3] Every student of Chinese Buddhist thoughts, art and architecture is greatly indebted to the Japanese scholars Tosio Nagahiro and Seiiti Mizuno for their valuable and monumental contribution regarding the Lung-men cave temples.

It was during the Shan-Kuei period (A.D. 517) and Chang-Kuang period (A.D. 519) under the regency of Dowageress Empress Ling T'ai-hou, the royal treasury possessed enormous wealth. There was a long period of economic and material prosperity. This economic prosperity and political stability helped the Empress to execute such splendid work of art.

There are mainly three types of donatory inscriptions which have come down to us and which reveal the circumstances that led to a social, political and religious transition. Firstly, the inscriptions donated by the ruling class, the nobility, specially by the Imperial family of the Northern Wei and other nobility belonging to the northern clan before. Secondly, there are a large number of inscriptions by common people, family members of the officials who were believers and directors of Buddhism and by monks and nuns. Thirdly, the inscriptions by the groups and leagues organised by the Buddhist monks. The first two types were made individually and the third one collectively[4].

From overall description of the first category of inscriptions and a large number of images it seems that most of these inscriptions were curved under the royal patronage. Special mention may be made here that the Empresses, the royal concubines and other ladies belonging to the royal family, mothers, wives of nobles made no less contribution for this creative work. From the stone records of Lung-men, we know that the oldest inscriptions of the cave Ku-yang-t'ung belonged to the 19th year of the T'ai-he period A.D. 494 and other inscriptions belonged to Ching-ming period A.D. 500-501, Chang-shih period A.D. 504-507 and the rest covering more than twenty seven years. After the third year of the Chang-kuang period, the Dynastic inscriptions of the To-ba Wei are to be seen in various caves of Lien-hua, Hui-shao, Wei-tze beside Ku-Yang cave.

The earliest inscription which still exists in the southern wall of the cave Ku-Yang mentions the name of Sun Ch'iu-sheng and two hundred other names. The inscription belonging to the 7th year of the T'ai-he period A.D. 483 says, "Let the country prosper forever and let the Three Jewels illuminate more shiningly than ever."[5]

Most of the inscriptions at the Lung-men caves are dedicated to the *Maitreya Bodhisattva* after the death of the donors' dear and near ones. Wei-Ch'ih Shih, the queen of Ch'ang-le erected a magnificient statue of *Maitreya* after the death of her son and the inscriptions which were dedicated to the image of *Maitreya* follows as, "Wei-Ch'ih, the wife of Chiu-Mu ling-liang, the King of Ch'ang-le and officer in the Imperial household, Lord in Waiting, after passing away of their beloved son erected an image of *Maitreya*. Her sincere prayer was that the soul of her bereaved son should be free from suffering of this world of sorrow and misery, should rest in heaven, the abode of eternal peace and his soul should be free from bondage of life and death. If she has to be born again, she prays, he should be born in heaven, the abode of the Buddha or if in this world again, should be born in a place of joy and freedom. If his soul is in distress, let the Buddha, she prays, by His grace save him. Let him be free from three lowest migrations – hell, hungry ghosts and beasts. Not only her son but the living beings be free from this place of horror."

The inscription dedicated by the grand-mother T'ai Fei hou after the death of her husband Chia lan-han the King of Kuang Ch'uan[6] as well as Chung-shih (Imperial Service) expresses the sorrows and tragedy of her life when husband and only son died. The inscriptions follows, "In my long circle of birth and death in difficult to traverse. I must be careful otherwise I would fall into the ice. I have faith only in the Buddha who would save me from all difficulties. I curve the ornate statue of Maitreya. I pray to the Buddha that this act of merit would give me good health. Let me have real consciousness, so that I could leave this world of Avidyā or ignorance and miseries. I pray for the long life of my grandson and his wife. I pray for the birth of their children, their prosperity and glory of the family. I pray for the safety and security of the Imperial throne, for the eternal and ever-lasting glory of the Crown, so that they propagate *Mahadharma* Ch'ao-fa.[7] Let all the beings who are in darkness of ignorance realize the greatness of the Buddha." This inscription shows her sincere devotion to the Buddha as well as the pathos of her heart, although she was held in high esteem in the society.

Besides the inscriptions by ruling classes, there are a number of inscriptions by Buddhist monks and nuns of the Northern Wei period. In carrying out the project of Lung-men the ruling classes, the nobility and the gentries were always advised by the active monks and nuns. In the catalogue of 'Stone Inscriptions' there are 189 inscriptions belonging to the Northern Wei Dynasty in Lung-men. Among these 189 inscriptions, 72 i.e. about 2/5 of the total were incised by the monks and nuns. At the early period of the history of Lung-men, there was a large community of monks, but there is no mention of nuns. But in the beginning of Yu-p'ing period (A.D. 508-512) of the Emperor Hsuan-wu, suddenly sprang up a large number of nuns who also contributed for the Lung-men cave project. In this field the pioneer was the Empress herself, followed by a number of ladies from royal houses and gentries. Many nunneries were established under the patronage of the Dowageress Empress Ling T'ai-hou. Images were erected and inscriptions were dedicated by nuns after the expiry of their sons, daughters and they prayed for the successful conjugal life of their children. Interestingly, these nuns did neither start their life as recluse nor did they enter into ecclesiastical order, but after many years of their married life they left home and joined the nunnery.

In the 22nd year of the T'ai-he period, the Bhikṣu Hui-Ch'ang incised the inscription on the northern wall of Ku-Yang-t'ung, "Buddha is dead, I consider that sincere endeavour has been made in the cause of sculpturing the images in the period of the Northern Wei Dynasty, I pray to the Buddha. let the soul of my beloved father be free from the bondage of this world and let him obtain salvation, I pray for the happiness of seven generations of parents and preceptors and let them be in Tusitā, the 4th *Devaloka.* If they are to reborn, let them be in the royal and noble families. I wish to share the Buddha's blessings with all mankind."

During the Northern Wei Dynasty, the monks, the believers of the faith assembled together in a group or association consisting of sometimes far more than 300 members and jointly spent enormous wealth for the construction of the cave temples. These associations of monks were known as Fa-she Religious Fraternity, I-hui Religious Society. The monk Shih fa Chen Ch'uan[8] of the temple Kuang-te along with other fellow brethren started religious activities in Lo-yang during the rules of the Emperor Hsiao ming and the Empress Ling T'ai-hou. The activities of these associations were not only limited in making images, holding religious meetings, copying *Sutras* but also advising people to repair temples and *stupas.*

In the 2nd year of Shan-Kuei period A.D. 519, the members of the Religious Society engraved inscription which says that the head of the Society spent about 900 yuan and each member of 25 fraternities spent 100 yuan of the construction of the Lung-men caves. There are dedicatory inscriptions (A.D. 570), on both the walls of the entrance of the Yao-Feng cave of Medical Prescriptions. The monk Kuang-tao constructed an image of *Vaiṣajyarāja Bodhisattva* or *Śākyamuni* (?) The prognosis, diagnosis, prescription for different discases, the names of medical herbs as well as prayers for longevity are inscribed.

In conclusion we can say from all these inscriptions, firstly that Buddhism which was extensively practiced in Lo-yang under the Northern Wei Dynasty was predominantly *Mahāyāna. Hīnayāna* the religion of *Śrāvakas* emphasizes the importance of self-interest whereas *Mahāyāna* the religion of *Bodhisattva* emphasizes altruism and sacrifice for the welfare of others. In the inscriptions donors hope to share the Buddha's blessings with all mankind and living creatures. This is a reflection of the spirit of *Mahāyāna* in contrast with the ideal of personal salvation of the *Śrāvakas*. These inscriptions clearly show that during this period *Mahāyāna* excelled *Hīnayāna*. Secondly, the prayers offered by the donors for the repose of ancestors' spirit well indicate how Buddhism was practiced inseparably with the universal observance of age-old custom of ancestor worship and strong morality of filial piety which characterize the Chinese family system. Buddhism during the Northern Wei succeeded in its early stage because the followers of the faith compromised this religion with Taoism and Confucianism. There was a tendency among the rich and aristocratic circles to sympathise with the three religions. Thirdly, Buddhism was apparently taken up by the upper strata of the society before it spread downward among masses. But the class distinction which was so deep-rooted in Chinese society was somewhat eased by the Northern Dynasty. Common religion united the rich and the poor, nobility and the common people and with the cooperation of the entire society the magnificient piece of Buddhist art at Lung-men was created.

Endnotes

1. Arthur F. Wright: Fo-t'u-teng, *Harvard Journal of Asiatic Studies* II. 1948, P. 356.
2. Rene Grousset, *Rise and Splendour of the Chinese Empire*, University of California Press, 1965.
3. Journal Lu-hsing-Tsa-chih Pa-ch'i
   Kenneth, K.S. *Ch'en Buddhism in China*, P. 171.
   Princeton University Press, 1964.
4. Lung-men Shih K'o-lu.
5. Wei-shu Shih-lao Chih.
6. The ruler of the Former Han Dynasty governed Kuang-Ch'uan it was known as Hsin-tu old I-chou, Shen-chou, Liang-chou area. (Han-Shu ti-li-chih. Topography in the Han Records). There was a big river flowing through Hsin-tu. So the name of the place is given as Kuang-Ch'uan, a long river.
7. *Saddharma. The wonderful law or truth of the Lotus Sūtra.*
8. *Taisho* Vol. 50. Shu-Kao-seng chuan.

* Miss Latika Lahiri is a lecturer in the Department of Buddhist Studies, University of Delhi, Delhi.

19

REASON AND AUTHORITY IN BUDDHISM AS A PHILOSOPHY

Kewal Krishan Mittal

Insofar as a I have understood Buddhism as a Philosophy, I must say, at the very outset, there is no place of authority in it. A well-known and oft-quoted statement attributed to the Buddha comes to my mind in this connection. "Believe nothing", says he, "because a so-called wise man said it. Believe nothing because the belief is generally held. Believe nothing because it is written in ancient books. Believe nothing because it is said to be a divine origin. Believe nothing because someone else believes it. But believe only what you yourself judge to be true."[1] It was in this spirit that he rejected the authority of the *Vedas* and did not hand down a scripture of his own to his followers.

It may be said that even though the Buddha did not accept any authority his followers surely did, may be, contrary to the advice of the Master. It is contended that the Buddha's word had been the final truth with the Buddhists.[2] May I humbly ask the scholars who maintain such a view as to whether do we possess an authentic record of his sayings? My own answer to the question is that we do not. It is a well known fact that his teachings were oral and were texts known as *Pāli*-canon or the *Tripiṭaka* texts came to be written not earlier than the passage of about a hundred years after the *Parinirvāṇa* (death) of the Buddha. Grave doubts have been expressed about their genuine representation of the 'words of the Buddha' *(Buddhavacana)*. It is not without some ground that George Grimm calls *Tripiṭaka* as 'a great falsification – a killing of the Buddha idea by its professed guardians.'[3] Winternitz informs us that the same is the view of Mrs. Rhys Davids, though she does not say it in so many words.[4] One need not agree with such a sweeping judgement to realize that, in so far as the authenticity of the *Tripiṭaka* texts is a matter of controversy they cannot be regarded as authoritative.

Any other texts, such for examples as the *Abhidharma* texts also do not fair better. Basing his view on a discussion on the subject among the *Theras* (the elder Monks) as reported in *Aṭṭhasālinī* – a famous Buddhist text, B. C. Law rightly, observes: "there would always be a difference of opinion among Buddhist scholars as to whether the *Abhidharma* books contain the genuine words of Buddha Gautama."[5]

The ideals of '*Pacceka Buddha* (each Buddha)' and '*Samāsama Buddha* (equal and the unequal Buddha)' as held by the *Hīnayāna* Buddhists were in line with their rejection of authority and represented a spirit of self reliance. The later ideal of *'Bodhisattva'* as upheld and propagated by the *Mahāyāna* Buddhists does seem to undermine the spirit of self-reliance but surely does not bring in the element of authority. The *Bodhisattva* is no doubt described as *'Sarvajña'* (all knowing) and *'Sarvajñatā of Buddha'* as also *'Kevalajñāna* or *Sakalajñāna* of Mahāvīra' are in a way the *Baudha* and the *Jaina* substitutes for the 'infallibility of the *Vedas*, as held by the *āstika* (orthodox) systems of Indian philosophy. But in so far as people are not advised to believe in the sayings of a *'Bodhisattva'* as much as it is emphasized that the *Bodhisattva* moved by *Mahākaruṇā* (great compassion) comes to help them merely by awakening in them the spark of enlightenment, the ideal of *Bodhisattva* does not amount to a return to authority. Besides the idea of 'postponing one's salvation till everyone else too gets it', does not go against the idea of *'Pacceka Buddha'*, in essence.

Coming to reason, I am inclined to affirm emphatically that Buddhism as a philosophy[6] is thoroughly rational.

It was their firm faith in reason that led the early Buddhists to deny the existence of self as a substantival entity. They did not fight shy in drawing logical or rational implications of 'the four noble truths' as enunciated and explained by the Buddha, however unpalatable to the popular taste.

It was a result of giving free reins to reason that Nāgārjuna, the propounder of *'Śūnyavāda'*, developed a dialectic where through he rationally denied that there was ever a *Buddha, Dharma or Saṅgha*[7]. He argued for a position that he called *'Madhyamā Pratipadā* (the Middle Way) or *Advayavāda* (non-dualism) which transcends the distinction between affirmation and negation,[8] purely on a rational basis.

The emphasis laid by the Buddhists on reason had a sharp reaction on those who stood for the authority of the *Vedas*. Some denied the utility of reason, others condemned it as something misleading, some others, however, adopted and adapted it to vindicate their scriptures. Kumārila Bhaṭṭa, for example, refused to grant that any one could ever know *'Dharma'* through reason. *Dharma* could only be known from the *Veda* according to him.[9] Surīśvara a *Vedānt* ācarya tells us that one who relies completely on reason, as the Buddhists do, is sure to plunge into darkness.[10] Gauḍapāda the celebrated teacher of Śaṅkarācārya who argues that the *Upaniṣad* teach the doctrines of *Ajātivāda* (non origination) and Buddhists through their pure-reasoning too reach the same conclusions.[11] Śaṅkara goes a step farther than his Guru (preceptor) when he says that if scripture is opposed to reason, it is not reason but scripture that should be rejected.[12] An argument going from the seen to unseen on the basis of analogy, in being nearer to experience, is to be rated higher than a statement made by a scripture about something far removed from experience, according to him.[13] Little wonder, therefore, if Śaṅkara earned the title of a *'Pracchanna Bauddha'* (A Buddhist in disguise).

Endnotes

1. *Aṅguttara Nikāya.*
2. A. B. Keith, *Buddhist Philosophy,* p. 33.
3. *Die Wissenschaft des Buddhismus* (Leipzig 1923), p. 2 note quoted by M. Winternitz – "*Self and non-self in early Buddhism*" – Jha Commemoration volume p. 456, footnote 1.
4. Ibid.
5. B. C. Law, *Historical Gleanings*, pp. 51-52.
6. I am underlining '*Buddhism as a Philosophy*' because I equally firmly hold that Buddhism as a religion is not and cannot (perhaps like every other religion) be thoroughly rational.
7. *Mūlamādhyamika-kārikā, Kārikā* XXIV.
8. Ibid.
9. *Tantravārtika* (Jha's translation – Bibliotheca Indica) Vol. I, pp. 165-8.
10. See his *Naiṣkarmya Siddhi* (Vavilla Press Madras) III *vākya* 90, III 99 ff.
11. See *Māṇḍūkya Kārikā* IV. 1-5 See also *Āgama Sāstra of Gauḍapāda* (Calcutta University) Introduction.
12. *Śaṅkara* in Introduction to his commentary on *Bṛhdāraṇyaka Upaniṣad* V. 1.1.
13. *Śaṅkara Bhāṣya* on *Brahmasūtra* 11. 1.4.

20

SHAMANISM AND BUDDHISM

*Sudha Sengupta**

Shamanism at present signifies witchcraft, sorcery, exorcism, devil-dancing, etc., and such kind of actions which are performed by a class of people to satisfy the eternal superstitious beliefs of people to attain certain objects, which are not supposed to be attained by any other normal means. Belief in the supernatural agencies like ghosts, demons and the like, and in the magic and miracles performed by people skilled in that art, is as old as the history of human race. Whenever any calamity like – disease, pestilence, enemity and the like, fell on people, which seemed difficult of impossible to be averted by ordinary human efforts, the help of supernatural elements was sought. The person or persons who acted as the connecting link between the supernatural elements and his human clients, are called the priests or the magicians. All the misfortunes were supposed to be caused by the evil eyes of some ghost or demon, and as these enemies could not be fought out with bare hands, some kind of witchcraft was needed to drive them away. For this purpose, a class of people were specially trained, who also had some natural aptitude for that. These people were respected with some awe and horror by their clients, as they had to perform various kinds of odd rituals to serve their purposes. This belief in demons and the office of the priests to overcome them, is prevalent throughout the world in different names from time immemorial. In India, the earliest known literature about it – the part of the Vedic texts known as *Atharvaveda* – is full of these accounts. The priests who performed these magical practices, were called the *Atharvans* in it.

The term '*Sāman*' occurs in the Tungus language, meaning a priest, a medicine-man or a spirit conjuror, from which the term *Shamanism* is derived to signify the indigenious religion of the Ural-Altaic people of North Asia and Europe. In the wider sense, this term designates certain type of religious practices, whose fundamental characteristics are found to be mostly identical with those practiced among other races of the world, far remote from each other, like the Red races of the North and South America, the races of Siberia, nay even the multitude of Indo-Chinese tribes. It presupposes belief in a multiplicity of spirits (animism) and in continued existence after death of individual souls (ancestor worship). The most distinctive features of *Shamanism* have to do with choice, initiation, techniques of those specialists in mediation between the world of spirits and the world of men, who are called Shamana. The office of *Shaman* may be hereditary, or acquired by, or bestowed upon a suitably endowed person after a period of intensive training. The *Shaman* may be epileptic or otherwise predisposed to fits and trances. On initiation, he is invested with dress and equipments. A *Shaman's* dress is elaborate and symbolical, while his indispensable instrument is the drum (or the tambourine), ornamented with esoteric symbols. Thereafter his functions are priestly, oracular, and medicinal. He offers sacrifices, foretells fortunes and cure diseases, in each case with the help of the spirits,[1] which are supposed to be mischievous and cause illness and other calamities. The *Shamans* invoke the spirits and the usual way of appeasing them are some fantastic ceremonies and convulsive dances.

The similarity of the term *Shaman* with *Pāli Samaṇa* (Sanskrit *Śramaṇa*) and the similarity of the religion with the magical practices of later Tāntric Buddhism – particularly those of Tibet, Mongolia, etc. – led to the belief that the *Shamans* are none other than the Buddhists in their transformation. According to some scholars, the *Śramaṇas* of a certain tribe in Central Asia, transformed themselves from hermits to *Shamans*. Max Mullar of Oxford wrote, '*Shamanism* found its way from India to Siberia via Tibet, China and Mongolia. Rules of the formation of magic figures, on the treatment of diseases by charms, incantations and other branches of *Shaman* witchcraft, are found in the *Tanjur'*. He further writes, 'the only trace of the influence of Buddhism among Chudic races, the Finn, Lapp, etc., is found in the name of their priests and sorcerers, the *Shamans'*.[2] A. H. Sayce writes, 'In Shamanism, so called from the *Shaman* or Sibarian sorcerer, who is himself but a transformed *Śramaṇa* or Buddhist missionary priest, we rise to a higher conception of religion.'[3]

The word *Shaman* is found in the Arabic records in the form '*Samaniyya*' to designate Indian and Bactrian Buddhists. In Firdausi's *Shahnama,* we find the term *Saman* in the sense of a worshipper of idols. There it evidently refers to the Indian Buddhists and has no connection with the Siberian *Shamans,* as the *Saman* in it says, 'our religion is one of peace and quiet, and fighting and slaying is prohibited, as well as all kinds of shedding of blood.'[4] In classical literature also, like the record of Megasthenes, we come across the term *Samanoj,* obviously meaning the Buddhists. The Turkish and ancient Mongol term for *Shaman* is Kaṃ, from which the Russians have derived the verb '*Kamlat*' meaning to *Shamanise,* to conjure, spell, prophesy.

Before the introduction of Buddhism, Tibet was dominated by an indigenous religion called *Bon* which was nothing but *Shamanism* with its necromantic cult, devil dancing, etc. So deep was the belief of the Tibetans in ghosts, demons, witchcraft, etc., that in the early stage of its inception, the pacific religion of Buddhism could not take root in its soil, notwithstanding the earnest efforts of its first promulgator, viz, the king Srong-tsan-Gampo. Even a few centuries later *Śāntarakṣita* was driven out of the country because he was against such rituals. It was only when Padmasambhava arrived with the full-fledged Tantric practices, that Buddhism could gain ground in Tibet, because the Tantric rituals suited to the temperament of the people there. That is why Padmasambhava is regarded as a great teacher in Tibet even today. Though Buddhist scriptures and philosophical texts went on to be studied, cultured and new treatises being written in subsequent periods, an undercurrent of old beliefs continued to flow. Like Taoism of China, the *Shamanist Bon* religion of Tibet also is intermingled with Buddhism. As in *Shamanism,* they make sacrifices, not only animal but sometimes human also, which are strictly forbidden in Buddhism. It is opposed to the *Lamaist* religion also, and the Lamaist rulers are prohibited to practice this age-old ritual, but, it is said, they do it secretly. "The reformed *Lamaist* church of the yellow-hat sect employs many rites which are transparently *Bon,* such as the necromantic expelling of the death-demon and the demon of sickness and much of their divination roles. The unreformed red-hat sects practice the old *Bon* rites to a much greater extent, including the erection of masts attached to dog's or sheep's skulls, 'to bar the door' to the earth and sky demons."[5]

The occurrence of *Shamanistic* elements in Tibetan Buddhism, especially the *Bon* religion, has been pointed out by many scholars. The Tibetan deities form a group of 'brothers' or 'sisters' comprising five, seven, nine or some other odd number. The same is found in the mythology of the *Shamanistic* divinity.[6] The use of drums as part of religious equipment by both the *Shamans* and the *Lamas,* are noticeable. The drum of course sometimes change into an eight spoked wheel under the influence of Buddhism. Affinity of dress and customs between the *Shaman* priests and the Tibetan priests are that 'their *Shamans* travel in rainbow to heaven.' In the rites of initiation these rainbows are represented by two ribbons of silk, one red and the other blue. Similar ideas are encountered in Tibetan Buddhism. The two yellow and red ribbons hanging at the sides of Tibetan paintings *(thang ka),* are called 'yellow' and the 'red rainbows'........"[7]

The above survey shows that *Shamanism,* though originally a religion of the Tungus and other Siberian aboriginals, spread into a much wider area and influenced other religions, especially Buddhism of Tibet and Mongolia. In fact, to generalize, it may be said that 'the *Shaman* belongs to no special form of belief, but holds a position somewhat intermediate between the medicine-man and wizard for the lower and the marabout and true priest of the higher, religious systems.'[8]

Endnotes

1. Brandon, S.G.F., *A Dictionary of Comparative Religion*, pp. 571-2.
2. Chips from a German workshop, vol. 1, pp. 233-4.
3. *Introduction to the Science of Languages*, vol. II., p. 293.
4. Hobson – Jobson, p. 820.
5. E.R.E., XII, p. 333.
6. Nebesky – Wojdowitz, *Demons and Oracles of Tibet*, p. 539.
7. Ibid, p. 552.
8. E.R.E., II. p. 120.

* Miss Sudha Sengupta is a lecturer in the Department of Buddhist Studies, University of Delhi, Delhi.

21

MEANING, ORIGIN AND THE DEVELOPMENT OF THE AVADĀNAS

*Sharmistha Sharma**

Muck ink is split on the subject as to what the exact meaning of the '*avadāna*' is. Right from the Vedic period, it has its appearance at different places with different shades of meaning. In the *Śatapatha Brāhmaṇa*[1], it has been used in the sense of a sacrificial thing *(hotavya dravya).* It is further mentioned that gods are pleased when '*avadāna*' is presented to them. In *Kātyāyana Śrautasūtra*[2], this word is applied for the portions of the *haviṣ* offered to the deities. It is also used in the sense of an act which makes one free from all the four debts, i.e. *deva-ṛna, ṛṣi-ṛna, pitṛ-ṛna* and *manuṣyāṛna*[3]. It is obvious that the act which is so powerful as to make one free from all the debts is certainly a noble act.

The classical Sanskrit literature also abounds in with the recurrent use of this word. The words of *Vālmiki, Kālidāsa, Bhāravi, Harṣa,* etc., are not altogether devoid of this word. In the *Rāmāyaṇa*[4] the word '*apadāna*'[5] occurs at so many places for illustrious or heroic deeds. In *aghuvaṁśa*[6], *Kumārasambhava*[7], *Kirātārjunīya*[8], *Naiṣadhīya-Carita*[9] and *Daśakumāra carita*[10], it has been used for heroic deeds. *Mallinātha* comments upon the meaning thus Vīrayāṇyevāvadānāni Bhāguri[11] also holds similar views about the meaning.

Winternitz[12] explains the meaning thus, "The word *avadāna* means a noteworthy deed" sometimes in a bad sense, but generally in the good sense of "a heroic deed", "a feat", with the Buddhists a "religious or moral feat" and then also the "story of a noteworthy deed or feat". Feer[13], in his French translation of the *Avadāna-śataka* writes that '*avadāna*' is an instruction which shows with facts the link which exists between an act and its inevitable consequences. In the preface to the *Avadāna-śataka* edited by J.S. Speyer, it is mentioned that outside the Buddhist world the Sanskrit word *avadāna* is used for illustrious actions or feats.[14] The editor further observes, "An *avadāna (apadāna)* is in proper sense something cut off; something selected." He quotes Hodgson, who gave definition of the word *avadāna* that it treats "of the fruit of actions or moral law of mundane existence."[15] J. J. Jones holds, "An *avadāna* is a tale in which the heroism or other virtue of a living character is explained by the Buddha as the result of a good deed performed in previous existence."[16] G. K. Nariman opines, "The word '*avadāna*' signifies a great religious or moral achievement as well as the history of a great achievement".[17]

After taking into consideration the above discussion we can safely conclude that *ava* prefixed to a noun also means noble, illustrious or heroic[18]. *Dāna* means the act of donating or giving. The act of giving is considered an act quite virtuous. Thus the compound '*avadāna*' means noble, illustrious or heroic act, in general, and the act of giving, in particular.[19]

A section of Buddhist literature is called *Avadāna* because it deals with the tales pertaining to noble deeds of either the Buddha or any of his disciples. These noble deeds generally consisted in supplying of food, incense, flowers, gold, etc., to the Lord and also in building of *stūpas, caityas,* etc.

When we go to the original sources of the *Avadāna,* we are reminded of the *Puṇyakathā* and the *Puṇyavipākakathā* which according to Kanga Takahata, may be taken as referring to these *Avadānas.* Referring to the development of the *Avadānas* from early Buddhist types of stories, he holds, "There exists instance of *Avadāna* being called alternatively *kathā* and since they are normally stories developed stage by stage describing acts of worship such as alms-giving or offering to the Buddha and the fruit borne by the merit thus acquired throughout past and subsequent existences, I think it not inappropriate to fit them in here. Looked at in this light, the *Avadāna* literature is a development from the early Buddhist types of stories concerning such matters as alms-giving, the moral precepts and the heavens into which human beings may be reborn......."[20]

Since almost all the *Avadānas* inculcate the idea that black deeds bear black fruits, white deeds bear white fruits and those mixed ones beget mixed fruits so they can rightly be called the '*karma-stories*' also.

As regards the origin of Indian story literature in general, we can find traces of stories in Vedic *Saṁhitās* which have been developed in *Brāhmaṇas* and *Upaniṣads.* In the *Ṛīgveda,* which is hailed to be the earliest literary composition of India, so many such *sūktas* are found in which a dialogue between two or more than two characters is depicted. These are called the *Saṁvāda-sūktas* and from the historical point of view these can rightly be claimed as the main sources of later story literature. In the *Purāṇas* these stories have changed to a considerable extent. In the *Rāmāyaṇa* and the *Mahābhārata,* too, the themes of the stories, drawn from the above mentioned ancient literature, are somewhat changed. The *Śukasaptati,* which contains several stories of parrots, the *Pañcatantra* fables, etc. form a precious treasure of stories from which story-tellers of other countries sought inspiration. These stories have been told and retold with a twist here and there. The Buddhists, too, carried the same tradition further in the form of the *Jātakas* and the *Avadānas.* Both are closely related to each other. Both concern tales told with the purpose of inculcating high morals. The *Jātakas* are acclaimed to be the fore-runners of the *Avadānas.* The question arises: if there already existed a vast section of literature called *Jātakas* to inculcate high morals among the laity, what use there was in introducing a new type of literature called *Avadānas* and that, too, with the same purpose? The question, no doubt, is very challenging. We can say in answer that the *Jātakas* generally related the glorious deeds of the *Bodhisattvas* who could offer their wife, children, flesh, blood and even body to those who needed them or who pretended to be in need of them. The common people could not be made familiar with the glorious deeds of the world-famed heroes (*Bodhisattvas*). They could not understand that what the great hero has done, they, too, can do. So there was a need for something humbler, i.e. the glorious deeds of some ordinary human beings with whom the common fold could make identity. The *Avadāna* literature served this purpose because in these stories the *Bodhisattva* was always either the hero or one of the characters occurring in the story.

Besides the glorious deeds, such as offering gifts to the *Saṅgha,* paying homage to the Lord and his ardent followers by offering them incense, flowers, silver, gold, jewels, honoring of *stūpas* and *caityas,* the performance of which brought glorious results, some wicked deeds such as non-practice of charity, abusing and disrespecting the Lord and his disciples, etc., which certainly brought wicked results, were also given expression in the *Avadāna* literature. Theoretical and idealistic descriptions of all good and no evil generally become incredible and hence without desired impact. So in order to fulfill the purpose of inculcating religious precepts and laying down moral rules of conduct which could moralise and regulate the life, the *Avadāna* type of literature was introduced.

Of all the available *Avadāna* texts, *Avadāna-śataka* is hailed to be the oldest. According to Wessillief[21], this book belongs to the first preaching period of *Śākyamuni,* indicating a high antiquity of the work. It cannot be dated after the 3rd century A.D., because it was translated into Chinese in the first half of the 3rd century A.D. At the same time it cannot be dated before the 1st century A.D., because in one of the *Avadānas* there is the mention of *Dīnara* as a coin.[22] History tells us that *Dīnāra* as a coin was introduced in the 1st century A.D.[23] So we can state that the *Avadāna-śataka* must have been composed sometimes either in the later half of the 1st century A.D. or in the first half of the 2nd century A.D. Dr. Hardayal[24] and Dr. M. A. Mahendale[25] have placed it in the 2nd century A.D.

The stories in the *Avadāna-śataka* are divided into ten sections each consisting of ten stories. Unfortunately the 5th story of first section is not found in the original Sanskrit, hence the whole text comprises of 99 stories instead of 100 which the very word 'Śataka' in the title denotes.

Chronologically speaking the *Divyāvadāna* comes next to the *Avadāna-śataka.* It seems that the book was not written in one period nor by one another. A number of authors must have brought together a variety of stories from different sources. As regards the original sources of the *Avadānas* in the *Divyāvadāna,* M. Huber held the view that out of the total number of 38 compiled under the title of the *Divyāvadāna,* there are as many as twenty *Avadānas* which have their counterparts in the *Dulva* (Tibetan *Vinaya*).[26] These are as follows: *Koṭikarṇa, Pūrṇa, Maitreya, Brāhmaṇadārikā, Stutibrāhmaṇa, Indrabrāhmaṇa, Nagarāvalambikā, Meṇḍhaka (1), Meṇḍhaka (2), Prātihāryasūtra, Svāgata, Māndhātā, Sahasodgata, Saṅgharakṣita, Nāgakumāra, Sudhanakumāra, Toyikāmaha, Rupāvati, Cūḍapakṣa, Rudrāyaṇa.* Among others, three stories, i.e. of *Māra* and Upagupta, Yaśas and the Gift of the half-*āmalaka* fruit are borrowed from the *Sūtrālaṅkāra* of *Aśvaghoṣa.* Many of the remaining stories are derived from the *Pāli* canon. The seventh chapter is an extract from the *Mahāparinirvāṇa-sūtra.* The story of *Pūrṇa,* who goes as an apostle to the savage land of *Śroṇaparantakas* corresponds to a well-known *Pāli Sūtra.*[27]

Though the book begins with the typical *Mahāyānic* benediction and does not contain many of the *Mahāyānic* elements in it, yet we cannot deny the fact that it decidedly belongs to one of the *Hīnayāna* schools, possibly the *Sarvāstivādin.*

Endnotes

1. *Śatapatha Brāhmaṇa* 1.7.2.6. अथ यदग्नौ जुहोति तदेनास्तदवदयते तस्मात् यत् किं चाग्नौ जुह्वति तदवदानं नाम।
2. *Kātyāyana-Śrautasūtra.* 1.9. पुरोडाशचर्वादेर्मध्यप्रदेशादेक्मगुण्ठपर्वमात्रं तिरश्चीनमवदानमवद्यति।
3. *Śrauta-koṣa,* अथातोऽवदानकल्पः चतुरुन्नयति चतुरवत्तं भवतीति।
4. *Rāmāyaṇa, Ayodhyā Kāṇḍa.*

   ततस्तु स्तुवतां तेषां मूतानां पाणिवादकाः,

   अपदानान्युदाहृत्य पाणिवादानवादयन् 65.4

   बलवन्तश्च कच्चित्ते मुख्या युद्धविशारदा;,

   दृष्टापदाना विक्रान्तास्त्वया सत्कृत्य मानिताः। 100.32
5. *Amarakoṣa,* अपदानमित्यपि पाठः
6. *Raghuvaṃśa,* 11 21. प्रपदस्त्रमवदानतोषितात्।
7. *Kumārasambhava,* 7.48 संगीयमानत्रिपुरावदानः
8. *Kirātārjunīya,* 3.43 वीर्यावदानेषु कृतावमर्षः
9. *Naiṣdhīya-carita,* वरप्रदानाय तवावदानौश्चिरं मदीया रसनोद्धुरेयम्।
10. *Daśakumāra-carita,* 3.43 तत्त्वत्पूर्वावदानेभ्यो
11. *Bhāguri,* पराक्रमोऽवदानं स्यात्
12. Winternitz, M., *A History of Indian Literature,* Vol. II., 1933, pp. 277-8.
13. Speyer, J. S. (Ed.) *Avadāna-śataka,* p. 1.
14. Ibid.
15. Ibid.

16. Jones, J. J. (Jr.) *Mahāvastu*, Vol. I. P. XIV.
17. Nariman, G. K. *Literary History of Sanskrit Buddhism*, 1923, p. 45.
18-19. For instance, अवभासः, अवदातः, अवपूर्णः, अवसेयः, अवदानः, etc.

"The central idea of the *avadāna* literature is *cittaprasāda* or spiritual cleansing, and what is inseparable from this is the practice of *dāna* or charity. Meeting Buddha, one performs various kinds of alms-giving and offering, and thus obtaining purification of mind avoids falling into evil destinies and attains final enlightenment. *Avadāna* is the explanation of this *Karma* in reference to previous and later existence and the practice of *dāna* is dealt with in most of the stories. The *avadānas* dealing with *Mātsarya* (avarice) merely stress the wickedness of it as opposed to the virtue of alms-giving. As the concluding words to many of the tales in *Avadāna-Śataka* we find the following words of the Buddha अयं अस्य देयधर्मो यो ममान्तिके चित्तप्रसादेति (scuh is one's gift which expresses the purity of his mind towards me), (*Avadāna-Śatak* pp. 7, 12, 22, 27, 35, 40, 46, 53, 62, 128, 135, 143, 147, 152, 157, 162, etc.). Since alms-giving is thus associated with the purity of mind, this gives rise to a thought that there was probably a period when the original meaning of *avadāna* was taken as being *'alms-giving'*.

20. Takahata, Kanga (Ed.) *Ratnamālāvadāna*, p. XIII.
21. Spayer, J. S. (Ed.) *Avadāna-śataka*, P. X.
22. Vaidya, P.L. (Ed.) *Avadāna-śataka*, LXXXIII. पाणिद्वये चास्य लक्षणाहतं कर्मविपाकजं दीनारद्वयम्
23. Semell, Journal of Royal Asiatic Society, London, 1904, "The use of the Roman word denarius, in its form of dīnār in early inscriptions is well known....introduced into India as early as the 1st century A.D."
24. Hardayal, *Bodhisattva Doctrine in Buddhist Sanskrit Literature*, P. 383.
25. Majumdar, R. C. *History and Culture of Indian People*, II, p. 208.
26. Banerjee, A.C., *Sarvāstivāda Literature*, p. 261.
27. Nariman, G.K., *Literary History of Sanskrit Buddhism*, 1923, p. 57.

---

* Dr. (Mrs.) Sharmistha Sharma is a lecturer in one of the Colleges of University of Delhi, Delhi.

22

A STUDY OF THE ORIGINS OF BUDDHIST MONASTIC EDUCATION

Sanghasen Singh

The Buddha was called the teacher of gods and men *(Satthādevamanussānaṁ)* by his disciples. If analysed critically, this statement signifies the role played by the Buddha in building up a powerful movement by mobilizing men at his command to bring an awareness among the people to change the society. The structure of the old decadent society was fast crumbling and a new society was emerging in its place. The earlier slave-owning society had outlived its utility and was fast becoming an obstacle in the growth of production. The fast changing production relations were reflected in the overwhelming desire of the people to have a change in the social set-up. A large number of religious leaders and social philosophers were seen on the scene in the sixth-fifth centuries B.C. The Buddha chose to be an instrument in this process of change. His powerful advocacy for change was reflected in his doctrine of *Aniccavāda* (Sanskrit, *Anityavāda,* i.e. theory of change) as against the theory of *Sassatavāda* (Sanskrit, *Śāśvatavāda,* i.e. theory of permanence) professed by the teachers of the *Vedas* and the *Upaniṣads.* In fact, the way the Buddha developed his set of ideas is clearly indicative of the fact that he was consciously theorizing for the newly emergent feudal system. The fact is borne by the evidences which show how the Buddha helped the emergent feudal lords[1] of his time. *Bimbisāra, Ajātasattu, Pasenadi,* etc., got direct and indirect help from the Buddha in consolidation of their powers and territories.[2] The Buddha, it seems, had reaslised the importance of this role from his early youth and hence his *Mahābhinikkhamaṇa* or renouncement of his household to lead the life of a recluse. After the attainment of his *'Bodhi'* or Enligtenment (which is nothing but the final attainment of maturity in his thinking and the fixation of the set of ideas which he intended to propound and propagate), he became, as depicted in the *Tipiṭaka,* one of the most mobile teachers. He was excessively zealous in collecting followers around him for the cause he had espoused. He went to the extent of compelling his own kith and kin to join his Order of monks even at the cost of embarrassing his own father.[3] This clearly shows the amount of his commitment to the cause.

The Buddha established his *'Saṅgha'* of the Order of monks, in the thirty-sixth year of his life and allowed, after a thorough scrutiny of the integrity and the motives, practically everybody to join it, irrespective of caste, creed and colour. As time passed, he acquired great popularity in the whole of *Majjha Maṇḍala* (an area comprised of roughly the whole of Uttar Pradesh, Bihar, southern parts of Nepal and some northern parts of Madhya Pradesh) and people from almost all castes joined his Order. With his new slogan of *cātuvaṇṇa-pārisuddhi* (emancipation of all the four varṇas), he attracted men from the lower strata of society in large numbers. The uncultured commoners with a spiritual bent of mind sought admission to the Order. But as is well known, they lacked training and education. Thus, they arose the urgent need of making arrangements for the education of the new entrants. On the other hand, we find references to cultured and otherwise-trained entrants who, however, needed a more complete knowledge of his teachings. The famous instance of *Assajī* is one of them. Having been I structured by the Master 'to walk on tour for the blessing, the happiness of *devas* and men.......'[4], *Assajī,* one of the five firsts, walked on the streets of *Rājagaha* for almsfood. On being struck by the 'spiritual radiance of his countenance', Sāriputta follows close after him and approaches him with queries regarding the *(Assaji's)* teacher and the *Dhamma* (faith) professed by him. When asked about the latter Assajī replied, "Now, I, friend, am new, not long gone forth, fresh to this *Dhamma* and Discipline. I am not able to teach you *Dhamma* in full, but I can tell you its purport briefly?"[5] This, it seems, must have been the position of all the Buddha's disciples with regard to his teachings and the Discipline (which developed later). This and the further instances regarding the want of full knowledge of the *Dhamma* and the *Vinaya* must have prompted the Buddha and his close disciples to consider the idea of imparting education to the new entrants. We also find instances of such people who having been brought for admission to the Order, were unable to answer even very simple and ordinary questions. Thus, the necessity to impart to them a sufficient knowledge before their admission was felt acutely. This led to the system of *Parivāsa* (probation period) meant for all except the *Jaṭilas*, and the *Sākiyas*, the Buddha's own kinsmen. The senior and worthy monks were allowed to keep one novice each with them for this purpose.[6] Thus, every monastery with a number of such monks became automatically a seat of learning. This, it seems, must have been the beginning of the monastic education in the Buddhist Order.

In order to understand the characteristics of the Buddhist monastic education, it is essential to understand the nature of the Buddha's social and religious movement. In order to achieve this goal, he organised his *'Saṅgha'* on purely democratic lines. The men and women (in course of time) who rallied to his cause were such, who could devote their time and energy whole heartedly without much hindrance from any quarter. They were unmarried whole timers. The training and education of this body of devoted workers was his first concern. He was fully conscious of the fact that untrained and misbehaved monks brought bad name to the Order and hence the danger to the very existence and development of the movement. He, therefore, gave full attention to the education and training of monks. These trained and educated monks, in their turn, imparted religious and sometimes secular education to even the laity. According to the *Sigālovāda-sutta*[7] of the *Dīgha Nikāya*, it was also the duty of the monks to give education and guidance to the lay devotees. On the other hand, no direct reference to the monks imparting education to the householders or their sons in the premises of the monasteries is found in the *Pāli* canon. The reference of *Takkasilā* in the *Jātaka* stories (which chronologically belong to a later period) as a great seat of learning, where students from far and wide would flock, does not prove the fact. At the same time, there is no dearth of such references, where the Buddha or his senior disciples are seen imparting religious as well as secular instruction to laymen. The *Sigālovāda-sutta,* mentioned above, is of course a significant example.

The lack of any systematic education of the laity was probably due to the fact that education was not universal in those days. It was not the concern of the state. The exploiting classes had the monopoly. It was, therefore, confined to the *Brāhmaṇas, Kṣatriyas* and to a section of *Vaiśyas,* particularly to those who were wealthy. But the religious and ecclesiastical education was the concern of the religious leaders. The professional and other types of secular education was conducted by guilds and institutions like *Takkasilā*. The *Jātaka* stories are replete with such instances where the sons and the wards of nobles and wealthy people were sent to far-off places for studies,[8] while the rest of the people were forced to be contented with the lot they were put to.

Although the education and training of the members of the religious orders were the direct concern of their leaders, but at the same time it was not possible for them to shut their eyes towards the laity. It is true that the laity did not live under a common roof with the monks, but they too were equally instrumental in the growth and expansion of the Order. In fact, the Order fully depended upon the goodwill of the laity for its support and subsistence. Guided by this factor the young Buddhist Order was vitally interested in the growth of a believing and pious laity. The Order, therefore, had laid down certain rules for the regulation of the life of laity. Certain duties towards the Order were also laid down, but the Order normally did not insist upon their fulfillment. The Buddhist laity was a loose body of devoted followers who were never brought under one discipline. But at the same time, we find references, to show that the Order sometimes did resort to certain methods which helped in bringing the laity under some control. It used to declare a boycott whereby 'the bowl was turned down' in respect of the offenders, for it meant the prohibition of giving and receiving gifts and instruction as between the two parties.[9] A comprehensive list of the duties of the laity is given in the *Sigālovāda-sutta,*[10] which classify them according to the several capacities or relationships that the householders have. The duties, for instance, of parents and children, of pupils and teachers, of laymen and monks are laid down. It is the duty of parents to have their children taught arts or sciences. "The pupil should honour his teachers by (1) rising in their presence, (2) ministering to them, (3) obeying them, (4) supplying their wants, (5) attention to instruction. The teacher should show his affection for his pupils by (1) training them in all that is good, (2) teaching them to hold knowledge fast, (3) instruction in science and lore, (4) speaking well of them to their friends and companions, (5) guarding them from danger.[11] According to the *Vinaya Piṭaka,*[12] the Buddha held discourses to the overseas of several townships under the rule and sovereignty of King *Bimbisāra,* in which he had highlighted the importance of 'giving, righteousness, heaven, the danger, worthlessness and depravity of lusts and the advantage of renunciation'. This, the Buddha did under the express desire of *Bimbisāra* himself.

It is a fact that the credit for compelling the Master to formulate the *Vinaya* code for the smooth functioning of the Order goes to the laymen. It were the laymen who, through their complaints about the unbecoming and unwholesome conduct of some of the monks, led the Buddha to prescribe certain rules for the monks. With the passage of time, these rules increased in number and hence the voluminous code of conduct for them. Thus, the interest taken by the laymen in the proper functioning of the Order is very significant. In fact, it was not possible to record the names of all the laymen and women in this connection. The names of King *Bimbisāra* and *Visākhā Migāramātā* are conspicuous in this respect. The credit for the suggestion of the introduction of the fortnightly *'Uposatha'* ceremony goes to *Bimbisāra.* It is a well-known fact that *'Uposatha'* as an institution had played a great role in educating and disciplining the monks of Buddhist Order. The procedure was that the monks of one *'Saṅgha' (Saṅgha* of a particular locality was defined on the basis of well-defined *Sīmā* or boundaries of its own) would assemble on the fourteenth and the full-moon day of each lunar month and account for their omissions and commissions during the preceding fortnight. If found guilty of a particular offence, the monk concerned would be penalized accordingly.[13] *Visākhā,* on the other hand, was instrumental in getting the approval of the Master for more than one robe to the monks during rains. We are in the dark regarding the names of those worthy laymen of *Kosambī,* who compelled the warring factions of the local monks to come to terms, when even the Buddha did not succeed in thrashing out the differences of those people and out of disgust retired to the *Pārileyyaka* forest. The name of the Emperor *Asoka* in the later period deserves mention. In the Bhabru Edict, he expressed his sincere solicitude for the long endurance of the good faith, and with that 'noble' end in view he selected seven Buddhist discourses[14] and commended them confidently to the monks, nuns and laity for their constant study and remembrance. This shows the keen interest taken by the laymen for the proper teaching and training of the monks of the Buddha's Order.

As a corollary to the question of education and training, there arose the problem of monastic settlement. The Buddha and his early disciples, it seems, got fully convinced in course of time that for a systematic course of education and training of monks somewhat congenial atmosphere was very essential. The impetus, in this respect, might have come other older and well-developed religious orders making their headway in the *Magadha* region, particularly in the area in and around *Rājagaha*. As mentioned earlier, *Bimbisāra* and the Buddha were partners in the development of a new social system. This necessitated *Bimbisāra* to come forward with the offer of a suitable and congenial place for the Buddha and his fraternity. The day after his arrival at *Rājagaha,* the Buddha accepted the King's invitation to a meal at the palace. The decision to bestow *Veluvana* on the Buddha was made in the light of its suitability to the Buddhist Order, because of its unique location. It was located at a place "not too far from the town, not too near, suitable for coming and going, easily accessible to all people, by day not too crowded, by night not exposed to noise and clamour, clean of the smell of people, hidden from men and well fitted to seclusion." In the history of the Buddhist Order, it was the first donation of an *ārāma* which the Buddha readily accepted and made it his normal and temporary place of stay. In the modern terminology, this happened to be the first central office of the organization which the Buddha had founded. This continued to be so till the development of *Sāvatthī,* which proved to be its rival. At the same time, this has to be borne in mind that in those days there was no concept of central office. In fact, because of his superior position in the Order, the Buddha himself was its central office. Wherever he used to stay even for a purely temporary period, the high and low in the Order would flock to that place for various organizational purposes. Significantly enough, it was during his stay here that *Sāriputta* and *Moggallāna* joined the Order.[15]

This new turn in the history of the Buddhist Order had a very wide impact. A large number of caves came into being in and around *Rājagaha.* In course of time, as the *Saṅgha* expanded in all its dimensions, the Buddha gave a clear sanction of five kinds of *leṇas* as fit for monks' dwelling under the name *vihāra, aḍḍhayoga, pāsāda, hammiya* and *guhā.*[16] They proved to be a great asset to the development of the Buddhist Order. It was because of this fact, probably, that the Buddha had often spoken very highly of the donation of *vihāras* to the Order. He, in fact, exhorted the rich publically "to give *vihāras* to the *Saṅgha* where, in safety and in peace to meditate and think at ease, the Buddha calls the best of gifts. Let them the able men, regarding their own weal, have pleasant monasteries built and lodge their learned men."[17] This call given by the Buddha had a salutary effect. The mercantile class came forward and loosened the strings of their money bags to build huge and palatial *vihāras* for the Buddhist fraternity. The association of this class with the Buddha and his movement was not an isolated and individual instance, but had developed as a conscious alliance of various forces to replace the old system with a new progressive one.

Endnotes

1. Cf. Rahul Sankrityayan: *Darśana-digdarśana.* (He talks of feudal lords waging war for the expansion of their territories).
2. Cf. the *Mahāvagga, Mahāparinibbāna-sutta,* etc.

3. Cf. for example, the initiation to the Order of Rāhula, Nanda, etc.
4. Cf. *The Book of the Discipline*, iv (tr.), I.B. Horner, p. 28.
5. Ibid, p. 53.
6. Ibid, p. 81.
7. Cf. *Dīgha Nikāya*, (Nalanda series) iii, 146.
8. Cf. e.g., *Jātaka* No. 252.
9. Cf. H. Oldenberg, *The Buddha, His Life, His Order*, pp. 383-4.
10. Cf. *Dīgha Nikāya*, (Nalanda series), ii. 146.
11. Ibid.
12. Cf. *Mahāvagga*, (Nalanda series), p. 200.
13. Cf. *Pātimokkha*.
14. Cf. *The Suttanipāta: Introduction*, (ed) U. *Dhammaratana*.
15. Cf. *Vinaya Piṭaka*, (ed) Oldenberg (Williams and Norgate) i, 42.
16. Cf. *Cullavagga* (Nalanda series), p. 239.
17. Ibid, p. 240.

23

संघरक्खित और उनका सुबोधालंकार

ब्रह्ममित्र अवस्थी

पालि-साहित्य के विशाल भण्डार में साहित्य-शास्त्र विषयक ग्रन्थों का प्राय: अभाव है। संभवत: इसका कारण बौद्ध आचार्यों का निर्वाण की ओर ही मुख्यत: उन्मुख होना है, जब कि काव्य अथवा काव्यशास्त्र में निर्वाण (अपर पर्याय मोक्ष) विषय अत्यन्त गौण है। इस प्रसंग में यह नहीं भूलना चाहिए कि काव्य और काव्य-शास्त्र के अनेक प्रयोजनों में मोक्ष का संयोजन बौद्ध आचार्यों की ही देन है, अन्यथा वाल्मीकि आदि प्राचीनतम कवियों की रचनाओं में उद्देश्य के रूप में केवल धर्म, अर्थ और काम का ही संकेत मिलता है।[1] भरत कृत नाट्यशास्त्र में केवल आठ रसों की चर्चा भी इसका ही प्रमाण है।[2]

पालि-साहित्य में काव्य-शास्त्र के आचार्य के रूप में हमें एक मात्र भिक्षु संघरक्खित का पता चलता है। मेजर जी. ई. फ्रेयर के अनुसार संघरक्खित प्रसिद्ध पालि-महावैयाकरण मोग्गलान से अभिन्न हैं। उनका दूसरा नाम मेधंकर है, जो सीलोन के प्रसिद्धतम बौद्ध विहार उदुम्बर-गिरि के भिक्षुओं की परम्परा में 13वीं शताब्दी में हुए थे। इनके गुरु का नाम सारिपुत्त या सील थेर था।[3]

'सोसाइटी इन मिडियवल सिलोन' के लेखक अरियपाल के अनुसार संघरक्खित थेर पराक्रम-बाहु (द्वितीय) के राज्यकाल में, जो साहित्यिक विकास की दृष्टि से सिलोन के इतिहास में स्वर्णकाल कहा जा सकता है, हुए थे[4] तथा उनके राज्यकाल के अनन्तर अर्थात् विजयबाहु (तृतीय) के राज्यकाल में (1227 से 1231 ई. तक के मध्यकाल में) डिम्बुलागल मेधंकर की सहायता से संघरक्खित ने विद्वानों की एक संगीति बुलाई थी, जिसमें धार्मिक पुस्तकों का संशोधन किया गया[5]।

'हिस्ट्री ऑफ सिलोन' के अनुसार मेधंकर महाथेर तथा महासामि संघरक्खित दोनों ही सारिपुत्त के शिष्य थे[6]। राजा पराक्रम-बाहु (प्रथम) की सभा में इनका अत्यधिक समादर था, तथा अपनी मृत्यु से पूर्व पराक्रम-बाहु (प्रथम) ने अपने उत्तराधिकारी पुत्र, विजयबाहु (तृतीय) को इनका सम्मान जारी रखने को कहा था[7]। विजयबाहु के शासन-काल में अपने गुरु सारिपुत्त की मृत्यु के अनन्तर संघरक्खित संघ-थेर (संघ के प्रधान) बने। यहीं उनके एक अन्य गुरु मोग्गलान महाथेर का भी संकेत मिलता है[8]। इस ग्रन्थ के अनुसार विजयबाहु (तृतीय) का शासनकाल 13वीं शताब्दी का पूर्वार्ध अर्थात् 1232 से 1234 ई. है। अत: संघरक्खित का स्थिति-काल भी तेरहवीं शताब्दी का पूर्वार्ध निश्चित मानना चाहिए।

उनके पारिवारिक जीवन के सम्बन्ध में केवल इतना ही पता चलता है कि उन्होंने विवाह के प्रसंग में यह पहले से ही निश्चिय कर रखा था कि वे उसी कन्या से विवाह करेंगे जो परिवार को देखभाल करने में पूर्ण समर्थ हो।[9]

उनके लिखे ग्रंथों में सुबोधालंकार, वुत्तोदय, सम्बन्धचिन्ता, सुसद्दसिद्धि, योगविनिच्छय तथा खुद्दक-सिक्खा-टीका का स्पष्ट पता चलता है, जिनमें प्रथम दो साहित्य-शास्त्र विषयक, सम्बन्धचिन्ता शब्द-शक्ति विषयक, सुसद्द-सिद्धि व्याकरण विषयक तथा शेष दो बौद्ध धर्म से सम्बन्धित धार्मिक ग्रन्थ हैं।

साहित्य-शास्त्र विषयक इनके दोनों ग्रन्थों में से वुत्तोदय में काव्यों में व्यवहृत होने वाले छन्दों को विस्तृत एवं सोदाहरण विवेचन किया गया है। सुबोधालंकार में काव्य-लक्षण, दोष-परिहार, गुण, अलंकार एवं रसादि का विवेचन प्राप्त होता है। पालि-भाषा में लिखा गया यह एक मात्र ग्रन्थ है, जिसमें काव्य के प्रायः समस्त उपादान तत्वों का विवेचन किया गया है।

तीन सौ इकहत्तर (371) कारिकाओं में रचित यह ग्रन्थ पांच परिच्छेदों में विभक्त है। जिनमें क्रमशः प्रथम में अड़सठ, द्वितीय में अड़तालीस, तृतीय में अड़तालीस, चतुर्थ में एक सौ अस्सी और पंचम में एकतीस कारिकाएं निबद्ध हैं। इनमें क्रमशः काव्य-लक्षण, दोष-विवेचन, दोष-परिहार के उपाय, गुणों का सोदाहरण परिचय, अलंकारों का भेद-प्रभेदों एवं उदाहरणों सहित परिचय विभाव अनुभाव सात्विकभाव व व्यभिचारिभावों की परिभाषाओं सहित परिगणन तथाश्रृंगार आदि नव रसों का परिचय उपनिबद्ध है।

आचार्य संघरक्खित ने पूर्वकालीन आचार्यों की रचनाओं में उपलब्ध सामग्री का भी यथेष्ट उपयोग किया है। ग्रन्थ के प्रारम्भ में राम शर्मा नामक आचार्य विशेष का उल्लेख है[10], जिनकी चर्चा आचार्य भामह ने भी अपने काव्यालंकार में की थी[11]। आदिपद से कुछ अन्य आचार्यों संभवतः भामह और दण्डी की ओर संकेत है। कुछ विद्वानों का विचार है कि सुबोधालंकार की रचना दण्डी के काव्यादर्श को आधार बनाकर की गयी है[12], किन्तु मैं इस विचार से सहमत नहीं हूं। इसका मुख्य कारण अनेक अलंकारों के नामों में पूर्ण अथवा आंशिक भेद, अलंकारों के विवेचन-क्रम में दण्डी-स्वीकृत क्रम का सर्वथा अभाव आदि है। आचार्य संघरक्खित काव्य में दोषों का अभाव न केवल नितान्त आवश्यक मानते हैं, अपितु दोषों के अभाव से उसमें गुणों की अनायास सत्ता स्वीकार करते हैं। संघरक्खित-कृत रसादि-विवेचन का दण्डी-कृत काव्यादर्श में सर्वथा अभाव ही है। अतः सुबोधालंकार को काव्यादर्श का अनुकरण मानना नितान्त अनुचित है। इतना अवश्य है कि अग्निपुराण और सरस्वतीकण्ठाभरण के समान सुबोधालंकार में भी अनेक अलंकारों की परिभाषाएं काव्यादर्शगत अलंकारों की परिभाषाओं से कुछ साम्य रखती हैं, किन्तु इस साम्य का आधार वर्ण्य विषय के धर्मों के कारण भी हो सकता है। संघरक्खित और दण्डी की मान्यताओं और प्रयोगों में अन्तर के कुछ उदाहरण द्रष्टव्य हैं-

संघरक्खित ने काव्य-पद के स्थान पर बन्ध-पद का प्रयोग किया है। उनके अनुसार भामह की भांति[13] दोषरहित शब्द और अर्थ के साहित्य का नाम बन्ध अर्थात् काव्य है[14]। दण्डी के अनुसार इष्टार्थ-व्यवच्छिन्ना पदावली काव्य है[15]। आचार्य कुन्तक भी शब्द और अर्थ के साहित्य को बन्ध अथवा काव्य स्वीकार करते हैं, यद्यपि उनके अनुसार उसे वक्र-कविव्यापार से युक्त अवश्य होना चाहिए[16]। यह काव्य पद्य, गद्य एवं मिश्र भेद से तीन प्रकार का है, तथा ये तीनों प्रकार निबद्ध और अनिबद्ध भेद से दो दो उपभेदों में विभक्त हो जाते हैं। यहाँ निबद्ध और अनिबद्ध से संघरक्खित का तात्पर्य कल्पना-प्रधान और ऐतिहासिक होना चाहिए। काव्य का यह उपविभाजन आचार्य संघरक्खित की मौलिक उद्भावना है।

संघरक्खित दण्डी और भामह की तरह ही काव्य में दोषों का अभाव आवश्यक मानते हैं। दण्डी के अनुसार दोष काव्य को उसी प्रकार तिरस्कार-योग्य बना देते हैं, जिस प्रकार कोढ़ शरीर को[17]। भामह दोष-युक्त कविता की उपमा कुपुत्र से देते हैं[18], तो संघरक्खित गुणों और आभूषणों से अलंकृत उस कन्या से जो अपने दोष विशेष के कारण विद्वानों में कभी प्रतिष्ठा नहीं कर पाती[19]। उनके अनुसार निर्दोष होने

पर वह रचना अलंकारों के अभाव में भी अनलंकृत किन्तु दोषों से रहित गुण-शालिनी कुल-वधू के समान आदरणीय होती है। क्योंकि वे मानते हैं। कि दोषों के अभाव में गुणों की सत्ता अनायास ही उजागर हो जाती है[20]।

संघरक्खित के अनुसार काव्य में पदवाक्य और अर्थ-भेद से दोष तीन प्रकार के हो सकते हैं, जबकि दण्डी और भामह ने दोषों का किसी प्रकार का भी विभाजन नहीं किया। इस प्रकार का विभाजन हमें सर्वप्रथम वामन की काव्यालंकार-सूत्रवृत्ति में उपलब्ध होता है[21]। संघरक्खित के अनुसार विरुद्धार्थान्तर, अध्यात्त, क्लिष्ट, विरोधि, नेश्य, विशेषणापेक्ष, हीनार्थक और अनर्थक ये आठ पददोष, एकार्थक, भग्नरीति अव्याकीर्ण, ग्राम्य, यतिहीन, अपक्रम, अतिव्युत्त, अपेतर्थ तथा सम्बन्ध स्पर्श ये नौ वाक्यदोष एवं अपक्रम, औचित्यहीन, भग्नरीति, संशय, ग्राम्य और दुष्टालंकृति ये छः अर्थदोष कहे जाते हैं[22]। स्मरणीय है कि इन्होंने वामन के अनुसार अर्थदोषों का पदार्थ और वाक्यार्थ-रूप विभाजन न कर केवल अर्थदोषी के अन्दर ही सबका परिगणन किया है। वामन के अनुसार असाधु, कष्ट (क्लिष्ट), ग्राम्य, अप्रतीत एवं अनर्थक पाँच पद-दोष, भिन्नवृत्त, यतिभ्रष्ट एवं विसन्धि तीन वाक्यदोष तथा अन्यार्थ, नेयार्थ, गूढ़ार्थ, अश्लील, क्लिष्ट (पदार्थगत) व्यर्थ, एकार्थ, सन्दिग्ध, अप्रयुक्त, अपक्रम, लोकशास्त्र (विद्या) विरुद्ध (वाक्यार्थ) भेद से ये ग्यारह अर्थदोष है। जबकि दण्डी और भामह दोनों ने ही अपार्थ, व्यर्थ, एकार्थ, सन्दिग्ध (ससंशय), अपक्रप, शब्द-हीन यतिभ्रष्ट, भिन्नवृत्त, विसन्धि एवं देशकालादि विरुद्ध भेद से दस काव्य-दोष स्वीकार किये थे। भामह ने इन दोषों में प्रतिज्ञा हेतु दृष्टान्त आदि शास्त्रीय तत्वों के अनिर्वाह को, जिन्हें विद्याविरुद्ध का ही प्रकार भेद कहा जा सकता है, स्वतन्त्र रूप से दोष के रूप में परिगणन किया था।

विवेचन-क्रम की दृष्टि से भामह और दण्डी ने दोष-प्रकरण को ग्रन्थ के अन्त में निबद्ध किया था, जबकि संघरक्खित ने सबसे पूर्व। वामनकृत काव्यालंकारसूत्रवृत्ति में रीति और गुणों के विवेचन के अनन्तर दोषों का विवेचन है जबकि सुबोधालंकार में दोष-विवेचन के अनन्तर गुणों का विवेचन किया गया है।

सुबोधालंकार के अनुसार काव्य में दस गुण हैं-प्रसाद, ओज, मधुरता, समता, सुकुमारता, श्लिष्ट, उदारता, कान्ति अर्थव्यक्ति, और समाधि[23]। भरतकृत नाट्यशास्त्र और दण्डीकृत काव्यादर्श में अविकलरूप से इन्हीं गुणों का वर्णन प्राप्त होता है[24], जबकि भामह माधुर्य, प्रसाद और ओज तीन गुण ही मानते हैं। दण्डी के गुण-विवेचन में श्लेष का स्थान सर्वप्रथम है और ओज का आठवाँ, जबकि संघरक्खित प्रसाद को सर्वप्रथम स्थान देते हैं, वे श्लेष को सुकुमारता के अनन्तर छठें स्थान पर रखते हैं। संघरक्खित ओज को द्वितीय स्थान पर रखते हैं, जबकि दण्डी प्रसाद को द्वितीय स्थान प्रदान करते हैं। इस आधार पर दण्डी और संघरक्खित की दृष्टि से गुण विशेष को महत्व देने के प्रसंग में पर्याप्त अन्तर प्रतीत होता है।

दण्डी और भामह की दृष्टि से अलंकार दो प्रकार के हैं- शब्दालंकार और अर्थालंकार। शब्दालंकारों में दोनों ने ही यमक और अनुप्रास को स्वीकार किया है, यद्यपि दण्डी अनुप्रास की चर्चा गुणों के प्रकरण में प्रथम परिच्छेद में तथा यमक की चर्चा दोष-विवेचन से पूर्व तृतीय परिच्छेद में करते हैं[25]। साथ ही वे इसी प्रकरण में चित्र तथा प्रहेलिका की भी चर्चा करते हैं। आचार्य संघरक्खित ने शब्दालंकारों की सर्वथा उपेक्षा की है। यही परम्परा हमें संस्कृत काव्य-शास्त्र के उत्तरकालीन आचार्य शोभकरमित्र, अप्पयदीक्षित, जगन्नाथ, विश्वेश्वर और भट्टदेवशंकर आदि में प्राप्त होती है। कालक्रम से अलंकार-शास्त्र का अध्ययन करने पर संघरक्खित ही इस परम्परा के प्रवर्तक कहे जा सकते हैं।

आचार्य संघरक्खित के अनुसार अर्थालंकार निम्नलिखित तैतीस हैं[26]। अतिसय (अतिशय), उपमा, रूपक, आवुत्ति (आवृत्ति), दीपक, आक्खेय (आक्षेप), अत्थन्तर-न्यास (अर्थान्तर-न्यास) व्यतिरेक,

विभावना हेतु, कम (क्रम-यथासंख्य), पियतर (प्रेयान्), समासवुत्ति (समासोक्ति), परिकल्पना (उत्प्रेक्षा), समाहित, परियाय-वुत्ति (पर्यायोक्ति) व्याजवण्णन (व्याजोक्ति), विसेस (विशेषोक्ति), रूळाहंकार (उर्जस्वि), सिलिस (श्लेष), तुल्ययोगिता निदस्सन (निदर्शना), महन्तत्थ (उदत्त), वंचना (अपह्नुति), अप्पकतत्थुति (अप्रस्तुत प्रशंसा), एकाबली, अञ्ञोञ्ञ (अन्योन्य), सहवुत्ति (सहोक्ति), भम (भ्रान्तिमान्), भाव, मिस्स (संकर-संसृष्टि) आशी और रसवन्त।

सुबोधालंकार में स्वीकृत अलंकारों में से महन्तत्थ, एकावली, भम व अञ्ञोञ्ञ चार अलंकार ऐसे हैं जो दण्डी के काव्यादर्श में स्वीकृत नहीं है। अन्य अलंकारों के बीच अन्तर्भाव अथवा भेदोपभेदों के बीच इनकी सत्ता खोजना दूसरी बात है। वंचना और परिकल्पना अलंकारों को दण्डी ने अपहनुति एवं उत्प्रेक्षा अलंकार नाम दिया था। इसके अतिरिक्त सुबोधालंकार-गत पियतर, समासवुत्ति, परियायवुत्ति, व्याजोपवण्ण, रूळाहंकार, अप्पकतत्थुति, सहवुत्ति, भाव और मिस्स के नाम भी कुछ अन्तर के साथ ही काव्यादर्श में उपलब्ध होते हैं[27]।

सुबोधालंकार में वर्णित समस्त अलंकारों के लक्षण एवं भेदोपभेद देना विस्तार भय से यहां उचित न होगा। किंतु इतना अवश्य कहा जा सकता है कि दण्डी और संघरक्खित द्वारा दिये गये लक्षणों में यदि कहीं साम्य प्रतीत होता है, तो वह लक्ष्य के धर्म के कारण है, अनुकरण के कारण नहीं।

सुबोधालंकार में अलंकारों के लक्षणों एवं भेद-प्रभेद की कल्पना में अनेक बार मौलिक अन्तर भी दृष्टिगोचर होता है। उदाहरणार्थ दण्डी के अनुसार लोकोत्तर विशेष की विपक्षा से किया गया कथन अतिश्योक्ति अलंकार है[28], जबकि संघरक्खित के अनुसार अतिश्योक्ति में विशेष का लोकोत्तर होना आवश्यक नहीं है, केवल अतिशयविशेष की प्रकाशक में उक्ति को भी अतिशय अलंकार कहा जा सकता है। यही कारण है कि इन्हें लोकातिक्रांत अतिशय अलंकार कहा जा सकता है। यही कारण है कि इन्हें लोकातिक्रांत अतिशय के साथ ही लौकिकातिशयोक्ति को भी अतिशयोक्ति के भेद के रूप में स्वीकार किया है[29]।

अलंकारों के भेद-प्रभेदों की कल्पना में भी दण्डी और संघरक्खित के बीच महान अन्तर परिलक्षित होता है। दण्डी ने उपमालंकार के धर्मोपमा आदि बाइस भेदों को स्वीकार किया था, जिनमें से संघरक्खित ने केवल चौदह भेदों की ही चर्चा की है। भेदों की कल्पना में विस्तार भय से कुछ की उपेक्षा कर देना स्वाभाविक हो सकता है किन्तु यहां वे सभी भेद छोड़ दिये गये हैं, जिन्हें आचार्य भामह ने अस्वीकृति प्रदान की है[30]। जिसके फलस्वरूप भेद-विशेष को छोड़ देने में मान्यता-भेद की कल्पना करना अनुचित न होगा। इस संदर्भ में यह भी स्मरणीय है कि आचार्य मेधावी-स्वीकृत सात उपमा दोषों की संघरक्खित ने भी पुष्टि की है[31]। जिनका भामह ने उल्लेख किया था[32], एवं दण्डी ने उन्हें स्पष्ट शब्दों में अस्वीकार किया था[33]।

आचार्य दण्डी ने रूपकालंकार का सर्वप्रथम विभाजन वाक्य-संघटन की दृष्टि से करते हुए समस्त-रूपक, व्यस्त-रूपक आदि भेद किये थे[34], जब कि संघरक्खित ने आरोप्यमाण और आरोपविषयों की सम्पूर्णता और अल्पता के आधार पर सर्वप्रथम समस्तवस्तु विषय एवं एक देश विवर्ति भेदों का परिगणन किया है, जो उत्तरकालीन आचार्यों द्वारा निर्विवाद रूप से स्वीकृत हुए हैं। उन्होंने परम्परा के अनुसार रूपकालंकार के अनन्त भेद कहते हुए समासोक्त रूपक की चर्चा अवश्य की है, किन्तु उसे विशेष महत्व प्रदान नहीं किया है[35]।

दीपकालंकार के प्रसंग में भी उन्होंने दण्डी-स्वीकृत जाति, द्रव्य, गुण एवं क्रियादीपक तथा विरुद्धार्थ,

एकार्थ एवं श्लिष्टार्थ दीपक भेदों की चर्चा नहीं की है। यही स्थिति आक्षेप अलंकार में है, आचार्य संघरक्खित ने अतीत, वर्त्तमान एवं अनागत भेद से आक्षेप अलंकार को तीन प्रकार का मानते हुए दण्डी-स्वीकृत धर्माक्षेप धर्म्याक्षेप आदि इक्कीस भेदों की पूर्णतः उपेक्षा की है। परिकप्पना (उत्प्रेक्षा) अलंकार में संघरक्खित ने क्रिया-परिकप्पना (क्रियोत्प्रेक्षा) आदि भेदों के साथ उपमाभ्यन्तरा परिकप्पना नामक भेद को स्वीकार किया है[36]। दण्डी जिसका उल्लेख करते हुए स्पष्ट शब्दों में खण्डन करते हैं[37]। इसके अतिरिक्त वंचना (अपह्नुति) अलंकार में दण्डी आदि आचार्यों ने विषयापह्नुति आदि भेदों को स्वीकार किया है[38], जबकि संघरक्खित ने इन भेदों की चर्चा किये बिना समवंचना एवं असमवंचना भेद से दो भेद स्वीकार किए हैं[39]। जिसके आधार पर यह स्वीकार करने में किसी को आपत्ति नहीं होनी चाहिए कि संघरक्खित ने सुबोधालंकार में दण्डी का अनुकरण नहीं किया है, जैसा कि हेरम्ब चटर्जी आदि कुछ विद्वान् स्वीकार करते हैं।

सुबोधालंकार में किए गए अलंकार-विवेचन तथा यथावसर पूर्वाचार्यों के स्वीकृत नामों के अन्तर में संघरक्खित की मौलिकता है। अथवा यदि उन पर किसी आचार्य विशेष का प्रभाव है तो यह आज खोज का विषय है। अधिक संभव है कि इनका सुबोधालंकार राम शर्मा (राम-समण) के ग्रंथ से प्रवर्तित परम्परा पर आधारित हो। जिनके नाम का उल्लेख ग्रंथ के आरम्भ में ही किया गया है[40]। इन राम शर्मा की चर्चा भामह ने भी काव्यालंकार में प्रहेलिका अलंकार के प्रसंग में की है। तथा उपमानाधिकत्व दोष का उदाहरण राम शर्मा के ग्रन्थ (अब तक अज्ञात) से संकलित किया है[41]।

ग्रन्थ के अन्तिम परिच्छेद में आचार्य संघरक्खित ने रस आदि का परिचयात्मक विवरण प्रस्तुत किया है। इस प्रकरण में उन्होंने स्थायिभाव, विभाव, अनुभाव, सात्विक एवं व्यभिचारिभावों की परिभाषाएं भी दी हैं, जो नाट्यशास्त्र में उपलब्ध परिभाषाओं का अनुसरण करती हैं। इनके द्वारा संकेतित रसानुभूति का सिद्धान्त नाट्यशास्त्र के भाष्य-कार अभिनवगुप्त की मान्यता से अभिन्न है[42]। नाट्यशास्त्र में आचार्य भरत ने केवल आठ रसों का स्वीकार किया था, जबकि आचार्य संघरक्खित शांत रस के साथ रसों की संख्या नौ मानते हैं। इस प्रसंगों में उनकी मान्यता आनन्दवर्द्धन, मम्मट आदि आचार्यों का अनुगमन करती है। रसों के अवान्तर भेदों में उन्होंने केवल हास्य के भेद प्रदर्शित किए हैं[43]। जो अन्य किसी ग्रन्थ में प्राप्त नहीं होते। रसों के अतिरिक्त संस्कृत काव्यशास्त्र के आचार्यों द्वारा स्वीकृत भाव, रसाभास, भावाभास, भावोदय, भावशान्ति, भावसन्धि और भवशवलता की चर्चा इन्होंने नहीं की है।

आचार्य संघरक्खित ने सुबोधालंकार में दोष, गुण, अलंकार आदि सभी प्रकरणों में प्रायः सभी उदाहरण स्वनिर्मित ही दिये हैं, जिससे उनकी कवित्व-प्रतिभा की सूचना मिलती है। कहीं कहीं इनके पद्यों में संस्कृत कवियों का भी स्पष्ट प्रभाव परिलक्षित होता है। जो इनकी स्वाध्यायशीलता की परिचायक है। इनके प्रायः सभी पद्यों में भगवान बुद्ध के प्रति भक्ति भाव की व्यंजना हुई है।

सुबोधालंकार पर अब तक हमें पांच टीकाओं का पता चला है। पहली टीका सुबोधालंकार-टीका नाम से वाचिस्सर नाम से प्रचलित किसी सिंघली भिक्षु के द्वारा 13वीं शताब्दी के उत्तरार्ध में लिखी गई थी[44]। भरत सिंह उपाध्याय के अनुसार इसके लेखक सारिपुत्त के शिष्य थे[45]। मललसीकर के अनुसार इन्हें 13वीं शताब्दी का उत्तरार्ध में होना चाहिए। एक अन्य टीका सुबोधालंकार-अभिनवटीका अनुराधपुर निवासी किसी अज्ञातनाम भिक्खु द्वारा लिखी गई थी। ये दोनों टीकाएं बर्मी लिपि में बौद्ध-शासन-समिति द्वारा प्रकाशित हो चुकी हैं। बर्मा में इस पर सन् 1880 में अलंकार-निस्सय नाम की टीका लिखी गई थी[46]। जिसके लेखक का नाम अज्ञात है। इसके अतिरिक्त काव्य-साहित्य-संग्रह नामक टीका 1872 में विन्दाभिसिर नामक बर्मी

लेखक द्वारा लिखी गई थी। डॉ. हेरम्ब चटर्जी के अनुसार इन टीकाओं के अतिरिक्त परिवार नाम की एक टीका सीलोनी भाषा में प्राप्त है, जो अब तक ताड़पत्र पर सीलोनी में ही सुरक्षित है, तथा अब तक उसका प्रकाशन न हो सका है तथा जो इस ग्रन्थ को स्पष्ट करने में पर्याप्त सहायक है[47]। इस ग्रन्थ का एक अनुवाद वर्तमान शताब्दी में भी भिक्खु अरियवंस द्वारा बंगला भाषा में किया गया है, जिसका प्रकाशन 1948 में कलकत्ता से हुआ है। किन्तु यह अनुवाद न तो विषय-विवेचन की दृष्टि से प्रौढ़ कहा जा सकता है और न ही अर्थ को स्पष्ट कराने में ही पूर्ण सक्षम है।

पालि साहित्य के विशाल भण्डार में अब तक उपलब्ध एक मात्र अलंकार-शास्त्रीय ग्रन्थ सुबोधालंकार प्रत्येक दृष्टि से अत्यन्त महत्वपूर्ण है। इस ग्रन्थ के मूल एवं टीकाओं के प्रकाश में आने से निस्संदेह अलंकार-शास्त्र के इतिहास में एक रिक्तता की पूर्ति होगी।

टिप्पणियां

1. अभिरामस्य रामस्य चरितं कर्त्तुमुद्यतः।
   कामार्थगुणसंयुक्तं धर्मार्थगुणविस्तरम् ।। रामायण, 1, 3, 7-8
2. नाट्यशास्त्र, 6, 115-116
3. बंगाल एशियाटिक सोसाइटी, कलकत्ता का जरनल (जे.ए.एस.बी.), 1875, पृ. 91
4. Society in Medieval Ceylon, p. 10
5. Ibid, p. 229
6. History of Ceylon, Vol. I (Part II), p. 745
7. Ibid, p. 618
8. Ibid, p. 770
9. Society in Medieval Ceylon, p. 294
10. रामसम्माद्यलंकारा सन्ति सन्तो पुरातना। सुबोधालंकार, 1, 1
11. भामह, काव्यालंकार, 2, 19, 58
12. Heramb Chatterjee, Comparative Studies in *Pāli* and Sanskrit Alankaras, preface, p. VI.
13. शब्दार्थौ सहितौ काव्यम्। भामह, काव्यालंकार, 1-8
14. बन्धो च नाम सद्दत्थ-सहिता दोसवज्जिता। सुबोधालंकार, 1, 8
15. काव्यं तावदिष्टार्थव्यवच्छिन्ना पदावली। काव्यादर्श, 1, 10
16. शब्दार्थौ सहितौ वक्रकविव्यापारशालिनौ ।
    बन्धे व्यवस्थितौ काव्यं तद्विताह्लादकारिणि ।।
17. यदल्पमपि नोपेक्ष्यं काव्ये दुष्टं कदाचन ।
    स्याद्वपुः सुन्दरमपि श्वित्रेणैकेन दुर्भगम् । काव्यादर्श, 1, 7
18. सर्वथा पदमप्येकं न निगाद्यमवद्यवत् ।
    विलक्षणाहिकाव्येन दुःसुतेनेव निन्द्यते ।। भामह, काव्यालंकार, 1, 11

19. गुणालंकारसंयुत्ता अपिदोसावलिंगिता।
पसंसिता न विञ्ञू हि सा कञ्ञा विवतादिसि। सुबोधालंकार, 1, 14

20. (क) सालंकारवियुत्तापि गुणयुक्ता मनोहरा ।
निद्दोसा दोसरहिता गुणयुत्ता वधूरिव ।। वही, पृ. 1, 16
(ख) निद्दोसा सब्बथा सायं सा गुणानमवेप्प किं। वही, 1, 15

21. काव्यालंकारसूत्र-वृत्ति-पद, 2, 3, 4; पदार्थदोष, 2, 2, 11
वाक्यदोष, 2, 3, 1; वाक्या., 2, 3, 9

22. विरुद्धन्तराध्यत्थकिलिट्ठानि विरोधि च,
नेय्यं विसेसनापेक्खं हीनत्थकमनत्थंक,
दोसं पदानं, वाक्यानं एकत्थं भग्गरीतिकं,
तथा व्याकिणणगम्यानियतिहीनकमव्युत्तं ।
अतिकुतमपेत्थं सम्बन्धफरुसं तथा।
अपक्कमं ओचित्यहीनं भग्गरीति ससंसयं ।
गम्मं दुट्ठालंकतीति दोसावाक्यत्थविस्सिता । सुबोधालंकार, 1, 8, 20-21

23. सुबोधालंकार, 3, 2

24. नाट्यशास्त्र, 17, 16; काव्यादर्श, 1, 41

25. काव्यादर्श, 1, 52-58; 3, 1-77

26. सुबोधालंकार, 4, 5-8

27. पियतर, प्रेयान्; समास, समासोक्ति; परियायवुत्ति, पर्यायोक्ति; व्याजोपवण्णनं, व्याजस्तुति; रूळाहकार, ऊर्जस्वी; अप्पकतत्थुति, अप्रस्तुतप्रशंसा; भाव, भाविक; मिस्स, संकीर्ण।

28. विपक्षया विशेषस्य लोकसीमातिवर्त्तिनः ।
असावतिशयोक्तिः स्यादलंकारोपमा यथा।। काव्यादर्श, 3, 212

29. पकासका विसेसस्स सियातिसयवुत्ति या ।
लोकातिक्कन्तविसया, लोकियाति च साद्विधा ।। सुबोधालंकार, 4, 10

30. यदुक्तंत्रिप्रकारत्वं तस्याः कैश्चिन्महात्मभिः ।
निन्दाप्रशंसाचिख्यासाभेदादत्राभिधीयते ।।
सामान्यगुणनिर्देशान्त्रयमप्युदितं ननु ।
मालोपमादिः सर्वोपि न ज्यायान्विस्तरो मुधा ।। भामह, काव्यालङ्कार, 2, 37-38

31. समुप्पेजेति धीमन्तं भिन्नलिंगादिकं तु यं ।
उपमा दूसनायालं एतं कत्थचितं यथा ।। सुबोधालंकार, 4, 42, (206)

32. हविता सम्भवो लिंगवचोभेदविपर्ययः ।
उपमानाधिकत्वं च तेनासदृशतापि च ।।
त एते उपमादोषाः सप्त मेधाविनोदिता ।। भामह, काव्यालंकार, 2, 39-40

33. काव्यादर्श, 2, 56
34. वही, 2, 67-97
35. सुबोधालंकार, 4, 50, 58, 62
36. वही, 4, 107. उपमाश्यन्तराथेन किरियादिवसेन च ... ।
37. काव्यादर्श, 2, 225-31
38. वही, 2, 304
39. सुबोधालंकार, 4, 155
40. रामसम्माद्यलंकारा सन्ति सन्तो पुरातना। सुबोधालंकार, 1, 1
41. भामह, काव्यालंकार, 2, 10; 2, 58.
42. नाट्यशास्त्र, 6, 15-16
43. सुबोधालंकार, 5, 21-22
44. उपाध्याय, पालि-साहित्य का इतिहास, पृ. 572
45. वही, पृ. 661
46. वही, पृ. 503
47. Heramb Chatterjee, Comparative Studies in *Pāli* and Sanskrit Alankaras, Preface, p. VII.

24

BOOK REVIEWS

Sectarianism and Religious Persecution in China

J. J. M. De Groot

Published by Literature House Ltd.
Taipei, Taiwan, 1963

This work deals with religious persecution and sectarianism in China from the 1st century A.D. (Han-period) to 1860 A.D. It is in two volumes and is divided into eighteen chapters. The works written by Confucius are classics in China. All religious doctrines, customs and ethics which did not get mention in them or did not conform to them were doomed to death at the hands of successive governments. So, all non-Confucian religions and sects such as Buddhism, Taoism, Christianity were subject to persecution.

Buddhism, being of altogether exotic origin, was often deprived of its right of existence. Throughout history it has been the object of persecution at the hands of Confucian sects. An edict issued by the Emperor Wu (reigned from A.D. 424 to 452) has been cited as an example. The second chapter deals with the edicts depicting anti-Buddhist and anti-Taoist attitude of the Chinese governments upto 17th century. The monks and nuns were asked to return to lay life, the property of the monasteries was confiscated, the clergy had to possess official diplomas and thus their number was restricted. The chapters IV to VII deal with various sects prevalent in China. Most of these sects had their origin in Buddhism and Taoism.

The second volume deals with the persecution of religions in the Ching period. The Imperial decrees and memorials regarding the persecution of Christianity tell about the expulsion of missionaries to port areas and the confiscation of their chapels. During this period many revolts occurred. The persecution of the religious sects is considered to be the cause of these revolts.

The object of the work is to warn Christian missionaries in China of the religious intolerance of Chinese Government. "Chinese state is most intolerant, the most persecuting of all earthly governments, a state which on account of ancient dogmatic principles in the system of political philosophy whereon it is based, could not do otherwise than brandish fire and sword in the face of every religious community or sect which since the days of Confucius has ventured to make its appearance in China." His main argument is that Chinese government had been intolerant to foreign religions. Had it been so, how could Buddhism, a foreign creed, gain popularity in China? Buddhist ideas had profound influence on the life and religious outlook of Chinese people. The total effect of Buddhism was to influence art and literature, to reinforce the native moral standards, to give the masses a conception of future life of rewards and punishments.

For Christianity, the Chinese policy of tolerance was the formidable obstacle to Christian missionary's success. Chinese people were not opposed to Christian faith, but "they were unwilling to grant it the exclusive title of belief." As Paul H. Clement puts it, "It (Christianity) offends everyone, it antagonizes every creed, it mingles with none because its fundamental tenets deny the existence of any other faith or standard of morality." Chinese government was secular and did not patronize any particular religion. An Imperial edict issues in 955 A.D. says, "The excellent religion of Buddha, of those absorbed in the Tao and of the Holy Sages (Confucianism) assist my dynasty in exhorting mankind to do what is good, and the benefits which for this reason they convey are very abundant." But at the same time, it cannot be denied that there was persecution of various sects from time to time. The decree issued on the 30th July 1817 by the Emperor Jen Tsung is an evidence. It says, "....ye mandarins ...... without reluctance and mercy crush in their birth all religious societies before they have time to develop." But, in fact, religious intolerance was not the cause. Some of the sects had become the refuge of rebels. In the name of religious societies, groups were formed for rebellious conspiracies. A decree issued on 22nd January, 1834 tells about the discovery of 339 pounds of gunpowder in the house of Wan Yuen-heng of Tien Chu Chiao (a society) in Honan.

At times, socio-economic reasons were behind such acts. In the year 955 A.D., the Emperor ordered that the bronze Buddha images be melted in order to cast in material into coins as the central government was short of coined money. When the number of monks and nuns increased to such an extent that there was shortage of productive labour and the economy was overburdened, the rulers had to put restrictions on the number of clergies.

Among the Christian missionaries also, the Catholic missionaries met much more opposition than the Protestants, as the Catholics concentrated upon building a Christian community. They even undermined government authority. Consequently, political system of Chinese government frowned upon such organization that demanded exclusive authority from the followers. Intervention of Pope infuriated the Emperor and the anti-Christian movement increased. Had Christians been tolerant like Buddhists, they would have been accepted in Chinese society.

-Kamlesh Jain

BOOK REVIEWS

Pupphañjali

By Sanghasena
Published by the Secretary, Pāli Parisad,
Mandir Marg, New Delhi, 1960, Price : Rs. 2.00

The book embodies a collection of verses, stories and essays written by the author at various occasions, while he was a student at Nava Nalanda Mahavihara, Nalanda (Bihar). These are: *Buddhasāsanuppatti* (The Origins of the Buddha's Religion), *Nālandā-paccabhiññāṇaṃ* (The Identification of Nalanda), *Milindapañhassa Itihāsikathā* (The Historicity of *Milindapañha*), *Holikā Jātakaṃ* (The Holikā *Jātaka*) and *Subhāsiṁsanaṃ* (Valedictory Address).

The author has dedicated the work to his teachers as is suggested by the very title, i.e. *Pupphañjali* (Salutation with flowers in the folded Palms). This has been made very clear in the dedication verse and the *Nidānakathā* (Preface). The book, although small, happens to be the first work of the author and if my knowledge of *Pāli* literature is any guide, is the only *Pāli* work in the second half of the twentieth century.

The first essay presents a brief description of the origin of Buddhism in ten abhorisms in purely Sanskrit *Sūtra* style. The second, i.e. *Nālandā paccabhiññāṇam* is in verses and was originally composed as the first section of a book, viz., *Nālandā-vaṁsa* which the author proposed and began to write, but could not complete. It is written in the famous narrative style of the *Pāli Vaṁsa* literature. The third is an essay on the historicity of the *Milindapañha.* It was read and discussed in a seminar at Nalanda. The fourth happens to be the Holikā *Jātaka.* This is based upon the flight of imagination of the author. According to the footnote, it was written in March, 1957 on the occasion of the Holi festival. The author has drawn the theme from Hindu mythology to prepare this *Jātaka.* The last one happens to be a poem written in honour of Prof. P. V. Bapat at the time of his farewell in April, 1960.

The author seems to be successful in imitating the *Pāli* canonical style. Significantly enough, the text begins with *Nidānakathā* and ends with *Uddāna.*

-S. R. Kulshreshtha

The Sphuṭārthā Śrīghanācārasaṅgraham-ṭīkā

By Sanghasena

Published by K. P. Jaispal Research Institute,
Patna, 1961 Price: Rs. 8.00

The work embodies the critical edition of the commentary, viz. the *Sphuṭārthā Śrīghanācārasaṅgraha-ṭikā* with preface, explanatory notes, index of proper names, technical words and verses. Wherever necessary, the words of the original work, viz. *Śrīghanācārasaṅgraha* (the text could not be traced in original or in translations) have been underlined in order to facilitate the understanding of the text.

The work happens to be a discussion on the code of conduct of the *Śrāmaṇeras* or novices with regard to ten śīlas. The work seems to be chronologically very late as regards to the development of Buddhism. The *Mahāyānic* influence is very much evident. In fact, the work seems to belong to the *Mahāsāṅghika* sect of Buddhism.

The controversy about the authorship of the work has not been solved satisfactorily. The name of the author was probably *Jayarakṣita* (vide the colophon of the text).

-S. R. Kulshreshtha

The Śrīghanācārasaṅgraha

By Sanghasena

Published by Maha Bodhi Society of India,
Mandir Marg, New Delhi, 1974, Price : Rs. 4.00

The work is a reconstruction of the text, the *Śrīghanācārasaṅgraha* (which could not be traced either in original or in translations). The basis of reconstruction has been the famous commentary on this text, viz. the *Sphuṭārthā Śrīghanācārasaṅgraha-ṭīkā.* It is a collection of two hundred verses. The indication of number was given in the original text itself, which has been quoted and commented upon by the author of the commentary. As the text of the commentary itself is faulty and lacuanic at various places, the author (of the present work) has done well in providing many probable gaps here and there. The subject matter of the text is the code of conduct of the *Śrāmṇeras* or novices.

In the preface the author gives the main features of the work. The dedication in verses by the author in the style of the text, is an indication of author's grip over the text. He seems to be totally sentimental in dedicating the text to the memory of Upāli, the greatest exponent of *Vinaya* in the history of Buddhist literature.

The text is provided with an index of technical words and proper names, which has added the utility of the text.

- *S. R. Kulshreshtha*

25

A BRIEF SURVEY OF BUDDHISM IN JAPAN

Sudha Sengupta

Japan is known to be a Buddhist country. So, to a student of Buddhism, it is nothing but natural to be inquisitive about the form of Buddhism prevalent and the influence exercised by it on the society of that country. One question is sometimes asked – if Buddhism is a religion why is it called with a local epithet – Japanese, Chinese, Ceylonese or for that matter, even specifically 'Indian'? Are all these 'Buddhisms, different from one another, it is only the name which is the same? The connoisseur's reply is both 'yes' and 'no'. These are not different in the sense that all of them are developed centering round (1) some fundamental principles of Buddhism and (2) as the main cult object.

A religion, moving from one country to other, undergoes considerable change, in order to mould itself suitable to the changing circumstances of the land of its adoption. A rolling stone might not gather any moss, but a rolling religion collects and assimilates many things from the local soil, which make its appearance quite different from the original one. And the further it travels, the more it changes its appearance, so that after it has traveled through a number of countries for a considerable time, it becomes very difficult to recognize it as the same old religion. Even in its own native place, there is considerable change in a religion after a few centuries, not to speak of any alien country where the atmosphere is completely different.

The form of Buddhism which reached Japan via China and Korea was basically *Mahāyāna*. This religion had been in these two countries, specially in China, for a long time and as is expected, imbibed numerous local ideas. Accepting this, Japan also twisted it here and there to make it suitable for their own atmosphere.

Shintoism, the original religion of Japan and Confucianism – religion imported from China, was already prevalent when Buddhism made its advent in Japan in the sixth century. Buddhism stole the heart of the people and was an established religion within a century with the help of royal patronages. There is, of course, a long history of its ups and downs during the subsequent centuries – because all the ruling heads in different periods were not very favourable to this religion – but it could not be eradicated from the country, as it had already taken its roots into the soil being mingled with the native religion Shintoism. This condition prevails even today. Eventually Buddhism had sixteen sects and numerous subjects in Japan many of which have become almost extinct but some of them are still quite active. Quite a number of ruling heads in different periods were great patrons of Buddhism which helped to raise it to the status of state religion. Special mention can be made of the name of prince Shotoku, who founded the oldest and most famous Buddhist temple of Horyuji at Nara and who is recognized by the Japanese people as playing the same role as Asoka did in India in propagating Buddhism, in Japan. He is credited with writing a number of commentaries on Buddhist scriptures. The Horyuji temple also possesses a set of very old – the oldest so far known – Sanskrit Buddhist Mss. from India. The sculptures and paintings in the Horyuji temple also bear distinct marks of antiquity and have much resemblance with those of India of the similar period. Particularly, the paintings resemble those of Ajanta to a great extent. It is interesting to note that there is a nunnery attached to the Horyuji temple, with a few inmates still living in it. The temple with its five-storied pagoda occupies a vast area and is very imposing in appearance.

Japan is studded with Buddhist temples. Almost all of them are wooden structures excepting one or two of most recent creation. Mention may be made of one recently made in Tokyo which has architectured designs resembling Chaitya-halls of Indian rock-cut cave temples. The biggest wooden construction in Japan or may be even in the world, is the double roofed hall of the great Founder in the Higashi or East Honganji temple at Kyoto – the headquarters of the Jodo-shin sect – one of the most popular sects of Japan. The hall in question enshrines a wooden image of Shinaran Shonin – the founder of this temple, which was carved by himself. The structure being wooden, all the temples have got slanting roofs, with more or less difference in other details in the general plan. The Kofukuji temple at Nagasaki shows Chinese influence in its design, it is also said to be made by Chinese people. The biggest enemy of these wooden structures is fire and many of these beautiful constructions were burnt once or more, but are renovated again. The Indian influence through Buddhism is detected in many aspects. The high alter in the temples in which the image of the Buddha is placed, is called the mount Sumeru. One of the features of the Shinto Shrine which differentiates them from the Buddhist temples, is the Torii or gateway which confronts every Shinto Shrine. This gateway, of bright vermillion colour, is a wooden construction, with two vertical pieces of wooden pillars sturmounted by two horizontal ones, both the ends of the upper one of which are a little slanting upwards, more or less resembling the design of Sanchi gateways. The name Torii also has come from Sanskrit Torana, they say. Interestingly enough, though this type of gateways is known as Buddhist gateways in India, they are conspicuously absent in any Buddhist temple in Japan, being meant exclusively for the Shinto Shrines. Of course, in some of the Buddhist temples, there is a small Shinto Shrine with a Toril in front, in the same compound, before the approach to the main temple. These temples might be significant in showing the transition period or the mingling of Shintoism with Buddhism (in a friendly way, both maintaining one's own individuality). In their daily life also the Japanese people have made a compromise with both the religions. The rituals during marriages and birth of children – for those who observe the orthodox way of life – are done in Shinto Shrines while after death, the rituals are followed in Buddhist way.

Another peculiarity of the Buddhist temples in Japan is, in each temple there is a very big brass bell sometimes enormously big – and just at the midnight of each last day of the year, when the New Year ushers in – all these bells throughout Japan will going 108 times, to drive away 108 types of evils, - according to Buddhist maxims. People visit both Buddhist temples and Shinto Shrines at this time onwards for a week.

As has already been said that the form of Buddhism which went to Japan, was Mahayana, which, by that time was incorporating some of the *Brāhmaṇical* gods and goddesses into its fold. We can trace a number of such *Brāhmaṇical* gods in the temples of Japan – but they have been changed to a great extent both in name and in form. A bronze sculpture kept in the Todaiji temple at Nara – where the world's biggest Bronze Buddha image is installed – resembles lord Krishna playing the flute, but it is called a *Bodhisattva* there. Wooden images of some gods bearing names equivalent to Indian Indra, Kuvera etc., placed at the corridor of 'Sanjusan Gendo' temple at Kyoto – are given demonlike fierce appearance. Another small bronze figure kept in a museum at Kamakura, resembles Indian Śiva in the pose of trampling a small human being under his feet – is explained as one of the guardian deities of a direction (dikpala). Instances can be multiplied. The Buddhist gods also have changed their forms. *Bodhisattva Avalokitesvara*, has become feminine with the name Kannon or the 'goddess of mercy' in many places. Of course, thousand in the temple of Sanjusan Gendo mentioned above, he is a male one, a thousand and one statues of which are kept in the temple. The central one can be called in Sanskrit as '*Ekadasamukha Sahasrabhuja Avalokitesvara*'. It has really eleven faces on the head and 21 pairs of hands which represent the thousand hands as possessing power equivalent to 1000 hands for protecting 25 worlds. On both sides of the central figure, there are five hundred images, bringing the number of 1000 images in total. It is believed that the lord Kannon can transform himself into 33 different forms, that is why the name of the temple is Sanju-san Gendo which means a hall for 33. *Bodhisattva Bhaisajyaguru* is also very popular as the 'divine healer', his image with a pot of medicine in his hand resembles that of *Bodhisattva Maitreya.* In the temples of those sects which believe in the Buddha *Śakyamuni* or any *Bodhisattva* – (the *Amitābha Buddha* is very popular, *Vairocana* also has got quite a number of devotees) – there are the images of the respective deities, while in the temples belonging to other sects like *Nichiren*, or its subjects, there is no image, but a lotus plant representing the '*Saddharma-pundarika*' which they worship. A number of Buddhist sects like *Nichiren* are after the name of its founder. *Nichiren* has got many other subsects of which one, the Sokagakkai, who claim to possess progressive or reformative views, and whose activities are more political than religions, has become very popular with a group people recently and their clientale is on the increase. Zen is one of the most popular Buddhist sects of Japan which corresponds to the *Chan* or *Dhyana* School of China, has a large number of devotees in its three subjects viz., *Soto, Rinzai* and *Obaku*, which are again sub-divided into different schools. This sect does not believe in the recitation of the name of the Buddha *Amitābha* or the *Lotus Sūtra* or any other ritual, but believes that enlightenment or *Buddhahood* can be attained by meditation which is called *Zazen*. In each temple area there is a special room for meditation for the inmates. The inmates may be permanent residents of the temple – which are very few, or boys or even girls from the devotee family who come for a short training, particularly during the vacation periods. *Zen* has gained so much popularity with western scholars that of late, they – both men and women – are seen to be living in small huts in *Zen* monasteries at Kamakura and other places, practicing *Zazen*. The process of Zazen briefly is: to sit erect and fix one's mind in any one object and meditate. This seems very much resembling the method of meditation prescribed in *Brāhmaṇic* scriptures from good old days. That age old system seems to have taken only a new form in Japan. Incidentally, it may be mentioned that meditation is nothing new in Buddhism, it was prescribed by the Buddha himself.

It is a paradox that Buddhism which arose as a protest against the *Brāhmaṇic* ritualism – culminated itself into the ritualistic practices of *Māhayāna* and finally of Tantrism even in its own country of origin. But though different kinds of ritualistic practices of Tantric Buddhism are heard of in India, the practice of performing fire sacrifice – homa or havanam as they are called – is yet unheard of to be practiced by the Buddhists in India. It seemed to be a monopoly of the followers of *Brāhmaṇic* rituals upto this day. The only Tantric Buddhist sect of Japan, the Shingon sect, follows the *Mahāvairocana* and other Tantric *Sūtras* and mystical practices of Tibetan Tantric Buddhism. It is interesting to note that followers of this and the Tendai sect, which is not essentially a Tantric sect, perform fire sacrifice they call '*goma*' – a transformation of the Sanskrit name '*Homa*'. The process of the performance, with a closer observation, seems almost similar to those performed by Brāhmaṇical practisers even today – with minor differences such as the arrangement of the pieces of wood in a rectangular way instead of a triangular way, using wax instead of butter or ghee – and such others. The '*Yantra*' or the pit of sacrifice, is different for the male or female deity; the one for the male is square while that for the female is round. The *mantras* and the postures of hands (*mudrā*) etc. are also very similar, the names of *Brāhmaṇical* deities of course are replaced by Buddhist gods. At any rate, there is no doubt that this system has been borrowed and adopted from the *Brāhmaṇic* system of performing fire sacrifices.

Japanese Buddhism in modern days, is more an object of culture and subject of research, than a living force among its adherents, particularly the new generation. There are still numerous active temples no doubt, many of them being very well-to-do. The heads of these institutions are called monks, though most of them are households and seldom 'monks' in our sense the term. They devote their times in many other activities than only looking after the temples. Many of them are engaged in educational activities. Usually they wear civil dresses but on ceremonial occasions, they put on some professional dress over which they hang a belt-like thing slantingly from one shoulder to another waist in somewhat similar way as the sacred-thread is worn, in which the emblem of the particular temple is embroidered. This is supposed to represent the full three-piece robes of monks. Almost every well-to-do temple has a children's school attached to it, which is very often looked after by the wife of the abbot. These monks or rather priests are held in high esteem. With almost every temple is attached a piece of land where the relies of members of the devotee families are preserved. Small stone monuments are made over them and sometimes there are some inscriptions also. Each family has its separate emblem and each has got separate corner to add its relic urns.

In these days of economic development and materialistic importance, religion usually remains in the background. But the Japanese people have taken religion so easily that it does not come in their way of life. In the same family, husband and wife may profess different religions – one Buddhist, another may be Christian – because Christianity now is an established religion in that country and Islam is also gradually creeping in into it. They live in quite harmony. In fact, religion particularly Buddhism, which is even today, a majority, is mingled with their life and culture so inseparably that it is hardly discernible and its influence is not at all to be undermined. The tea ceremony and flower arrangement, - two most well known Japanese arts, without which a modern lady's accomplishments are not perfect, - are contributions of the Zen Buddhism. Many other qualities – which have become Japan's national characteristics – their very modest behaviour, their military – like discipline, their diligence and preservence, their apparent indifference to worldly miseries (the Japanese people have to inform the death of their near and dear one with a similing face), and above all, their gentle manners (normally the Japanese people are very quite) and many other features of their daily life–are all the contributions of religion and Buddhism has got a lion's share in it.

26

NĀGĀRJUNA'S MESSAGE FOR THE IGNORANT

Kewal Krishan Mittal[1]

In an attempt to understand and appreciate the message of Nāgārjuna for the ignorant, I present to the scholars of Buddhist Studies a free English rendering of a short treatise attributed to the sage. The treatise is available in its Tibetan Version in the Tibetan *Tripiṭaka,* B-Stan-Hgyur Volume XCV (95th) on page 69-70 (Peking edition). The same, it is believed, is a Tibetan translation of the original in Sanskrit accomplished by Pandita Ananda and Lokacaksu Grags-jor-shes-rab. The title of the original is somewhat as: 'A Prakaraṇa names Abuddha-Bodhaka'. My rendering of the title and all, done with the help of my friend and colleague Sh. L. Jamspal (who is now in the United States), is:

A Treatise Named the Enlightener of the Unlightened.

Having Saluted Manjuśree, the flawless ocean of qualities, I will explicate the following by way of compassion for the ignorant, to make them understand the essential truth (the Tattva) that they know not:

The tasks are four: To know the alien view point; to refute the same; to know one's own theory (siddhānta); and to establish, elucidate and elaborate the same.

Now, what is the alien view-point? They say, there is a Soul (ātmā) that is permanent (nitya), ubiquitous (vibhu), one (eka), doer (karttā) and enjoyer (Bhoktā). This has to be refuted as under:-

We can ask what is a Soul (ātmā)? The Skandhas (the *Constituents, supports*) can not be regarded as Soul in so far as they are subject to *production* (*utpatti* janya) and *destruction* (vināśaśila). The Soul can not be other than the Skandhas because the former and the latter cannot be seen as distinct in the same way as a pot (ghaṭa) from the cloth (paṭa). We cannot imagine their relation to be of the kind obtains between the supported and the Support i.e., the one that obtains between the water and the pot.[2] The situation cannot be described as that represented between the grain of rice and its husk. The Soul is not inherent in the skandhas as the latter are many (whereas the soul is regarded as one). The Soul cannot be said to be possessed of the Skandhas (Skandha-yukta) in the way (a pesson called) Devadatta may be said to be possessed of a cow gau-yukta.

The aliens (Paravādis or Tīrthikas) say that if we do not accept (the existence of) a Soul there would be a lack of relationship between an action (Karma), like giving away (dāna), and its result (Karmaphala). It would be something like the fate of the tail, horns and hoofs etc. of a dead cow (none of the remains).

Listen now, of the special example that we offer: We go on having fear from a snake seen mistakenly for a rope, in a semi-lighted night, so long as we do not examine the situation, with the help of a lamp, and realize that what we have been viewing as a snake and of what we were in mortal fear, is nothing but a projection (āropana) on a rope. Similarly so long as we remain ignorant the connection between our doings and their results (Karma and the *Karma*phala) seems to be lasting. But this is not only an example of the removal of false identification of the elements (*dharma*s or skandhas) with a person or a bodily being (Pudgala-nairātmya). For, in this example, the opponent (Pūrvapakṣin) can say that the rope is there alright, our reply is that the rope must be analysed into its strands. Each of them, too, is also dependent on atoms and as such none of them can be said to have a reality. The atoms cannot be themselves regarded as persistent entities as they, too, are composed of the portions of directions (digāṁśas). But should we say that there is nothing? We can not say so because nothingness (*abhāva*) cannot be conceived except in terms of something positive or existing (bhāva). One who understands the being (bhāva) and non-having (*abhāva*) understands that there is no reality of the elements either (*dharma*nairātmya).

Here, we can raise a question as to how can there be production (utpāda), persistence (Sthiti) and destruction (vyaya or bhaṅga)? Is production possible? If it is, and is without persistence and destruction then anything and everything including the here's horn shall be possible. If someone says, 'let there be persistence', how can it be there or of what there is the persistence without production and destruction? If he says 'there is destruction', how can that be or what can meet destruction without having been produced and persisting? If the three (utpāda, dhrūvya and vyaya) are taken as simultaneous that would be patently wrong or impossible as these processes contradict each other like light and darkness.

The vijñānavādīs (the idealists) speak of the existence of vijñāna (consciousness). If there is such an existence of consciousness then we must expose its nature (*Svarūpa*) and its nature is not of one but of many kinds, because of the many-ness (multiplicity) of the objects of consciousness (viṣaya-bhinnatā). If the nature of vijñāna is not unitary (ekarasa) or uniform then it can not be that of many (anektā) or multiform as we can not think of the many (aneka) without reference to the one (eka). Vijñāna can not be said to be born of itself, of something else, of both itself and the other, and yet can not also be uncaused (ahetuka).

If all this (Soul, consciousness, Skandhas, etc.) is not of what there is existence then? This all is like a fire brand (alātcakra) miraculous (*Māyārupī*) creation (nirmāna), a dreamlike appearance (Svapnavat), moonshine shadow (udaka candra), vapourous air (vāṣpa) distant echo (pratidhvani), mirage (mrgamaīcikā) and a cloud (megha). We have nothing to remove or reject and nothing to establish;

If righteousness is rightly viewed;

Release one gets, unpursued.

Here all is unapprehended (anupalbdha) and in this unapprehension (*anupalabdhi*) itself there is all light. If unapprehension of the intellect is realized then unapprehension of all would be realized.

Endnotes

1. The paper had been submitted for a Seminar organised by the Institute of Tibetan Higher Studies, Sarnath (Varanasi).
2. The text here is obscure as the relata mentioned are water and cloth.

27

STUDIES IN BUDDHISM
A Brief Review

G. B. Upreti

Buddhism as a religion and philosophy was known in the West even before the 19th century. But systematic studies were taken up only from the beginning of the 19th century when a few competent scholars studied, edited and translated some original Buddhist texts into various European languages.[1] General surveys of Buddhism were made by scholars like Burnouf, Bishop P. Brigandet, R. Spence Hardy, H. Oldenburg, R.L. Mitra, H. Kern and Max Muller.[2] However, all these scholars were excelled by T.W. Rhys Davids who studied Buddhism for about half a century and produced many brilliant articles, introductory notes to the *Suttas* and some good monographs.[3] His death in 1922 closed the first phase of researches on Buddhism. This phase was totally dominated by the European scholars, the reasons for which were obvious: First, there was intellectual and scientific backwardness of the colonial people. Secondly, on their part, the European scholars were motivated by a sense of urgent need to know and understand the spiritual super-structure of the colonial world and in some cases to support their own religious, philosophical and ideological beliefs. The 19th century was a crucial point in the history of the development of human thought. Science and religion were at loggerheads and the latter was already a dying force. However, the interested social forces were still undaunted and vigorous attempts were made to prove that religion if divested of its dogmas and superstitions is basically not anti-science, Buddhism was forwarded to prove this point.[4]

The second phase is mainly notable for three developments. First, joining of the fray by the colonial or erstwhile colonial scholars. Secondly, diversification of opinion on the nature of Buddhism. Lastly, the prominence of bourgeois democratic interpretation of Buddhism. The outstanding names of this phase are those of Stcherbatsky, Max Weber, Poussin, Sylvan Levy, D. D. Kosambi, Tatakusu, B. M. Barua, A. B. Keith, E. B. Thomas, Suzuki, Nakamura, N. Dutta, Rahul Sankritayayan, Bapat, Vaidya and Malalasekera. The Indian scholars who belonged to this phase were mostly guided by the ideas of bourgeois democracy.

The third and last phase began with the entrance of the Marxists. Rahul Sankrityayan had done some work on such lines but D.D. Kosambi was the first to study *Buddhism in relation to the changes in the means and relations of production.* Further enquiries on these lines are being made by D. P. Chattopadhyaya and R. S. Sharma. Many young scholars disillusioned with the bourgeois democratic ideals and in search of new avenues of knowledge and disciplined thinking are adopting Marxist approach toward Buddhism. However, the earlier traditions continue and both theologians and idealists are trying to check the tide.

So much work has been done on Buddhism that it is impossible to analyse the contributions and opinions of individual scholars. *The Shinso Hanayama Bibliography on Buddhism* published in 1961 covers 836 pages. Many important contributions have been made after the publication of this work. In such a state of affairs the best possible course is to evaluate various trends, approaches and interpretations. A few such attempts were made earlier by scholars like Edward Conze and Sangharakshita. But both these scholars are neo-converts to Buddhism and have a characteristic disdain for science. The approach adopted in the *2500 years of Buddhism* is purely descriptive. Our approach is basically different and tries to study and analyse various points of view in their historical perspective.

The most popular and common place point of view is that Buddhism was purely a code of ethics and morality. This school can be called the *ethico-moral school of Buddhism.* It insists that only the *Theravāda* is genuine and other forms of Buddhism are degenerate, corrupt and false. The two great masters of this school were H. Oldenberg and T. W. Rhys Davids, The former emphasized its monastic character and the latter social. Oldenberg's views were shared by his compatriot Max Weber and many other who asserted that Buddhism had no political or socio-economic content. This view was challenged by many scholars like Max Muller, Thomas, Eliot, Macdonell and Bapat who, like Rhys Davids, were convinced that Buddhism was closely connected with social change and reforms. In their zeal some scholars went so far as to prove that Buddhism was a democratic and revolutionary movement. Notwithstanding the differences, the school as a whole represents the viewpoint of the European liberal bourgeoisie and its counterparts in other countries.

The main drawbacks of this school of thinking are as follows: First, Buddhism was not seen in its historical setting but in its deviation degeneration and corruption. Secondly, the movement was studied squarely on the basis of the *Pāli* texts and in this process comparative approach and stratification of the texts were relegated to secondary place. Lastly, integrated approach was not adopted which resulted in vague and sweeping generalizations.

The second school can be called *the metaphysical school.* According to this school the central conception of Buddhism is *dharma* (a metaphysical category), The code of ethics and morality is a minor and insignificant part of the whole scheme. It depends mainly on the *abhidharma* for its source material. Scholars like Stcherbatsky, Poussin, Rosenberg and Sylvan Levy subscribe to this view. The school had its early seat in pre-revolutionary Russia where democratic tradition was not very strong. The metaphysical approach was a typical reaction against the ethico-moral scheme of Buddhism. The optimistic and secular outlook of the 19th century was already giving way to the pessimistic and metaphysical outlook of the 20th century Europe.

The main problems of this school are as follows. First, philosophy is treated in abstraction and with a metaphysical basis. Secondly the *abhidharma* which existed only in rudimentary from during the lifetime of the Buddha was used as the chief source material. Lastly, a balance was not struck between the *Pāli* and Sanskrit traditions. If the first school was squarely built on the *Pāli* sources, this school had its foundation as well as superstructure in Sanskrit tradition.

We will call the third school as *the conservative school.* Its proponents asserted that the Buddha did not challenge the basic religious and philosophical tenets of Hinduism. For instance, the idea of soul in the absolute sense was never discredited. In other words, Buddhism came to fulfill and not to destroy. But as a true Hindu the Buddha protested against the social and religious evils which had crept into the Hindu society in the course of many centuries and tried to restore its pristine purity. The two great masters of this school were S. Radhakrishnan and Anand Coomarswamy.

In this school of thinking the most noticeable flaw is the casual and abstract treatment of the social forces. The conflict centres round the intellectual discussions of the sophists and social thinkers rather than concrete material situation. This has given the Buddha the stature of a superhuman intellectual giant and social forces have become subservient to him. Such an attitude takes objectivity out of history. Secondly, the scholars are so keen to make Buddhism a part of ancient Brahmanism that they seek the concept of soul were it really does not exist. Finally, this school is not only anti-materialist but also ultra-conservative.

The next school can be called the *psycho-religious school.* The most prominent scholar of this school was Mrs. C. A. F. Rhys Davids who insisted that 'Buddhism is a religion of development of the human will'. She also suggested that early Buddhism was not a monastic religion but a popular religion asserting soul and god. The idea of pre-canonical Buddhism was supported by Schayer, Regamey, Mary Falk, etc. The positive contribution of this school is persistent insistence on stratification of the religious texts.

But this stratification of the Buddhist canon with a religious bias is certainly misleading. Selections made by Mrs. Rhys Davids to illustrate her point of view are fragmentary and ambiguous. Finally, her insistence on psychological explanation made other more important facts secondary or expendable. This approach seems to represent a reaction against the ethico-moral scheme of Buddhism. Again this school, like the metaphysical school, represents the pessimistic and metaphysical outlook of the twentieth century Europe.

The theological school takes many and diverse forms: Sometimes it concentrates on doctrinal disputes between the Hinayanists and Mahayanists or exoterics and esoterics; and at others it takes the form of a comparative study of religions by liberal or fanatic theologians. Recently it has appeared in another form among the neo-converts of the West. The most vocal representatives of this recent trend are Edward Conze and Sangharakshita. They advise us to make science subservient to religion and exclude spiritual phenomena from the purview of science.

Such an approach to Buddhism is not only irrational but also motivated. It is a subtle attempt of the imperialists to make anti-science propaganda among the developing nations of Asia.

Finally, to come to *the Marxist school.* For the Marxists religion is a type of consciousness. The consciousness can be analysed only by understanding the concrete base which gave birth to it. The base consists of the means and relation of production, i.e. economic and technological development and the nature of class struggle arising out of property relations. In dealing with Buddhism the Marxists are guided by the basic premise. Consequently, an integrated approach has been adopted. The origin, development, decline and final disappearance of Buddhism from India are not explained away by such simple devices of morality or lack of it, royal patronage or antipathy, etc. by a historical analysis of the different stages. As a result new problems along with possible answer are being put forth. In some cases old questions are being examined afresh. Thus the Marxist school has opened a new and fresh avenue of knowledge from the students of Buddhism.

Endnotes

1. Bapat, P.V. (ed.), *2500 Years of Buddhism*, p. 380.
2. Ibid.
3. Ibid. pp. 384-385.
4. See, for instance, Huxley's striking definition of Buddhism in his Romance Lecture, 1893. "A system which knows no god in the western sense; which denies a soul to man; which counts the belief in immortality a blunder and the hope of it a sin; which refuses any efficacy to prayer and sacrifice; which bids men look to nothing but their own efforts for salvation; which in its original purity knew nothing of vows of obedience and never sought the aid of the secular arm; yet spread over a considerable moiety of the old world with marvelous rapidity and is still with whatever base and mixture of foreign superstitions the dominant creed of a large fraction of mankind". (Quoted by Charles Eliot, *Hinduism and Buddhism,* 1, X(iv).

28

HARṢA
A Śaiva or a Buddhist?

Rakesh

The common-place notion about Harsa being a Buddhist was questioned by Dr. R.C. Majumdar who called him a pious and devoted 'Satva'.[1] This view was refuted by Dr. Dashrath Sharma who on the testimony of Yuan chwang and certain passage of Bāṇa's *Harṣacarita* calls Harṣa a devoted Buddhist.[2]

Most of the writers on Harṣa admit that he was originally a Śaiva and remained so up to the twenty-fifth year of his reign.[3] The epigraphic sources belonging to the early part of Harṣa's reign calls him a *Parama-Māheśvara.*[4] In his Sonepat Copper-seal, we see a reclining Nāndi. In fact, Harṣa belonged to a family which was known for its liberal tendencies in religion.[5] Beside being sun-worshippers, the family was also devoted to Lord Śiva. There is ample evidence to support this in Bāṇa's *Harṣacarita.* Thus, we can safely presume that Harṣa by birth, as also in his younger days, was under the influence of Hinduism or Brhmanism as opposed to Buddhism. Even before setting out on his conquests Harṣa, 'with deep devotion offered worship to the adorable Nīlohita.[6] In the dramas *Ratnāvalī* and *Priyadarśikā*, attributed to Harṣa, the benedictory verses mention the chief deities of Brāhmaṇism. Besides there are passages in these dramas suggesting king's interest in the performance of sacrifices by Brāhmiṇs as the sign of the people's progress and efficiency in administration.

Harṣa's inclinations towards Buddhism must have commenced quite early in his life. His brother Rājyavardhana, himself a '*Paramasaugata*', may have exercised some influence on him. Harṣa's plans to meet Divākaramitra, a Brāhmin turned Buddhist, clearly reveal his interest in Buddhism.[7] Again, Harṣa while dissuading his sister from becoming a Buddhist nun, not only arranges for her instruction in the philosophy of the *Tathāgata* but promises also to don along with her the red robes of a *Bhikṣu* as soon as he had finished his self-appointed task of punishing his brother's murderer, Śaśāṅka, the ruler of Gauṛa.[8] By the time it fell to his lot to become the king, the change in Harṣa's religious learnings had become quite evident. Harṣa's reluctance to accept the throne and his subsequent decision to accept it after due consultations with *Bodhisattva Avalokiteśvara*[9] demonstrate further his unmistakable leanings towards Buddhism. Harṣa's interest in Buddhism must have only increased after meeting Divkarmitra who formally consecrated him.[10]

Harṣa's interest in Buddhism and his active support to its cause is revealed to us from the work of Yuan-chwang. Harṣa called the Kannauj Assembly mainly in order to give due publicity to the doctrines of *Mahāyāna* school of Buddhism. His devotion to Buddhism is further made more explicit by the Prayāga Assembly. An account of this Assembly leaves us in no doubt that by 643 A.D. Śiva had gone to the third place in Harṣa's estimation. Harṣa's own plays tell a similar story. While his plays *Ratnāvalī* and *Priyadarśikā* show no influence of Buddhism. *Nāgānanda*, the last and maturest of his plays reflects the great change in his religious outlook. It begins with salutations to the Buddha, deals with the life of a *Bodhisattva* and preaches in uncompromising terms the noble doctrines of *Ahiṁsā*. Harṣa's patronage of Buddhism is further illustrated by the yearly Buddhist Assemblies he summoned,[11] his enshrinement of Buddha tooth-relic procured from Kashmir in a monastery built near Kannauj[12], his gift of a temple to the Nalanda convent, and his erection of topes and monasteries at the sacred places of Buddhism.

While Harṣa's interest in Buddhism thus stands clearly established he can't be called a Buddhist ruler in the same sense as we understand AŚoka and even Kaniṣka. True to his family tradition, Harṣa was initially wedded to Hinduism or Brāhmanism, more particularly Śaivism. Subsequently, we find a change in his religion leanings and his advocacy of Buddhism. But at no stage in his career, however, he was intolerant to any religion or sect. Though Yuan Chwang may give such an impression, it is doubtful if Harṣa ever treated with scant respect the orther religious sects.[13] Harṣa's support to Buddhism never detracted him from the path of religious liberalism which is clearly evidenced by the Prayāga Assembly held as late as 643 A.D.

It is futile to paint Harṣa either as a devout Śaiva or even as a devout Buddhist. He could profess his allegiance to both at one and the same without antagonizing either of them. In fact, by pronouncing the policy of religious toleration, Harṣa was simply identifying himself with the main currents of religious thinking in this period. Yuan Chwang's account makes it very clear that the dominant tendency in religion during this period was that of syncretism. This was more pronounced in the case of Buddhism and Śaivism which were greatly influenced by Tantricism and developed some common characteristics which brought them nearer. The above contention can be amply illustrated by the following informative remarks of Yuan Chwang in his description of MO-LO-KU-TA.

"......By the side of the lake was a stone Deva-palace frequented by Kuam-tzu-tsai Pusa (Avalokiteśvara). Devotees, risking life, brave water and mountain to see the p'usa, but only a few succeed in reaching the shrine. To the people at the foot of the mountain who pray for a sight of the p'usa, he appears sometimes as a *Pāṣupata Tīrthika*, or as Māheśvara, and consoles the suppliant with this answer...."[14]

Endnotes

1. *Classical Age*, Bhartiya Vidya Bhawan series, pp. 119-120.
2. Dasharath Sharma: '*Harṣa: A Buddhist*' Gautama Buddha, 25th centenary, Vol., 1956 (Ed. M. N. Law).
3. See R.S. Tripathi's '*History of Kanauj*', p. 163.
4. Madhuban and Bānskhera Copper-Plates of Harṣa.
5. Harṣa's Nālanda and Sonepat copper seals refer to his brother Rājyavardhana as '*Parama-saugata*' and his father Prabhakaravardhana as '*Paramādityabhakta*'.
6. *Harsacarita*. pp. 202.
7. Bāṇa's Harṣacarita. Ch. VIII.
8. Harṣacarita Ch. VIII.
9. Watters: *On Yuan Chwang's Travels in India*. p. 343.
10. Bāṇa, Ch. VIII.
11. Watters, p. 344.
12. Ibid., p. 352.
13. Yuan Chwang's description of Harṣa dressed as Śakra holding a precious canopy and Bhāskaravarman as Brahma-rāja holding chāmara going on either side of the elephant carrying the Buddha image in the Prayāga Assembly is a flight of imagination obsessed as he was with the superiority of Buddhism.
14. Ibid., Vol. II, p. 229.

29

THE TREATMENT OF THE SELF (ĀTMAN) IN MĀDHYAMIKA PHILOSOPHY *

Peter Della Santina

In the eighteenth chapter of Ācārya Nāgārjuna's *Mūlamādhyamakakārikā,* entitled *Ātmaparīkṣā*, or as it has been rendered in Tibetan, *Ātmadharmaparīkṣā*, contained an exhaustive examination of the concept of the 'self'. The *Prasannapadā* of Ācārya Candrakīrti, a commentary to the *Prajñāmūla,* is indispensable if one would hope to appreciate the significance of Nāgārjuna's arguments which, in the cryptic style of the verses, is often obscured. In the eighteenth chapter of the *Prajñāmūla* there exhibited the concern with soteriology which so characterizes the philosophical systems of India. It is Nāgārjuna's purpose to dismantle dialectically the categories of thought so that insight, or wisdom (*prajñā*), may arise. The real is transcendent to thought, which though erroneous conceptualization, obscures and falsifies it. Ignorance is productive of bondage and, as such, its removal is imperative. Both the doctrines of self and not-self, if posited absolutely, distort the real. Hence Ācārya Nāgārjuna is careful to demonstrate their inapplicability to the absolute which is non-descriptive and non-dual.

In the opening *Kārikā* of the chapter Nāgārjuna writes "If the self (*ātman*) is constitutive of the aggregates (*skandhas*), it will be endowed with the nature of origination and destruction. If it is other than the skandhas, it will be endowed with the latter's characteristics.* Nāgārjuna begins by examining the relationally dependent entities; the self and the aggregates, characteristically in terms of identity and difference. In the opening line of his commentary to the chapter, Candrakīrti writes, "If it is said, 'Afflictions, deeds, individuals, agents, and fruits are all not real (*atavattaṃ*), only a fairy city, then how is one to penetrate the real'? It is replied, 'Not relying upon anything as a support, either internal or external, by putting an end to the sense of self and self-identity (*ahaṃkāra* and *mamakāra*), here there is the real'." Going on to quote from the *Mādhyamakāvatāra,* the author of the commentary says, "All afflictions and faults arise from the view of real individuality (*satkāyadṛṣṭi*). Having known through insight selves and their objects, the saint simply rejects the self. The view of real individuality is the root of *Saṃsāra*. When one does not grasp a self, one abandons the view of real individuality. Through abandoning the view of real individuality all afflictions are dispelled". Thus the soteriological motivation underlying the treatment of the self in the *Mādhyamika* is immediately made evident as is the existential character of erroneous views which, as the commentary says, are the root of the phenomenal world.

The commentary then proceed to state that the self is the object of ahmkāra and to examine whether it, the object of *ahaṃkāra*, be of the nature of the aggregates or different from them. In this way the alternative modes of conceiving two relationally dependent entities are indicated. The author of the commentary writes, "If it is contended that the aggregates are the atman, then the self will be originated and annihilated because the aggregates are originated and annihilated. However this is unacceptable, for through the 'reduction and absurdum' (*atiprasaṅga*) there will emerge the fault of a plurality of selves. Further, at the time of liberation the self will necessarily be annihilated because the aggregates are annihilated". The *Mādhyamika* wishes to establish that the self and the aggregates are not intelligible in terms of identity. For if the self were identical with the aggregates, it must necessarily lose all those predicates which are peculiarly its own.

Having disposed of the first alternative, Candrakīrti goes on to say, "If the aggregates are not the self, then the self apart from the aggregates is likewise not admitted. If the self is different from the aggregates, then it will be devoid of the characteristics of the aggregates....The aggregates arise from causes and conditions. Hence they are originated. They are characterized by origination, duration and annihilation. If, as you assert, the self be devoid of the characteristics of the aggregates, then the self will not be endowed with origination, duration and annihilation. Whatever is, thus, is not existent, therefore, unconditioned like a sky-flower or like *Nirvāṇa*". In this way the *Mādhyamika* exposes the inapplicability of the concept of the self as predicated absolutely. The self, if deprived of empirical predicates, is a wholly empty expression. An unconditional self is unintelligible, and so the silence of the *Mādhyamika* with regard to the absolute must be admitted to be preferable. Candrakīrti goes on to write, "The false inference of selves is obtained through false imagination only. The self is imagined through ignorance." The self and the aggregates are mutually dependent entities. They are intelligible neither in terms of identity nor difference, hence they are not established. The author of the commentary writes, "Having grasped a mirror the reflection of one's own face is seen, but, absolutely, there is nothing. Similarly, having grasped a support *ahaṁkāra* is perceived, but, absolutely, there is nothing. Just as when the mirror is not grasped one's own face is not seen, so apart from the aggregates the self is not seen".

Nāgārjuna writes in the second *Kārikā*, "Where the self does not exist, how could there be a selfhood (*ātmya*). From the fact that the self and the selfhood are in their basic nature quiescent, there is no self-identity (*mama*) or individuality (*ahaṁkāra*)". Candrakīrti goes on to write, "Not having obtained the self but only its name, the five aggregates, the support of the self, are surely not obtained...In this way, having understood the insubstantiality of the self, the saint should certainly understand the insubstantiality of things or of the aggregates pertaining to the self. The five aggregates originate from *ahaṁkāra*, but as *ahaṁkāra* is objectively not real, how is what has arisen from an unreal seed possible? Having seen the five aggregates as false, *ahaṁkāra* is dispelled. Having dispelled *ahaṁkāra*, again the aggregates will not arise...One who is far from right knowledge of the self and selfhood, falsely imputes the aggregates, but for one who is close to right knowledge the aggregates do not appear...Like a mirage, the self and the aggregates are not seen objectively. Therefore, the self and selfhood are not grasped by one who dwells near to the ultimate vision." Thus the commentary explains, through the non-apprehension of the self and the aggregates, free from *ahaṁkāra* and *mamakāra*, the saint is produced.

In the third *Kārikā* Nāgārjuna writes, "Any entity whose individuality and self-identity does not exist, whosoever sees it with non-individuality and non-self-identity, cannot see or grasp the truth". The commentary says, "Some think there is a saint endowed with the idea of non-individuality and non-self-identity. Hence there must be an individual, the saint. Thus the self as well as the aggregates are established, but it is not so. One who perceives non-individuality and non-self-identity does not see. The self and the aggregates are never apprehended in their own-being. Apart from these, how are non-self-identity and non-individuality apprehended?" What is in its own-being not existent cannot be conceived of as non-self-identity and non-individuality. Thus, Candrakīrti writes, "The child who conceives of the *dharmas* of *śūnyatā* also enters into a wrong path. He would explain through characters the truth of emptiness." Nāgārjuna's argument in the third *Kārikā* is undoubtedly directed against the schools of the *Hīnayāna* who upheld the reality of non-self-identity and non-individuality.

In the fourth *Kārikā* Nāgārjuna writes, "Grasping ceases to be where, internally and externally, the ideas of individuality and non-self-identity are destroyed. From the cessation of grasping the cessation of birth also follows". Thus, again, the soteriological function of the dialectic is clearly shown. Candrakīrti, quoting from sūtra, writes, "The view of real individuality is the root cause from which all afflictions arise. The view of real individuality is abandoned through nonapprehension of the self and selfhood."

In the fifth *Kārikā* Nāgārjuna directly indicates the aim of the *Mādhyamika* dialectic when he writes, "There is liberation from the destruction of *karmic* afflictions which are but conceptualizations. These arise from mere conceptual play (*parapañca*) which is in turn banished in *śūnyatā*". Here, again, attention may be drawn to the existential character of *avidyā* or, in this case, thought construction (parapañca) in Buddhist philosophy. Candrakīrti writes in the commentary, "By putting an end to afflictions and deeds, birth is put an end to. Conditioned by the extinction of grasping, becoming does not occur. Having once extinguished becoming, how are birth, old age and death, etc., possible? Therefore there is liberation when afflictions and deeds are extinguished... Deeds and afflictions are only imaginary. This thought construction is extinguished in emptiness. Form, etc., are conceived of incorrectly by common people. Then attachment, etc., ensure. Attachment, aversion and delusion arise from conceptualization". Again the author of the commentary writes, "Knowledge and the object of knowledge, the expression and the expressed, agent and action, jug, cloth, crown, chariot, form, feeling, woman, man, profit, loss, happiness, pain, fame, notoriety, praise, blame, etc., these conceptions are beginningless and arise through conceptual play. Seeing all these phenomenal though constructions as in their own-being, emptiness, they are extinguished in *śūnyatā*. How? The net of imagination, which has been just described, results from relying upon things as supports... Not entering into the thought construction of an object, erroneous thought construction is not engaged in. Not entering into the net of imagination, by means of attachment to the self and selfhood, the heap of afflictions, the root of which is the view of real individuality, will not arise...In this way, the saint on the stage of the realization of *śūnyatā* does not apprehend altogether the aggregates, elements and sense spheres.....In this way, only *śūnyatā* is characterised by the extinction of all thought construction. Therefore, it is called *Nirvāṇa*".

It may be suggested that the sixth *Kārikā* of the chapter under consideration is central to an understanding of the treatment of the self in the *Mādhyamika* system. In the sixth *Kārikā* Nāgārjuna indicates the inapplicability of the concepts of self and not-self to the real. Also, as will be shown through Candrakīrti's commentary, *Mādhyamika* resolves the apparent contradictions which exist between the various utterances of the Buddha on the subject of the self, through the division of texts into expedient, or indirect (*neyārtha*), and final, or direct (*nītārtha*), testimony. Thus Nāgārjuna writes, "The Buddha has provisionally employed the term atman and instructed on the true idea of *anātman*. He has also taught that no abstract entity such as atman or *anātman* exists". Candrakīrti writes quoting from the *Dhamma*pada, "*The self is the lord of the self. Who will be the lord of another*? The wise man can obtain heaven through subduing himself. *The self is the lord of the self. Who will be the lord of* *another?* The self is the witness of good conduct and bad". It is quite likely that this quotation is representative of an argument employed in support of their doctrine, by either the *Vāstiputriyas* or the *Āryasamhitās*. The *Mādhyamika* replies, "Did not the Buddha also say this, 'Here there are no beings and no selves, but these elements are endowed with causes'. "Further, poses the question whether no contradiction exists between the divergent citations just adduced and answers in the negative. As he says, "Generally the Buddha in His speech made use of many distinctions like those of *neyārtha* and *nītārtha*". The author goes on to described the position of the *Cārvākas*. He says that some accept only the four elements, i.e. earth, water, fire and air. They maintain that just as the combination of boiled rice, water and yeast produces, after maturation, an intoxicating beverage, so in the womb the commingling of the paternal element with the maternal gives rise to consciousness. He writes, "Pre-existence, subsequent existence and liberation are denied...There is no effect which results from virtuous and non-virtuous actions performed. There is no Being, no miraculous birth, etc. Disparaging these, striving for the sublime fruits of heaven and liberation is relinquished and continuously doing only non-virtuous actions, one is always liable to fall into the great precipice of hell, etc. In this world sometimes the Buddha said, "The self exits", He employed the term self in order to remove these erroneous views, because he wished to rescue people from these great sins...The Buddha wished to benefit persons of inferior, moderate and superior ability. Wishing to free those of inferior ability who commit non-virtuous actions from sin, the Buddha employed the term atman to this kind worldly, but not absolutely. Thus he rightly refuted the doctrine of nihilism, *ahetuäda.*" Next the commentary treats of the employment of the concept of not-self. Thus Candrakīrti writes, "One who is bound loosely by the very strong rope of the view of the self (ātmadṛṣṭi), like a bound bird which can fly only for some way, who does virtuous actions and avoids non-virtuous actions, he too cannot escape from the three worlds. Though he traverses *Saṃsāra* he cannot enter the blissful city of liberation which is free from old age and death. To cause these disciples of moderate ability of loosen their attachment to the view of real individuality and to produce the thought of *Nirvāṇa*, the Buddha taught *anātman.* To those who have practiced in former lives, who have confidence in and understand the exalted and profound truth, whose seed has ripened and whose *Nirvāṇa* is very near, to these superior disciples who have relinquished affection for the self, and who are able to have confidence in and understand the most profound speech of the Lord of Sages, the Buddha taught that no entity, such as self or not self, exists. As the view of the self is not real, therefore the Buddha declared, 'There is neither any *ātman* nor any *anātman*'. Thus, says the *Ratnakotrum,* Oh Kashyapa, the atman is one extreme, *nairātmya* is another extreme. That which is the middle way, avoiding these two extremes, is formless, unperceivable, nonabiding, nonapprehendable, nondescriptive, uncontained, it is called, Oh Kasyapa, madhyamāpratipadā, the middle way. This is the truth of the elements of existence'. Or in the Ratnvali, "Neither *ātman* or *anātman* is demonstrated from the standpoint of absolute truth. The great *Muṇi* asked us not to hold views based on *ātman* and *anātman.* The Muni said that which is seen and heard is neither true nor false. There is a position, so there is a counter position (*pakṣa, pratipakṣha*). Neither of them is real". Thus, it is seen that the *Mādhyamika* explicitly denies the two alternatives of *ātman* and *anātman.* Neither can be predicated of the real which is transcendent to thought.

Nāgārjuna writes in the seventh *Kārikā,* "Where mind's functional realm ceases, the realm of words also ceases, for indeed the essence of existence (*dharmatā*) is like *Nirvāṇa,* without origination and destruction". It is clear that in this verse Nāgārjuna seeks to indicate the inapplicability of language to the absolute, a point which is elaborated in Candrakīrti's commentary. Thus he writes, "The nature of the elements of existence, unoriginated and undestroyed, is like *Nirvāṇa.* Therefore the mind is not existent. In the absence of thought activity, how will there be the ascription of signs? In the absence of this, how will there be expression? Hence Lord Buddha was correct in remaining silent.....Thought construction is extinguished in emptiness. Why is thought construction extinguished in emptiness, because the absolute is inexpressible.......Apprehending neither internal nor external things, individuality and self-identity, which are always within and without, are extinguished. This is the real. Why can the real not be expressed? Because it is devoid of any object of mind".

Again, in the eight, verse of the chapter Nāgārjuna writes, "Everything is suchness, both suchness and not suchness, and neither suchness nor not suchness. This is Buddha's teaching". In this verse Nāgārjuna introduces the Catuṣkoṭi for which the *Mādhyamika* is renowned. It is interesting that he should choose for the subject of dialectical analysis the concept of suchness (*tathatā*) which might so easily be taken as definitive of the absolute itself. The commentary says, "The nature of the elements of existence, unoriginated and undestroyed, is like *Nirvāṇa.* In the nature of the elements of existence there is the functional activity of neither speech nor mind. Yet people are unable to understand this without demonstration. That people may understand empirical truth is certainly made use of." Quoting from the Catuḥśataka, he writes, "Without worldly usage, one cannot approach the world." To illustrate this point Nāgārjuna himself wrote in the *Madhyamakaśāstra,* "Without relying upon empirical truth, the absolute, is not taught. Without arriving at the absolute, *Nirvāṇa* is not attained," Thus the *Mādhyamika* utilizes the two standpoints, that of the empiric and that of the absolute.

In the ninth *Kārikā* Nāgārjuna writes, "Unconditioned, quitescent, nonconceptualised by conceptual play, nondiscriminated, and nondifferentiated, these are the characteristics of reality." In his commentary Candrakīrti is careful to demonstrate that the predicates of the real, mentioned in the verse, are only provisional. Thus he writes, "The real is inexpressible, because it is devoid of an object of mind.....However, in accordance with conventional truth, empirical reality is accepted. Through false imputation, characteristic marks are spoken of ". With regard to the absolute, silence is the most appropriate language.

In the tenth *Kārikā* Nāgārjuna writes, "Any existence which is relational is indeed neither identical nor different from the related object. Therefore it is neither interruption nor constancy". Again, in this *Kārikā* the two alternative modes of interpreting related phenomena are indicated by the author. It is a central tenet with the *Mādhyamika* that any two entities which cannot be understood either in terms of identity or difference are neither of them established. Candrakīrti writes in the commentary. "Depending upon a seed, earth and other conditions, a rice sprout arises. It cannot be said that very seed is that very sprout. That seed is not that sprout because, through the 'reduction and absurdum', the producer and the produced will be identical. Similarly, the father and the son will also be identical. Again, if not different on the occasion of the sprout, the seed will also be seen. Along with the seed the sprout will also be grasped. If the nondestruction of the seed is admitted, it will then be permanent. In this way, the doctrine of eternalism (*śāśvatavāda*) is seen through the 'reductio and absurdum' to be greatly defective....Nor can it be said that they are different. The sprout is not absolutely different from the seed. If absolutely different, then, by the 'reductio and absurdum', the sprout would originate even apart from the seed." The preceding lines contain in brief the *Mādhyamika's* criticism of the doctrines of *satkāryavāda* and *asatkāryavāda*, pre-existent and nonexistent effect. The subject is treated, exhaustively by Nāgārjuna in the opening chapter of his *Prajñāmūla,* and is also frequently met within Nāgārjuna's other works, like the *Ratnāvali* and *Śūnyatāsaptati.* The relation between cause and effect, as has been shown, is unintelligible either in terms of identity or difference. The relation between cause and effect for Nāgārjuna is inexpressible. In the *Pratityasamutpādahṛdayakārikā* he illustrates it by means of examples like those of a lamp, a mirror, an echo, etc.

In the eleventh *Kārikā* Nāgārjuna writes, "Nonidentity, nondifferentiation, noninterruption and noncontinuity, these are the immortal teachings of the world's patron, Buddha". Candrakīrti writes in his commentary, "The disciples who understand this immortal and ultimate teaching, through the practice of the three heaps – morality, concentration and wisdom – will, without doubt, attain *Nirvāṇa* which is characterised by the extinction of old age and death".

In the concluding verse Nāgārjuna writes, where the accomplished the Buddhas do not appear and the *śrāvakas* cease to be, the enlightened mind of the *Pratyekabuddha* comes forth from the independent disengagement from the self." The verse, as Dr. Kenneth Inada indicates, suggests that all beings are potential *Pratyekabuddhas* capable of independently realizing the truth. As with respect to this verse, Candrakīrti's commentary is occupied principally with the refutation of rival Buddhist schools on point which have little direct bearing on the subject in hand, so it has not been quoted further.

In its treatment of the self the *Mādhyamika* exhibits its characteristic philosophic attitude. Nāgārjuna and Candrakīrti stress the nondescriptive nature of the real. They persistently demonstrate the inapplicability of empirical concepts to the absolute. Hence the *Mādhyamika* is rigorous in its rejection of the various formulations which pretend to represent an accurate characterization of the real.

In the preceding pages it has been seen that the *Mādhyamika* systematically rejects the doctrines of eternalism and nihilism, of pre-existent effect and non-existent effect, and of self and not-self. The self for the *Mādhyamika* cannot be predicated absolutely, because the absolute is transcendent to thought. As the self is never apprehended in its own-being, it is a phenomenal concept only, and thus its utility must necessarily be limited to the sphere of the relative. Alternatively, neither can the doctrine of not-self, which is but the corrective for the falsely imputed notion of a self, be predicated of the real. It too is a relative concept only.

Buddhism can be divided into two aspects. One has reference to the sphere of the relative and is characterised, in brief, by the Buddha as *ahiṃsā*, noninterference. The other conduces to liberation and is described by Āryadeva as *śūnyatā*. While the self doubtlessly exercises a legitimate function within the limits of the former, it is the principal impediment to the realization of the latter and, as such, its abandonment is essential.

---

* The *Kārikās* from the *Prajñāmūla*, excluding the ninth, used in this work are taken from Dr. Kenneth K. Inada's translation of the text. *Nāgārjuna, A Translation of his Mūlamādhyamakakārikā with an Introductory Essay*, The Ho kuseido Press, Tokyo, 1970, pp. 113-116.

30

ĀCĀRYA NĀGĀRJUNA AND HIS SUHṚLLEKHA

Jay Goldenberg

Ācārya Nāgārjuna holds an almost unequalled place among the ranks of those Buddhist saints who expounded the teaching of the Buddha Śākyamuni for the benefit of the world. As prophesied in the *Laṅkāvatāra Sūtra* the *Mañjuśrimūlakalpa Tantra,* as well as in several other discourses of the Buddha, Ācārya Nāgārjuna revolutionized the interpretation of the doctrine of the Enlightened one which was current at his time and lent it a vitality and dynamism which has continued to sustain it event to our day among the votaries of the *Mahāyāna.* The revolution which Ācārya Nāgārjuna accomplished within the fold of Buddhism was not, as some might think, a radical departure from the original doctrine of the Buddha Śākyamuni. On the contrary, the adherents of the *Madhyamīka* school are undoubtedly justified in asserting that their interpretation represents the true import of the doctrine of the Buddha and the essence of Buddhism. Although it is not our purpose here to substantiate this claim, it may simply be said that its truth has not escaped the notice of competent scholars in the field.

Given the majesty of Ācārya Nāgārjuna's name and the importance of the role which he played in the development of Buddhist thought, it is not surprising that the story of his life and achievements, as traditionally told, should partake of the fabulous and the legendary. In recounting the life of the Ācārya, his biographers have invariably included elements which, though undoubtedly facts of religious history, are difficult to establish in actuality.

Ācārya Nāgārjuna lived sometime during the last quarter of the first century C.E. This is evident from his acknowledged friendship with a king of the Satavahana line of Andhra. The king, Gautamiputra Śatakarni, son of queen, Bala Śhri, was the only one of his line to embrace Buddhism, and it was for him that Ācārya Nāgārjuna wrote the *Suhṛllekha* and *Ratnavali.* That the king in question reigned at about the time indicated is certain from the evidence of present archaeological discoveries[1]. The traditional biographers agree that the Ācārya was born in a brahmin family of south India. The Tibetan accounts state that at his birth, astrologers prophesied that the child would not live beyond the age of seven. Unable to beat the sight of his premature death, the accounts tell us, his parents sent the boy to a Buddhist monastery, where – by reciting the *Aparimitayu Dharani* – he succeeded in escaping his fate. The account given by Kumārajīva of Ācārya Nāgārjuna's early life differs substantially from that of the

Tibetan biographers. It is mentioned here only because it is presumably earlier than the latter, and so perhaps deserves consideration. Kumārajīva writes that in his youth Ācārya Nāgārjuna was overcome with lust and through the art of invisibility seduced women in the royal palaces. Once, however, he narrowly escaped death at the hands of the guards, an experience which led him to dwell upon the Buddha's teaching that desire is the foremost cause of suffering. As a result, according to Kumārajīva, the Ācārya entered the Buddhist order. Thereafter, the Tibetan accounts state, Nāgārjuna became a student of Rāhulabhadra[1] who was then abbot of the great university at Nalanda.

Virtually all the traditional biographers agree that Ācārya Nāgārjuna procured some *Prajñāpāramitā sūtras* from the Nāgas. Though some have suggested that this term may have been used to indicate a band of great yogis, the exact significance of the reference remains uncertain. Finally, Ācārya Nāgārjuna seems to have spent the latter part of his life at the monastery built for him by his friend and patron, king Gautamiputra at Shri Parvata. Although the accounts given of the manner of the Ācārya's death differ with regard to detail, they agree in that Nāgārjuna consented to his own death at the hands of the son of king Gautamiputra.

Ācārya Nāgārjuna was an accomplished master of Buddhist doctrine. He wrote voluminously on almost every aspect of Buddhist philosophy and religion. Although Ācārya Nāgārjuna has rightly won widespread acclaim as the foremost exponent of the 'middle', 'way', or *Madhyamapratipada,* and as a master of dialectic, his writings also include works on *Vinaya,* on *Tantra,* on the career of the *Bodhisattva,* and on the practice of the *Paramitāyāna.* Among the latter are counted his commentary on the *Daśabhūmikasūtra,* the *Sutrasamuccaya* and others. Ācārya Nāgārjuna also wrote works of a highly devotional character, such as the *Catuhstava.* It is lamentable that thus far so few of the writings of the Ācārya have been made available in English translation.

The *Suhṛllekha,* of Ācārya Nāgārjuna is a concise and comprehensive summary of Buddhist teaching. It can generally be said to belong to a class of texts which later came to be called, in Tibet, those of the graduated path or *lam. rim.* The works of Nāgārjuna, most especially the *Sūtrasamuccaya,* but also to a lesser degree the *Suhṛllekha,* were the forerunners of a multitude of texts which can be classed under the name *lam. rim.* They include such works as the *Shikshasamuccya* of Shāntideva, *The Jewel Ornament of liberation* of Sgam. po. pa and *The Clarification of the Thought of the Sage* of the Sākya Pandita Kunga Gyaltsen Pal Zangpo. It is not surprising that the concise style and comprehensive content of a work like Nāgārjuna's *Suhṛllekha* should have rendered it so popular as a vehicle for conveying in brief the teaching of Buddhism. That the *Suhṛllekha* enjoyed such popularity even in India is evident from the account of the Chinese pilgrim I-Tsing who visited India in the 7th century, for he writes, "In India students learn this epostle in verse early in the course of instruction, but the most devout make it their special object of study throughout their lives"[3]. Today, also, the *Suhṛllekha* enjoys widespread popularity among Tibetans who use it with regularity as a basic manual for teaching Buddhist *Dharma.* The comprehensive character of the work, though short, renders it highly suitable for use as an introduction to the whole of Buddhism. As it was written principally for laymen, addressed as it was to the Satavāhana king with whom Nāgārjuna shared a life long friendship, the teachings it encompasses can be appreciated by a wide spectrum of readers with varying interests. Though scholars and academicians seeking clarification of abstruce points of the doctrine of the Mādhyamikas may find little to satisfy them in the *Suhṛllekha,* those who desire a concise and comprehensive manual of instruction in the doctrine and practice of Buddhist philosophy and religion will surely not be disappointed.

Though the *Suhṛllekha* contains elements which belong specifically to the *Mahāyāna,* much of its content comprises a common foundation which both the *Hīnayāna* and *Mahāyāna* share. The letter commences with an invocation to cultivate faith in that which is pre-eminent and exalted, such as the Buddha, *Dharma* and *Sangha.* As Nāgārjuna says in the fourth verse, "You should bring to mind the six things of remembrance: the Enlightened One, His Teaching, the Noble Assembly, giving, morality and gods; the heap of qualities of each of these six recollections was well-taught by the Conqueror". There follows a lengthy summary of ethical and religious precepts which, if adhered to, result in birth in the fortunate realms of men and gods, as Ācārya Nāgārjuna writes, "....morality is said to be the foundation of all virtues, just as the earth is (the support of both) animate and inanimate things". Again, in the fifteenth verse it states, "Since there is no Penance like patience, you must give anger no opportunity to arise. The Buddha said that by giving up anger, one will attain the irreversible stage", and in the twenty-second verse, "Protect the unsteady mind just as (you would protect) learning, a son, a treasure, or life; withdraw the mind from sensual pleasures just as (you would withdraw yourself) from a vicious (snake), poison, a weapon, an enemy or fire". The injunctions and prohibition set forth in the text are accompanied by practices which are to be employed to counteract non-virtuous propensities. As Ārya Nāgārjuna says in the fortieth verse, "Always meditate rightly on love, compassion, joy and equanimity....". Again, in the thirty-fourth verse it states, "The Preceptors of gods and men said that satisfaction is the most excellent among all riches, so always be satisfied; if content though possessing no wealth, one is truly rich", and in the thirty-eight verse, "Understand food to be like medicine, neither use it with hatred, nor attachment, nor might, pride or beauty, but solely for maintaining the body", of equal importance is the portion of the text designed to remove erroneous views produced from ignorance, for morality practiced in ignorance does not result in liberation. Thus Arya Nāgārjuna says in the twenty-eighth verse, "The person possessing high caste, beautiful form and learning is no respected if he lacks wisdom and morality; however, one who possesses these two qualities, even though lacking the other qualities, is worshipped". However, through the combination of morality and wisdom, the understanding of emptiness, liberation is attained. This emptiness, the Ultimate Truth, is revealed through erroneous views. Therefore, Ācārya Nāgārjuna says in the twenty-seventh verse, "Be skilled in rightly perceiving things with the understanding of the Ultimate (Truth), for there is no other practice possessing comparable quality". Again, in the fiftieth verse it states, "Know that the aggregates originated neither from chance, time, Nature, intrinsic character, God, nor without cause, but ignorant deeds and craving", and in the forty-ninth verse. "Thus it has been said, 'The form is not the self, the self does not possess the form, the self does not dwell in the form, and the form does not dwell in the self', in this manner also understand the four remaining aggregates as empty".

Death, impermanence and opportune conditions form the subject matter for the subsequent verses of the text. Since life is transient like a bubble of water caught by the wind, Nāgārjuna exhorts the reader, who has obtained the opportune conditions which are prerequisites for the practice of *Dharma*, to strive for liberation without delay. Thus the Ācārya says in the fifty-nine verse, "O lord of men, make this (human life) fruitful by practicing the Holy *Dharma*, for it is more difficult to obtain a human birth from animal states than for a tortoise to place (its neck) in the aperature of a wooden yoke which are in the same ocean". Again, in the sixtieth verse it states, "Having obtained a human birth, one who commits sins is more foolish than one who fills a jewel adorned golden vessel with vomit", and in the sixty-third and sixty-fourth verses, "Whoever is born as a heretic, animal, hungry ghost, hell being, barbarian, fool, long-lived deity, or where there is no teaching from a Buddha is declared to be born in the eight faulty and unfavorable (states). Having gotten the opportunity to be free from them, then strive to put an end to birth". If this human birth is not properly utilized, then one will continue to experience the sufferings of the six realms of *Saṃsāra* which are then described by Nāgārjuna. Such descriptions are commonly met within texts of this kind. They are designed to produce a revulsion for worldly existence and a desire for liberation. The reader meeting with these descriptions for the first time should be warned against dismissing them as fanciful imagination, for they perform a vitally important function in the process of liberation. Since the highest goal of freedom and enlightenment cannot be achieved unless and until attachment to the world is relinquished, the detailed descriptions of the manifold sufferings experienced are necessary in order to produce that renunciation which is essential to tread the path to liberation. It should be remembered that the 'truth of suffering' is the first of the Four Noble Truths and the very cornerstone of the Buddhist religion. Therefore, in order to show the suffering of Saṃsāra as a whole, and man's suffering in particular, Nāgārjuna's says in the sixty-fifth verse, "Grieve over *Saṃsāra* which is the source of manifold sufferings, such as destitution of what is desired, death, disease, old age, etc., and also listen to some of its faults". To illustrate the uncertain of *Saṃsāra*, it is stated in the sixty-ninth verse, "Having become Indra, deserving the reverence (of) the world, (one) will again fall to the earth on account of the force of (previous) deeds; even having become an universal monarch, (one) will become a servant of a servant in *Saṃsāra*". As an example of the suffering experienced in the seventy-eighth verse says, "There some are pressed like sesamum; similarly, others are ground into fine powder; some are cut by saws; likewise, others are split by the very sharp blades of terrible". To show the suffering of animals, Nāgārjuna writes in the ninetieth verse, "Some are killed for pearls, wool, bones, meat, or skin; while others, powerless, are employed by kicking, striking, whipping, or prodding with iron hooks. In verse ninty-five, we see an example of the suffering of the hungry ghosts, "For them even the moon is hot in the summertime, while even the sun is cold in the winter; tree become fruitless and rivers dry up if only looked upon by them". Concerning the gods, in the ninty-eighth verse it is said, "Also, (as a result) of the great pleasures in the heavens, the suffering of death and transmigration is greater; having contemplated thus, nobles should not crave for heaven which will come to an end". Finally, Nāgārjuna says of the suffering found in the realm of the demigods or *Asuras*, "Also among the demigods, there is great mental suffering because of natural hostility toward the splendor of the gods; though they are also intelligent, the truth is not seen due to the veil of (their) *Karma*".

Ācārya Nāgārjuna's letter concludes with a description of the path and the unequalled result to be gained through its practice. Morality, concentration and the wisdom arising from the understanding of the precious doctrine of Interdependent Origination comprise the path resulting in the exalted state of a *Bodhisattva* or Buddha. Thus, concerning the path to liberation Nāgārjuna writes in the one hundred and sixth verse, "These seven limbs of enlightenment – mindfulness, discrimination of things (*dharmas*), energy, joy, purification, trance and evenmindness – are the accumulation of virtue which is the cause of obtaining *Nirvaṇa*". Again, in the one hundred and twelfth verse it is stated, "This (doctrine of) Interdependent Origination is the profound and precious treasure of the teaching of the Conqueror; one who rightly sees this (Interdependent Origination) sees the most excellent Buddha, the Knower of Reality", and in verses one hundred and fourteen and fifteen the Four Noble Truths are stated thus, "This birth is suffering; craving is called the great source of that (suffering); its cessation is liberation; and the path to attain that (liberation) is the Noble Eightfold Path. So in this way, always try to realize the Four Noble Truths, for even laymen dwelling the lap of prosperity cross the river of the defilements by this knowledge". Concerning the exalted result of *Bodhisattvahood* or *Buddhahood*, verses one hundred and twenty and one hundred and twenty-one state, "Born (like) Arya Avalokitesvara aidding through (his) conduct many stricken people and dispelling disease, old age, attachment and hatred, dwell for limitless lifetimes like the Protector of the World, the Blessed One Amitābha in His Buddhafield". Then, Ārya Nāgārjuna concludes the *Suhṛllekha* with the following two verse, "Having spread to the gods' realms, the sky and on the earth (your) great unblemished fame arising from wisdom, morality and giving, having surely subdued the delight of gods in heaven and men on earth in the enjoyment of excellent maidens, and having gained the Lordship of the Conquerors extinguishing the arising of fear and death for multitudes of living beings afflicted by the defilements, attain the faultless, ageless, fearless state (which is) peaceful, only nominal and transcendent".

Hence, as was said before, Ācārya Nāgārjuna's *Suhṛllekha* provides the aspirant who wishes to be acquainted with the essentials of the Buddhist path to liberation with a comprehensive summary of the principles of the Buddhist religion. The foundation of correct moral conduct and right understanding of the truth free from the obscurations of ignorance results in a transcendent model of being in which not only is freedom from bondage and ignorance achieved, but also the capacity to nurture and mature all living beings that they may also attain enlightenment.

Endnotes

1. See *Nagarjuna's philosophy* by K.V. Ramanan, Bharatiya Vidya Prakashan, Varanasi, India, 1971, p. 25.
2. Rahulabhadra is also known as the Mahasiddha Saraha.
3. *A Record of the Buddhist Religion as Practised in India and the Malay Archipelago (A.D. 671-695)* by I-Tsing, translated by J. Takakusu, pub. Munshiram Manoharlal, Delhi, India, 1966, p. 162.

31

THE CHINESE PILGRIMS ON THE INDIAN BUDDHIST MONASTIC EDUCATION

Sanghasen Singh

The studies in the motivation of the Indian Buddhist missionaries and the Chinese Buddhist Pilgrims may provide us a clue to understand the social and political conditions obtained in India and China in those days. Why was this exchange of travelers from one country to the other? What were the social forces which were instrumental in paving the way for such hazardous travels? The Buddhist missionaries and pilgrims had to overcome innumerable obstacles before reaching their destination. As their accounts go, they had to cross rivers, valleys, mountains and so on, while encountering with all sorts of beasts and hostile tribal people. Why and what for all those troubles?

The biographical notes found here and there in the account of the Indian Buddhist missionaries and the Chinese Buddhist pilgrims show that both countries were coming closer to each other in the early centuries of the Christian era and the most important blinding force was the developing trade relation between the countries. The Buddhist saints there, knowingly or unknowingly, paving the way for a very smooth can cordial transaction between the two great people.

However, after the establishment of the *Saṅgha* or the Buddhist Order in China, there arose problems in the Buddhist fraternity there. By that time, Buddhism was divided into various schools and sects in its homeland. It reflected very clearly on the *Saṅgha* of China as well. Beginning with Fa-hsien, we find him very much obsessed with the task of collecting texts of *Vinaya* in India, which could help them in understanding and resolving *Vinayic* questions and problems which used to crop up off and on. Yuan Chwang, on the other hand, was more interested in the studies of the philosophical tenets of the schools and sects of Buddhism. I-tsing, the last of the great Chinese pilgrims, had, more or less, similar objectives as those of the general monastic education of the Buddhist monks and nuns, with particular reference to the *Vinaya* as a whole.

Fa-hsien visited India from A.D. 399 to 414. He left behind a vivid description of the functioning of the monasteries in various parts of India. After visiting Bhid in Punjab, he proceeded downwards in the south-east direction along the river Yamunā and reached Mathurā, one of the most important and prosperous Buddhist centre in those days. According to his account, the religion was flourishing there. He observed that there were as many as twenty monasteries on both the banks of the Yamunā with about three thousand monks residing there. Several Kings, traders and bankers not only built many monasteries there, but also endowed them with land grants for their maintenance. As Fa-hsien was mainly a student of *Vinaya*, his observations about the religious practices seem to be more authentic. One of the characteristic features of the monasteries there, was that they had been occupied by such monks who would recite *sūtras* in the monasteries, sit in meditation and perform other pious deeds. The original *Vinaya* rules regarding incoming monks were very promptly observed. Due courtesies were shown to them and everything possible was done to make their stay comfortable. Another important feature of the monastic culture there was the practice of erection of *stūpas* not only in memory of Sāriputra, Moggallāna and *Ānanda*, but in honour of many more reciters of *Sūtra, Vinaya* and *Abhidharma*. According to this account, the practice of *Varṣāvāsa* or rain-retreat was still in vogue, more or less, in the same fashion.

By the time of Fa-hsien, we notice a very significant development in the life of the Order. The monks and nuns, it seems, had developed their own intellectual groups on the basis of their intellectual affiliations with the life and teachings of the famous disciples of the Buddha. This point is clear by the fact that a set of particular monks and nuns would worship the *stūpas* of particular teachers only. Fa-hsien very clearly mentions that the nuns would worship the *stūpa* of *Ānanda*, novices that of Rāhula, students of *Abhidharma* and *Vinaya* those of the teachers of *Abhidharma* and *Vinaya* respectively. The group of *Mahāyānists* would worship *Prajñāpāramitā*, *Mañjuśrī* and *Avalokiteśvara*. The fascination for their earliest specialists in their own field, the espousers of their own cause or ideal in the pursuit of monastic life is traceable in its rudimentary form in the early life of the Order, but the clear-cut intellectual division on the basis of their likings and dislikings was a new development in the Order. This practice was witnessed by Yuan Chwang as well, who visited India nearly two centuries after Fa-hsien. N. Dutta goes a step further by enumerating this practice to be one of the causes of growth of sects in Buddhism.[1]

During the period when Fa-hsien visited India, Pāṭaliputra occupied prominent position in the sphere of monastic education and learning. He mentions two grand monasteries there, one belonging to *Mahāyāna* and the other to *Hīnayāna*. The total number of monks residing in those monasteries were nearly six or seven hundred. One noteworthy point with regard to the monasteries of Pāṭaliputra was that they attracted both the full-fledged monks and the unordained and untrained novices. Secondly, they came to these monasteries from far and wide. Although the Pāṭaliputra monasteries had already become reputed as great centres of advanced studies, yet the Buddhist leaders had not lost sight of the interests of the younger elements in the Order, who, in course of time, had to take up the leadership of those monasteries. This could come about only because of the association of the far-framed and far-sighted teachers of the highest order. This fact can be testified by the following statement of Fa-hsien. "The rules of demeanour and the scholastic arrangements in them are worthy of observation. *Śramaṇas* of highest virtue from all quarters and student inquirers wishing to find out truth and the grounds of it, all resort to these monasteries."[2]

Fa-hsien was a keen observer and, as mentioned above, was very much particular to notice if the *Vinayic* rules were fully observed. Wherever he went, this point had been uppermost in his mind. His observations about the three monasteries at Gayā are on these lines. He showered praises on the efficiency of these centres of studies in the following words, "The disciplinary rules are strictly observed by them. The laws regulating their demeanour in sitting, rising, and entering when the others are assembled, are those which have been practiced by all the saints since the Buddha was in the world down to the present day."[3] Thus, according to him, the *Vinaya* rules were strictly observed there. The resident-monks of these monasteries were equally concerned with the studies and meditation. The fact is evident from his further observation. "The regular business of the monks is to perform acts of meritorious virtue, to recite their *Sūtras,* and to sit wrapt in meditation."[4]

From the observations of Fa-hsien, it appears, the mode of instruction in respect of *Vinaya* in most of the monasteries in India had been oral. There had been dearth of written material. He found teachers in various parts of India, more particularly in the northern India, instructing *Vinaya* rules by oral transmission only. Fa-hsien was, in fact, greatly disappointed in this respect. Before reaching India, he had expected that he would be able to get vast material on *Vinaya* to copy and transcribe,[5] but to his utter disappointment he could find nowhere except in two places, i.e. in the Mahāyāna monastery at Pāṭaliputra and in the monasteries at Tāmralipti. There would have been two reasons behind his phenomenon. Either the study of *Vinaya* was not given that much importance as that of the *Sūtras* and the *Abhidharma,* or the tradition to study *Vinaya* with the aid of written literature had developed only in the eastern part of the country and not in the north and north-west. It seems, the practice of meeting together in the common room or hall of the monastery for the purposes of religious discourses and discussions had continued upto the time of Fa-hsien. He mentions, "All the monks come together in a great assembly and preach the law."[6] Their meetings, it is presumed, would have been mostly for carrying out the *Vinayic* rules, the *uposatha* being the most important among them.

The next famous Chinese monk-scholar who visited India was Yuan Chwang (Hsuan-tsang of the English historians). He had been here during a period from A.D. 629 to 645. His evidences are very valuable to us in the sense that he left us with a vast record of the systems of education which was prevalent in those days in the monasteries of India.

Although Fa-hsien too had mentioned that the monasteries in India were divided clearly on the lines of the sects, but Yuan Chwang's descriptions draw much more sharper lines of distinction among them. Even the curricula of studies in the monasteries used to be drawn on the basis of the tenets of the sect they belonged to. Yuan Chwang mentions as many as eighteen sects of Buddhism under the grand division of *Hīnayāna* and *Mahāyāna*. According to him, the monks and monasteries were very clearly divided on the basis of these sects or the schools of thought which developed on the teachings of the individual sects. In the field of the *Vinaya*, the course of studies comprised the five redactions of the *Vinaya* of *Hīnayāna* school under the names of *Dharma*gupta, Mahīśāsaka, Kāśyapīya, *Sarvāstivāda* and Mahāsanghika.[7]

Another very notable feature of the monastic education at the time of Yuan Chwang was the fact that the studies of the monks in the monasteries included even such subjects which did not fall within the limits of Buddhist religious life. According to the traveler, a monk in the monastery of Laghman had produced a work on magical invocations,[8] while at the same time, some monks in the monasteries of Udyana had distinguished themselves as 'experts in magical extorcisms'. The observations of the great Chinese traveler raise some very fundamental questions. Did Buddhism deteriorate to such an extent in nearly two centuries after the visit of Fa-hsien, or were there existent such trends in the monastic Order at the time of Fa-hsien as well, which he did not clearly mention and discuss as he was a *Vinaya* expert and the highlighting of *Vinayic* purity was his main concern. He did not want to condition the minds of his Chinese readers and thereby hasten the process of deterioration there too. Yuan Chwang, on the other hand, being more forthright, described the weakness of his own religion in so many words.

During the time of the visit of Yuan Chwang in India, it appears comparatively more stress was laid on developing power of debate and exposition. A graduated course was described for the learner to prepare himself to give a performance of his oration in public meetings, possibly in the presence of a galaxy of learned scholars of the time. Yuan Chwang makes a mention of certain tests which used to be held, most probably under the patronage of the rulers of those days. This fact is evident from the following statement, "The Brethren are often assembled for discussion to test intellectual capacity to reject the worthless and to advance the intelligent. Those who bring forward (or, according to some texts, estimate aright) fine points in philosophy, and give subtle principles their proper place, who are ornate in diction and accurate in refined distinctions, ride richly caparisoned elephants preceded and followed by a host of attendants. But as for those to whom religious teaching has been offered in vain, who have been defeated in discussion, who are deficient in doctrine and redundant in speech, perverting the sense while keeping the language, the faces of such are promptly daubed with red and white clay, their bodies are covered with dirt and they are driven out to the wilds or thrown into the ditches".[9]

Here, it seems, the traveler resorts to a high degree of exaggeration in order to show the importance of such tests and examinations. Besides this, there used to be conducted internal tests as well. This, normally, used to be for the purpose of assigning hierarchy among the inmates of the monastery or the members of one community of monks. This had been an innovation in the functioning of the Order. The traditional method of assigning hierarchy seems to have been replaced by this type of intensive tests where the power of the exposition of the philosophical thoughts used to be the only criterion. It means that by this time the age-old *Vinaya* practices had ceased to be as important as learning, if not more. The superiority of the latter had been proved to be unavoidable. This fact is testified by the following comments of the traveler, "The Brother who expounds orally one treatise (or class of scripture in the Buddhist canon), whether *Vinaya, Abhidharma,* or *Sūtra,* is exempted from serving under the Prior; he who expounds two is invested with the outfit of a Superior; he who expounds three has Brethren deputed to assist him; he who expounds four has lay servants assigned to him; he who expounds five rides an elephant; he who expounds six rides and has surrounding retinue."[10] This state of affairs in monastic education might have been either due to further development in the Order during the two centuries which elapsed since Fa-hsien left India, or due to their own biases – one emphasizing upon the *Vinaya* and the other on the philosophical thoughts.

The traveler has given in his account an approximate number of the famous monasteries, nearly five thousand or so. It shows the extent to which emphasis was laid on higher education and training in the monastic life. As regards the location and general surroundings of the monastic establishments, one important feature is noticeable. A great many famous monasteries sprang up and developed in the vicinity of one another in the same locality. The monasteries of Nālandā and Tilośikā, for instance, were situated at a distance of only twenty miles from each other. Thus, according to the account of the traveler. Magadha occupied the highest position as regards extensive and intensive spread of monastic education.

The third famous Chinese traveler was I-tsing, who happened to visit India in A.D. 672, very closely after Yuan Chwang who left for his homeland in A.D. 645. His mission to visit India, it seems, was, more or less, based upon similar objectives as those of Fa-hsien. He really supplemented the account of Yuan Chwang who failed to reflect all aspects of Buddhism. To mention a few, Yuan Chwang could not draw a picture of Vinayic practices, divergences in the code of conduct of various sects, etc.

The emphasis of elementary and general education was, more or less, the same as that during the period when Yuan Chwang visited India. I-tsing mentions the study of five Vidyās as the pre-requisite before entering the realm of higher education. The higher learning, according to him, amounted to specialization in one or the other branches of knowledge.

A new feature in the monastic education is noticeable at the time of I-tsing. The emphasis on the study of the Science of Grammar was very great. There used to be advanced and specialized course in this field, which was rightly considered to be a part of secular education. Those who succeeded in completing such courses were designated as *Bahuśruta'* (one who learns much by way of hearing or one who knows much of Śruti). It is also worth noting that both monks and laymen were welcome to such courses. The association of laymen in higher monastic education shows a new trend which had developed by this time in the life of the Order[11]. Besides the Grammatical Science, the monasteries provided specialization in *Vinaya* and philosophical studies. Two monasteries which were extraordinarily famous for higher learning in this respect were, Nālandā in central India and Valabhī in western India.[12]

It seems, by the time of I-tsing, the shape of monastic education had changed considerably. Besides provision for religious studies, as mentioned above, there used to be secular section attached to these monasteries, where even the lay people were admitted for education, and training. The students admitted to this section were designated as Brahmacārīs who obviously had not renounced the world for the time being. It seems to be the first historical evidence in the life of the Buddhist Order, which testifies the admission of laymen in the premises of the monasteries in a systematic way. The lay people on their part, made full use of this provision. They used to be entrusted to the monks and got regular instructions from them.[13] It means that the resident-monks, in fact, had to master religious as well as secular subjects in order to be able to instruct the two set of students attached to them. Proficiency in both, was a must for them to be really called *Bahuśruta.*

I-tsing has further mentioned a very startling fact about the monastic education of his time. The monks participated in the intellectual contests held at the kings' 'House of Debate' for the sake of proving their talents in practical administration. After having met success there, they even entered the services of the kings. Had a convention developed in those days that after their education even the monks had the choice to adopt any sort of occupation?[14] Was such course open to them? How is it that such an important fact does not find mention in the accounts of Yuan Chwang who visited India just only two and a half decade before? There can be two explanations to this tricky question. Either that I-tsing account reflects his own imaginations based upon the type of administrative examinations open to all in China without any sort of distinction, or that the earlier travelers were extraordinarily cautious in drawing the picture of monastic life in such a way that no fact could even indirectly reflect upon the character of monks in a derisive manner and thereby tarnish their images in any way. I-tsing mentions yet another section of students who were unordained. They got admission in the monasteries and studied Buddhist scriptures under the guidance of the resident-monks. They were designated as Māṇavas who had the potentially of becoming monks in course of time.[15] This new institution of admitting laymen into the monasteries served two immediate purposes. On the first instance, their services were utilized by the monasteries as pages under monks and secondly, their aspirations were sometimes aroused to such an extent that they renounced the world and became monks. This fact is further substantiated by the evidences available in the Sphuṭārthā Śrīghanācārasaṅgraham-ṭīkā. The text under reference was composed probably in the sixth or seventh centuries A.D. According to the author of this text, the practice was fully in vogue at that time.[16]

This secular section, although sharing roof of the monasteries with the acclesiastical ones, did not enjoy free feeding and other privileges. They had to provide their own boarding expenses or they to compensate it with some sort manual work for the monasteries.

This secular section, although sharing roof of the monasteries with the acclesiastical ones, did not enjoy free feeding and other privileges. They had to provide their own boarding expenses or they had to compensate it with some sort of manual work for the monasteries. Sometimes these monasteries accepted special grants for feeding the unordained section. The details of this secular section of the monastic life leads us to a very important question of explaining the possibility of the social factors which were influencing the course of events in those days. It is very clear that by the emergence of *Mahāyāna* Buddhism, the early emphasis on ascetic life gradually subsided and gave place to the concept of Gṛhī *Bodhisattvas.* It seems, the lay people asserted their right to have equality in the matter of pursuit of spiritual life. The impact of and rivalry with Brahmanism and many more religious orders, led the Buddhist leaders to revise the basic tenets of their religion, and thereby change the rules of the monastic life. But at the same time, it does not mean that the lay devotees could acquire complete equality with the monks. After all monkhood had become vested interest for those whom it served and suited. This fact is very clear by the simple hands of the monks and the actual leadership of the Order was provided with from amongst those who were ordained and none else. In the field of scholarship as well, those who gained eminence, were invariably the monks themselves who had the leisure to study as they had renounced the world and stayed in monastic establishments.

The account of I-tsing speaks, more or less, on the same lines about the importance of the power of debate and exposition. The great monk-scholars spent years together to develop this art and thereby attained the honour of their times, because of the simple fact that they would, "oppose the heretics as they would drive away beasts (deer) in the middle of the plain and explain away disputations as boiling water melts frost." The successful debaters and disputants received glorious tributes from people all over 'Jambudvīpa'. They attained rare fame. In this respect, I-tsing's list of great monk-scholars is very much significant. He names only a few who flourished and rose to the top in different eras. "Such were Nāgārjuna, Deva, Aśvaghoṣa of an early age; Vasubandhu, Asaṅga, *Saṅgha*bhadra, Bhāvaviveka in the middle ages; and Jina, *Dharma*pāla, Dharmakīrti, Śīlabhadra, Siṁhacandra, Sthiramati, Guṇamati, Prajñāgupta, Guṇaprabha, Jinaprabha of later years." Besides this, I-tsing has supplied us with another list of rare monk-scholars who attained distinction not only in 'Jambudvipa' but also in China, the beloved land of the Chinese travelers. They were Kāśyapa-mātaṅga, *Dharma*rakṣa (who were the first Indian Buddhist monk-scholars to visit China in as early as A.D. 67), Kumārajiva (who reached China in about A.D. 401 and translated fifty Sanskrit texts into Chinese) and Paramārtha (who visited China in A.D. 548 and translated as many as thirty-one works).

This intellectual interaction between India and China was, in fact, the culmination of the excellence of monastic education and culture of these two great countries of the world. Of course, the prime-mover had been the social forces, as mentioned above. Under this process, innumerable monk-scholars had been attracted to the task of dissemination of knowledge to the people living in places far and wide. They thereby enriched the cultures of both the countries and the people. The copious accounts of the Chinese monk-travellers and scholars reflect this point to a very large extent.

Endnotes

1. Cf. N. Dutta, Development of Buddhism in Uttar Pradesh, p. 311.
2. Cf. J. Legge, A Record of the Buddhist Kingdoms, (1886), p. 9.
3. Cf. Ibid. p. 89-90.

4. Cf. Ibid, p. 44.
5. Cf. Ibid, p. 98.
6. Cf. Ibid, p. 45.
7. Cf. Thomas Watters, On Yuan Chwang's Travels in India, Vol. I, p. 226.
8. Cf. Ibid, p. 182.
9. Cf. Ibid, p. 162.
10. Cf. Ibid.
11. Cf. Takakusu, A Record of the Buddhist Religion By I-tsing, p. 169.
12. Cf. Ibid, p. 180.
13. Cf. Ibid, 177.
14. Cf. Ibid, p. 106.
15. Cf. Ibid, p. 178.
16. Cf. Ibid, p. 105.

32

AN APPRAISAL OF "THE NEGATIVE DIALECTICSS : A STUDY OF THE NEGATIVE DIALECTICISM IN INDIAN PHILOSOPHY BY DHIRENDRA SHARMA."

V. K. Bharadwaja

Consider the judgement 'It is raining'. If it describes the fact that it is raining, it is said to be true; otherwise it is false. Consider now another judgement 'It is not raining'. Apparently, it describes what is not the case; and it is said to be true when it does this, otherwise it is false. The puzzling question is: How can a negative judgement describe what is not the case? Or, how can we assert that a negative judgement is true when it describes something which is not the something (even when that something is not the case), then it is really not a negative judgement; and if it describes nothing, then a negative judgement really is not a judgement at all. It is the assumption of the paradox that a judgement *qua* judgement must be descriptive of reality.

Dr. Sharma's book is a study of the *Nyāya-Vaiśesika*, the *Mīmāṁsaka*, and the Buddhist attempts to solve this paradox. The method employed is dialectical in the sense of critical examination. It is partly for this reason and partly for the reason that the author desires to show that the principle of *ahiṃsā* is based on the dialectics of negation that he calls his book "*The Negative Dialectics*". I make this observation only to caution the reader against its misleading title. It is misleading at least to my mind. I wish I am wholly mistaken in this impression. But when I mentioned about this book to a friend of mine, he was at once reminded of the post Marxian German social scientist, T.W. Adorno's book *Negative Dialectics.* It is noteworthy that the book is dedicated to "The Questioning Youth of the United States of America who were imprisoned for their opposition to the United States' aggressions in Vietnam, Laos, and Cambodia. It is they who have reaffirmed my faith the future of mankind".

During the past one decade (covering the period from 1965 to 1975) I have come across three published studies on the logic of negation. First is Janki Ballabha Bhattacharyya's *Negation* (Calcutta, 1965): Second, *The Navya-Doctrine of Negation*: The Semantics and Ontology of Negative Statement in *Navya-Nyāya* philosophy by Bimal Krishna Matilal (Cambridge, Massachussetts 1968) and third is the study under review. The last two are the best of the three. Matilal's is analytical and confined to the *Navya-Nyāya*; while Dr. Sharma's is mainly historical and dialectical, and it covers a much wider field than does Matilal's book, by including a discussion of the *Mīmāṃsā* and the Buddhist views on negation. Janki Ballabha Bhattacharyy's study is much older than the year of its publication suggests. To my mind, its focus is not very clear, though it covers almost the whole of Indian philosophy so far as the notion of negation is concerned. I wish very much that the author had sufficiently revised his manuscript (it was like the other two a doctoral dissertation) before sending it to the press.

Dr. Sharma's book consists of six chapters to which are added an excellent bibliography, a two-page glossary of Sanskrit terms, and indices of proper names and Sanskrit terms and expression. The first chapter is introductory and provides a historical background of the realist ontology of negative dialectics. The second chapter is devoted to a discussion of the "Logical meaning of negation." The phrase "Logical meaning" is not clear; but what he does in this chapter is a detailed discussion of the *Anupalabdhi Pramāṇa* of the later *Mīmāṁsakas* and the post-Dharmakīrti Buddhist thesis that the negative judgement really is an inferential judgement. In the third chapter the author analyzes the various kinds of negations following the *Nyāya-Vaiśesika* tradition. Also, it is here that he introduces the idea of interpreting the Law of double negation as "the dialectical basis for the renowned Indian doctrine of *ahiṃsā*" (pp. 59-60). The fourth chapter, in the reviewer's opinion is by far the most important in the book. It is devoted to an illuminating discussion on the epistemology of negation. The author takes into account the *Navya-Nyāya* view that the negative judgement is essentially a perceptual judgement and also the controversial distinction between Kumārila Bhaṭṭa's notion of the *abhāva pramāṇa* and the different notions of *anupalabdhi* held by the Buddhists and the *Prabhākara Mīmāmsakas* (p. 88-92). The fifth chapter includes the Buddhist theory of *apoha*; and the last chapter is devoted to a detailed statement of the author's conclusions.

I said above that this book is a study of the *Nyāya-Vaiśesika* the *Mīmāmsaka*, and the Buddhist attempts to solve the problems concerning the paradox of the negative judgement. According to the author, the early *Nyāya-Vaiśesika* philosophers, Gautama, Kaṇāda, and Praśastapāda, postulated the whole world of negative facts in order to account for the descriptivity and truth of negative judgments. They in their writings implied the acceptance of *abhāva*. For, "apart from the problem of negative judgement, postulation of the negative reality was necessary for their doctrines of Emancipation and Causality" (p. 117). It was this need that "led them to elevate *abhāva* to the status of a category or an entity" (p. 6). *Apavarga* or *niḥśreyas* is negation of pain which in turn is the negation of happiness. Thus, the ultimate value is described in terms of negation. Similarly, notion of *kārya* is defined in terms fo *prāgabhavā*. Accepting *kārya* as *prāgabhavā* and not recognizing the notion of *abhāva* would have been inconsistent. Again, if negation were not real, how could *apavarga* or *niḥśreyasa* be described negatively? To avoid both these difficulties they accepted *abhāva* explicitly in the later *Nyāya-Vaiśesika* literature. But, as the author shows, it is wrong to say that the early *Nyāya-Vaiśesika* did not regard *abhāva* as *padārtha*: only they did not do this in so many words.

From the fact that *abhāva* is a *padārtha*, it follows that it is a *prameya* (knowable). It is in this sense that *abhāva* is one of the seven *padārtha*s accepted by the post-*Uddyottakara Nyāya-Vaiśesika* logicians. Once we regard *abhāva* as a *prameya*, we may ask the question: How do we know it? To this question, we have two different types of answers. The *first* is given by the *Navya-Nyāya* philosophers. On their view, *abhāva* is known perceptuily. We know, for instance, that the book is not on the table by the same *pramāṇa* (here *pratyakṣa pramāṇa*) as we know that the book is on the table. No additional *pramāṇa* is needed; nor is any inference involved in such a perception. The *second* type of answer comes from the later Buddhists like Dharmakīrti. For them the fact there is no book on the table is known inferentially and not perceptually, however complex that perception might be. It is only on the basis of not seeing the book on the table that we infer the judgement 'The book is not on the table'. The pattern of inference is as follows:

(1) The standard conditions of the perceptibility of *x* in a place *y* at a time *z* are satisfied.

(2) But, what we are perceiving in *y* at *z* is the *bare* surface of *y*.

(3) If *x* were there in *y* at *z*, it would have been perceptible. It follows that (4) there is no *x* in *y* at *z*.

In this argument (1) to (3) constitute *niṣedha hetu* (evidence or reason) for asserting the inferendum, namely, the *abhāva* of *x* in *y* at *z*. Dharmakīrti includes this analysis of negative judgement under *anumāna* (inference); while the *Prabhākara Mīmāmsakas* regard the cognition of *abhāva* as a matter of *anupalabdhi*, not of *pratyakṣa* as the *Navya-Nyāya* philosophers hold, or a matter of *pramāṇābhāva*, as the Bhāṭṭa *Mīmāmsakas* do. Dr. Sharma takes pain to differentiate the notion of *pramāṇābhāva* from that of *anupalabdhi*, and points out that historians of Indian logic, like Dasgupta, Radhakrishnan, and Sinha have failed to segregate these two fundamentally different notions and consequently have also failed to realize the enormous influence of the Buddhist logic on the thinkers of the *Brāhmaṇic* tradition (p. 121 – 125).

What is his own solution of the paradox of the negative judgement? In their early writings at least the Indian realists "were not concerned with the propositional character of negation. Rather they were involved in ontological and epistemological problems connected with it" (p. 117). They tended to subscribe to the assumption of the paradox that a negative judgement must describe some facts which make it true, or else it is not a judgement at all. Dr. Sharma denies this assumption. Rightly, too, he is in sympathy with the Buddhist thinker who in his opinion "conceives the factual and the function of logic in such a manner that the necessity of postulating of negative objects does not arise. Negation rightly remains in the domain of logic rather than falling in the trap of ontological myriad" (p. 121).

The author connects the discussion of *abhāva* to the three cardinal tenets of Indian philosophy: (1) The theory of *asatkāryavāda*; (2) the theory of non-violence of *ahiṃsā*, and (3) the theory of *mokṣa*, *apavarga*, *niḥśreyas*, or *nirvāṇa*. The theory of *asatkāryavāda* has for its foundations the notion of *abhāva* (this I have said above) such that it is a mistake to suppose that the *Nyāya-Vaiśesika* thinkers accepted *asatkāryavāda* without accepting *abhāva* as a *padārtha*. The theory of *ahiṃsā* follows the law of double negation. *Hiṃsā* is the negation of love and compassion (*karuṇā*) is *ahiṃsā*. Thus, to practice *ahiṃsā* is to act on the principle of love and compassion. Similarly about the theory of *mokṣa* (Sumum Bonum). *Duhkha* or pain is the same as the negation of *Sukha* or happiness; and the negation of *duhkha* or pain is *moksa*, *apavarga*, *niḥśrreyas*, or *nirvāṇa*.

I wonder if this thesis about the logic of double negation would work. To my mind, it fails historically; for, many of the Indian thinkers who spoke of *apavarga*, *niḥśreyas*, or *nirvāṇa* did not regard these notions as synonymous with the notion of *ānanda*, *sukha*, or happiness. I have in mind, for example, the early Buddhists, the *Nyāya* thinkers with the exception of *Bhāsarvajñā*, the author of the *Nyāya-sāra*, and also the *Vaiśeṣikas*. Most of these philosophers structured their conception of the ultimate value negatively, in general in terms of the absence of *dukkha* or suffering. *As a philosophical thesis* also, the construction of the law of double negation as the basis of *mokṣa* or *ahiṃsā* fails. The reason is not far to seek. He appears to have taken *hiṃsā* and *ahiṃsā*, for instance, as two contradictory notions, whereas they are only contrary and not contradictory. For, the worlds of *hiṃsā* and *ahiṃsā* are mutually exclusive, but not jointly exhaustive. This is shown in the following table:

A	*B*	*C*
Hiṃsā Kill!	A*hiṃsā* Do not kill !	Prema and Karuṇā Love and have compassion !

It is possible that a person subscribes to the principle of *A* or to the principle of *B* but does not subscribe to the principle of *C*. That *B* and *C* can go together needs no argument. But it is also possible that *A* and *C* may in fact go hand in hand; at least the state of affairs in which they may do so is not inconceivable, as for example, in the case of mercy killing.

Two more points need mention here. *One:* Dr. Sharma suggests that *mokṣa* originally was a sociological concept developed as a conceptual panacea for all human pain and suffering. And, he regards Gautama the Buddha as the first social philosopher to focus Indian wisdom on the question of the suffering of mankind. True, These two theses are far reaching significance both historically and also from the point of view of the development of the ethico-religious ideals found in Indian philosophy. One wishes that further research is done in this very fertile field of sociology of knowledge. *Two:* A couple of pages are devoted to a sentimental mention of Miss Joan Baez to show that the principle of *ahiṃsā* has been accepted by the thousands of youth of America who have rejected individual and social violence in that country. If this mention is aimed only at indicating and also encouraging the recent cultural influence of India on the American people, fine. But, then its relevance to the study of the notion of *abhāva* is not very obvious.

Technically, the book is very well produced: good paper, good print, and good get-up. However, there are several misprints scattered throughout the book.

Finally, I join hands with the author in affirming that "this work claims the consideration of the historians of Indian philosophy and culture"(p. xiii). I would add that no Indian philosopher can afford to ignore this excellent study of the negative dialectics in Indian philosophy if he or she wants to find a real good book rich in material on the subject.

33

BUDDHA JAYANTI SMĀRIKĀ (1976) (IN HINDI)

By Shri M. C. Bauddha, Permanand, M. S. Sambharwal and Bhoop Singh

Published by Dr. Ambedkar Bauddha Adhyayan Sansthan, "Buddha Vihar", J. J. Colony, Wazirpur, Delhi, containing 70 pages. This has no price printed therein.

The souvenir under review contains nine critical essays on different aspects of the *Dhamma*. These essays are full of information specially suited to the current trends of our society. In the second article entitled *"Bauddh Vāṅmaya Me Nāri"* written by Shri Rasik Behari Manjul, the social and moral status given to women in the Buddhistic literature has specially been stressed. It has also been magnificently brought out that a women can attain the highest virtue and value of life, 'the *Nirvāṇa*' as per the ancient and the modern Buddhistic doctrine in India.

The most important and the historic article of this souvenir is *"Kaise Bauddh Dharma Bharat Se Luptapraya Hua"* written by Shri Ram Das Suman. In this article the author has brought to light some of the unknown causes responsible for the downfall of Buddhism in India. This is a remarkable piece of research which should go a long way to inspire the brilliant scholars of Buddhism all over the world. Shri Suman deserves a rich tribute for his scholarly talent as evidenced by this article.

Advocate Shri Sambharwal's article entitled *"Dr. Ambedkar Bauddha Hee Kion Bane"* is another excellent piece of literature. In this article the author has highlighted some new points for the first time. Shri Mool Chand Bauddh's article entitled *"Bodhisattva Baba Saheb Ambedkar"* should interest the common man.

The attempts of Shri Bhoop Singh, Bhagwan Singh Rawat, Jodhalal Shah and Kalicharan Gautam are appreciable. The article of Mrs. Vimla Bhatnagar is a memorable picture of the Buddhistic Society in India.

On the whole, the souvenir is commendable from the view point of its research value and readability. This collection before the modern thinkers of Buddhism in itself is a star view.

The Institute deserves to be congratulated for bringing out the remarkable piece of literature. I strongly recommend the volume to be carefully read by all interested in Buddhism.

- *R. B. SAXENA*

35

भिक्षु जगदीश काश्यप

भिक्षु कौण्डिन्य

जब हम भारत में बौद्ध-साहित्य और पालि भाषा का नाम लेते हैं, तब हमारे सामने तीन पण्डितों के नाम आते हैं। वे हैं : महापण्डित राहुल सांकृत्यायन, भिक्षु जगदीश काश्यप और भदन्त आनन्द कोसल्यायन।

पूज्य जगदीश काश्यप का जन्म बिहार प्रान्त के गया जिले के रौनिया गाँव में सन् 1909 ई. में एक कायस्थ परिवार में हुआ था। उनकी शिक्षा रांची, पटना और हिन्दू विश्वविद्यालय, वाराणसी में हुई थी। शिक्षा समाप्त कर उन्होंने वैद्यनाथ धाम (बिहार) के गुरुकुल महाविद्यालय में सन् 1932-33 तक अध्यापन कार्य किया। सन् 1934 ई. में देश भ्रमण के लिए निकले और लंका गए। लंका में वे बौद्ध विनय अनुसार उपसम्पन्न होकर भिक्षु हुए। उनका मूल नाम जगदीश नारायण था, काश्यप उनका गोत्र है। लंका के विद्यालंकार परिवेश में उन्होंने पालि भाषा और बौद्ध साहित्य का विशेष रूप से अध्ययन किया।

पूज्य काश्यपजी ने अपने बौद्ध धर्म के प्रति प्रेम के कारण निश्चय किया कि, "मुझे समग्र बौद्ध देशों का भ्रमण कर बौद्ध धर्म का ज्ञान बढ़ाना चाहिए"। वे इसी निश्चय के अनुसार सन् 1935-36 ई. में मलाया तथा बर्मा देश गए। वहाँ के बौद्ध समाज और संस्कृति की स्थिति का अध्ययन किया और साथ ही साथ स्वयं उसका प्रचार भी किया। इन देशों के बाद वे चिनांग और सिंगापुर में धर्मोपदेशक के रूप में रहे। तब फिर वे लंका लौटे।

इस प्रकार बौद्ध साहित्य और संस्कृति का अध्ययन करने के बाद वे स्वदेश लौटे, तब वे जहाँ तथागत बुद्ध ने प्रथम 'धर्मचक्र प्रवर्तन' का उपदेश दिया था, उस पुण्य स्थान, सारनाथ में रहने लगे और वहाँ एक माध्यमिक विद्यालय की स्थापना की और वहीं अध्यापन करते रहे। सन् 1940 से 1950 ई. तक योग्यतापूर्वक काम करते रहे।

पूज्य काश्यपजी के प्रयत्न के फलस्वरूप 1951 ई. में संसार प्रसिद्ध नालन्दा में बिहार सरकार ने बौद्ध साहित्य के अध्ययन तथा शोध के लिए नव नालन्दा महाविहार नामक शोध संस्थान की स्थापना की। बिहार सरकार के अनुरोध पर वे नालन्दा में संस्थापक-निर्देशक हुए। नालन्दा संस्थान में रहते हुए उन्होंने बौद्ध साहित्य-पालि-त्रिपिटक को देवनागरी लिपि में प्रकाशन की योजना बनाई। उसके बाद उन्होंने नालन्दा संस्थान का पद छोड़ कर वाराणसी में त्रिपिटक के मुद्रण का व्यवस्था भार ग्रहण कर लिया। जिसका कार्य बनारस में हुआ। उसके बाद वे वाराणसेय संस्कृत विश्वविद्यालय में पालि विभाग के अध्यक्ष भी रहे।

पूज्य भिक्षु जगदीश काश्यप उन बौद्ध भिक्षुओं में से थे, जिनकी कीर्ति समस्त बौद्ध जगत में फैली हुई है। उनके विद्वान शिष्य सारे बौद्ध जगत में हैं। वे बड़े-बड़े पदों की शोभा बढ़ा रहे हैं। वे 'अखिल भारतीय भिक्षु-संघ के संघ-नायक' थे। भारत के गिने-चुने भिक्षुओं में आपकी विशेष प्रतिष्ठा है। वे जिस तरह बौद्ध सिद्धान्त के उपदेशक के रूप में अपनी वक्तृत्व शक्ति के लिए प्रसिद्ध थे, उससे भी अधिक उच्चकोटि के बौद्ध ग्रन्थों के प्रणेता के रूप में प्रतिष्ठित थे।

उन्होंने महत्वपूर्ण भूमिका सहित पालि के दर्जनों ग्रन्थों का हिन्दी और अंग्रेजी में सम्पादन और अनुवाद किया था। उनके अनूदित और मौलिक कुछ ग्रन्थ निम्नलिखित हैं:

1. संयुक्तनिकाय
2. उदान
3. मिलिन्द-प्रश्न
4. दीर्घ-निकाय (महापण्डित राहुल सांकृत्यायन के साथ)
5. पालि महाव्याकरण (मौलिक ग्रन्थ, इस व्याकरण के विद्वानों में ऊँचा स्थान है।)
6. The *Abhidhamma* Philosophy (अभिधर्म जैसे विषय को अति सुबोध और सरल पद्धति से लिखा गया है। यही ग्रन्थ आज बौद्ध धर्म के अंग्रेजी जानकार विद्यार्थियों के लिए सहज प्राप्य है।)
7. Buddhism for Everybody
8. पाश्चात्य तर्कशास्त्र, आदि

इस प्रकार पालि साहित्य और बौद्ध दर्शन के पण्डित होने के साथ ही उन्होंने हिन्दी साहित्य के विद्वानों में भी ख्याति प्राप्त की थी।

लंका, बर्मा, थाईलैण्ड, कम्बोडिया आदि में राष्ट्रधर्म बौद्ध-स्थविरवाद है, जिसका सर्वमान्य ग्रन्थ है 'पालि-त्रिपिटक'। उन देशों में उनकी अपनी अपनी लिपियों में समय-समय पर त्रिपिटक के सुन्दर से सुन्दर संस्करण प्रकाशित होते रहे हैं। लंदन की 'पालि-टैक्स्ट सोसायटी' ने भी 'त्रिपिटक' के अधिकांश भाग का प्रकाशन रोमन लिपि में किया था। इस अभाव की पूर्ति के उद्देश्य से केन्द्रीय तथा बिहार सरकार के संयुक्त प्रयत्न से सम्पूर्ण 'पालि-त्रिपिटक' को देवनागरी लिपि में सम्पादित तथा मुद्रित करने की योजना स्वीकृत की गई। प्रायः चार-चार सौ पृष्ठों वाले 41 खण्डों में त्रिपिटक का प्रकाशन हुआ है। इसे पूर्ण करने का भार नालन्दा के 'देवनागरी त्रिपिटक प्रकाशन विभाग' को सौंपा गया। इन 41 खण्ड त्रिपिटक का सम्पादन पूज्य भिक्षु जगदीश काश्यप जी ने किया।

पुनः सन् 1964 से 1972 तक काश्यपजी नवनालन्दा महाविहार (नालन्दा) शोध-संस्थान के निदेशक रहे। इस संस्थान में विश्व के विभिन्न बौद्ध राष्ट्रों के पण्डित आकर अध्ययन करते हैं। अब ज्ञान के महान पुजारी पूज्य काश्यपजी नहीं रहे। 28 जनवरी 1976 को राजगीर में उनका देहावसान हो गया।

35

LIFE AND TEACHINGS OF MAHĀVĪRA

Anukul Chandra Banerjee

Jainism evolved at a very early period of Indo-Aryan history. The Buddhist records attest the importance and high antiquity of Jainism. Jainism claims that it was founded by Ṛṣabha many a long century ago and that its first teacher was followed by the twenty-three others of whom Pārśvanātha was the twenty-third being followed by Mahāvīra, the last Tīrthaṅkara, Pārśvanātha, the historical founder of Jainsim, was known to his contemporaries as the peoples' favourite (puriṣādāṇiya). In the Jaina tradition of Tīrthaṅkaras, the role played by Mahāvīra was that of the last reformer as he developed new points of view. He introduced *Pañca-yāna-dharma* for a very strict code of mental and physical discipline in Jaina monarchism. All the rules of religious life which Mahāvīra had observed were intended to be a practical aid to the perfect knowledge and attainment of the self.

Mahāvīra was born in the town of Kundananagara, a suburb of Vaiśālī. So he was called Veśālie (Vaiśālika), a citizen of Vaiśālī. He was the son of Kṣatriya Siddhārtha who was otherwise named Śreyamśa. His mother was Kṣatriyāṇi Triṣalā, also known as Videhadattā. She was a sister to Cetaka of Videha, at whose call all the Licchavīs and Mallas rallied together. Nigaṇṭha Nāṭaputta was the name by which Mahāvīra was also known to his followers as well as to his other contemporaries. He was Nigaṇṭha (*nirgrantha*) as he was outwardly unclothed and inwardly free from all worldly bonds and ties. His parents gave his name as Vardhamāna or Prosperous One, because with his birth the wealth, fame and merit of the family increased. He was also called Mahāvīra for his fortitude and hardihood and also for his strictly adhering to the rules of penance. He, was equally known as *Jñātṛputra* (Nāṭaputta) or scion of the Jñāṭṛ clan, *Śāsananāyaka* or Head of the Order.

He had a reflective turn of mind since his boyhood. He meditated upon the misery that filled the earth and sought to discover the means to permanent release from this eternal and inevitable suffering. Mahāvīra renounced the world at the age of thirty and he went out to establish a universal religion of love and amity. In his long sojourn he practiced asceticism and meditation, had to face hardship in calmness. The rural rustics troubled him on various ways but he endured the trouble without any resentment. With equanimity he bore, underwent and suffered all pleasant and unpleasant occurrences. Though ill-treated he engaged himself in meditation very calmly. Thus, as the hero at the head of a battle, he proceeded on the road to deliverance. He exerted himself for the stoppage of the defilement of *Karma*. He guarded his thoughts, words, acts and senses, and restrained the impulses for the purification of the soul. In short, he had cut off all earthly ties, and was not stained by any worldliness.

After twelve years of penance and meditation as an ascetic he attained Jinahood at the age of forty-two. He then reached the highest knowledge, omniscience, called *Kaivalya* which is infinite, supreme, unobstructed and complete. He had solved the cause of human misery and preached it to the world.

During the thirty years of his career as a Teacher he traversed thousands of miles covering Bihar, Uttar Pradesh and some portions of Bengal. Urged by the favour of missionary zeal he preached the ancient doctrine of the *Nirgranthas*. His clarion call roused many thousands of people from their torpid slumber. His religious life had the special attraction to the followers. He lived and moved among men and disseminated among all his ineffable spiritual experience that awakened the dormant energies of the soul. His followers pursued the course of life for eternal freedom from the bondage of *Karmas*.

In the Tirthaṅkra's life time there were four powerful monarchies in northern India and the rest of the country was divided into the principalities of several oligarchical or republican clans. Magadha, Kośala, Vatsa and Avanti were the four powerful kingdoms where reigned Śreṇika Bimbisāra, Prasenajita, Udayana and Caṇḍa Pradyota respectively. Among the republican clans of Kṣatrīyas, the two most powerful were Vajji-Licchavīs and the Mallas. He had the royal patronage from kings like Kuniya Cetaka, Seniya, Pajjota, Udayana and others. According to Buddhist texts, king Śreṇika Bimbisāra of Magadha paid a glowing tribute to Mahāvīra and he with his wives, servants and relatives became a firm believer in the law of the Jaina Tīrthaṅkara. Prince Abhaya of Magadha, Siṁha, a Licchavi general, the Ugras and the Bhogas were among the most prominent of the earliest converts. King Cetaka, maternal uncle of Mahāvīra, was the most powerful king of Videha. He had seven daughters, the eldest one was married to king Udayana of Vatsa, the youngest to king śreṇika Bimbisāra of Magadha, who joined the religious Order of Mahāvīra, the other four were married in one or the other royal family of eastern India. It is thus evident that princesses helped much in the propagation of Jainism in northern India. The venerable ascetic visited Vāṇijagrāma, Campā, Bārāṇasī, Alabhi, Kampīlayapura, Palāspura, Rajagṛha, Śrāvasti, Pāvā, Mithilā, Bhadrika and Punītabhūmī. In all these places the great lay disciples and lay supporters of his Order both male and female, are all mentioned as persons of opulence and influence and they are noted for their piety and devotion.

Thus Mahāvīra in his lifetime, according to *Kalpa Sūtra* had an excellent community of sixteen thousand recluses, thirty-eight thousand nuns and one hundred fifty nine thousand lay disciples. Undoubtedly this shows the popularity and the personality of Mahāvīra and his sect.

Mahāvīra preached his doctrine in *Ardha-Māgadhi*, the language of then people. The sacred books of the Jaina *Āgamas* are all worded in *Ardha-Māgadhi*. These books are the oldest known literary monument that we find even today. The current speech of the people indeed received an impetus from the master. His later followers, the chief disciples known as Gaṇadhāras, who were all well-versed in sacred texts also contributed much to the later literary development.

The religious order founded by Pārśva enjoyed the reputation of a high and rigid standard of conduct. The *Cāturyāma Saṁvara* or four-fold restraint was regarded as a distinctive feature of their discipline. He made four moral precepts binding upon his followers. The four moral virtues of a Jaina recluse are: (i) the recluse will be free from passion and desire, (ii) he should keep himself aloof from all kinds of traffic, (iii) he should get rid of all *parigrahas* (ideas of possession) and (iv) he should remain absorbed in meditation. As a reformer of Pārśva's religion, Mahāvīra added a fifth, viz., the vow of chastity. The definite path prescribed by Mahāvīra for the realization of the world of absolute happiness consisted in the abstinence from the idea of killing, the idea of theft, the idea of lying, the idea of unchastity and the like. He also restricted the practice of religious suicide by slow starvation only to those who followed his personal example. The gift of supernormal vision was no monopoly of any Order or caste or sex. In this matter, Mahāvīra made no distinction between men and men or between men and women.

His very first principle of *ahiṁsā* or non-harming had a visible effect on the disposition of men. This compassionate attitude leads to a higher life. The beasts, birds, reptiles and fishes were left unharmed, men gave up the eating of meat and fish. The laws of the country were modified and humanized. It was this principle of compassion that encouraged philanthropic and humanitarian deeds and people came forward with the noble mission for the welfare of the beings.

Mahāvīra was an exponent of the doctrine of action (*Kiriyāvāda*). Whatsoever a man experiences, whether it is pleasant or painful, neither pleasant nor painful, is due to his *Karma* (totality of deeds) in the past. Through penance (*tapasā*) the force of past deeds is exhausted and the effect of fresh deeds is not accumulated and the stoppage of the future course of rebirth is assured. According to Mahāvīra, the practice of penance involved three kinds of daṇḍa or self-inflicted punishment: bodily, vocal and mental. Thus it awakened the consciousness that liberation was not a gift of favour but an attainment within human possibility and this salvation was assured to all without distinction of caste or creed or sex. Mahāvīra's great message to mankind is that *Karma* is everything and on the destruction of *Karma* the future happiness depends.

The ultimate object of Jainism is *Nirvāṇa* which is otherwise called *mokṣa*, liberation. *Nirvāṇa* is the attainment of the highest state of sanctification. It is the eternal place, but difficult to approach. To attain that blissful state of the soul equanimity of the mind is indispensable and that state of the mind ultimately rests on concentration. To get rid of the continual cycle of birth and death, we have to contemplate on blissfulness, truthfulness, honesty, chastity, purity of body and mind.

The question of world peace is the most important problem facing humanity. The perfection of man is to be recognized as the highest problem before the progressive humanity. Mahāvīra's contribution to the spiritual and cultural advancement to humanity is vast, outstanding and beyond measure. His life and teachings have influenced of the daily lives and aspirations of the millions. The blissfulness of the entire being, according to Mahāvīra, is to be attained through sufferings and sacrifices, love and kindness – this is his message to humanity. There is something in Jainism that directly appeals to our finer feelings and commands respect. Unlike Buddhism, Jainism did not develop into a world religion though it has still been a living force in India.

Endnotes

1. B.C. Law, *Mahāvīra, His Life and Teachings.*
2. H. Jacobi, *Jaina Kalpasūtra (S.B.E.).*
3. S.B. Deo, *History of Jaina Monachism.*
4. J.L. Jaini, *Outline of Jainism.*
5. M. L. Mehta, *Jaina Psychology.*

36

REFLECTIONS ON AESTHETICS FROM A BUDDHIST POINT OF VIEW*

G. C. Pande

Beginning as a moral, mystical and monastic religion, Buddhism inspired over the centuries the creation of a vast world of art and literature as also of learning and philosophy. The religious matrix of Buddhism proved equally effective in inspiring aesthetic creativity as much as philosophical reflection. The emergence of Buddhism may, thus, be viewed as that of a powerful moral and spiritual force which created for its expression a multidimensional world of culture, as vast as it was subtle. To under the essential unity of Buddhist inspiration ubiquitously present in all its diverse creations, we must turn, not to its well-defined but everdisputed and reinterpreted dogmas, but to that fundamental spiritual experience which made Gautama the Buddha. It is here that Buddhist art and Philosophy meet, each seeking to express this central experience in its own characteristic manner.[2] The heart of Buddhism is mystical and that mystical point of view underlies Buddhist art and philosophy. Neither Buddhist philosophy nor Buddhist mysticism should be held to be dead and finished in so for as they are conceived as historical expressions of the foundational experience which alone must be deemed as the creative and perennial *Natura Naturans* of the Buddhist cultural world. Coomaraswamy and Suzuki illustrate how attention to the fundamental inspirational source leads to fresh creativity. In focusing attention on the spiritual ground and meaning of Buddhist art, Coomaraswamy has placed Buddhist philosophy as well as art in a new perspective viz., that of *Philosophia perennis.* In Coomaraswamy's writings, thus, one can discern the first adumbration of a spiritual Aesthetic drawing at once on classical, Christian and Buddhist sources.[3] For a variety of reasons, however, this effort has not been continued. Among these reasons the most important has been the very character of contemporary aesthetic consciousness. It is proposed here to consider some of its dilemmas in the light of Buddhist philosophy conceived as a developing system of thought issuing out of the matrix of Buddhist experience.

If there are no Buddhist treatises on Aesthetics, that is so because 'Aesthetics', like 'Art' itself, is a cultural category the significance of which changes with culture. The dividing lines between the branches of thought, learning and specialized activities are only the self-articulations of cultural awareness and keep shifting historically. They do not represent natural provinces of the mind.[1] Theology and Mysticism, Psychology, Logic and Philosophy are, for example, sharply distinguished today but it would be vain to search for these distinctions in the older Buddhist tradition. Similarly, the attempt to think of art as a wholly autonomous world and of aesthetics as a distinct and independent realm of speculation is, again, a recent tendency hardly two centuries old. For Buddhism man's pilgrimage from the City of Righteousness *(Dhamma-nagaraṁ)* to the City of Quiescence *(Nibbāna-nagaraṁ)* is the ultimate context in terms of which all thought and action must find their meaning and formulation. There is no place here for 'ethics' or for 'aesthetics' if they are to be treated as concerned with autonomous values lying outside the concrete and integral whole of man's spiritual development. As the conceptual analysis of this spiritual experience, Buddhist philosophy must be at once an ethic, a metaphysic and an aesthetic.[2] It will not be an aesthetic only if aesthetics were concerned with something inessential and accidental to spiritual life, or if only a system based on the empirical study of the arts were to be called aesthetics. If Aesthetics is the philosophy of Beauty, and Beauty one of the major and perennial dimensions of Value like Goodness, Truth or Pleasure, any spiritual philosophy is bound to reckon with it.

In fact, the modern tendency with respect to art and aesthetics is only the modern dominance of a perennial tendency. Plato contrasts the rational use of the Arts with their subservience to irrational pleasures and it is obvious that he is referring to his contemporary state of art. Buddhaghoṣa is the *Visuddhimaggo* similarly condemns the arts which simply pander to the senses and Vasubandhu in the *Abhidharmakoṣa* clearly distinguishes the music which appeals to 'vulgar taste' *(grāmya-rasopasaṁhita)* from the music which is 'liberating' *(naiṣkarmyopa-saṁhita).* In canonical writings a clear distinction is made between the 'restful' and lucent beauty of natural scenery conducive to contemplation or the serene and radiant beauty of the face of a person touched by spiritual inspiration, on the one hand, and the seductive attractiveness of sensual beauty on the other.[3] It is, of course, clearly recognized, as for example by Asvaghoṣa, that relationship between sensuous beauty and desire is not a direct causal relationship but is meditated by imagination and habit.[4] It is not a condemnation of beauty or art as such but of beauty and art in the service of sense-enjoyment. The Buddhist emphasis on an analytical and critical attitude to sensations is anti-Hedonistic but not anti-aesthetic in the true sense.

It may be objected here that we must not confuse between moral and aesthetic categories. Art has its own distinctive 'aesthetic' value in the light of which it must be judged. Art has no goal to serve beyond itself. There is undoubtedly a distinction between the vulgar and the refined in art but it is more a matter of the mode of expression than of social or moral content. From the aesthetic point of view the subservience of the arts to sensuality would be as bad as its subservience to morality, theology or religion. A didactic art would be no better than any commercial or sensual art. Sensuousness may, indeed, turn out to be one of the essential elements of art. Whether we turn out to be one of the essential elements of art. Whether we turn to the *Saundarānanda* of Aśvaghoṣa of the sculptures of Sanchi or the paintings of Ajanta, we meet with pictures of glowing sensuousness. Again, the epithet 'spiritual' is ambiguous. If it refers to the human spirit, generally as it does in Hegel or even in common literary parlance in the West, non-religious art could also be spiritual. If, however, by the word 'spiritual' we mean 'religious' or 'mystical', to say that art expresses spiritual experience would then be begging the question. In fact, the most distinctive achievement of the West since, the 18th century has been to liberate the human spirit from its religious pre-occupation. Since the Middle Ages human self-awareness has freed itself from the trammels of religious dogma and a new humanistic and secular self-awareness has gradually come into its own and has been seeking to remodel the traditional cultural world to find an adequate expression for itself. Morality and ethical reflection have sought to be free from the prescriptions of the Church or revelation. Similarly, the philosophical search for truth has sought to base itself on the principles of reason and the accumulated experience of the sciences. It is in this very context that art has sought to develop as a new mode of exploring the worlds of sensibility and humanistic values. Aesthetics, again, has sought to unite the different arts as parts of an autonomous realm, governed by values of its own. It has been argued as, for example, by Bosanquet in his *History of Aesthetic* that this discovery of the distinctness of aesthetic value from other values with which it is often found mixed up in practice, it is result of a gradual deepening and maturity of aesthetic insight. Aesthetics itself is the result of this developed stage of aesthetic consciousness which was lacking in earlier times. Bosanquet, following Hegel, has indeed argued that an adequate notion of beauty was not reached till the Romantic Revolution which completed the older notion of Beauty in terms of formal perfection by adding to it the notion of 'Characteristic expressiveness' and simultaneously enriched the notion of art by adding Imagination to Reason as the faculty responsible for making or creating the work of art.

Kant remains the pivotal figure in this transition. Just as he sought to rehabilitate scientific knowledge by redefining philosophy, he gave the most serious philosophical expression to the romantic consciousness of art as essentially an activity of the imagination distinct both from practical as well as theoretical activity. Art is neither moral nor immoral, neither true nor false. Nevertheless, it is not purely subjective or arbitrary. Aesthetic judgement inevitably seeks universality and that is why aesthetic criticism remains significant. It may be worthwhile to consider the exact words of Kant in his *Critique of Judgement* to appreciate this position which is now so commonly held: "In order to decide whether anything is beautiful or not, we refer the representation, not by the Understanding to the Object for cognition but, by the Imagination (perhaps in conjuction with the Understanding) to the subject, and its feeling of pleasure and pain. The judgement of taste is therefore not a judgement of cognition, and is consequently not logical but aesthetical, by which we understand that whose determining ground can be *no other than subjective.*" Kant goes on to observe that the satisfaction which determines the judgement of taste is wholly disinterested. This satisfaction is distinguishable from the satisfaction of pleasant sensations as well the satisfaction in the good. "The Pleasant, the Beautiful, and the Good, designate then, three different relations of representations to the feeling of pleasure and pain, in reference to which we distinguish from each other objects or methods of representating them". The Pleasant and the Good have both a reference to the faculty of desire and involve an interest in the being of the object. On the other hand, the judgment of taste is merely *contemplative*; that is, it is a judgement, which indifferent as regards the being of the object, compares its character with the feeling of pleasure and pain. Nor is this contemplation based on concepts. While hedonistic judgements are purely subjective, moral judgements represent the object by means of a concept. Aesthetic judgment involves a non-conceptual, imaginative and subjective universality.[5]

This amoralistic point of view on art, which identifies beauty with the activity of the imagination to please within the conditions of taste without reference to desire, obviously needs something which at once non-causal and non-conceptual. As is well known, Kant brings in the idea of general purposiveness and teleology. It is doubtful, however, if the awareness of purpose can really be separated from desires and emotions which Kant so meticulously excludes. This aspect received more attention within the Indian tradition where as aesthetic theory closely resembling this was evolved in Kashmir between the sixth and the tenth centuries A.D. The *Rasa* theory also regards aesthetic enjoyment as quite distinct from the enjoyment of pleasures or the practical satisfaction of desires or the pursuit of theoretical knowledge. Here, again, judgement is made to depend on taste (*sahṛdayatā*). On the other hand, in the theory of *Rasa* the role of desires and emotions is perceived more clearly. Art experience is distinguished from actual experience by being imaginative rather than actual. There is no dependence here on the causal operation of the object. The art object is a sign or representation which functions evocatively. The imaginative spectacle which is relished emotions of the spectator. Just as art dissolves things into images, it dissolves the habitual *persona* of the subject. This is the source of the disinterestedness and apparent universality of the experience. The content of this felt experience – objective and subjective images – serves only as an occasion for the revelation of the inner blissful nature of consciousness. Aesthetic enjoyment thus turns out to be a return of consciousness upon itself, an experience where the self reaches a deeper awareness of itself through a new vision of life and nature and the consequent reintegration of the personality.

There are two basic questions involved in such accounts: (1) Whether by regarding art as an imaginative creation we can sufficiently distinguish it from practical and theoretical activity so as to free it from moral and cognitive categories; (2) Can we regard aesthetic value as *sui generic*? Can we say that the greatness or value of art depends just on the presence or degree of what is distinctive to art? Or rather that art is one of the media for the realization of values in general? At the outset we may consider the fact that aesthetic experience is not limited to art alone. The spectacle of natural beauty is well known to excite, the same kind of reaction as any work of art. The experience of the mystic in so far it has been expressed in poetry or art has often appeared to be an experience of beauty. The experience of romantic love, again, has a close parallel to aesthetic experience. Perhaps it may be said that imagination entering into a hightened and vivid awareness. Bosanquet has argued that 'nature' here differs from 'art' principally in degree, both being the media of human perception and imagination. Whether we regard art as a limitation of nature or natural beauty as an imaginatively apprehended spectacle out of nature where every man is his own artist, it is obvious that we are postulating a universally present faculty in the human mind of which the operation is spontaneous but of which the laws are scarcely known. To adequately meet the situation it is sometimes proposed to describe artistic imagination as creative imagination. And then to further explain the source of this creativity it has had to be assumed that imagination is not simply a reproductive and associative faculty but an intuitive faculty apprehending profound spiritual truths so that a work of creative imagination becomes a revelation. While empathy and creative imagination thus play a crucial part in an attempt to distinguish the aesthetic from ordinary experience as also in the attempt to explain the creation of the works of art, neither aesthetics nor psychology, as they have been current in the West, have been in a position to suitably connect these concepts with a metaphysics that would explain how imagination can really be creative or capable of seeing truth, or how, in short, works of imagination may be works of real value or truth. The contribution of Buddhist thinking at this point can be of inesteemable value.

So long as we regard the human experience as an interaction between bodies or between bodies and the mind, we would continue to face difficulty in explaining the every fact of knowledge. External objects or bodies may exert a causal influence on the human senses and produce a reaction in them. But, from this situation of physical causation, how is one to move to the cognition of the object which is a wholly mental phenomenon? To connect the content of knowledge with the sensible affect of the external object, it has been usual to interpolate the image which corresponds to the sensuous affect and simultaneously represents the object for the mind. At this level of the image, the continuous stream of momentary influences exerted by the external object undergoes a process of synthesis where memory plays a part, and then increasing verbalization replaces the image by a concept which enters into cognitive thought. All such and similar hypotheses which seek to bridge and gulf between sense and thought, between physical interaction and mental knowledge, continue to suffer from dialectical difficulties which realistic epistemologies have been quick to raise against representationist empiricism or semi-representationist 'critical' theories. Realism, on its part, unfortunately can neither explain the all important facts of error and illusion nor the apprehension of beauty which, like goodness, can not be reduced to objects or their qualities. Idealistic theories have suggested that through the operation of universal reason in nature as well as in the human mind there is a pre-established harmony between the forms of reality and the forms of knowledge. This also rules out error and illusion except as stages in the development of true knowledge.

The basic tendency of Buddhist philosophy is to discard the substantiality of the bodies as well as of the mind. Along with a substantial mind, goes out a faculty psychology as well as unknowable objects and subjects transcending the bounds of experience. The mind is a natural image-maker which functions at several levels and has several dimensions or aspects all the time. Imagination, feeling, will, judgement, are inseparable from apprehension or representation. Experience begins with images which are ultimately projections from within the mind governed by the inner dynamism of desire. The problem is not to give an explanation for imaginative experience or for the creativity of imagination within a given solid world of practical and cognitive reality, but to explain the meaning of practical reality and cognitive truth within an incessant process of insubstantial phantasmagoria *(abhūta-parikalpa).* Even the *Vaibhāṣikas* and the *Sautrāntikas* accept that sense perception includes *svabhāva-vikalpa* and that sense perception depends not only on the sense but also on the *manodhātu.* No sooner is one of the tenses impressed with an external causal agency, the mind itself if alerted *(āvajjana)* and receives *(sampaṭicchana)* an image which it scans *(saṁtīraṇa)*, verbalizes and classifies *(voṭṭhapana)* adjudges and feels *(javana).* The habitual picture of the world and the self are themselves dependent on this process of imagination. Cognitive truth in this sense belongs only to trains of images *(vikalpa-santāna)* such as have been found pragamatically reliable *(avīsamvādaka).* The imaginative experience of value, then is not something irrelevant to reality as it is experienced in knowledge an action but the restoration to experience of a deeper reality which is only fragmentarily encountered in the life of action governed by habit and desires or only abstractly and partially apprehended in terms of relations and exclusions (*apoha*) or indirect reference, in cognition or theory. Experience begins with a transcendental imagination which posits spatio-temporal objects and experiencing selves. This is the radical though illusive creativity of the mind. After this projection of distinct objects and subjects, of *svabhāvas* on the canvas of *śūnyatā,* instead of the original or luminous nature of the mind, we have experience as *abhūta-parikalpa.* Within this, imagination again works in two ways: an *abhinirūpaṇa-vikalpa* or conceptual construction and *anusmṛti-vikalpa* or a synthesis by virtue of memory or apperception. These workings of the imagination constantly enter into theoretical and practical activity. However, since they modify the sensuous image by joining it to memories and words or other signs they serve to take away the vividness of immediacy. In generating theoretically and practically useful ideas they make experience more determinate but less vivid. Now, the most important characteristic of aesthetic imagination is its vividness, its capacity of not just informing or instructing but of inducing an experience as if it has directly or immediately taken place. The creativity of imagination in art does not lie in inventing chimeras but in giving the quality of direct experience to what might otherwise be apprehended only dimly or abstractly through half-forgotten memories or the negativities of concept *vyāvṛtti*. In this role imagination is known in Buddhist Philosophy as *bhāvanā* leading to intuition *(Sākṣātkāra)*. What is called genius or *Paṭibhāna* is itself the result of past *bhāvanā*. *Bhāvanā* literally means 'causing to be', an activity of the mind by which ideas appear to become real.

As *Jñānaśri* has remarked, it is well known how emotions normally tend to induce *bhāvanā* in the sense of a train of ideas and images leading to a vivid inward experience[6]. But the result of such *bhāvanā* has no more value than the emotions which lead up to it. The value of imaginative intuition apparently depends on the value of the idea which is the subject of the *bhāvanā*. The purpose of imaginative intuition, if is to be valuable, cannot certainly be a vivid *reproduction* of sensuous immediacy. If what is normally perceived with the vividness of sense-experience were to be re-experienced with vividness in imagination, it would a vain re-enactment. In fact, imaginative intuition cannot normally represent actual existents except as an illusive experience. Where it excels over both sense-perception as well as conceptual knowledge is in its ability of vividly realize general ideas or deeper features of reality through the medium of the images referring to common experience. For example, common perception shows impermanent things and although imaginative intuition cannot show the things themselves more vividly, nevertheless, it can reveal the impermanence of things through their images much more vividly than common experience. We observe good and bad people in life. The intuition which we reach through a sustained imaginative process such as arises when we are absorbed for example, in a novel, presents to us more vividly not actual persons but the goodness or evil or the complexity of their characters. What we have here to use the language of Jñānaśri is a *dharma-sākṣātkāra* not *dharmi-sākṣātkāra*. Our experience of the real world is elevated into an experience of human truth or value through the sustained application of imagination which leads to the intuition that is called aesthetic experience.

We can now attempt to answer the two questions which were raised earlier. If by saying that art is an imaginative, not a theoretical or practical activity, it is sought to be implied that art avoids all jugdement of reality or forming of attitudes and characters, the assertion must be plainly rejected. Art experience as intuition is not indeterminate. It is not less than a conceptual judgement or theory. On the other hand, by vividly *realizing* an idea it turns a jugement about reality into an experience which tends to leave an abiding impression on the mind and character. Intuition includes both vividness and determination and since it influences the formation of character, it cannot be held amoral. Of course, if art were an act of idle imagination, devoid of all conviction and commitment of any moving insight, if it were something merely superficial or technical, it would remain morally non-descript. That is why while Vasubandhu describes poetry as an activity proceeding from a design *(yoga-paravrattam-karma)* and hence moral or immoral as intimations *(vijñapti)* generally are, he describes mechanical arts and crafts *(śīlpasthāna)* as morally indeterminate *(anivrtāvyākṛta)*. In music, again he distinguishes morally good from bad depending on whether it serves to inflame the passion or leads to liberation from them. Art as an activity is not insignificant in its effect on character. Consequently it cannot be amoral except on pain of being inconsequential. Art is not like nature leaving every percipient free to react in his own way: art is *designed* to facilitate a certain kind of attitude towards things.

It may be objected that this amounts to didacticism which has been often condemned by sensitive critics and artists. It is undoubtedly true that where the work of art seeks to communicate a truth which the artist has only realized as an abstract or conceptual truth and his intention plainly supervenes on his work as something external and accidental to it, his work would truly merit rejection. It seeks to instruct but not through the image it creates. On the other hand, can any great work of art be created without communicating a profound knowledge of man or nature of the supernatural? Can anyone say that the epic of Aśvaghoṣa cease to be poetry of the highest order simply because he intends to convey the spiritual experience of the Buddha? In the early images of the Buddha or *Bodhisattva* from Gāndhāra we can notice the disconnection between the image and the idea. But, images from the Gupta period convey the luminous silence of the Buddha through the very image itself. Here *lakṣaṇa* and *pratimā* or *bimba* have coalesced into one harmonious unity. The *bimba* is a sensuous presentation or image, the *lakṣaṇas* and *mudrās* indicate the *idea* of a 'great man' as enlightened: It is the fusion of the two which produces an image worthy of being contemplated in worship. Such an image arises worthy of being contemplated in worship. Such an image arises from a profound imaginative intuition on the part of the artist. That is why the standing injunction to the artist in the Buddhist and Indian Tradition was to contemplate and then make according to the vision. The *Aṭṭhasālinī* postulates a *Cittasaññā* or *picture-idea* behind the *Cittakiriya* or the actual painting.

It is not being suggested that the work of art should concern itself with only certain kinds of objects or things. What is being said is that the ideas and attitudes which it reveals must be valuable. For example, Dostoevsky's *Crime and Punishment* deals with a thief, a murderer, a prostitute. Nevertheless, what it reveals is the nature of sin and the power of love to absolve it. There are some works of art which bring out the power of evil in so far as evil is often insidious and not always recognized for what it is. Such a representation has value.

Nevertheless, if the evil is not revealed as such but merely its power is intimated, it would be difficult not to condemn such a work as either leading to distaste or seduction.

With respect to the second question raised earlier we may begin by considering whether the value of a work of art depends simply on those features which distinguish the work of art from other things. A tuning fork can produce a pure musical note but it is without any musical value. A simple folk-tune or a display of attractive colours or a faultless metrical composition may have all the formal and distinctive characteristics of art but one would hardly consider them examples of great art. The greatness or value of any work of art depends on precisely those reasons for which we hold *anything* to be really valuable or great. The distinctiveness of art-experience only distinguishes it from common practical or cognitive experience but not from any kind of vivid or felt intuition. A vivid dream or a mystical vision or the experience of love, for example, have the same kind of intuitive and felt quality as a work of art tends to reveal in its experience. How we evaluate these experiences depends on how we evaluate things in general in the context of human life and seeking. It is true that within the work of art we may adjudge its success or failure, its power or weakness, by the vividness and the magnitude of the experience it tends to produce. Nevertheless, all powerful and vivid art-experiences can not be held to be of the same value. The greatest works of the art derive their value from revealing the highest values of their age or of all ages.

I. A. Richards has stated that in order to avoid being duped by sentimentally or other temporary influences distorting the judgement, he would like to recall such basic truths as death and impermanence before commencing to study a poem.[7] The important thing to recollect here is that merely conventional or commonly held values or attitudes should not be allowed to become the criteria of judgement or value in any aesthetic experience. In this respect the Buddhists upheld the highest standard. The truths of impermanence, impersonality and the misery of the human condition were for them the essential realizations for any realization of true value. The realization of value at its highest was held to be an experience of illumination, an experience which saw the relativity of conditioned phenomena as also the ineffable quiescence of the unconditioned. The poems of the monks and nuns included in the *Pāli* canon are poignant expressions of such moments of illumination, each moment expressed in terms of a concrete and individualized image. It may be felt that an art which is thus motivated will tend to be ascetic and other worldly and exclude the richness of human life and experience. This would be a grave misunderstanding because the effect of illumination is not the annihilation of the world but its transfiguration. The world that is projected by the mind under the influence of ignorance and passions become transfigured when the mind is illumined. This is the Buddhist doctrine of *parāvṛtti*.[8] The peculiar and distinctive value of art lies in forshadowing, however, dimly and temporarily, this sense of illumination and transfiguration. Even the meanest reader of a great poem tends to undergo in some measure this experience, of realizing a new significance becoming enlightened and experiencing the freedom and the bliss that accompany it in sharing the vision of a transfigured world. There are immense degrees in which the works of art achieve this effect and hence there are levels and levels of artistic achievements. Where the effects of illumination, liberation and transfiguration are achieved but insignificantly, very often the image of worldly life and pleasures are presented with great gusto and power. For examples, the works of Boccacoio or Rabelais acquire significance only in the negative context of doing away with a narrow and inhibited view of life. Nevertheless, such works cannot compare with the Gospel or the *Buddhacarita.* It is necessary in this context to emphasize that the proper appreciation of any work of art may also require an adequate training on the part of its public. In this sense the responsibility of a critic is heavy. Artists and critics together form and educate the taste of the public and hence moral responsibility attaches to them equally.

To sum up, from the Buddhist point of view art cannot be held to non-moral except where insignificant, nor can be essence of art be discovered anywhere except in imaginative intuition, and the value of art must ultimately be judged by its capacity to illuminate, liberate and transfigure the psyche. The concept of *Śilapasthāna* and *Vijñapti, Lakṣaṇa* and *Pramāṇa, Pratibhāna* and *bimba, Vikalpa* and *Pratibhāna, Bhāvnā* and *Parāvṛtti,* are some of the Buddhist notions which contain profound intimations for any aesthetic philosophy.

Endnotes

1. Philosophy or *Abhidharma* is included in *Prajñā* while Art is to be included under *Upāya,* esp.
2. *Bhāvanā. Prajñā* and Bhāvanā diverge as Reason and Imagination but come together as intuition.
3. See especially, *Figures of Speech or Figures of Thought,* London, 1946.
4. Cf. my *'Meaning and Process of Culture'* (Agra 1972).
5. Whether *Dharma* is interpreted ontologically or phenomenologically as, e.g. by Rosenberg in his *Die Probleme der buddhistischen Philosophie,* the subject matter of *Abhidharma* remains comprehensive and includes being, consciousness and value.
6. See my *'Early Buddhist Notion of Beauty'* in Rajasthan University Studies in History, 1963.
7. Cf. *Saundarānanda,* 13.49-51.
8. *Critique of Judgement,* tr. J. M. Bernard (London, 1931), pp. 45 ff.
9. On the place of *Rasa* theory within a general value theory, see my Mūlya *Mīmāṃsā,* (RHGA, Jaipur).
10. E.g *Abhidharmakośabhāsya,* (Patna 1967), p. 275.
11. See, e.g. Asanga's *Mahāyānasūtrālankāra,* cf. the distinction made in the *Milindapanho* between *Rasa-patisamvedana and Rasarāga-patisamvedana.*

---

* Buddha Jayanti Lecture delivered under the auspics of the All India Philosophy Congress, 1975.

37

BUDDHIST VIEW OF OMNISCIENCE
Religious, Philosophical, Scientific, or......?*

Kewal Krishan Mittal

One can understand the credo of a theist having, on faith, a belief in Omniscience of God along with his Omnipotence and Omnipresence but the Buddhist insistence on the 'Omniscience (Sarvajnatā) of the Buddha' is not easy to grasp. The idea of the omniscience is brought forth, in a religion, in order to inculcate authority and arouse faith or to lure converts. There is little place for authority in Buddhism and scanty evidence of the use of the notion as a bait for faith-fishing. We have against authority a well known and oft quoted statement attributed to the Buddha himself. "Believe nothing," says he, "because a so-called wise man said it. Believe nothing because the belief is generally held. Believe nothing because it is written in ancient books. Believe nothing because it is said to be of a divine origin. Believe nothing because someone else believes it. Believe nothing because it comes from an honourable preceptor. But believe only what you yourself judge to be true."[2] Little wonder, therefore, if despite a statement maintaining that the Buddha knows more than even Brahma, the god of creation[3], there is not one from him matching that of Lord Krishna where-in the latter has said, "Surrendering all duties to Me, seek refuge in Me alone. I shall absolve you of all sins."[4]

His death bed advice to each of his followers, 'Be a light unto thyself', is indicative, if of anything, of the fact that the claim of omniscience is not preferred by the Buddha for himself alone but for each and every person who comes to attain bodhi (enlightenment). It is in this context that we can understand the Hinayāna ideals of 'Pacceka Buddha (Each a Buddha)' and the 'Sammāsam buddha. The *Mahāyāna* ideal of a '*Bodhisattva* (the Buddha Essence' too wherein omniscience is an obvious achievement among some other attainments of the person who becomes a *Bodhisattva* – is an ideal, despite all its emphasis on altruism through 'Great-Compassion (Mahākarunā)', for any and every individual i.e. an individualistic and humanistic ideal.

Considerations as the above suggest that the Buddhist use of the word omniscient is distinctly different in meaning from that of the one by the theists. But one is surely baffled to see almost all the references to the omniscient one, in the Buddhist literature, directly or indirectly pointing to the person Sākyamuṇī, Gautama Buddha, the Founder of the Religion.[1]

The *Jātaka* stories suggesting the 're-incarnation (*Avatāra*) idea' re-inforce the view that as a religious notion omniscience is understood by the Buddhists in much the same way as by the theists. Scholars like Kern[2], Poussin[3] and Keith[4] are pursuing this line of thinking, it seems, when they are maintaining that faith plays a role in Buddhism of much more importance than is usually granted. But after a careful perusal of the texts which these scholars have cited or based their views on, one is sure to agree with K.N. Jayatilleke that they are not entitled to hold such a view since they misinterpret the Buddhist view of omniscience.[5] Even as a religious notion, omniscience as understood by the Buddhists has to be distinct in meaning in so far as it is seldom combined with the notions of omnipotence and omnipresence except through a remote implication.

The present author is not aware if there is any thought-system in the West that recognizes anything philosophical about the notion of omniscience but he can observe, without fear of contradiction, that in India there are not only as many as four distinct systems of Philosophy that regard the notion as integral to their thought but even presystematic, vedic and upanisadic thought has something significant to say about it. The systems are *Jainism, Advaita Vedānta, Sāṃkhya* and, of course, Buddhism. They all hold that the final goal of their conception in each cases, respectively *Kevalīpada* or *Kevalajñāna, Mokṣa, Kaivalya* and *Nirvāṇa* can be achieved through knowledge and their unstated argument is that saying knowledge would not be knowledge if it were not 'knowledge of all' i.e. 'omniscience'. The differences in their views of omniscience rest on the differences in their conceptions of 'knowledge' and interpretations of 'all'. As regards the conception of knowledge, Jainism stands alone in considering the same in a naturalistic way, though in an interverted manner in so far the ordinary sensory-perception is regarded as indirect in comparison to *Kevalajñāna* which alone is taken as direct perception. In Jainism alone one hears of incomplete and complete knowledge (*Vikala* and *Sakalajñāna*) in the quantitative sense – may be due to partial or full removal of the Karmic veil of knowledge (*Jnānāvaraṇa*). In the other three knowledge is conceived in such a way that one cannot, strictly speaking, talk of its acquiring in full or piecemeal. Knowledge is such that either you have it or you do not. It is a matter of realization of confirmation which can occur in a flash. Such a conception of knowledge, since it is held commonly by the *Advaita Vedāntins, Sāṃkhyites* and the Buddhists and has got its echo in the Vedic and *Upaniṣadic* thought, makes for a common approach to the question of omniscience among the *Advaitins, Sāmkhyites, Upaniṣadic* thinkers and the Buddhists. The differences in their views narrow down on interpretation of 'all' or are determined by metaphysical considerations.

There is no need to argue that there is a close concurrence between the Vedic and *Upaniṣadic* and the Buddhist ideas of 'omniscience' as the same has been shown by a competent scholar already.[6] What can be attempted here then is to contrast the Buddhist view with the Jaina one and distinguish it from that of the *Advaitin* and the *Sāmkhyite*. The Jaina view, that has been consistently maintained and concertedly defended by Ācārya after *Jaina-ācārya*,[7] stands in total contrast with the Buddhist view. We find it criticized and ridiculed at many a place in the Buddhist *Nikāyas*.[8] It is their native-realistic view of knowledge and a literal interpretation of 'all' as all that amounts to an assertion that the omniscient, sleeping or waking, standing or walking, knows everything in all its details, lurid or excellent – that has specifically been criticized. It is said in so many words that 'there is no recluse or *brāhmiṇa* who would know or see everything *all at once* – for such a thing is impossible'[9]. It is interesting to note that even while rejecting omniscience of the Jaina conception, the Buddha maintains in the same breath a distinct possibility of an omniscient in the words, "Those who say that the recluse Gotama denies that their can be a recluse or brāhmin who would claim to be an omniscient, all seeing and having an infinite knowledge and vision, for such a thing is impossible, are not reporting me accurately and are accusing me of saying what is untrue and false". The Jaina idea of 'all' is too full to be of precise philosophical significance. Their view of omniscience, therefore, seems to be more boldly religious than philosophical. Infinite knowledge (*Anantajñāna*), with them always accompanies. Infinite observation (*Ananta-Darśana*), Infinite-power (*Ananta-vīrya*) and Infinite-bliss (*Ananta-Aiśvarya*).

For the *Advaita-Vedāntina* 'to know all' is to experience (*Brahmānubhāva*) that unsublatable (*Abādhita*) Reality that remains uncharacterized even by epithets such as Sat (Being), Citta (Consciousness) and *Ānanda* (Bliss). In such a knowledge, the knower and known become one (*Brahmātma-ekatva*). Knower-known distinction transcended 'omniscience' passes beyond understanding. To indicate such an impasse that we are thus lead into by the *Advaitin*'s view. One may rightly say with S. S. Surya Narayan Śaśtri, "Omniscience as knowership is not real since there is nothing to know; Omniscience as knowledge is real, but there is nothing to know."[10] Granting further that 'the former is not the latter but necessarily fulfils itself in the latter'[11], the present author is tempted to observe that whatever may be the religio-mystic significance of such a view of omniscience, as a philosophical notion it does seem to be utterly vacuous.

The Buddhist view chooses the middle course between the two extreme views put forth by the Jainas and the *Advaitins* and moves somewhat close to that presented by the *Sāṃkhya* thinkers. It is true that Buddhist thinkers, such, for example, as Śāntarakṣita, the celebrated author of *Tattvasaṅgraha* who devotes an entire chapter consisting of as many as 522 verses to an 'Examination of the Person of Supernormal Vision' wherein he states (verses 3124 to 3246) and answers (verses 3247 to 3646) all the objections against the Buddhist view of omniscience,[12] especially argue that not Kapila, the propounder of *Sāṃkhya* ideas but the Buddha alone is the omniscient (*sarvajñā*).[13] The two views are close in so far as they not only hold a common conception of knowledge, as already pointed out, but also proceed on similar lines in their interpretation of 'all' in terms of a basic principle or principles. They seem to betray an unwitting acceptance of the scientific assumptions of 'limited independent variety', 'uniformity of Nature', 'Regularity of Sequence' and 'Convergence to simplicity with diminution of extent' etc.[14] Yet there is an important difference in their views. In searching the basic principle the *Sāṃkhya* lays emphasis on the common and essential and thus adopts the positive procedure while the Buddhist lay emphasis on rejecting the irrelevant in true spirit of *'Neti-Neti'* of the *Upaniṣads.* 'To know all' for the *Sāṃkhya* is 'To know uniformly transforming dynamic Nature (*Prakṛti*) constituted and characterised by three characteristics (*Guṇas*) of Inertia (*Tamas*), Momentum (*Rajas*) and Equilibrium (*Sattva*) in any of its manifold forms from the grossest, blade of grass, to the sublest, faculty of intellect.[15]

The Buddhist interpretation of 'all' presents itself in three phases related to the spheres of Morality, psycho-physical experiences and the universe at large and is marked by a negative tone of expression except, in a way, in the case of second phase. For, if it talks in the first of 'all' is suffering (*Sarvaṁ Duḥkhaṁ*)', 'all its impermanent (*Sarvaṁ, anityaṃ*)', and 'all is non-substatial (*Sarvaṁ-anātmaṃ*) then in the third of *Nissvabhāvatā*' and '*Śūnyatā*'[16] only the second it classifies 'all' in terms of 'Five-supports (Pañca-sakandha i.e. *rūpa, vijñāna, Samjñā, Vedanā* and *samrakā*)', 'Twelve-Bases (*Dwādaśāyatna* i.e. *Cakṣu* and the *Cākṣas, Śrotra* and the Śrotrās etc.)' or the 'Eighteen Elements (*Aṣṭadaśadhātūs* i.e. 12 *āyatāanas* and their respective conscious products such as *cakṣu-vijñāna, śrotrvijñāna* etc.).[17]

The Buddhist view of omniscience is scientific in the sense of not being summative but one that holds a confirmatory key or a touch stone to all ordinary knowledge. No scientist lays personal claim to omniscience nor does he specifically speak of the omniscience of anyone else yet in so far as the not only does not deny the possibility of an omniscient but also affirms the same by holding out that there is nothing in principle, that cannot be brought in the perview of science. It is in this context that we can understand the observation 'that neither did Buddha claim omniscience nor was omniscience claimed of the Buddha until the very latest stratum in the *Pāli* canon'[18] together with Buddha's specific refusal to deny the possibility of an omniscient recluse or brāhmin.[19] Scientists are not unaware of the 'limitations of the science'[20] but they do not deter them from the path of knowledge and they come forward even to calculate the 'indeterminacy, correct upto a statistical fraction. The possibility of omniscience is kept intact.

In such a sort of view of omniscience the future is known as not only future i.e. possible but also holding infinite possibilities each of which can become an actuality and the same can be determined or predicted (but not forced). It is not difficult to avoid in this case that fatal mistake which makes the scholars see something in Omniscience as detrimental to 'Freedom of the will'.

Summing up, it may be pointed out that the Buddhist view of Omniscience is neither, strictly speaking, scientific, nor philosophic and not even religious and yet it has overtones of each one of them.

Endnotes

1. *Aṅguttara Nikāya* I. 189.
2. *Dīgha Nikāya* I, 17-18;
3. *Bhagvadgita* XVIII. 66.
4. See Satkari Mukherjee, "*The Omniscient as the Founder of a Religion*" – Nava Nalanda Mahavihara Research Publication Part II (1960) pp 1-44.
5. *Manual of Buddhism*, p. 50.
6. Poussin, *Buddhism* (Third edition 1925) p. 132.
7. *Buddhist Philosophy*, p. 33.
8. K. N. Jayatilleke, *Early Buddhist Theory of Knowledge*, pp. 376-80.
9. Ananda K. Coomaraswamy "*Rebirth and Omniscience in Pāli Buddhism*" – Indian Culture III 1936 pp. 19-34.
10. See for example *Majjhima Nikāya* I. 519.
11. Ibid II. 127, See Jayatilleke op. cit. p. 203 as also p. 468.
12. Ibid II.
13. S. S. Surya Narayan Sastri, "*Omniscience*" The Indian Historical Quartery, Vol. XIV. No. 1, 1938 p. 292.
14. Ibid.
15. For a paraphrasing of the main arguments, see Esther A. Sclomon, "*The Problem of Omniscience* (Sarvajnatva)" The Adyar Library Bulletin Vol. XXVI, 1962, p. 36-77.
16. Tattva Saṅgraha Verses 3345-47 in answer to Verse 3149.
17. Of L.S. Stebbing *A Modern Introduction to Logic* (Serventh edn.) pp, 406-414.
18. Of *Saṃkhya Kārika* 54, 56.
19. It is not easy to translate these two words.
20. Stcherbatsky, *The Central Conception of Buddhism and the Meaning of the Word "Dharma"*, p.5; *Saṃyutta-Nikāya* iv-15-17; *Viśuddhimagga*, Ch. XIV; warren' Buddhism in Translation p. 158; Mrs. Rhys Davids, *Buddhist Psychology* p. 41.

* Paper presented at International Seminar on Buddhism, Magadh University, Bodh Gaya (Feb. 14-19, 1972).

38

HISTORY OF BUDDHISM IN MONGOLIA
A Preliminary Survey *

Piotr Klafkowski

Although we are more or less sure that there was the first spread of Buddhism in Mongolia much earlier than we know at present, the so-called Sogdian propagation, we cannot tell much about it. We only may state that Buddhism came to Mongolia with the Sogdian people sometimes probably around the VII century. The Sogdians were of Iranian origin. At the time of their arrival in Mongolian lands they had to encounter the strong influence of the Nestorian Christian church, quite firmly established there by Nestorian exiles from the Byzantine Empire. The traces of these religious fightings, where the three systems met – Nestorian Christianity, Iranian Buddhism and Mongolian native *Shamanism* – have been found in one of the most important Mongolian historical texts, *The Sacred History of the Mongols* (coming from the XIII century) by the eminent Soviet historian *Lev Gumilov*, in his book *"Searching for the Never-Existing Empire"*. This book, gives the best interpretation of the *Secret History of the Mongols* is based on the excellent Polish translation by *Stanislaw Kaluzynski,* titled *"Tajna Historia Mongolow."*

(Polish translation titled "Sladami Cywillzacji Wielkiego Stepu" – as the author does not have a copy with him, it is difficult to give the exact date of the publication of the Polish edition but, to the best of the author's memory, it was published by the State Publishing Institute PIW, Warsaw, ca. 1972.)

We may assume that the final result of the fights between the Buddhists and the Nestorians in Mongolia was the Shamanist native religious take-over, completed by the time of Temujin's becoming the Chengis Khan in 1206.

When the great Mongol Empire was at the peak of its power, *Godan*, the son of Ogodei, the son of Chengis Khan (i.e. the grandson of the great Chengis Khan) started a great march on Tibet. The council of the Tibetan monasteries immediately realized that Tibet was too weak to offer any resistance to the advancing Mongols. The only way left was to negotiate, and for that reason a special envoy was dispatched to Godan, in the name of *Kun dGa'a rGyal mTshan* (1182-1251), whose name pronounces Kunga Gyaltsen, but who has passed to history as Śākya Paṇḍita. The Mongols, converted by him to the Buddhist faith of the Old (unreformed) church, entered Tibet not as conquerors but as protectors. After Śākya Paṇḍita's death his nephew, *'aPhags Pa bLo Gros rGyal mTshan* (1235-1280, known as *Phagspa*) was invited by Kubilai Khan in 1253 as an Imperial Teacher and, when Kubilai officially became the ruler in 1260, Phagspa became his official chief advisor for Tibetan and Buddhist affairs. He is also reputed to have invented the famous Mongolian square script, known after his name. Phagspa's diaries od 1271 mention a foreign friend of Kubilai Khan, who, by all probability, must have been *Marco Polo.**

Gradually the attitude of the Mongols towards the Tibetans started changing. While the relations between Śākya Paṇḍita and Godan were of a lord-subject nature, the relations between Phagspa and Kubilai were of the Patron-priest one, which shows the change of the Mongol attitude to the Tibetan Buddhist church.

An interesting insight into Phagspa's methods on completing the conversion of the Mongols may be given. In the year 1267, when Phagspa was called to Mongolia, he left dressed in Mongol clothes. Chomden Rigral, the abbot of the Narthang monastery, felt it not to be good and wrote Phagspa the following lines:

"Lord Buddha's sun-like face is now clouded by the Kargyu teachings, the officials are not good and the people are deprived of peace and happiness.

When they see their beloved Lamas dressing up and behaving like the Hor barbarians, someone does not understand these lines he cannot be exceptional, even when he claims so."

The key-word in this stanza was *"exceptional"*, which is Tibetan is just *"Phagspa."*

Phagspa himself proved to be a sharp-witted one, writing in his answer the following lines:

"Even Lord Buddha himself has said that the Doctrine will have its ups and downs and that the happiness of the people depends on their *Karma*, not their officials stating to prove to the Mongols that we are right I must become one of them. If someone does not understand these lines he must indeed be of a scattered knowledge."

The word for *"scattered knowledge"* in Tibetan is just *"rigral."* The above letters are to be found in the *gDung Rabs* or the *History of the Sakyas, Sakya Sumbum* vol. 7 (see the reading list).

After the death of Kubilai Khan the Śākya hegemony in the Mongol Empire did not last long. The Emperor died in 1295, and only 55 years later, in 1350, the Central Tibetan province of *dBus* fell under the rule of the *Phag Mc Drug Pa* family. The Mongol Empire itself collapsed in 1386.

The texts dealing with the various events of the period is the *Sa sKya Pa'I bKa'a 'aBum* commonly referred to as the *Sakya Sumbum* or the collected works of the five great scholars of the Sakya Monastery. The whole collection amounts to 15 volumes, divided as follows:

1. Kun dGa'a sNying Po's (1092-1158) works – vols. 1-2.
2. bSod Nams rTses Mo's (1142-1182) works – vols. 3-5.
3. Grags Pa rGyal mTshan's (1147-1216) works – vols. 6-9.
4. Kun dGa'a rGyal mTshan's (1182-1251) works – vols. 10-12.
5. 'aPhags Pa bLo Gros rGyal mTshan's (1235-1280) works –vols. 13-15.

The whole collection is analysed by the famous Soviet Tibetologist, Vostrikov in his book "*Tibetan Historical Literature*" (For further details please consult the reading list).

After the fall of the Mongol Empire both Tibet and Mongolia were reduced to small states, divided into many parts by the local monasteries (Tibet) or petty khans (Mongolia). The unified Sakya sect power was on the decline, and there was a great need of some far reaching reforms in the Buddhist church of the day, or of organizing a new force within it. This need was realized by *bLo bZang Grags Pa* immortal under the nickname of *bTsang Kha Pa* (1357 Kumbum – 1419 Galdan), who created the new sect of Tibetan Buddhism – the Gelugpa or Yellow Hat sect – and managed to make it a leading religious political power of the day. In 1409 he founded the first monastery of this sect, named *dG'a dDan* (Galdhan), near Lhasa.

After the death of Tsong Kha Pa (as he is commonly referred to in simplified Tibetan spelling), his successive incarnations became the Dalai Lamas of Lhasa. As the process of emergence of the Dalai Lamas to both religious and political power in Tibet is not wholly relevant to the present study, the author will limit himself to giving only their names in phonetic Tibetan spelling. The role of the Third and Fourth Dalai Lamas in the process of emergence of the Jetsundamba Khutuktus of Urga will be dealt with in the next section. We may as well quote here the title of the superb study by Tsepon W.D. Shakabpa "*Tibet, A Political History*", Yale 1967, and its revised and enlarged version (approximately three times as big as the original one) titled "*A Political History of Tibet*" in Tibetan, two volumes, published by the author in Kalimpong, 1976. These two books will give any interested reader a good insight into the background of the Dalai Lama system.

The Dalai Lama appeared in the following order:

I. Gedun Truppa of Tashilunpo – 1391-1474.

II. Gedun Gyatso – 1475-1542.

III. Sonam Gyatso – 1543-1588 – the first Dalai Lama to have received this title from Altan Khan in 1577.

IV. Yonten Gyatso – 1589-1617 – the great-grandson of Altan Khan, brought up in Mongolia at the time of the religious fights in Tibet.

V. Ngawang Lobsang Gyatso, the Great Fifth – 1617-1682 – the first Dalai Lama to exercise full political power over Tibet.

VI. Tsangyang Gyatso – the only officially deposed Dalai Lama, one of the most eminent lyrical poets of Tibet – 1683-1706.

VII. VIII, IX, X, XI and XII Dalai Lamas either died before ascending to power or were poisoned by their respective regents and had not any influence on the history of Mongolia. All the details about them are found in *Shakbpa's* books.

XIII. Ngawang Lobsang Thubten Gyatso the Great Thirteenth Dalai Lama who gave Tibet independence and whose 1913 declaration of Tibetan independence was an example to be followed by the Mongols in 1921-1933.

XIV. Tensing Gyatso (born 1935) – in India since 1959 – the present Dalai Lama, sometimes reputed to be the last one on the basis of some mysterious ancient prophecy; has his headquarters in Dharamsala, Kangra District, Himachal Pradesh.

The origin of the Jetsundamba Khutukus of Urga – the supreme lamaist Pontiffs of Mongolia – may be put at the time of the Great Fifth Dalai Lama of Lhasa. In the process of de force unification of the whole Tibet under his supremacy of both religious and political character, he was aided by the Mongolian *Gusri Khan (died* 1655), who continued the policy of his predecessor *Altan Khan* who was helping the IV Dalai Lama. In 1659, when the Mongol tribes of the Koko Nor region were fighting each other, the Great Fifth Dalai Lama arranged the peace mission which ended the fights. The Great Fifth died in 1682.

And thus we are passing now to the most interesting part of our study. In the year 1635, one year after the death of Ligdan the last of the great Khans, a boy was born in the family of Tushiyetu Khan. The boy's name was *Dzanzanbazar,* and from the earliest childhood his life was accompanied by miracles and omens, proving that the the boy must have been an extremely important incarnation. The Great Fifth Dalai Lama on receiving the account of the boy's wisdom, proclaimed him to be the incarnation of Tārānātha. According to another tradition, Dzanzanbazar was the incarnation of the Mongolian Lama *Maidari Khutuku* (1592-1653). However, the authoritative Mongolian chronicle *Erdeni-yin Tobei* (1620) does not confirm this claim. Be it as it was, in 1650 the fifteen year old Dzanzanbazar (whose name, incidentally, is the Mongolia pronunciation of the Sanskrit *Jñānavajra*) visited Tibet and spoke to the Great

Fifth. The Dalai Lama, amazed by the boy's knowledge, gave him the Tibetan name of *bStan Pa'i rGyal bTsan dPal bZang Po* (Tanpi Gyaltsen Palzang Po in simplified spelling) and the title of *rJe bTsun Dam Pa Hutuk-tu* (Jetsundamba Khutuku – The Precious Man of Great Wisdom). In 1652 the Great Kurultai (the council of the Mongolian tribes) of the Khalkha Mongols, needing a strong leader to protect the unity of the people, granted him the supreme political authority over all Mongols and the throne of Urga. From then on the boy was known as *Bogdo Gegen* or the Living Buddha of Urga; another of his famous names was *Ondur Gegen*. All his successive incarnations at the *Hu Re Chen Mo* or the Great Monastery of Urga were known under the names of Bogdo Gegens or Jetsundamba Khutuktus. In 1688, to stop the Oirat invasion of Galdan Qhotshotu Khan, Ondur Gegen accepted the sovereignty of the Manchu Emperor *Taifin Abakai* (born 1654, ruled 1661-1722, better known under the Chinese name of his ruling era *K'ang-His*). In 1691 he visited Peking and was received with utmost honours by the Manchu Emperor. To gain as many merits for his future lives as it was only possible, he is reputed to have copied the whole Kanjur three times and the Tanjur one time. He died in 1723.

The complete list of the Jetsundamba Khutuktus based on the *"Eminent Polymaths of Mongolia"* now follows:

I. Ondur Gegen Dzanzanbazar – 1635-1723.

II. Lobsang Damba Dongmi – 1724-1757.

III. Ishi Damba Nima – 1758-1773.

IV. Lobsang Dubdan Wangchug – 1775-1813.

V. Jibchun Lobzang Chultum Jigmed – 1815-1840.

VI. Jibchun Lobzang Baldah Damba – 1843-1848.

VII. Jibchun Ngawang Choji Ji Wangchug Trinle Gyamcho Jetsun Ngawang Choskyi Jig Wangchug Drimed Gyatso – 1850-68.

VIII. Jibchun Choskyi Nima Tensin Wangchug – 1870 – 1924 - the last and the most controversial of them all, fought the Chinese in 1909/12 and the Russians in 1919/21, the man who created Mongolia's independence, the friend and protector of the famous "Mad Baron" Roman von Ungern-Stern-berg who occupied Urga on February 3, 1921.

The long tradition of the Mongolian lamas of encyclopedic knowledge and writing in Tibetan ends in the person of *bLo bZang rTa mGrin*, commonly referred to as Tsawa Tamdin. He was born in the Gobi Desert in 1867. A child of genius, he is reputed to have learnt the Doctrine at the age of four. He traveled extensively all over Mongolia, rediscovering and reactivating the old centres of Buddhist faith. In 1906 he was consecrated as the Urga Khambo – the Supreme Pontiff of Urga. In 1915-1919 he was devoted to history and wrote the last two Tibetan language chronicles of Mongolian Buddhism – the *gSer Gyi Deb Ther* ("The Golden Annals", see the reading list). In 1922 he founded a Tantric College in Urga, and in 1926 – the *bKa'h gDams Chos Gling* (Kadam Choling) Buddhist Monastery. In 1935 he established the Mongolian college of the Losalling Monastery. Deeply loved by all the Mongols, he attained Nirvana in 1937. His complete works in 15 volumes are being published from New Delhi by this Mongolian Lama Guru Deva.

The first parts of the Kanjur were translated into Mongolian at the time of the Emperor *Khaisan Kulug* (1308-1311) of the Mongolian Imperial Dynasty of China. The most famous translator of that time was *Chos kyi'od Zer.*

This process was continued at the time of *Tumed Altan Khan* (1507-1582), when Siregetu Guushi Chorjiva and others translated most of the Tibetan Kanjur into Mongolian.

In 1628-29, by the order of *Ligdan Khan* (1604-1634), the whole Kanjur was codified and calligraphed in gold and silver letters. It consisted, then of 113 volumes (as confirmed by the Mongolian chronicles *Altan Eriqe of* 1887 and *Bolor Eriqe* of 1774-75). The work on that edition was commenced at the *Quotala Bayasyu Monastery.* The editorial committee of 35 scholars was supervised by *Kun dGa'a o'd Zer.*

On the Imperial order of the Emperor *Taifin Abakai* (Chinese name of his ruling era was K'ang-His), in 1717-1720 the whole Kanjur of Ligdan Khan was revised, reset in order to achieve the auspicious number of 108 volumes, and cut into new printing blocks. In 1718 at the *Dolonor Monastery* the text underwent the final revisions and the calligraphers could start their work. By 1720 the complete Kanjur blocks were cut and ready for printing. This edition, the so-called *Imperial Red Edition* of the Mongolian Kanjur, was finally published by the end of 1720. A complete copy of this edition exists in the archives of the International Academy of Indian Culture, New Delhi, and is now in the process of publication.

It is a little risky to include Buryat-Mongolian and Siberian. Buddhism here because, although closely related to our main topic, the Siberian Buddhist studies are still a new field, relatively little worked out. We may begin with the year 1660 (which roughly coincides with the Great Fifth Dalai Lama and Ondur Gegen), when the first arrivals from Khalkha Mongolia arrived in Buryatia; it is very probable that they were the refugees after the same incidents which made Ondur Gegen the first Jetsundamba Khutuktu. In 1667 the immigrants from Khalkha and the native Buryats (who were there already much earlier, although their origin is still uncertain) became a part of the *Vierkhnieudinsk* (now Ulan Ude) District of Russia. The inflow of the lamas from both Mongolia proper and Tibet into the new area was constantly increasing – for example 150 Tibetan lamas came to Buryatia in the year 1720 alone. They obtained their Russian citizenship in 1752. The supreme lama of Buryatia, since 1760, was the *Pandita Khambo Lama* – and the first one was *Dambarajiya Zayayin.* He died in 1777. Later on, in 1812, Alexander the Tzar of Russia sent a personal letter to the Pandita Khambo Lama asking him to conduct special prayers on the intention of defeating Napolean. The successful (as it seemed) prayer and the subsequent defeat of Napolean made it easier for the Buryat people to establish new monasteries, and in the year 1831only six of them were established. In 1848 the first Buryat *Cham* dance was performed at the *Iruge* Monastery. Finally, on *May* 15, 1853, the Pandita Khambo Lama was made the supreme lama of the whole Eastern Siberia. Earlier, in 1810, the famous *Aginsk* Monastery was built, which together with the *Ivolginsk* Monastery are the best known Buryat Buddhist temples of today. The Buddhist church and faith of the modern Soviet Buryatia receive the state support and have every possibility to flourish within the new social system of the USSR.

* The famous Venetian traveler also mentions in his book the personal lama of Kubilai, but does not give his name; yet we may assume that these two great men of East and West may have met personally.

39

THE MATERIAL MILIEU OF THE DAŚABHŪMIKA-SŪTRA

Kalpana Upreti

The *Daśabhūmikasūtra,* also known as *Daśabhūmisvara, Daśabhūmikaśāstra and Daśabhūmaka,* is one of the nine *Dharmas* or *Vaipulyasūtras* of the Mahāyānists. The contents of the work are essentially ethico-religious and metaphysical in character, and consist of harangues to the devotees in 'Sesquipedalian phraseology and gorgeous metaphor' as to how an aspirant to *Buddhahood* has to gradually develop his spiritual stature. The name of the author of the text, like many other *Mahāyāna* texts, is not known. Fortunately our position in regard to the date of the text is more satisfactory. The first Chinese translation of the text was prepared by *Dharma*rakṣa in 297 A.D.[1] This translation however does not include the *Gāthā* portion. This omission has rightly induced the scholars to conclude that this portion is a later addition.[2] The prose portion, which was already well systematized before the close of the 3rd century A.D., can be put approximately in the first two centuries of the Christian era, coinciding with the *Kuṣāna* rule in northern India and that of the *Sātavāhanas* in the Deccan.

The nature of the work is such that we can not expect much data on the contemporary socio-economic conditions. The similies, metaphorical usages and certain terms which recur very often, however, give us a broad and general idea about the material milieu of this age. Recently the archaeologists and historians have emphasized the accelerated process of urbanization during this period.[3] According to R. S. Sharma : "If we leave out the Harappa phase, archaeology makes it evident that Kuṣana India saw the highest peak of urbanization. Excavations at Sonkh (Mathurā) have revealed seven levels of Gupta structure ... Apparently this phase saw not only the peak of urbanization, but also of crafts, commerce and monetary economy."[4] At another place he remarks: "The *Sātavāhanas* who ruled over the Deccan were equipped with all those material components which Mauryas possessed in the earlier period in northern India, namely the profuse use of coins and iron tools. What further distinguished their rule was the enormous trade with the Mediterranean region and the influence of the Roman coins coupled with the rise of urban settlements in the Deccan on a huge scale".[5] The textual evidence at our disposal is not ample enough to support or contradict such general statements. However, the few available references clearly indicate to a state of society in which urban economy and value system played a prominent role.[6]

The word *grāma* has been used very rarely. In two instances it has been used to denote the basic social unit and at one place it has a metaphoric usage. The rural culture has been viewed through the eyes of the sophisticated city-dweller and the language of the former has been called *grāmyā* (rustic) in a derogatory sense.[7] In contrast to this, the language spoken by the urban elite is called *paurī* (sauve, elegant and refined).[8] Thus a clearcut distinction is made between a village rustic and a sophisticated city-dweller; and of course, the author identifies himself with the latter. This was in contradistinction with the stand taken by the authors of the *Dharmasūtras* who were favourably disposed to the rural culture[9] but in complete consonance with the stand of early Buddhists[10] who thrived and prospered with the growth of the urban centres. The terms and expressions referring specifically to village economy are very few. Cane-groves (Veṇu-vana), sugar cane-groves (lkṣu-vana), reed-groves (Nāḍa-vana), sesame-groves (Tila-vana) and rice-farms (Śāli-vana) are reerred to.[11] There is also a reference to the ripening of the crops.[12] Such statements, however, are very general and do not betray an intimate knowledge of the author with the village economy.

In contrast to this, the terms and expressions related to the city life and its economic activity are not only numerous but also betray the author's close acquaintance and familiarity with the urban mode of life and economy. The words like *Nagara, Nigama, Janapada, Rāṣṭra, Rājadhānī,* though used in stock phrases,[13] have specific meaning as is well attested by the contemporary inscriptions. Precious metals and stones, like *Hiraṇya, Suvarṇa, Maṇi* (gem), *Muktā* (pearl), *Vaidūrya* (lapislazuli), *Śaṅkha* (mother of pearl), *Śilā* (crystal), *Pravāla* (coral), *Jambunada-suvarṇas, Aśmagarbha* (emerald), *Jātarūpa, Rajat,*[14] *Musāragalva*[15] (sapphire or emerald) used by the urban craftsman for manufacturing various types of ornaments.[16] This enriched the technique of lapidary. At one place ten types of refinements or qualities of an excellent gem are enumerated.[17] Even the *Bodhisattvas* are named after various types of jewels. Refrences to trade and mercantile activity, especially maritime trade, are numerous. In fact the illustrative sentences and phrases, in the form of similies and metaphors, make it very clear that the author had very profound knowledge of marine phenomena. He was not only acquainted with the basic characteristics of an ocean[18] but also with the monsoon winds[19] (vātamaṇḍa, vātamaṇḍali) and cloud formation.[20] The sea is called *Sāgara, mahāsāgara, samudra* and *mahāsamudra* and the ship as *pota*[21] or *mahāyāna pātra.*[22] Some of the *Bodhisattvas* are named after *Samudra* or *Sāgara.* Trade through land routes organised by leading traders, is also referred to. The precautions which the caravan leaders had to take for safe journey are also mentioned.[23] Branches of learning like Calculations *(gaṇanā),* Numerals *(Saṁkhyā),* Counting of coins *(Mudrā),* Scripts *(Lipiśāstra),* working out mathematical problems *(Nikṣepa)* closely related to commerce were usually learnt by those who aspired for a mercantile career.[24]

Lastly, it would also be highly relevant to point out that luxuries like grand vehicles, male and female slaves: maintenance of gardens etc., enjoyments of arts like poetry, drama, anecdotes, dance, music and mythical stories[25] were essentially urban phenomena. The accumulation of the surplus products in urban areas in a few hands led to such conspicuous consumption and pomp and show by the rich classes with its anti-thesis namely, the poverty, misery and degradation of the rural and urban producing but exploited masses. Thus the *Mahāyāna* Buddhism of which the *Daśabhūmika-Sūtra* is a scripture, represented *fin-de-siecle* of the reversed world consciousness of an age in which the differences between the village and city, on the one hand, and between haves and have-nots, on the other, had become very acute and antagonistic.

Endnotes

1. M. Winternitz, *A History of Indian Literature,* English Trans. Vol. II, p. 328.
2. P. L. Vaidya (Ed.), *Daśabhūmika Sūtra* (Intro.) P.I.
3. This view seems to be based on concrete facts, and sound and scientific reasoning.
4. General President's Address, 36th Session, Indian History Congress, P.7.
5. *Aspects of Political Ideas and Institutions in Ancient India,* 2nd Ed. P. 20.
6. The other Buddhist Sanskrit works like *Mahāvastu, Avadānśataka* and *Divyāvadāna* are more informative in this regard than the work begin utilized for this paper.
7. Daśa, p. 15.
8. Ibid.
9. *Baudhāyana Dharmasūtra,* ii, 6.33.
10. *Pārājika* (Nalanda Ed.), p. 25; *Cullavagga* (Nalanda Ed.), p. 193.
11. *Daśa,* P. 63.
12. P. 41.
13. PP. 12, 29.
14. PP. 12, 13, 18, 25, 29, 40, 55, etc.
15. PP. 13, 18.
16. PP. 29, 35, etc.
17. P. 66.
18. Ibid.
19. P. 44.
20. P. 60.
21. Ibid.
22. P. 40.

23. P. 13.
24. P. 5, 29.
25. Ibid.

40

BOOK REVIEWS

The Conception of Buddhist Nirvāṇa

By Th. Stcherbatsky

Published by Motilal Banarasidas, Delhi. 1977.

'Old is gold' – this old adage can be very appropriately applied to Theodore Stcherbatsky's 'The Conception of Buddhist *Nirvāṇa*'. A name which is almost a catch-word in the list of Buddhist scholasticism. Stcherbatsky's contribution to the field of Buddhist Logic and Philosophy is well appreciated by the students of Buddhist Philosophy since the publication of his works. Its importance has not diminished in the least with the passing of time. His 'Conception of Buddhist *Nirvāṇa*' was long out of print. Messers Motilal Banarasidas has done a commendable service in publishing the book in a new form which will satisfy the long-felt need of the scholars of Buddhism. The editorial work by Dr. Jaidev Singh not only adds to its importance, but gives a new light to it which helps the reader to comprehend the most difficult topic of *Mādhyamika* philosophy – which becomes more and more interesting as one goes deeper into it. Our thanks go to the editor as well as to the publisher.

S. Sengupta

Buddhavijayakāvyam

by Professor Shanti Bhikshu Shastri

Published by the author himself, Shanti Sadan, Saran Lodge Area, Lakkar Bazar Marg, Solon – 173212 (H.P.)

The work entitled *Buddhavijayakāvyam* is an epic poem composed by one of the most renowned scholars of Sanskrit and Buddhist Studies. It elaborately depicts the life of the Buddha together with his philosophical and religious doctrines. In fact, the work is written in the tradition of the great poet Aśvaghoṣa who composed two epic poems entitled the *Buddhacarita* and the *Saundarananda*. The entire poem has been written in a dialect of Sanskrit which became standardized in the hoary past and was grammaticised in course of time by

Pānini, the first known grammarian of the language. Following Aśvaghoṣa's tradition, he has freely used words and terms common in Buddhology. One may come across some words of the older dialectics as well, but according to the author's own admission, the same have been used with certain specific purpose. The author seems to be responsive to the problems of printing technology as he has used the *anusvāra* in place of the fifth letters of *vargas* save 'n' in the interior of the words. He has made this point clear in his preface. As if in order to provide justification for the same, he cites manuscript writing tradition in this context.

The number of verses in this work run into five thousand and one hundred. The same are divided into hundred cantos. The metre used in the work is *Anuṣṭubh,* but towards the end of each canto, the author gives one verse in the *Vaṁsastha Vṛtta.* The story of the life of the Master from his *Bodhisattvahood* to the attainment of the *Mahāparinibbāna* has been retold by the author in an extraordinarily simple language with easily understandable diction. The main sentiment *(rasa)* happens to be *Bhakti* or devotion which the author seems to testify by his own words in the following verse –

Cittaṁ priṇayituṁ cārucarcā seyamatṛpyataḥ.

Buddhapūjaiva hīnasya vibhavairmama vāṅmayī.

(XIV, 8)

The other sentiments also find their due place such as *Sṛaṅgāra, Karuṇa* and even *Hāsya* in one or two places. But the author seems to be excessively careful in their use, more particularly in the cause of *Sṛaṅgāra* which has not been allowed to trespass into the realm of vulgarity.

The philosophical ideas depicted in the poem reflect the *Theravāda* tradition, but the author has freely and skillfully interwoven the *Mahāyāna* viewpoints at specific occasions. The Buddha's human form has touched the heart of the author to such an extent that he seems to be over conscious in depicting him as a human being. But it does not mean that the author has lost sight of the supernatural contexts. Wherever such occasions come across, he gives full play of his poetic imagination and sores very high in his flight, but the human aspiration of the Buddha seem to constantly haunt him and remind him to be always on his guard. To him his efforts in this context had been in the direction of the cultivation of *Bodhicitta* or Enlightened mind. On the whole, one cannot resist his temptation in passing his judgement on this work of the highest order in the field of Sanskrit poetry where Vālmikī and Kālidāsa had left their footprints, to be a work written in the old tradition of the Buddhist poets.

Sanghasen Singh

41

PĀLI LITERATURE
A Critique

Anukul Chandra Banerjee

There is no denying the fact that the Buddhist literature is chiefly embedded in *Pāli* – a study of which gives us a true and clear picture of the culture and heritage of ancient India.

Pāli is the language of canonical literature of *Theravāda* Buddhism. The huge mass of the canonical literature consists of collections of speeches or conversations or sayings, narratives and rules of the order. This is technically called the *Tipiṭaka* in the Buddhist literature. It consists of three *Piṭakas*, viz., *Vinayapiṭaka*, *Suttapiṭaka* and *Abhidhammapiṭaka*.

The *Vinayapiṭaka* contains rules of discipline guiding the lives of the Buddhist monks and nuns. The rules and regulations were promulgated by Buddha himself during the early period as the occasion arose. The *Vinayapiṭaka* comprises the following texts:

(i) The *Suttavibhaṅga* consisting of (a) *Mahāvibhaṅga* and (b) *Bhikkhunīvibhaṅga*:

(ii) The *Khandhaka* comprising (a) *Mahāvagga* and (b) *Cullavagga*:

(iii) The *Parivāra* or the *Parivārapāṭha*.

The *Suttavibhaṅga* tells us in a sort of historical introduction how, when and why the particular rule in question came to be laid down. The words of the rule are given in full, followed by a very ancient word for word commentary, which in its turn is succeeded by further explanations and discussions on doubtful points. It comprises (a) *Mahāvibhaṅga* which has eight chapters dealing with eight classes of transgressions against discipline and (b) *Bhikkhunivibhaṅga*, a shorter work, being a commentary on the code for the nuns.

The *Patimokkha* which is included in *Suttavibhaṅga*, is the nucleus of the *Vinayapiṭaka*. It deals with the ecclesiastical offences requiring confession and explanation. In other words, it contains a set of rules to be observed by the members of the *Saṅgha* (Order) in their daily life. There are two codes – one for the *bhikkhus* (monks) called the *Bhikkhupātimokkha*, and the other for the bhikkhunis (nuns) known as the *Bhikkhunīpātimokkha*. The former consists of eight sections containing 227 offences, while the latter only seven section comprising 311.

The *Khandhakas* comprise two divisions, viz. (a) *Mahāvagga* and (b) *Cullavagga.* They form a sort of continuation and supplement to the *Suttavibhaṅga.* The *Mahāvagga,* in ten chapters, furnishes us with the story of the formation of the *Saṅgha,* rules for admission into the Order, the mode of life during the rains, observance of the *Pavāraṇā* and the *Kaṭhinā* ceremonies, food, clothing, seats, conveyance, medicaments, dress and the like.

The *Suttapiṭaka* contains prose dialogue, legends, pithy sayings and verses. It is the primary source for the doctrine of Buddha. It incorporates the greatest literary works of Buddhism. It consists of five *Nikāyas* or collections, viz., *Dīgha, Majjhima, Saṁyutta, Aṅguttara* and *Khuddaka.* The *Dighanikāya* is indeed a collection of long discourses and is divided into three parts: (a) *Sīlakkhandha,* (b) *Mahāvagga* and (c) *Pātheya* or *Pāṭikavagga.* It contains thirty-four suttas, each of which deals elaborately with one or more points of Buddhism. The *Majjhimanikāya* which is divided into three books, each consisting of fifty suttas is indeed the collection of discourses of medium length. The discourses of this *Nikāya* cover almost all the points of early Buddhism and throw a flood of light on the life of the Buddhist monks. *Brāhmaṇical* conception of sacrifices, various forms of asceticism and relation of Buddhism to Jainism. The *Saṁyuttanikāya* is the third collection of the *Suttapiṭaka.* It is a compilation of suttas with their main bearings on psycho-ethical and philosophical problems. It is divided into the five main *vaggas* and 56 sections called *Saṁyuttas.* The *Aṅguttaranikāyas* is the collection distinguished by numerical groupings of *dhammas* arranged serially in an ascending order. The importance of this text lies in its application on a comprehensive scale to the numerical scheme of mnemonics as enunciated in the *Kumārapañha.* The *Khuddakanikāya* which is the last division of the *Suttapiṭaka* consists of fifteen independent treatises belonging to different periods. It is composed for the most part in verses and includes the following books, viz., *Khuddakapāṭha, Dhammapada, Udāna, Itivuttaka, Suttanipāta, Vimānavatthu, Petavatthu, Theragāthā, Therīgāthā, Jātaka, Niddesa, Paṭisambhidāmagga, Apadāna, Buddhavaṁsa* and *Cariyāpiṭaka.* The Khuddakapāṭha is a book of the minor sayings and consists of nine short texts. The *Dhammapada* contains the sublime teachings of Buddha. It contains 423 verses divided into 26 *vaggas* or chapters. The *Udāna* which is a treatise containing Buddhist stories and sentences divided into eight *vaggas* or chapters. The Itivuttaka is a book of quotations of the authoritative sayings of Buddha. The *Suttanipāta* composed in verse contains important traces of early Buddhism, recognizable from its language, style and contents. The *Vimānavatthu* supplies in verses a graphic description of some celestial abodes enjoyed by the gods for having done meritorious deeds while on earth as human beings. The *Petavatthu,* on the other hand, consists of short poems, illustrating the belief in the existence of life beyond death, sufferings after death for having done evil deeds while on earth. The *Theragātha* and *Therīgāthā* are two collections of poems, some of which are believed to have been sung by theras or therīs during the lifetime of Buddha and others immediately after his great demise. The *Jātaka* contains birth-stories of Buddha in verse. It further comprises fables, fairy tales short anecdotes, moral narratives, etc. It is very valuable as regards literature and art. The *Niddesa* which is divided into two parts, *Mahāniddesa* and *Cullaniddesa*, contains detailed explanation by Sāriputta of 33 suttas belonging to the last two *vaggas* of the *Suttanipāta*. The *Paṭisambhidāmagga* comprises three *vaggas* or chapters. Each of the *vaggas* further consists of ten topics or *Kathās*. The *Apadāna* is an anthology of legends in verse describing great deeds of 550 male members and 40 female members of the Buddhist Order. The *Buddhavaṁsa* gives in verse an account of twenty four Buddhas supposed to have preceded the historical Gotama Buddha. It is probably a mere poetical expansion of some short prose history of the previous Buddhas. The *Cariyāpiṭaka*, a post-Aśokan work, signifies a canonical collection of stories illustrating the modes in which the *Bodhisatta* practices the *cariyā* or conduct.

The *Abhidhammapiṭaka* which is the third division of the *Tipiṭaka* treats of the same topics as the *Suttapiṭaka* and differs from that collection only in being more scholastic. It follows a progressive scheme of treatment, the *mātikas* or *uddesas* are followed by the niddesa and comprises the following works, viz., *Dhammasaṅgaṇi*, *Vibhaṅga*, *Kathāvatthu*, *Puggalapaññatti*, *Dhātukathā*, *Yamaka* and *Paṭṭhāna*. The *Dhammasaṅgaṇi* means co-enumeration of *Dhamma* and is 'in great part an analysis of the psychological and psycho-physical data of ethics'. It is indeed a manual or text-book, and not a treatise or disquisition elaborated and rendered attractive and edifying after the manner of most of the *Suttapiṭaka*. The *Vibhaṅga* or exposition usually deals with the different categories and formulas treated of in the *Dhammasaṅgaṇi*. The *Kathāvatthu* is a book of debate on matters of theology and philosophy. It is undoubtedly a work of the Aśokan age and was composed by Moggaliputta Tissa Thera, President of the Third Buddhist Council. The *Puggalapaññatti* which throws some light on several obscure Buddhist terms and phrases was probably composed after the *Nikāyas*. The *Dhātukathā* discusses the mental characteristics most likely to be found in conjunction with converted and earnest folk. It can hardly be regarded as an independent treatise. Its purpose is to serve as a supplement to the *Dhammasaṅgaṇi*. The *Yamaka* deals with matters of psychological, ethical and eschatological interest. The *Paṭṭhāna* which is called the book of causes, consists of three divisions. The twenty four paccayas or causal relations are enumerated therein.

The canonical literature apart, there are also a large number of non-canonical works. Among them the *Milindapañha* deserves our special attention. Most probably it originated in North-West India. It contains a learned dialogue between king Milinda and Venerable monk Nāgasena. The *Nettipakaraṇa* is another important text. It consists of connected treatment of the whole of the teaching of Buddha. The major portion of the non-canonical *Pāli* texts, however, contains commentaries on *Pāli Tipiṭaka* works composed by Buddhaghoṣa, *Dhammapāla* and others. There are also a few works on history, grammar, rhetoric and prosody. Lastly, the *Visuddhimaga*, a small encyclopedia on early Buddhism, is a remarkable contribution to the Buddhist literature by Buddhaghoṣa.

Pāli is, indeed, the main stream of Buddhist thought and culture. It contains works mostly of religious nature. Considered from the point of view of antiquity these works of Buddhist literature stand unparalleled for their sublime thoughts, superb intellectual treatment and unique literary excellences. They may easily be compared and best productions of the European literature. They, thus, occupy an enviable position in the annals of world literature.

42

CONTRIBUTION OF SOUTH-EAST ASIA TO PĀLI LITERATURE

Sanghasen Singh

Pāli literature is the only complete source which provides systematic materials for the study of at least one branch of Buddhist Studies. Two schools of thought, which claim to be the earliest, viz. *Vibhajjavāda* and *Theravāda*, find full representation in this literature. The literature of *Theravāda* as a religious sect also flourished through the *Pāli* language. Insistence on *Vibhajjavāda* in some of the discourses of the Buddha leads one to believe that there was a school of thought, if not a sect, which put excessive emphasis on the analytical approach to the study of the elements (*dhammas*)[1]. There might have been Buddhist masters after masters who upheld this school of thought. Even Moggaliputta Tissa, the convenor and president of the Third Buddhist Council which was held in the third century B.C. probably belonged to the ranks of monk-scholars of this lien of thought. However, as it seems to be probable, these two aforesaid schools of thought merged into one in course of time and continued with *Pāli* (earlier name being Māgadhī)[2] as the vehicle of their expression. Although this language originated and developed in India in the Magadha region[3], the later literature which developed in this language had Sri Lanka and Burma as the countries of its adoption. In fact, if one goes to the extent of saying that *Pāli* literature is the product of South-east Asia in general and Sri Lanka-Burma in particular, his statement will not be totally false. Although it is a fact that the Buddha's words are enshrined in the *Tipiṭaka*, which he delivered to his disciples in the *Majjhamaṇḍala*[4], i.e. the region which was traversed by him during his life time were successively recited and compiled in three earlier councils at Rājagaha, Vesāli and Pāṭaliputta, but the same were finally compiled and committed to writing for the first time in Sri Lanka in the first century B.C. (28-29 B.C.) under the patronage of the king, Vaṭṭagāmaṇi Abhaya. Thus even the *Tipiṭaka* literature owes its transmission and preservation to Sri Lanka. As regards the composition, transmission and preservation of the rest of *Pāli* literatuare it is evidently clear that Sri Lanka's role is superb. In fact, the position is such that it should be far more convenient and worthwhile to name only those texts which are not ascribed for their origin to Sri Lanka. The contribution of Burma is also significant in this respect. Countries like Thailand, Cambodia, Laos, Vietnam have also contributed to the sum total of the vast *Pāli* literature extant today. Thus, on the whole, barring the role of India, which was the original homeland of *Pāli* language and literature, the role of the following countries may be put in descending order – Sri Lanka, Burma, Thailand, Cambodia, Laos, Vietnam and so on.

Of the post-canonical literature, *Milindapañha* is one of the earlier texts[5]. This seems to the only important text of later *Pāli* literature which originated in a place outside Sri Lanka and Burma. Some smaller texts, or works of lesser importance did not find their origin in India and other parts of South-east Asia other than Sri Lanka-Burma, but their role and area of influence are very limited. *Uttaraviniccaya, Vinayaviniccaya, Abhidhammāvatāra*, etc. may be cited as some examples. According to the *Theravāda* tradition, both Buddhadatta and Buddhaghoṣa, the great authors of *Aṭṭhakathā* literature, flourished in India[6], but lived in Sri Lanka for considerably long time for their study and writing of the truth, the overall position does not change. That is to say, it will have to be accepted that the *Aṭṭhakathā* literature was the product of Sri Lanka. But in this regard one fact will have to be borne in mind that the impact of Indian literature on every aspect of *Pāli* literature is visible even to a layman. As regards the recent additions to *Pāli* literature from India, the names of *Visuddhimaggadīpikā* and *Navanīta Ṭīkā* by *Dhamma*nanda Kosambi may be cited as significant examples. The latter is the latest *Pāli* commentary on the *Abhidhammaṭṭhasaṅgaha*. Another small but significant text is the *Pupphañjali* by Sanghasen Singh* of Delhi University (published in 1960).

Out of the vast *Pāli* literatuare which was written in South-east Asia as detailed above, the majority belongs to Sri Lanka. But a significant part of it originated in Burma as well. For instance, the Saddanīti school of *Pāli* grammar, a large amount of *Abhidhamma* literature and so on originated and developed in Burma. In fact, in case of *Abhidhamma* literature and the claim on *Abhidhammic* practices, Burma is still retaining its pre-eminently superior position.

One more point merits mention here. There is a strong tradition in Sri Lanka[8] that the Buddha visited that country[8] and sojourned there in order to preach certain discourses to the Sri Lanka people. It could not be historically proved so far, nor there is any possibility to do so, considering the geographical conditions and the limited geographical knowledge of the people of the northern India at the time of the Buddha. Thus the credit of the origin and development of the *Tipiṭaka* literature remains with the *Majjhamaṇḍala*. The following table may be cited to view the vast *Pāli* literature in a glance:

Endnotes

1. The later *Theravāda* authors seem to be at pains to assert that *Vibhajjavāda* was none other than the *Theravāda*. According to the *Mahāvaṃsa*, the Blessed One was called the Vibhajjavādī in order to distinguish him from the rest of the *Vādas* (religious and philosophical views) of his time. Cf. *Mahāvaṃsa*, Gāthās, 271-272.
2. Māgadhī (literally, one belonging to the Magadha region) was the earlier name given to *Pāli* language in which the Buddha was supposed to have spoken and the later exegetical works were

written by many known and unknown authors. The language was known as Māgadhī Bhāsā/ Nīrutti/Tanti. It was in the 13th/14th century A.D. that the word *Pāli* could be used to connote the language known as *Pāli* today. The usage of the word *Pāli* in Buddhaghoṣa's works is found in the sense of the words of the Buddha, i.e. the contents of the *Tipiṭaka* in contrast to the word *Aṭṭhakathā*, e.g. *Pālimattamidhānītaṁ natthi aṭṭhakathā idha.*

3. See M. Winternitz, History of Indian Literature, Vol. II.
4. An area comprising of roughly Uttar Pradesh, Bihar, Southern parts of Nepal and a small portion of northern Madhya Pradesh.
5. See M. Winternitz, History of Indian Literature, Vol. II.
6. See Buddhaghosuppatti.
7. See Shanti Bhikshu Shastri, Buddha-Vijaya-Kāvya.
8. Unconcerned with the tradition of Sri Lanka, the author/authors of *Saddarma-laṅkāvatāra-sūtra* (the text belongs to the *Mahāyāna* Scripture whose date of composition cannot be ascribed to a period prior to the 3rd/4th centuries A.D.) describe the visit of the Buddha to Lanka island. Although the location of that island is said to have been in the ocean, the description seems to be about an imaginary island known as Lanka which was inhabitated by the *Rākṣasas*, *Asuras* and so on. Rāvaṇa was the lord of the *Rākṣasas*.

43

A SURVEY OF THE STUDIES ON BUDDHIST SECTS

N. N. Bhattacharya

The fact that there was a long time-gap between the days of the Buddha and the formation of canonical literature, that the present three-fold division was artificial, made only after the actual production of the majority of the texts concerned, and that something must have existed as the original canon before the days of Aśoka has been taken seriously into account by all critical and competent scholars of Buddhism. All of them unanimously hold that a comparative study of the texts belonging to different Buddhist sects is necessary to settle up the points of resemblance and divergence in their contents by which a chronological stratification for the reconstruction of the history of the earliest phase of Buddhism, which will throw new light on the origin and development of the Buddhist sects, will be possible and that some idea of the original Buddhist canon, supposed to have existed before the days of Aśoka, can be obtained.

From this viewpoint scholars have tried and are trying to make some formulations on pre-Aśokan Buddhism. Although unfortunately nothing positive has transpired as yet, owing to the paucity of materials, in recent years some research works have come out which purport to throw significant light on this problem. Such works[1] show on the one hand the difficulties in the sources of our knowledge in Buddhism, the problem of the original canon before the days of Aśoka, and on the other attempt to reconstruct the process through which the original texts were formed, on the basis of the internal evidence furnished by the surviving texts themselves. The present forms of the texts and, where texts are not available, or available only in fragments, those of the translations, bear testimony of additions, interpolations and accretions, and since there was no centralized control to prevent this, they came to disagree on numerous points. The questions to which we are confronted are these: To what extent do their disagreements affect the fundamental doctrines? To what extent these are responsible for the emergence of the Buddhist sects of the subsequent period?

Earlier scholars like Remusat and Schmidt drew all information for the sectarian studies respectively from Chinese and Tibeto-Mongolian sources which were secondary products. Burnouf depended more on the Sanskrit sources of the later period, although he had some idea of the then practically unexplored pali sources. The discovery and publication of the entire *Pāli* canon of the Ceylonese *Theravāda* school revolutionized the study of Buddhism. It claimed to be the actual word of the Buddha, and it was on the material of this canon that expositions of Buddhism were written by the *Pāli* scholars. Despite the correct idea on the basis of the Chinese and Tibetan translations of the existence of a complete Sanskrit canon of the *Sarvāstivādins*, fragments of which are now coming to light, the claim of the Sanskritists remained feeble until Vallee Poussin and Stcherbatksy pointed out that the mere existence of complete *Theravāda* canon in *Pāli* does not prove its relative, antiquity and primitivity. Subsequent researchers prove that, although some *Pāli* works were translated into Sanskrit, the major portion of the canon of the *Sarvāstivāda* and kindred schools were translated into Sanskrit not from the *Pāli* of the Theravādins, but from the *Prākrita* dialects in which they were originally composed. Even the *Pāli* canon might be the development of a still earlier canon composed in any form of *Prākrita*, a third source, probably a Māgadhī original.

Recent Buddhist researches, according to Edward Conze, have brought to light more facts about the *Sarvāstivādins* and the *Mahāsaṅghikas* showing that their materials are as important as the *Pāli* sources in regard to the early history of Buddhism[2]. Hofinger examined eight canonical accounts of the Council of Vaiśālī and came to the conclusion that the one in the *Mahāsaṅghika Vinaya* is the oldest of all. Some of the contents of the canon must be quite early, while others are rather late. Before the arrangement of the canon into *Tripiṭaka*, there were probably only the *Dharma* and *Vinaya*, the former divided into twelve or nine classes. It is not impossible that before the days of Aśoka there was a work called *Skandhaka* which divided and arranged the materials concerning monastic rules[3]. But can we distinguish within the accepted *Tripiṭaka* things which are earlier and later? So far as the *Pāli* texts are concerned, this is, however, possible to a certain extent.

The study of the Buddhist sects is further complicated by the lack of our knowledge regarding the original contents of Buddhism. Many of the authoritative works make widely divergent and sometimes totally opposite claims about the original teachings of the Buddha. Texts belonging to different schools which purport to contain the original teachings of the Buddha cannot also be accepted on various reasons at their face value.[4] The stories of schisms as recorded in different texts belonging to different schools of Buddhism appear more arbitrary than historical, and the causes of doctrinal differences up held by each school in its own way appear to be quite mythical and the imaginary for the lack of our knowledge about the real perspective. This history of Buddhism in India therefore requires a new appraisal in which more emphasis should be given on causes and objective conditions leading to the schisms within the Buddhist church, to the migrations of different schools and sects, to the compromise with the existing local religions and kindred local developments of Buddhism and so on. At present we have to remain satisfied only with a survey of our existing knowledge of this subject which is expected to throw some light on what has been done and what remains to be done.

It is interesting to note that from the earliest period of researches in Buddhism, attention of the scholars was drawn to the appearance of the Buddhist sects in India[5]. Earlier writers on this subject had to depend mainly on the *Pāli* sources, that is, the *Sthaviravāda* or *Theravāda* school, although fragmentary Sanskrit sources, and their translations into Chinese, and Tibetan were of some help to them. In the beginning of the present century, S. Beal, on the basis of Chinese sources, wrote on the *Vinaya* of the *Dharmaguptaka* sect. In 1925, J. Masuda published the translation of the Chinese version of Vasumitra's treatise on eighteen sects of Buddhism in India which was supplemented by the Tibetan texts on the eighteen schools by Bhavya and Vinītadeva[6]. On the basis of the available materials of the twenties of this century and especially of Vasumitra's accounts, Paul Demieville was able to throw in 1931 some new light on the origin of the Buddhist sects[7]. The Tibetan texts on the eighteen schools written by Bhavya and Vinītadeva are known respectively as *Nikāyabhedavibhagṅa* and *Samayabhedopararcana-cakra*. These texts represent a different tradition which is virtually in opposition to that found in the *Pāli* sources.

The discovery and utilization of the texts and commentaries of the *Sarvāstivāda*, *Mūlasarvāstivāda*, *Sautrāntika Sāmmitīya*, *Dharmaguptaka*, and *Bahuśrutīya* schools undoubtedly marked a progress in the study of the Buddhist sects. So far as the *Sarvāstivāda* texts are concerned Kātyāyanīputra's *Jñānaprasthāna*,[8] Ghoṣaka's *Abhidharmāmṛtara-saśāstra*[9] Saṅgharakṣa's *Yogācārabhūmi*[10], *Abhidharmadīpa* and *vibhāṣāprabhāvrtti*[11] deserve special mention. H.W. Baily's edition of the Khotanese texts in three volumes, which came out during the years 1946-56, served a very important purpose in the study of the Buddhist sects. A good number of the *Sarvāstivādin Dīgha Nikāya Sūtras* have been published by the Deutsche Academic der Wissenchaften Zu Berlin in recent years[12]. Much information about the *Sarvāstivādin* texts, mainly on the basis of Tibetan sources, has been given in Banerjee's work on *Sarvāstivāda* literature, which, however, ignores the Central Asian sources.[13] Of the Sāmmitīyas we have a very important text known as *Āśraprajñapti* or *Sāmmitiya Nikāya Śāstra*[14]. Of the *Mūlasarvāstivāda* texts we have the *Dharamasamuccaya*[15] and the *Saddharmasmṛtyupasthāna*[16]. There are several commentaries on the *Prātimokṣasūtra* and one on the *Bhikṣuṇīprātimokṣā* of the *Mūlasarvāstivādins* in Tibetan versions.[17] A. Bareau's French translation of Vasumitra's *Samayabhedopararcanacakra* has been proved very useful for the study of the *Dharmaguptaka* school.[18] Pa-Chow's comparative study of the *Prātimokṣa* has uncovered much of the doctrinal aspects of this sect[19].

So far as the Chinese sources are concerned. Hirakawa's study of the *Vinaya Piṭaka*, which came out in 1960, is very important.[20] In Chinese we have a vast *Tripiṭaka* consisting primarily of the translations of the Indian texts. But these works are vague about their affiliations and it is really difficult to establish their schools. In Chinese we have the *Mahāsaṅghika* recensin of the *Vinaya* which, when compared with that of the *Sthaviravāda*, shows close agreement as regards to the *Prātimokṣa* rules. According to Hirakawa, the close agreement of the *Vinayas* of the two schools shows that during the first schism both of them remained conservative, but their offshoots became unorthodox. Unfortunately, we have no *Mahāsaṅghika Āgama* (*Sūtra*) in Chinese, and if such things come into light they are expected to agree more closely with the *Sthaviravāda* than with its offshoots like the *Sarvāstivāda*, *Dharmaguptaka*, etc. The essential problems of the Chinese sources had previously been dealt with by Japanese scholars like Akanuma, Matsumoto, and Tatsuyama from whose researches we have been informed that the Chinese version of the *Dīrghāgama (Dīgha Nikāya)* can not be attributed to any specific school, although the usual conjecture is that it belongs to the *Dharmaguptaka* school, and that the versions of the *Madhyama* and *Saṁyukta* belong mostly to the *Sarvāstivāda*, *Ekottara (Aṅguttara)* has been attributed to the *Dharmaguptakas* by Matsumoto and to the *Mahāsaṅghikas*, especially to its *Prajñaptivāda* offshoot, by Akanuma. Of the numerous Chinese versions of individual *sūtras*, the determination of their affiliation is practically an impossible work.

Most of the historical works on Buddhism contain chapters on Buddhist sects. All the materials relating to the eighteen sects containing in different Buddhist traditions were known to all of us in a rather chaotic condition, but some recent works especially of A. Bareau (1955)[21] and N. Dutta (1970)[22] deserve special mention because in these we find historical attempt of bringing order into this chaos. Bareau has dealt with the different traditions about the origin of sects chronologically into three epochs, the first consisting of the sects mentioned in the *Dīpavaṁsa*, the second of those mentioned in the Sāmmitiya tradition of Bhavya and the third of those mentioned in the Kashmirian sources like the Chinese translation of *Śāriputraparipṛcchā* of the *Mahāsaṅghikas*, the *Samayabhedopararcanacakra* of Vasumitra and *Mañjuśri-paripṛcchā* available only in Chinese translation. Dutt has made not only an analytical study of the treatises of Vasumitra, Bhavya and Vinītadeva in presenting the history of the Buddhist sect but also of the *Kathāvatthu* and its commentary by Buddhaghoṣa as well as of the *Abhidharmakośavyākhyā*, an excellent edition of which was published by Wogihara, and the *Sāmmitiya-nikāyaśastra*, translated from the Chinese by Venkataramanan, and the Gilgit Manuscripts III, edited and published by Dutt himself, containing the original Mūlasarvāstivāda *Vinaya* and also the *Jñānaprasthāna* partially restored by Śānti Bhikṣu. In addition he has taken into account Hiuen Tsang's and I-tsing's observations on the dispersal of the Buddhist sects in India and also the epigraphical records.

Two other works, written respectively by Lamotte[23] and Warder[24], should also be mentioned in this connection. In these works study of the Buddhist sects only forms a part, and the accounts given in them, though precise, contain a very critical assessment of the previous researches on this subject. Lamotte has furnished us with a tabular statement of the geographical distribution of the several schools on the basis of inscriptions discovered so far. He has also taken into account an important *Pāli Abhidhamma* text known as the *Kathāvatthu* which presents the doctrines of the opponents, the exponents of the non-*Theravāda* schools. Warder's account of the eighteen sects is mainly based on Lamotte though he has made an improvement upon it by his own researches. Warder's main purpose is to show that all the eighteen schools of early Buddhism elaborated their doctrines out of a common kernel. The geographical distribution of the sects has been brought in relation to the doctrinal peculiarities of each of them.

Endnotes

1. Cf. E. Mayeda, *History of the Foundation of the Original Buddhist Texts,* Tokyo 1964; G. C. Pande, *Studies in the Origins of Buddhism,* New Delhi 1974, 17 ff.
2. E. Conze, *Thirty Years of Buddhist Research,* London 1967, 1-32.
3. This view was advanced by F. Frauwallner in his *Earliest Vinaya and the Beginnings of Buddhist Literature,* Rome 1956.
4. A. K. Warder, *Introduction to Pali,* London 1963, *intro.* XI.
5. The earliest article on Buddhist sects was written by St. Julien "Listes diverses des noms des dix-huit sects du bouddhisme" in *Journal Asiatique* (1859). This was followed by V. Vasilev (W. Wassiljew) *Der Buddhismus* (1860), T.W. Rhys Davids and H. Oldenberg, *Vinaya Piṭaka* in *Sacred Books of the East* (1881), H. Kern, *Manual of Indian Buddhism* (1884), I.P. Minayeff, *Buddhizm* (1884), H. Oldenberg "Buddhistieshe Studien" in *ZDMG*, LII (1898), Lad de la Vallee Poussin (1905) in *Encyclopedia of Religion and Ethics,* IV, 79-184 and in *Le Museon,* VI, 30-37, O. Franke in *Journal of the Pāli Text Society* (1908), W. Geiger, *intro.* to the *Mahāvaṁsa,* etc.
6. *Asia major,* II, 1925.
7. P. Demieville in *Melanges Chinois bouddhiques,* I, 1931.
8. Retranslated from Chinese to Sanskrit by Śānti Bhikṣu, Viśvabhāratī 1955.
9. Retranslated by Śānti Bhikṣu, Vissśvabhāratī 1953.
10. Translated by Demieville in *Bulletin de I'Ecole francaised, Extreme Orient,* 1954.
11. Ed. from an incomplete Sanskrit text by Jaini, Jayaswal Research Institute, Patna 1959.
12. Here we should refer to Waldschmidt's edition of *Catuṣpariṣat* (1952, 1957, 1962), *Mahāvadāna* (1952-1956), *Mahāparinirvāṇa* (1950-51) and other *Sūtras* and to Mittal's and Schlingloff's edition of the *Dasottara* (1957, 1962). Fragments of *Nidāna-saṁyukta,* belonging to the *Sarvāstivādin Samyukta Nikāya* have been edited by Tripathi (1962) and *Pvaretāadān* by Bechert (1961). Fragments from the *Sarvāstivādin Vinayavibhaṅga* have been edited by Rosen (1959) and those from *Vinaynvastu* by Hartel (1956). The latter was partly edited by Dutt *(Gilgit Manuscripts, VII, parts I-IV).*
13. A.C. Banerjee, *Sarvāstivāda Literature,* Calcutta 1957. A good number of *Sūtras* belonging to the *Sarvāstivādins* are included in the Tibetan *Tripiṭaka* and these were originally edited and published by L. Feer. Besides the *Sarvāstivādin Vinaya,* the Tibetan sources contain *Abhidharma* works like the *Prajñaptisāra* and commentaries an the *Tripiṭaka* like the *Abhidharmāvatāra* and *Sārasamuccaya.*

14. Eng. tr. by K. Venkataramanan in *Viśvabhārati Annals,* V. 1953.

15. First five chs. ed. by Lin Li-kouang, Paris, Musee Guimet 1946 with corresponding Chinese and Tibetan versions and a French translation.

16. Study of this *Sūtra* by Lin Li-Kouang. *L'Aidememoire de la vraie Loi,* Paris, Musee guimet 1949.

17. Reference should be made in this connection to Vinītadeva's *Vinayavibhaṅgāpadavyākhyāna* and Kalyāṇamitra's *Vinaya-vastuṭīkā.* There are a number of other commentaries or manuals of Mūlasarvāstivādin *Vinaya* available in Tibetan, such as *Vinayasaṅgraham* of Viśeṣamitra, *Śrāmaṇera-kārikā* and *vṛtti* of Śākyaprabha, etc. the *Avadānaśataka* has been edited from the Mūlasarvāstivādin *Vinaya* by Hofinger (1964). Banerjee edited the *Prātimokṣasūtra* of the *Mūlasarvāstivādins* in *Indian Historical Quarterly* (1953).

18. A Bareau in *Journal Asiatique* (1954), 235 ff; cf his tr. of the *Nikāyabhedavibhaṅgavyākhyāna* in *ibid* (1956), 162 ff., 192 ff.

19. Pa-Chow, *A Comparative Study of the Prātimokṣa* Visvabharati, Sino-Indian Cultural Society, 1955.

20. *Ritsuzo no Kenkyū,* Tokyo 1960.

21. A. Bareau, *Les Sectes bouqhiques du petit Vehicule,* Saigon 1955.

22. N. Dutt, *Buddhist Sects,* Calcutta 1970.

23. E. Lamotte, *Histoire du Bouddhismc Indien,* Louvain 1956.

24. A. K. Warder, *Indian Buddhism,* Delhi 1970, 288-351.

44

THE ORIGIN AND DEVELOPMENT OF THE BUDDHIST PHILOSOPHICAL SCHOOLS

G. G. Gyatso

That which determines a person as Buddhist is not the place of birth nor membership of a particular community nor by any external considerations, but rather by one's internal mental attitude. One is called a Buddhist who fearing the suffering of the world, i.e., of the three lower realms of existence-that of the animals, the hungry ghosts and of hell beings-possesses faith in and goes to take refuge to the triple Gem (*Buddha, Dharma* and *Saṅgha*). The Buddha is the teacher of the doctrine. It may be thought that in as much as the Buddha has passed into Parinirvāṇa, it is not possible to go for refuge to him. However, anyone who teaches the doctrine rightly may be regarded as the Buddha, such a teacher has three characteristics. First, he is altogether without faults. Second, he is endowed with all qualities. Third, the view which he teaches is one which does not affirm the eternality and independence of the self or ego.

The Buddhist doctrine arose from the teachings of the Buddha who having produced the enlightenment thought, accumulated the two heaps of merit and wisdom (i.e. *Pūnya* and Jnana Sambhara) achieved enlightenment on the *Vajrāsana* at Buddhagaya. Thereafter at Sarnath the Buddha performed the first turning of the wheel of the doctrine for the five ascetics. The first turning of the wheel of the doctrine consisted of the demonstration of the Four Noble Truths. At the Vulture Peak the Buddha turned the wheel of the doctrine for the second time which consisted of the demonstration of the signless *dharma* as found in the *Prajñā-pāramitā* literature. Finally the Buddha performed the third turnngi of the wheel of the *dharma* at Vaisāli which consisted of the exact explanation of good and evil actions and their consequences.

Based upon the teachings of the Buddha revealed by these three turning of the wheels of the *dharma*, ancient Buddhist scholars developed slightly differing interpretations according to their individual capabilities. Thus the four Buddhist schools, i.e., *Vaibhāṣika, Sautrāntika; Cittamātrika* and *Mādhyamika* were formed. Also the teachings of the Buddha are divided into three vehicles (*Yānas*) *Srāvakayāna, Pratyekabuddhayāna* and *Bodhisattvayāna* which concerned the concept of the path. The aim of all the three *Yānas* is the attainment of liberation.

The *Śrāvakas* are those who having listened to the teachings of the Buddha, Strive for freedom from sufferings. The *Pratyekabuddhas* are those who themselves realize their own liberation. Finally the *Bodhisattvas* are those who renouncing their own interest, strive for the attainment of Buddhahood and enlightenment for the sake of all sentient beings.

The accomplishment of all three *Yānas* requires the study of the three *Piṭakas*: *Sutta Piṭaka, Vinaya Piṭaka* and *Abhidhamma Piṭaka*. Based upon the study of the three *Piṭakas* the four Buddhist schools were evolved. First the *Vaibhāsikas*, which is one of the two schools of *Hīnayāna*, do not accept self consciousness. However they accept that external objects are truly established. One who holds this view is called a *Vaibhāṣika*. A representative of the school was Vasubandhu who explained the doctrine of the *Vaibhāṣika* in the *Abhidharmakoṣa*.

All the four Buddhist schools believed that they were avoiding the two extremes of eternalism and nihilism, *Śaśvatavāda* and *Ucchedavāda* and so were following the middle path. The *Vaibhāṣikas* maintained that in as much as when the effect is produced the cause is extinguished, the extreme of eternalism is avoided. On the other hand, when the cause is extinguished the effect is produced. Thus the extreme of nihilism is avoided.

The *Sautrāntikas* accepted both self consciousness and external objects to be truly established. One who holds this view is termed a *Sautrāntika*. There exists also a division among the *Sautrāntikas*, between those who follow strictly scriptural authority strictly rely upon the *Abhidharmakoṣa* while those who affirm the importance of reason follow the seven logical treatises composed by the Indian masters. The *Sautrāntikas* also believed that their doctrine avoided the two extreme of eternalism and nihilism. They affirmed that in as much as the continuity of mental phenomena (*Saṃskāras*) is not broken the extreme of nihilism is avoided. On the other hand they affirmed that phenomena were at every instant subject to destruction so they avoided the extreme of eternalism.

The *Cittamātrika* did not accept the existence of external objects. However, they accepted the *paratantrabhāva* to be truly established. Such a one is called a *Cittamātrika*. The *Cittamātrika* also like the *Vaibhāṣikas* and *Sautrāntikas* believe that their doctrine avoided the two extremes. In as much as they rejected the true existence of what was imputed (*Parikalpita*) they avoided the extreme of eternalism. However, by accepting the true existence of the *paratantrabhāva* they avoided the extreme of nihilism. A *Cittamātrika* is one who accepts that all the *dharmas* are nothing but the essence of mind (*citta*).

The *Mādhyamika* who is also called a follower of '*nihsvabhāvada*' is one who does not accept any element (*dharma*) to be truly established. He is called a *Mādhyamika* because he follows the middle way by avoiding the two extremes of eternalism and nihilism. He avoids the two extremes in that he accepts that all elements exist conventionally (*Vyavahāra*). Thus avoiding the extreme of nihilism. At the same time he rejects the ultimate (*Paramārtha*) existence of all elements thereby avoiding the extreme of eternalism. The *Mādhyamika* school is divided into two sub-sects-the *Svatāntrika-Mādhyamika* and the *Prāsangika-Mādhyamika*. A *Svatāntrika-Mādhyamika* is so called because he accepts conventionally that all elements (*dharmas*) are established by virtue of their own characteristic marks (*Lakṣana*). The *Svatāntrika-Mādhyamika* school is further divided into two schools the *Yogācāra-Svatāntrika-Mādhyamika* and the *Sautrāntika-Svatāntrika-Mādhyamika*. A representative of the former is Santaraksita, a representative of the latter is Bhavaviveka. The *Yogācāra-Svatāntrika-Mādhyamikas* do not accept self consciousness but do accept external objects. The *Svatāntrika-Mādhyamikas* believe that all entities are included within the two truths. A jar which exists to common sense is an example of the phenomenal truth (*saṃvṛitisatya*), the fact that the jar is not truly established constitutes the ultimate truth (*Paramārthasatya*). According to the *Svatāntrikas* a thing can be said to be truly established if when it analysed it can be said to exist apart from dependence upon any producing condition.

For the *Svatāntrika-Mādhyamikas* the insubstantiality of the individual (*Pudgala nairātmya*) has two aspects, a gross aspect and a subtle one. In so far as the gross aspect is concerned the view of all the four schools is identical. The gross aspect of the insubstantiality of the individual consists of the knowledge that the personality is not eternal and not independent. The subtle aspect is the recognition that the personality is not an independent object which exists independent of the five *skandhas*. The insubstantiality of elements (*dharma-nairatmya*) also has a gross and a subtle aspect. The gross aspect is the recognition that form and the consciousness which apprehends form are one object that is to say that they are empty of another object. The subtle aspect is the recognition that all *dharmas* are empty of anything truly established.

The *Prāsangika-Mādhyamikas* are those who do not accept even conventionally the existence of things established by virtue of their characteristic marks. Such an exponent of the doctrine of *nihsvabhāva* is called a *Prāsangika*. Representatives of this school are Buddhapālita, Chandrakīrti and Santideva. For the *Prāsangika-Mādhyamika* all entities which appear in experience such as a jar constitute the phenomenal truth (*saṃvṛitisatya*). The fact they are empty in their own being (*svabhāva*) constitute the ultimate truth (*Paramārthasatya*). The doctrine of the *Prāsangika-Mādhyamikas* can be understood through a careful study of the works of Buddhapalita and Chandrakirti such as the *Mādhyamakāvatāra*. There likewise exist many commentaries to these works.

The *Prāsangika-Mādhyamika* school represents the highest development of Buddhist philosophy based upon the exposition of the *sūtras*. Each succeeding school developed its exposition out of the criticism of an earlier standpoint and each of these successive positions had an indispensable role to play in the development of Buddhist thought. For instance the initial uncritical formulation was that of the *Vaibhāṣikas*. The *Sautrāntikas* developed their position out of a criticism of the standpoint of the *Vaibhāṣikas*. The *Cittamātrika* having appreciated the standpoint of the *Sautrāntikas* developed their doctrine out of a criticism of the latter. Again the *Svatāntrika-Mādhyamikas* pushed the critical development of Buddhist philosophy further through a criticism of the *Cittamātrika*. Finally the *Prāsangika-Mādhyamika* system was evolved out of a criticism of all the foregoing schools ending with that of the *Svatāntrika-Mādhyamikas*. Thus the *Prāsangika-Mādhyamika* school embodies the ultimate development of Buddhist thought and is a completely consistant critical philosophy. Nonetheless the doctrines of all the schools were necessary for the ultimate emergence of the *Prāsangika* doctrines. Each of them represents a stage in the successive development of Buddhist thought.

45

THE GROTTOES OF MAI-CHI MOUNTAIN*

Translation from original Chinese

Latika Lahiri

The primitive people lived mostly in natural caves of limestone on the cliff. But later on, the Buddhist caves in China and elsewhere were hewn out by human labour. The tombs on the cliff of mountains like Chia-ting[2], P'eng-shan[3], Ch'ung-ch'ing[4], etc. recently discovered are the examples of rock-cut caves by human labour. With the introduction of Buddhism in China, cave temples were continuously hewn out of rocks. The orthodox and folk form of tombs were combined together resulting in the creation of most significant and glorious style of cave arts in China. All the caves from various places of Sin-kiang in the west to Kan-su, Sze-ch'uan, Shen-his, Ho-nan upto Shan-tung down south some places in Chiang-su unceasingly presented a brilliant splendour that cannot be compared with a flash of light coming from far distance.

Among the caves, Tun-huang[5], Mai-chi Shan, Yun-Kang[6], Lung-men[7], etc. are remarkable. The art of making cave temples originated and very well developed according to the contemporary local style. Our sculptures (Chinese) carved religious statues on hard, inflexible stones wherever these were available. The images are generally of Buddha, *Bodhisattvas*, guardian deities, flying Apsarās, devotees offering worship, etc. The sculptors described various legends and folk-lore, *Jātakas* tales (Buddha's previous birth stories) and different events of Buddha's present life. The images of Yun-Kang, Lung-men and other cave temples on the mountain T'ien-Lung (Heavenly Dragon) are of the same style and they are the supreme creation of the talented artists. From the time of the Northern Wei' (5th Century A.D.) to the last year of the Ming period[8] (the 2nd half of the 17th century) we find a continuous history of sculptures.

In this story region it is practically very difficult to carve on the hard rocks but the Chinese artists have created prolific and brilliant mural paintings. They have also made use of clay and created many clay Buddha images, starting from *Bodhisattvas* to flying *Apsarās*. The grottoes of Mai-chi-shan also bear the testimony of the same style of the cave of Thousand Buddhas at Tun-huang. Many scholars have already been working on the mural paintings but the images which are still preserved in these caves are very recently introduced to the public. The mural paintings of Mai-chi are like the numerous paintings of Tun-huang but unfortunately the existing monuments are not in perfect condition as those of Tun-huang. At the base (of Mai-chi) clay images were made from the beginning of the 5th century A.D. onwards. The small images are not to be reckoned with but the bigger images have been placed along with Thousand Buddhas images. In doing research in history of Chinese sculpture, these are absolutely important treasures.

The art of modeling an idol and the stone carving were developed side by side with dawn of history. The wooden figures[1] of men and women buried with the dead (some with fetters and handcuffs) found in the burial ground of An-yang[2] belonging to the 17th century before Christ, that is about 4000 years ago. On the stone-tablets of the graves of important personages nothing has been recorded down. But all the wooden figures and figurines, earthen wares, terracottas belonging to various dynasties beginning from 2nd century B.C. to the period of Ming dynasty (17th century A.D.) thus covering 2,000 years, are indispensable materials for research.

The grottoes of Mai-chi-shan is to the south-east of the district T'ien-shui[3] in Kan-su province. It is about 45 li from the district T'ien-shui. Mai-chi is the western range of the Ch'in-ling[4] mountain. After going 35 li towards south-east from T'ien-shui, one finds comparatively better and even road which leads to the opening of the mountain pass of Mai-chi. Following the course of the circuitous road along the bank of a rivulet and again after 10 li of walk, one can behold the colossal Buddha figure rising up from the surface of beautiful peak of mountain. The lofty peak looks like a seat of small pagodas. This peak has some characteristics. In shape it is conical. The base is comparatively narrow which very much looks like wheat-straw piled up in countryside. So from ancient times the local people call it Mai-chi mountain.

During the time of the Five Dynasties[5] Ch'ueh-ming edited "The Pleasant Talks of the Members of Han-lin Academy".

(Yu-teng-Wen-hua) which says "the range of Mai-chi surpasses even Ch'ing-Wei, a large tributary of the Yellow river in Shen-si, in the north and south it gradually expands on both the sides. The range extends up to 500 li, half of it, is Mai-chi. It looks like a lump of stone. The shape and appearance of Mai-chi was known like this to the people. It has many names, one of these is Half-blue sky, and the other the Midst of Precipice. The images of Buddha have been chiseled out and thousand niches are hollowed out of stone. Though it is the product of human labour but some times it seems as if it has been created by the Devas. This short passage may be seen in 'T'ai-p'ing-kuang-chi' Chapter 397. The Chung-ting-shou-fu. Chapter 48 also refers to then name of Yu-teng-hua. The writer said that the 39th year of the Hsin-wei period of the T'ang ruler, coincides with the second year of the Kan-shih period of the Emperor Yun of the posterior Han Dynasty. This was written in the 10th century A.D. This is the earliest reference of the cave temple of the Mai-chi mountain which is made known to the world at present. But the beginning of these Buddhist rock-cut temples and monasteries was made in much earlier period. The Biography of Eminent Monks of the Liang Dynasty[6] says that during the time of the Yung-ch'u period, the monk T'an-hung spent many rainy retreats on the Mai-chi mountain. After some years, the monk Hsuan-kao reached Mai-chi and had joined meeting with T'an-hung. They lived together in great amity and friendship for common cause. There were more than three hundred disciples studying under them. This shows the glorious and flourishing period of educational system prevalent there. In the cave No. 115 of the Mai-chi even now one can see the faint traces of inscriptions of ancient period that belongs to the nineth month of the third year of the Ching-ming period (A.D. 502) of the Emperor Hsuan-Wu of the Northern-Wei dynasty.

Chang Yuan-po constructed a monastery on the mountain and inscribed his vow in very elegant and lucid language. In the following years during the period of Pao-ting and T'ien-pe[7] of the Northern Chou Dynasty Tu-Li-yun of Ta-tu[8] of Ch'in-chou[9] hewn out seven Buddhist niches for his departed father. The celebrated writer Yu-hsin composed a paragraph on his behalf. This has been inscribed on the Buddhist nich of Mai-chi at the prefectural city of T'ien-shui of Ch'in-shou. It is still to be seen in the 12th chapter of Yuan-p'i-I-wang, the original stone-tablet is already destroyed. This is the most clear and illustrious section regarding Mai-chi. Later on, during the time of the Sui, the T'ang, the Five Dynasties, the Sung, the Ming and the Ch'ing, they carved beautiful niches and (frescos) images. Only during the time of the Yuan Dynasty nothing has been added over there.

The Mai-chi mountain is 142 metres high. The total number of niches or shrines compiled by the 'Team' and the polished sculptures painted plastered are 194 in number. But in the early period of Mai-chi's history the number was many more.

The middle part of Mai-chi had fallen due to land slide; consequently the caves have been divided into two sections, the Eastern and the Western Cliff. The flyover and the tunnels which are repaired by the Team, have also been into two sections. Some of the most important caves belonging to the Eastern and Western cliff have been narrated below:-

Among the Eastern caves, the most important in the *Nirvāṇa* cave, the corridor of Thousand Buddhas. On the San-hua (scattered flowers) terrace there is a pavilion of seven Buddhas and in the Niu-erh, Calf-Hall there is also the same pavilion with seven Buddhas. The plan is really monolithic.

The *Nirvāṇa* cave (No. 1 Mai-chi) was hewn out during the later part of the Northern-Wei Dynasty (beginning of the 6th century A.D.). The special significance of this cave is that it has six stone pillars in front in a row. As a matter of fact, it looks like graves of Sze-ch'uan. The images had been repaired during the time of the Ming Dynasty but these still maintain the original style of the Northern-Wei Dynasty.

The corridor of Thousand Buddhas was hewn out during the Northern-Wei period (5th century A.D.), the length of which, from one end to the other, is 32 ft. (ie, 72 Chinese metres). The rows of clay images of Buddhas have been very closely carved on the barren womb (middle part of the mountain) in front of the cliff in two tiers, upper and lower. About 258 such types of Buddha images still exist. Many of them have been plastered and repaired during the later periods but there are few images which still retain their original form.

The pavilion of Seven Buddhas on the San-hua cave is the monolithic structure among all the caves of Mai-chi. A steep pavilion with seven separate chambers supported by eight long pillars had been carved out in Han style on the wall of the over hanging cliff which is 50 metres high from the base. In between every two long pillars there is a niche of Buddha. This has been mentioned by Yu-hsin in the 'Inscriptions on the niches of Buddha at Mai-chi'. There he mentioned that Li Chun-hsin, the governor of Ta-tu registered as a native of Su-chih, a devout Buddhist lived as a recluse under a tree, carved seven Buddha niches on the walls of the south cliff as an act of piety and to make offerings for his departed father. Similarly he also built a *stūpa.* "It looks as if someone has worked at quartz-crystal and appears like a magnificent full moon, a glowing fresh lotus. It manifests the luminous Sumeru (the central mountain peak of the Buddhist universe). People enjoyed the fragrant smell. In this wildworld they opened a hall to expound the doctrine which is like a fragrant mountain. This is more peaceful and quiet abode of the Buddha."

At the extremities of each of these Seven Buddhist niches on the wall, there are seven borders on the wall, and in each of the borders there are frescos of four celestial musicians ie., *Gandharvas.* Some playing music, some offering incense and some scattering flowers. Preservation of these relics are being properly done. These seven beautiful paintings on the strip of the wall belong to comparatively later period. The style of the painting is of the Sui[10] and the early part of the T'ang period[11]. There are about seventyfive clay images in this cave. The image of the Devarāja (Indra) was repaired during the Sung period[12], some of the Buddha and *Bodhisattva* images were repaired during the time of the Ming and the following Ch'ing period[13].

Niu-erh Hall (Mai-chi No. 5) is smaller than that of the Seven Buddha Pavillion, there are four pillars built in Han style, in between two pillars there are three Buddhist niches. Each of the heavenly flower slabs of the niches contains beautiful mural painting. On the top of the pillars a square peck-shaped box carved which is worth mentioning. Though the image of the Devaraja at the base of the Niu-erh Hall had been repaired during the time of the Ming rulers, the powerful and majestic demeanour still greatly moves the human heart.

The series of chambers of the Han style in the thirtieth cave of Mai-chi, the cave chambers and the style of stone-pillars are fully preserved. From these construction and architectural designs, it is easily presumed that it belonged to the Han nationality. These were not transplanted from India. The cave No. 43 of Mai-chi has four stone pillars but a part of the pillars has already been destroyed. The top of the pillars have been sculptured with *Padmāsana Buddhas*. Under the stone caves and between the top of the pillars, the peck-shaped boxes are not used, instead of that the images of the Buddha light streaming from precious jewels were carved.

In this style and expression we can find a unique example of synthesis of Indian and Chinese fine arts.

The three most important caves hewn out on the Western Cliff belonged to the last period of the Northern-wei Dynasty (beginning of the 6th century A.D.). Among these caves, the longest one is the Hall of Thousand Buddhas. It is also called Stone Tablet-cave (Mai-chi cave No. 133). The inner construction of the cave is very complicated. The Book Yu-tengYen-hua says "After ascending the Western pavilion with the help of suspended ladder, there are thousand and ten thousand chambers. Those who tried on secondary cause, *Partyayas*, and voidness (*Śūnyatā*) will not dare to turn their head to look. This leads to the top of the mountain having ten thousand *Bodhisattva* hall which had been hollowed out of rocks. The halls of ancient and comparatively later periods are extremely big. The carved beams, painted pillars, carved beams of the roofs, the lintels of doors are all chiseled out of rocks. It is said in the "T'ai-p'ing-kuang-chi"chuan 397, the Ten Thousand *Bodhisattva* Hall which has been mentioned here in nothing but the Hall of Thousand Buddhas. The 3½ ft high standing Buddhā in welcoming posture at the main entrance, was sculptured during the time of the T'ang and was repaired during the Sung period. This image of Buddha expresses profound compassion and tranquility. Two hands are joined in a very relaxed way to welcome the guests, particularly it creates benign, delicate and gentle feelings. This image is mostly elegant and highly esteemed, it is the best creation of the artists.

The thousand Buddha images have been stripped off by off robbers and bandits. In the gaṛbhagrha (inner chamber) of the cave there are more than twenty pedestals for images. Among these, 18 five pieces of stone-tablets, one of these tablets bears the sketch of most touching stories regarding the propagation of Buddhism. It is devoted to the incident in the Lotus Sūtra, the Bible of the *Mahāyāna*, where Śākyamuni by the power of his prerching caused *Prabhūturatna*, a Buddha of ancient past to appear beside him.

Going ahead up to the top of the covered way along the precipice on the west, one can get the highest place, the Deva Hall cave. On the top of the western wall of the Deva Hall there is faint remnants of the poem of Wang Jen-wu, the post of the later T'ang period. It says – "ascending the highest peak if one suspends 10,000 ft ladder in space one can ordinarily share the uniformity of white cloud. In front of the caves, the rows of mountains look very small. The setting Sun bisects equally the top of the Deva Hall. The peak is inaccessible and the road is dangerous. So very few people go there. The ancient grottoes are very strong and everlasting which are going to remain permanently. I want to transmit the names on the horizon, so I earnestly raise my hand brushing away the stone". On the fore wall of the Deva Hall there is an exceptionally beautiful mural painting depicting a battle scene.

The 127th cave of Mai-chi is the smallest of all the three big caves, but it has a number of mural paintings. The 165th cave was also hewn out during the time of the Northern-wei Dynasty but it went under major repair during the Sung period, majority of the images are greatly influenced by the Sung style. There are images of two women offering prayers in the "Temple of Statues" belonging to the Sung period. Stuccos are plentiful, the divine feeling in them is very life-like, they have fluttering dresses. These are actually masterpieces among all the sculptures belonging to the 12th century A.D. This class of sculptures are very rare to find in previous periods. Recently the ancient temple in the Ancestral Hall of the Chin on the Tzai-ling range in Shan-his and at Mai-chi are the rare objects have been unearthed.

The research of the Mai-chi mountain very recently started. It was one of the greatest heart centre of Buddha's religion; this place was not almost unknown to the people. Every year when the time of festival arrives there was no dirth of people going to that distant mountain to offer prayers and burn incense in the temple.

All these wall paintings, clay images, sculptures and the Buddhist texts that have come down to us always remind the artistic skill and dexterity of these artists.

Endnotes

1. Sze-ch'uan, forming also the district city Le-shan, Lat. 29°34' Long. 104°00'
2. District in Mei chou in Sze-ch'uan, Lat. 30°15', Long. 103°44'
3. Chung king in Sze-ch'uan, forming also the district city of Pa, Lat. 29°34' Long 106°50'
4. Post-town near An-hsi, in Kan-su Province, Lat. 39°40', Long. 95°05. About 30 li west of the Capital.
5. In Ta-tung, Inner Mongolia, modern Shen-si province.
6. In Ho-nan
7. House of Toba, Northern Wei dynasty A.D. 386-532.
8. A.D. 1368-1644.
9. In ancient times bundles of straws were made to represent human beings called Ch'u-ling (Straw soul). These straw bundles were then carried to grave and buried along with the deads as their attendants. During the time of the Chou dynasty (1122-256 B.C.) wooden figures of men and women having springs in them by which they could move easily were buried with the deads. Later on, the practice of living persons became common, vide Mencions, Chapter III, 6.

10. District in Hsu-chou Fu. Kiang-su (Chiang-su), Lat. 34°29', Long. 116°41'
11. A prefecture in Kan-su, Lat. 34°56'; Long. 104°44'.
12. A range of mountain in South Shen-si.
13. A.D. 907-960. Posterior Liang, A.D. 907-923, Posterior T'ang A.D. 923-936, Posterior Chin A.D. 936-947, Posterior Han A.D. 947-951, Posterior Chou A.D. 951-960.
14. A.D. 502-557.
15. The Emperor Wu-ti started these two eras in 561 and 566 A.D. respectively.
16. Peking, an Imperial prefecture in Chihli. Lat. 39°57', Long. 116°29'. It was called Ta-tu during the time of the Yuan Dynasty.
17. A.D. 581-618.
18. A.D. 618-907.
19. A.D. 960-1127 (North) A.D. 1127-1279 (South).
20. A.D. 1644-1912.

---

* Buddha Jayanti Lecture delivered under the auspics of the All India Philosophy Congress, 1975.

46

TIME IN NYĀYA-VAIŚEṢIKA AND VAIBHĀṢIKA-SAUTRĀNTIKA

Hari Shankar Prasad

Proofs for the Existence of Time: The Nyāya-Vaiśeṣika View

Nyāya and *Vaiśeṣika* are the realistic and pluralistic systems. They admit nine substances (*dravyas*)[1] – earth, water, fire, air, ether, time, space, soul and *manas* which comprise all kinds of material and immaterial things. The substances are grounds of qualities and action, and are coexistent material causes of all composite things produced from it[2]. Substance is the substratum of qualities (*guṇāśrayo dravyaṁ*). Four of these substances – earth, water, fire and air – constitute the material world and are non-eternal. Remaining five substances – ether, time, space, *manas* and soul – are divided into two groups. Ether, time and space are non-psychic, all-pervading (*vibhu*), imperceptible, one, infinite, eternal, and are common container of all material things. These substances have the characteristics of eternity, independence and ultimate particularity[3]. The other two substances – *manas* and soul – are psychic. They have many individuals and so they possess universals. Time and space are the instrumental causes of all produced things[4]. All activities of the phenomena, and our all the experiences are presented in time and space.

Now the question arises: How is the time known? What is the proof for the existence of time? As time does not possess any physical or psychical quality, it is not an object of perception, but it is known through inference only. The *Vaiśeṣika* asserts that the notions of the priority and posteriority, simultaneity and non-simutaniety, and soon and later are the grounds for the knowledge of time[5].

Here we will have to see in what sense the terms priority and posteriority are used. Actually priority (temporal elderliness) does not mean that it contains a large amount of time and posteriority (temporal youngerness) that of a smaller amount. According to the *Vaiśeṣika*, priority and posteriority are the qualities which are found in the produced things. They are related to the solar revolutions. The priority shows the larger number of the solar motions and the posterity that of smaller number. When we say that x is prior to y or vice versa, y is posterior to x, it means that x has witnessed larger number of solar revolutions than y[6].

But how can x (or y or any produced object) be related with the solar revolution? No direct relation is possible through the relation of inherence (*samavāya*), for the revolution of the sun confines to itself. The relation of conjunction (*saṁyoga*) also is not possible between them, because both are at a very large distance from each other. But as we know priority and posteriority imply the relation of x and solar motion, and as there is no direct relation between them, there may be an indirect relation or a connecting link.[7]

Now what is this indirect thing which connects x with the solar revolution? It must be a substance. Only a substance can be in conjunction both with x and the solar motion[8], because conjunction is possible only among the substances[9]. Again this substance should be omnipresent in dimension, individual in character so that it may be connected with all substances. Though ether and soul are two all-pervading substances, they cannot serve the purpose. The connecting link should be such that it may be in relation to both x and the revolution of the sun and also have the capacity to relate them with each other. Neither ether nor soul possess this capacity. If ether has this capacity, it would be possible for a particular stroke, producing sound in one drum, to be shifted to other drums and to produce sound in them also, because ether is an ubiquitous substance. Again if the soul had it, it would create different properties in things arbitrarily, e.g., the fragrance of the flower would be perceived in table, and the yellow colour of gold in a white lily[10].

The above absurdity shows that the ether and soul lack this capacity to be a connecting link and a direct relation is impossible. The *Vaiśeṣika*, therefore, sets forth a special substance which serves the end. And this substance is Time.

Now one may raise an objection regarding time that if time is granted to possess the capacity of connecting the two substances, it is not free from the qualities of producing the different attributes in the other substances in a most confusing way like ether and soul, for time also is ubiquitous in character. Thus time should also be restrained from this position. Keeping this difficulty in view *Vaiśeṣika* asserts that the existence of time as an indirect connecting link is proved by the reductio and absurdum argument against the other two possible substances – ether and soul. Again, in the present context the required capacity of time is posited by the same argument which broves the existence of time itself as a substance. Here is, therefore, no chance of mutual change of properties among the substances, if time is established as the medium of connecting the individual object and the solar motion[11].

Likewise, the concepts of simultaneity and non-simultaneity, soon and later are the logical substratum for the knowledge of the existence of time through inference. Simultaneity signifies the relation of two or more events with a particular solar evolution, and the non-simulataneity connotes such relation with two or more different solar revolutions. Soon or late of an event is also understood by the relation of the particular event with a greater or smaller number of solar revolutions[12]. Thus, we see that all these relations are possible only through the meditation of time, and institute the logical grounds for the inference of time.

But here all the *Vaiśeṣika* scholars are not in agreement. Śrīdhara, in his *Nyāya Kandali*, has a different approach to the inference of time. He out and out denies the possibility of establishing a relation between the notions of priority and posteriority, etc. and the solar revolutions. These notions cannot be explained by reference to solar motion, because no relation is possible between the produced things, which possess the qualities of priority and posteriority, and solar motion[13]. He is also against admitting time as a connecting link. Time itself is the cause of these notions such as, priority and posteriority, etc.[14]

One may say that to co-exist (sah*abhāva*) is simultaneity (*yaugapadya*) but not 'relating to one time' (*eka-kālikatva*). But it is not, according to Śrīdhara, true, because without conceding time the word 'co-exist' (*saha*) has no meaning. That which has not yet originated, that which continues to exist and that which ceases to be, all these three have no contradiction among themselves. Now the question arises – if time is one, why is there difference between these experiences? This is because of the difference of causes (*sāmagribhedā*). The cognition of the origination of one thing and the existence of another by the same knowledge gives the notions of priority and posteriority. And these notions arise from the cooperating cause (*sahakārikāraṇa*) time[15].

Further time is explained in terms of causality. Without granting the existence of time the emergence of everything will be impossible. An ever-existing thing like *ākāśa* is uncaused and is thus timelessly existent. Again, an every non-existing thing like round-square is also uncausable and is thus timelessly non-existent. As the *Vaiśeṣika* propounds the theory of *asatkāryavāda*, the only possibility where the causation may be applied to is the thing which is produced after having been previously non-existent (prāgasat). Only temporal or conditional things are causable. If there is no time, there is no event, no production[16] and there will be only two things either absolutely ever-existent like *ākāśa*, or absolutely ever non-existent like round-square and hence, there is no third possibility. Thus, we see causality is only intelligible by reference to time[17].

Change also gives the knowledge of time. It is time which takes us inexorably from birth to death. Different states of modifications from one state to another indicate the passage of time. Through different physical states of an old man and young one we infer the existence of time[18]. Without admitting time change is inexplicable.

Vallabha maintains that this view is very old[19]. He, like Vatsyāyana[20], advances another argument for the existence of time. The knowledge, he asserts, of the existence or being of a thing gives the notion of time. For example, 'Man exists', 'Cow exists', etc. denote the existence of something. 'Existentness' or 'Presentness' (*vartamānatva*) in general convey the idea of time[21]. Again, Vallabha clarifying his position puts forth that 'isness' (*astitva*) and presentness (*vartamānatva*) are two different things[22]. 'There is a man' does the necessarily imply that there is a man in reality. But when we say that 'the man exists', it necessarily implies the existence or presence of the man and thus gives the knowledge of the existence of time through inference[23].

Perception of Time is not Possible

Unlike *Bhaṭṭa Mīmāṁsā* and *Vedānta Nyāya-Vaiśeṣika* maintains that time cannot be an object of perception, because a substance to be perceived must possess a non-infinitesimal (*mahattva*) and a manifest form (*udbhūtarūpatva*). A substance is of atomic character and an atom cannot be perceived as it is infinitesimal, and time lacks the sensible or visible form. The knowledge of time is completely a matter of inference based on the priority and posteriority, simultaneity and non-simultaneity, soon and late. But here there is a difficulty. Though finite times or durations we infer the infinite time. Suppose we have no knowledge of finite times, then it would be impossible to infer the one, infinite, eternal time.

Gaṅgeśa in his Tattvacintāmaṇi observes that the present is conceived through finite determinants, because points of time (*kṣaṇāḥ*) are not perceivable.[24] The same statement is also found in *Nyāya-vārttika-tātparya-ṭīkā* and *Kusumāñjali.*[25] The 'present' in *Nyāya-Vaiśeṣika* is admitted as duration, not as infinitesimal (sūkṣma).

Nyāya-Vaiśeṣika conceive time as an external and all-pervading substance which is the receptum of the whole universe (*jagatām āśryaḥ*). An external thing cannot come within the range of sense-organs and so cannot be perceived. This is the reason why they do not admit time as an object of perception. Śrīdhara[26] maintains that the direct perception of time is not possible, but as a qualification of objects it is known. In *Padārthadharma-Saṅgraha*, it is stated that time is normally imperceptible, but perceptible supernormally.[27]

Measurement of Time

Nyāya-Vaiśeṣika admits two kinds of time – the infinite, eternal time (*mahākāla*) and the finite time (*khaṇḍa kāla*). Infinite time is an undivided whole. The finite time is a relative or empirical time, which is measured by the duration of an object or an action. It has only a practical value. The *Nyāya* does not accept the latter as an objective entity, but it arises from the association of absolute time with something else. It is infinite time which appears as finite when measured by the finite duration of an object or an action[28]. The same infinite and absolute time is called past, present and future through such associations, as the same person may be said to be father, son, brother, etc., from different points of view.[29]

The standard for the measurement of finite time is the daily solar revolution (*Sūrya parispanda*). B. N. Seal gives the following account for the measurement of time[30]:

The *Siddhānta-śiromaṇi* gives the following measures of time:

30 *kṣaṇas* = 1 day, 30 *kāṣthās* = 1 *kalā*

2 *Ghaṭikās* = 1 *kṣana*, 18 *Nimeṣas* = 1 *kāṣṭhā*

30 *kalās* = 1 *Ghaṭikā*, 30 *Tatparas* = 1 *Nimeṣa*

And 100 *Trutis* = 1 *Tatpara*

This makes a *Truti* of time equal to 1/33750 of a second, which is nearly the measure of the *Paramāṇu* of time as given in the *Viṣṇu Purāṇa* (vide *Bhāskara's Siddhānta-śiromaṇi, Kālamānā-dhyāya*).

The above measures were in use among the astronomers, but the physicists computed according to the following table given both in Udayana's Kiraṇāvali and Śrīdhara's *Nyāya-*kandali:

30 *Muhurtas* = 1 day (24 hours)

30 *Kalās* = 1 *Muhurta*, 2 *Lavas* = 1 *Nimeśa*

30 *Kāṣṭha* = 1 *Kalā*, 2 *Kṣaṇas* = 1 Lava

18 *Nimeṣa* = 1 *Kāṣtha*

Kṣaṇadvayaṁ lavaḥ prok to nimeṣastu lavadvayaṁ,

Aṣtadaśanīmeṣāstu kāṣthā triṁśattu tāḥ kalā.

Triṁśatkalā muhurtaḥ syāt triṁśadrātryahanī ca te.

(Udayana, Kiraṇvali)

This makes 1 *kṣaṇa* of the *Nyāya-Vaiśeṣika* equal to 2/45 of a second. The *Nyāya* assumes that the unit of physical change (or the time occupied by any single antecedent step in a causal series before the succeeding step is ushered in) is equal to a *kṣaṇa* (or 2/45 of a second).

The solar day was taken as a natural measure or division of time. In the *Nyāya-Vaiśeṣika* school the day of twenty-four hours (solar) is stated to contain 30 X 30 X 30 X 18 X 2 X 2 units of time *kṣaṇas*. The *Nyāya* unit of time, therefore, measures 2/45 of a second. The smallest measure of time mentioned by the astronomers is the *Truti*, which is 1/33750 of a second.

The Nyāya View of Present Time as Duration

There are two schools of thought about the present time – one denies it and the other admits it as duration and absolute time. The former is the opponent group[31] and the latter is *Nyāya*. The *Nyāya-sūtra* of Gautama with Vātsyāyana's commentary contains an exposition of the argument between the opponent and the *Nyāya* concerning the present time. It is divided into two parts – *pūrvapakṣa* and *uttarapakṣa*. In the first the opponent puts forward his views and then he is answered by *Nyāya*[32].

The opponent will assert that there is no present, because the ground of the practical division of time is 'action'. An action starts at one stage and stops at another. When the action is in operation either some part of it is finished, or some part of it is yet to be. That which is finished is past and that which has yet to be is future. There is no third one such as present. For example, a fruit is falling from the tree. At any point of its journey there are only two things. Above the point there is the path through which it has fallen and the time connected with it is past time; and below the point there is the path through which it has yet to fall and the time connected with it is future time. There is no third path with which we may connect the time as present. Hence, there is no present time.

The *Nyāya* affirms that time is not denoted by path or space[33]. It is denoted only by action itself[34], for example, 'falling'. When the action of falling ceases, it is past time; when the action is yet to be, it is future time and when the action is observed in operation in an object, it is present time. If the action of falling does not characterize an object, whose cessation or origination will be said? Past time is in relation to the action that has ceased; future time to the action that the object is falling, it is connected with action. And this relation of an object and action gives the notion of present time[35]. When the object is in action (*kriyā sambandha*) that is present time. When we say, the fruit is falling' the period, from the moment it starts falling to the moment it ceases to fall is present time. And if that is not admitted the other two (past and future) also depending on it would themselves collapse.

Again, without admitting present, past and future also cannot be proved mutually[36]. If past and future are dependent on each other only then present can be abrogated. But this is not so. Neither the past is independent on the future, nor the future on the past. Because it would be impossible to say how the past is proved in reference to future, or how the future is proved in reference to past. From what standpoint is it past or future? So the present cannot be repudiated.

The opponent may raise the objection that just as 'short' and 'long', 'high lands' and 'low lands', 'light' and 'darkness' are relative, the past and future also depend on each other.

But this position, say *Naiyāyikas*, is illogical. First of all, no specific reason is given for this[37]. Without proper reason only illustrations will not suffice. Again, there are counter-illustrations which contradict this supposition, such as colour and touch, odour and taste, are not mutually dependent. Mutual dependence proves neither, because when one is absent, the other is also absent and thus both will cease to be[38].

Present time is denoted by being of an objct also[39], e.g., substance exists, quality exists, action exists.

The perception arises from the sense-contact with present objects[40]. That which is non-existent cannot come into contact with the senses, and the opponent does not admit that anything is present. Thus, the means of perception, the object of perception and the perceptual knowledge – all are dismissed. And if perception is denied there can be no inference or verbal testimony, which are based on it. If all means of knowledge are spurned, there can be no knowledge of anything.

Present time is conceived in two ways – first by the being of objects, i.e., 'there is a substance', secondly by a series of actions, i.e., 'cooking' or 'cutting'[41]. There are two kinds of series of actions. One is a series of different actions but serving single purpose, e.g., 'cooking' which includes putting of the pot on the oven, pouring the water in it, washing the rice and to put it in the pot, collecting the fuel and inserting it into the oven, kindling the fire, stirring with ladle, pouring out of the scum (gruel) of boiled rice and taking down the pot on the ground. The other is a series of repetitions of the same action, e.g., 'cutting'. In this action a man repeatedly lifts up an axe and strikes with it on a piece of wood. Both the series of actions, from putting the pot on the oven to taking it down and from the beginning of cutting the wood to the end unless it is cut, indicate the present time.

Nyāya[42] further maintains that there may be the state of having been acted upon and the state of going to be acted upon, a two-fold apprehension of present time results. A stories of actions which is yet to begin indicates the future time, e.g., 'he will cook'; the cessation of the series followed by its result indicates the past time, e.g. 'he cooked'; and a series of actions which is still in progress gives the conception of present time, e.g., 'he cooks'. A complete action consists of three states – (1) the state which has ceased to be, (2) the state which has yet to be, and (3) the state which is going on. All these three states of time are included in a series of actions, and are recognized in reference to present time[43], such as 'he cooks' or 'it is cooked'.

Thus, the present time is conceived in two ways – (1) as having been dissociated from past and future or by the being of an object, e.g., 'there is a substance' and (2) as having been associated with them, e.g., 'cooking' or 'cutting', which denotes the perpetual series of actions, which comprises all the three states of time. Thus, we see, present time exists.

Nyāya sets forth that it is action itself which serves as the index of empirical or finite time. In the above example given by Vātsyāyana, a falling object indicates three things – the fruit that falls, the path or space through which it falls, and the action of falling. Of these, the space and the fruit remain the same when falling. They cannot be said to denote time. It is only action of falling which can be explained so[44].

This notion of action being the index of time, implies the conception of the present as duration. Again, it is said that all actions must last for at least four instants[45]. Instantaneous action is not possible at all. The duration of present cannot be less than four instants but it may be more. According to the atomism of the system, 'action' is supposed to operate through 'disjunction' and 'conjunction' each of which occupies two instants[46].

The being of an object (not associated with action) also indicate present time. This is the absolute mode of the present which is perceived as unassociated with the past and future. The relative mode of the present is described as associated with the past and the future and is indicated by the continuity of action. According to Ācārya Viśvanātha the substance of an object never ceases to be present[47]. Though the qualities of that object undergo different changes. Take, for example, a jar. It is black before baking and red after baking. Its colour changes from black to red but its substance persists throughout the same. 'In the strict logic, however, the time-determination are to be understood as predicated of different qualities or actions, and not of the substance'.[48]

Thus, we may say that the present is always a duration, though it cannot be objectively determined. Its breadth may vary from person to person. It is not necessarily the same whenever present time is apprehended. 'These variations, however, being necessitated by purely pragmatic considerations, can only be provisional and do not affect the absolute mode of the present.[49]

The *Vaibhāṣika* school of Buddhism also admits the reality of time. But while the *Nyāya-Vaiśeṣika* maintains that the time is an independent, infinite, all-pervasive, unique, imperceptible and absolute time by propounding four theories of change, such as – change as the transformation of modes (*bhāvanyathātva*) of an element (*dharma*), change in the aspects of the element (*lakṣaṇānyathātva*), change of the states of the element (*avasthānyathātva*) and change as a temporal relativity (*anyathānyathātva*). All these theories are in agreement that the essence of the *dharma* remains the same throughout the change. Time in the *Vaibhāṣikas* is based on the *kāritra* (of the *dharma*) which is the potency of projecting the results (*phalākṣepa-śakti*). When the *dharma* has not yet attained its *kāritra* it is future, when it has attained its *kāritra* it is present and when its *kāritra* has ceased to be is past.[50]

But as we have seen in *Nyāya-Vaiśeṣika* such divisions as past, present and future or second, minute and hour, etc. are *khaṇḍa-kāla* (relative or empirical time). It is only for practical use. It is not an objective entity, it arises from the association of absolute time (*mahākāla*). Time in *Nyāya-Vaiśeṣika* is objectively real (dravya-sat), but in the *Vaibhāsikas* it is conceptually real (*prajñapti-sat*) as the *Sautrāntikas* put it.[51] The *Vaibhāṣikas*' theory of three time-epocks (*traikālyavāda*) has been vehemently criticized by the *Sautrāntikas*[52]. The controversy between the two requires a detailed study which calls for separate treatment is not possible to give here.

Endnotes

1. *Pṛthivyāpastejo vāyurākaśam Kālo digātmā mana iti dravyāni*, V.S. (*Vaiśeṣika Sūtra*) 1.1.5.
2. *Kriyāgunavat samavāyikaraṇam dravyam* – V. S. 1.1.15.
3. *Nityatva, anaśritatva, antyaviśesavatva* – *Padārthadharmasaṅgraha* of Praśastapāda, pp. 20.21.
4. Ibid. p. 25.
5. V.S., ii. 2.6.
6. *Sūryodayāstamayakriyā pracayālpattvabahutvaviśiśṭāpīnḍādeva paratvā-paratve bhaviśyataḥ kṛtamatra dravyāntareṇa Kalencti cet.* – *Nyāyavartimatātaparyatīka*, Kashi Sanskrit series, 1982, p. 404. (onward NVTT)
7. *Na ca sūryagatiḥ sakśatpinḍasambadha, nāpi samyuktasamavāyaḥ sambhavati piṇdasūryayoḥ samyogābhāvat….Evam caitādṛśamekam dravyam svikāryam yadyāvatpiṇdasūryasambadham* – *Kiranāvalibhāskara*, Sarsvati Bhavan Texts, Benares, 1920, p. 137.
8. "The relation is expressed as 'svasamyuktasamyukta *samavāya*', i.e. inherence (of motion) in a substratum which is in conjunction with something which is in conjunction with the individual in question" – Studies in *Nyaya-Vaisesika Metaphysics*, S. Bhadhuri, Bhandarkar Oriental Research Institute, Poona, 1975, p. 185.
9. *Dravyadravayayoreva samyogah.*
10. *Na ākāśasya svapratyasattimātreṇa…sphatikamanerūparañjanaprasaṇgāt Kiraṇāvali, Bibliotheca Indica*, The Asiatic Society, Calcutta, 1956, pp. 351-352.

Sa ca sambandhaḥ samyogādirna sambhavatīti kāla eva sambandha ghaṭakaḥ kalpyate – Sidphānta Muktāvali, 45.

11. *Kiranāvali Bhāskara*, p. 138 (op. cit.), *Kiranāvali*, op. cit. p. 352.

12. *Nyāyavārttikatātparyatīkā* op. cit. – II. 1.39, p. 281; *Kiranāvali*, op. cit. p. 353.

13. *Ādityaparivarttanaṇipīyastvabhūyastvanibandhano yuvasthavirayoḥ parāparavyavahara ityeke, tadayuktam, āditya parivarttanasya yuvasthavirayoḥ smabandhābhāvādasambaddhasya nimittatve cātiprasaṇgāt* – *Nyāyakandali*, Varanaseya Sanskrit Visvavidyalaya, Varanasi, 1963, p. 156. (onward NK).

14. *Tasmādyadatra nimittam sa kāla iti* – Ibid.

15. Ibid.

16. *Asati tasmin vastūtpādabhāvāt* – Ibid.

17. Ibid, p. 158.

18. *Yuvasthavirayoḥ śarīrāvasthābhedena tatkāraṇatayā kālasamyogoe – numiyate* – Ibid.

19. *Esa tavaccirantanaḥ panthāḥ* - *Nyāyalīlāvatī*, Ghowkhamba Sanskrit Series, No. 355, 1927, p. 293.

20. *Nyāya-sūtra and Vatsyāyana's commentary* –II. 1.41.

21. *Kalopi sarvatrābhinnākaravartamāna pratyayavedyaḥ* - Ibid. p. 310.

22. *Astitvam vartamānatvamiti cenna* – Ibid, p. 310.

23. *Vide detail Nyāyalīlāvatī*, op. cit. pp. 310-312.

24. "*....Kśaṇānām attndriyatvāt, sthūlopādhim ādāya vartamānatva – grahat* ...." – *Pratyaksa-Cintamani* – p. 380.

25. NVTT, p. 21 (Chowkhamba, 1925).

    "*Kṣaṇopādhīnām anākalanāt*" – *Kusumāñjali*, st. 4, p. 5 (As. Soc. Ed.).

26. NK, op. cit., p. 158.

27. *Asmadvistanām tu yoginām yogajadharm, ānugrhītena manasā svātmāntarākāśa dik-kāla paramāṇuvāyumanassu tatsamavetaguṇakrama-sāmānayaviśeśeśu samvāye cāvitatham svarūpadarśanumutapadyate* – *Padarthadharma, samgraha*, Chowkhamba Sanskrit series, Benares, 1924-31, p. 553.

28. *Karikavali, Kārika*, 45 and *Muktāvali* thereon.

29. *Yathaikasmin puruse anekasambandhabhedanvidhāyinyabhinne pita putro bhrāteti pratyayā bhavanti tadvadekaḥ Kālaḥ Kāryakaraṇaviśeśāpekśaḥ paraparādipratyayaheturiti* – *Nyāya Vārtika*, Benares edition, 1916, p. 253.

30. '*The Positive Sciences of the Ancient Hindus*' – Sir B. N. Seal, Motilal Banarasidass, Delhi, 1958, pp. 76-77, 148.

31. Here the opponent is *Mādhyamika* as S. Radhakrishnan observes, *Indian Philosophy*, Vol. I, p. 142. But Sadananda Bhaduri disagrees with this by saying. "this view, however, cannot at present be affiliated to any school of philosophy. In the days of the *Nyāya-sūtra* and of the *Mahābhāsya* there seems to have been in existence a class of thinkers who denied the present. These thinkers might have been Buddhists, as some are inclined to think, but there is no conclusive evidence in favour of such a supposition, for the *Kathāvathu* and other earlier Buddhists' work testify to divergent opinions among the Buddhist sects on the three denominations of time. Some modern scholars are of opinion that the view criticized in *Nyāya-sūtra* represents Nāgārjuna's position. This is evidently wrong, for according to Nāgārjuna, the past, present and future are equally unreal, whereas the

view under consideration is that of a realist who believes in the reality of the past and future, though not of the present'. Studies in *Nyāya-Vaiśeśika Metaphysics*, Sadanand Bhaduri, Bhandarkar Oriental Research Institute, Poona, 1975, p. 207.

32. *Nyāya-sutra of Gautama with the commentary of Vātsyāyana*, 2.1.39-2.1.43. (Onward cited as Vatsyayana).
33. *Nādhvavyaṇga kālah* – Vātsyāyana, 2.1.40.
34. *Kriya Vyaṇgyaḥ* (Kālaḥ) – Ibid.
35. *Kriyādravyayoḥ sambandham gṛhṇāti vartamānaḥ Kālaḥ* - Ibid.
36. *Nyāya-sūtra*, 2.1.41.
37. *Viśeśahetvabhāvāt* – *Vātsyāyana*, 2.1.41.
38. *Yasmādekābhave'nyatarābhavādubhayabhavaḥ* - Ibid.
39. *Arthasadbhāvavyangyascāyam vartamānah kālah*, 2.1.42. Ibid.
40. *Pratyakśamindriyārthasannikarsajam*
41. *Ubhayathā ca vartamānaḥ Kālo grhyate Kvacidarthasadbhāvavyaṇgyah. Yathā's stidravyamiti. Kvacit KriyāsantānaVyaṇgyah. Yathā pacati. Chinnattīti* – Ibid.
42. *Nyāya-sūtra* – 2.1.43.
43. *Tadevam kriyāsamtānasthastraikālyasamāhāraḥ pacati pacyate iti vartamāngrahaṇena grhyate* – Ibid.
44. *Nyāya-Vārttika* – 2.1.40.
45. *Dinakarīya on Muktavali*, 1.45: *Prathamakarmaṇah kśaṇacatuśṭayā-vathāyinaḥ.*
46. Vide *Indian Logic and Atomism*, A. B. Keith, pp. 190 and 223.
47. *Nyāyasūtra Vṛtti* – 2.1.43.
48. S. Bhaduri – op. cit. p. 211.
49. Ibid. p. 212.
50. *Kāritrāt pracyuto' tītah, tat prāpto varttamānaḥ, tadaprāpto'nagataḥ.* – *Tattvasaṅgraha of Sāntaraksita and its commentary* by Kamalasila, Gaekwad Oriental Series No. xxx, P. 508.
51. *Bhavatu Kāritram prajnaptisat, tatkṛtam cāpyadhvavyavasthānam, tataśca ko dośaḥ* - Ibid, p. 510.
52. *Abhidharmakośa – bhāśya of Vasubandhu and Sphutārthā of Yaśomitra.* V, 24-26.

47

विज्ञानवाद एवं वैज्ञानिक चिंतन*

केवलकृष्ण मित्तल

आरम्भ में ही, यह स्पष्ट कर देना आवश्यक है कि मैं वैज्ञानिक चिन्तन को दार्शनिक चिन्तन की एक विधा मानते हुए ही, विज्ञानवाद के आलोक में, उसके प्रजनन और विकास के मुख्य आयामों पर एक विहंगम दृष्टि डालने का साहस करूंगा। ऐसा करने में मेरा आशय किसी दूर की कौड़ी लाने का नहीं अपितु विज्ञानवाद और वैज्ञानिक चिंतन दोनों में ही मूल रूप से आये शब्द 'विज्ञान' के अर्थ-साम्य सम्बन्धी कौतूहल की शान्ति मात्र है।

वस्तुतः विज्ञान जिस अर्थ में विज्ञानवाद में प्रयुक्त हुआ है वह एकदम व्यापक और अनूठा है। एक ओर तो वह उन सब अर्थों से भिन्न है जिनका व्यवहार पालि साहित्य में शब्द 'विञ्ञाण' - विज्ञान के पर्यायवाची के प्रयोग से हुआ है और दूसरी ओर यह अपने आप में इतना व्यापक है कि उन सभी अर्थों को सहज ही समाहित करता है।

पालि टैक्सट सोसायटी द्वारा प्राचीन पालि इंगलिश कोष के अनुसार विञ्ञाण का प्रयोग पालि साहित्य में मुख्यतः पांच विभिन्न अर्थों में हुआ है।

1. रूप, वेदना, संज्ञा और संस्कार के साथ एक स्कन्ध के रूप में
2. पृथ्वी, जल, अग्नि, वायु और आकाश के साथ धातु की भूमिका में
3. प्रतीत्यसमुत्पाद के उदाहरण स्वरूप द्वादशनिदान रूपी भवचक्र की तीसरी कड़ी- अविद्या और संस्कार से परिवेष्टित-नाम रूप की जननी के परिवेश में।
4. पुनर्जन्म के आधारभूत, कर्म क्षेत्र के उस बीज के रूप में जिसे जीवन प्रवाह के आहार (अन्न, भूत-द्रव्य) की संज्ञा दी जाती है और जिसका कार्य कर्म संस्कारों को एक जीवन से दूसरे जीवन में ले जाने का है।
5. चक्षु एवं चक्षुर्विषय, श्रोता एवं श्रोता-विषय आदि के परस्पर संपर्क से उत्पन्न कृत फल रूपी उस समुदाय के रूप में जिसे काया विञ्ञाण अर्थात् संवेदक और संवेद्य के संयोग से उत्पन्न उसका संवित् अथवा संवेदन कहा जाता है।

विज्ञानवाद को मान्य विज्ञान के व्यापक अर्थ की दृष्टि से तो न केवल रूप, वेदना, संज्ञा और संस्कार, पृथ्वी, जल, अग्नि, वायु और आकाश, वरन अविद्या संस्कार, नाम-रूप, षडायतन, स्पर्श, वेदना, तृष्णा,

उपादान, भव, जाति और जरामरण, संवेदक, संवेद्य और संवेदन भी सबके सब विज्ञान रूपी ज्वाला (विद्युत) के स्फुलिंग (तरंगे) मात्र हैं। ऐसा मानने पर विज्ञान को चित्त अथवा मन के पर्याय के रूप में स्वीकार किया जाता है, जैसा कि संयुक्तनिकाय 95, में उल्लेख है।

विज्ञान को मन अथवा चित्त के साथ एकार्थक मानने पर ऊपर वर्णित 'विञ्ञाण' के विभिन्नार्थक प्रयोगों में से चौथा अर्थात् "आहार" भी स्वतः ही इस व्यापक अर्थ में सहज ही समाहित होता हुआ तो प्रतीत होता है किन्तु तनिक विचार करने पर "आहार-रूप-विज्ञान" अपने आप में "विज्ञान" को और तदानुसार विज्ञानवाद की दो परस्पर भिन्न अवधारणाओं के व्यामिश्रण की सम्भावना को भी उत्पन्न करता है। अतः यह ध्यान रखना अत्यावश्यक है कि विज्ञान को मृत्यु और पुनर्जन्म के बीच की कड़ी मानते हुए भी हम बौद्धदर्शन की मूलभूत धारणाओं-अनित्यता अनात्म और प्रतीत्यसमुत्पाद को स्मरण रखें। बौद्ध-विज्ञानवाद के अनुसार मन अथवा चित्त से हमारा आश्य कदाचित् ऐसे तत्व से नहीं होना चाहिए जो नित्य आत्मस्वरूप एवं स्वतः स्फूर्त हो। इसलिये मज्झिमनिकाय 258 में विञ्ञाण की इस प्रकार की कल्पना की कड़ी आलोचना हुई है जिसका विस्तार एवं विश्लेषण (जाने या अनजाने) श्रीलंका के एक विद्वान D. H. De. A. Wijesekhara ने अपने तीन

1. "(वैदिक यक्ष एवं पालि यक्ख का दार्शनिक अर्थघटन)"
2. "(वैदिक गन्धर्व तथा पालि गन्धब्ब)"
3. "(थेरवाद बौद्धमत में विञ्ञाण की अवधारणा)"

(University of Ceylon Review vol. 1 2 p. 24, vol. III p. to Journal of the American Oriental Society 85, 1964 pp. 254-9)

लेखों में प्रकाशित किया है। मन अथवा चित्त का अर्थ यहाँ पर ऐसी प्रवाहमान मननक्रिया अथवा चिद्क्रिया है जो जन्म जन्मान्तरों में चलते रहने पर भी - सम्भवतः इसी कारण से ही -अनित्य एवं अनात्म रूप प्रतीत्यसमुत्पन्नता की द्योतक है। दीघ निकाय तथा संयुक्त निकाय में इसकी चर्चा इसी रूप में उपलब्ध होती है। विज्ञान को इस प्रकार समझने पर ही ऐसा कहा जा सकता है कि परिनिष्पन्न, परिकल्पित एवं परतन्त्र विज्ञान समान रूप से विज्ञान की विधायें हैं।

प्रश्न हो सकता है विज्ञानवाद एवं वैज्ञानिक चिन्तन की चर्चा में पालि साहित्य में प्रयुक्त विञ्ञाण शब्द के अर्थ विवेचन का क्या प्रयोजन है? ऐसा मैंने इसलिये किया है कि एक तो मैं "विज्ञान" शब्द के आधुनिक प्रयोग की विलक्षणता का प्रगाढ़ करना चाहता हूँ और दूसरी बात यह कहना चाहता हूं कि जिस प्रकार विज्ञानवाद में प्रयुक्त विज्ञान पाली साहित्य में प्रयुक्त विज्ञान (विञ्ञाण) से भिन्न किन्तु अपने में उसे सामने वाला है उसी प्रकार विज्ञान का आधुनिक प्रयोग भी विज्ञानवादी प्रयोग में समाहित अर्थ में स्वीकार किया जा सकता है, आवश्यकता है धैर्यपूर्ण विज्ञान के प्रजनन और विकास के इतिहास और (अब

तक के इतिहास द्वारा पहुंचे) निष्कर्ष के अवलोकन की। विज्ञान की विज्ञानवादी धारणा के बीज हम पहले के अर्थात् पालि साहित्य में देख सकते हैं। ''विञ्ञाण'' के प्रथम प्रयोगों और उसमें निहित विज्ञानवादी धारणा के विकास में कुछ एक शताब्दियों का अन्तर है। पालि साहित्य के विद्वानों को (उस साहित्य ही के आधार पर) निरालम्बन ज्ञान अथवा विज्ञान की बात आज भी जिस प्रकार नहीं जंचती ठीक उसी प्रकार विज्ञान के आधुनिक प्रयोग की विज्ञानवादी धारणा से अत्यन्त निकटता की बात उन वैज्ञानिक चिंतकों को नहीं जंचती जिन्होंने विज्ञान के विकास की प्रक्रिया को उसके लगभग 400 वर्ष के इतिहास में से अंतिम 50 वर्षों के इतिहास पर ध्यान नहीं दिया है।

लोक मानस में जो विज्ञान की धारणा प्रचलित है, निश्चय ही, उसका विज्ञानवादी धारणा से कदाचित् कोई भी सम्बन्ध नहीं है ऐसा स्वाभाविक ही है क्योंकि लोकमानस दार्शनिक चिन्तकों की भूमिका से सदा पीछे ही चलता है। मुझे ऐसा लगता है कि जो कोई भी वैज्ञानिक चिन्तक अथवा दार्शनिक चिंतक विज्ञान के आधुनिकतम रूप को जानता समझता है उसे विज्ञानवादी धारणा और वैज्ञानिक धारण (धारणा) में गहरा सम्बन्ध देखने में तनिक भी कोई कठिनाई नहीं होगी।

वैज्ञानिक चिंतन का सूत्रपात गैलिल्यो के चिंतन से लगभग सोलहवीं शताब्दी के मध्य काल में हुआ। तब से लेकर लगभग 300, 325 वर्षों तक हमारे सामने अनेक वैज्ञानिकों के प्रयत्न प्रयास से विज्ञान का एक निश्चित स्वरूप प्रकाश में आया है जिसके मोटे रूप से दो पक्ष हैं- एक विज्ञान की पद्धति सम्बन्धी तथा दूसरा उसके अध्ययन विषय सम्बन्धी। उन दोनों पक्षों में तब तक एक विरोधाभास बना रहा जब तक कि वैज्ञानिकों ने यह नहीं पहचाना कि उनका अध्ययन-विषय उनकी पद्धति द्वारा उद्‌घाटित है अथवा किसी पूर्वाग्रह पर आधारित हैं। इस प्रकार की पहचान पिछले लगभग 50, 60 वर्षों के वैज्ञानिक विकास द्वारा सम्भव हुई है। आनन्द की बात यह है कि पहला पक्ष आरम्भ से ही विज्ञानवाद को मान्य एवं उसकी मान्यता के अत्यन्त अनुकूल अथवा अनुरूप पड़ा है और उसका महत्व वैज्ञानिक चिंतन में उत्तरोत्तर बढ़ा ही है कम नहीं हुआ, और दूसरा जो कि विज्ञानवादी धारण के एकदम प्रतिकूल पड़ता था उसने कुछ इस प्रकार का पलटा खाया है कि आज विज्ञान को भौतिकवाद का समर्थक व पोषक-जैसा कि उसे लगभग तीन सौ बरसों तक माना जाता रहा है- न मानकर कुछ दार्शनिक एवं वैज्ञानिक एक या दूसरे प्रकार के विज्ञानवाद का ही प्रवर्धन करता हुआ घोषित कर रहे हैं।

विज्ञान का लोक प्रचलित लक्षण तो है एक ऐसा अध्ययन। अनुशासन जो न केवल कला एवं धर्म से ही वरन् विज्ञानवादी इत्यादि सभी दर्शन व्यवस्थाओं तथा अनुशासनों से भिन्न है, जिसका एक विशेष स्वरूप है, कार्यपद्धति है और क्षेत्र है। इस अर्थ में इसे विशिष्ट ज्ञान कहा जा सकता है। क्योंकि विज्ञान केवल सांसारिक गतिविधि को ही जानने समझने का दावा करता है इसलिए कोई-कोई विज्ञान को विपरीत ज्ञान अर्थात् परम तत्व के ज्ञान (परा विद्या) की अपेक्षा अपरा विद्या भी मानते समझते हैं। किन्तु विज्ञान का लक्षण जो गैलिल्यो को मान्य था और आज तक के सभी वैज्ञानिकों को मान्य है वह है एक ऐसा ज्ञान

जिसे निरीक्षण एवं परीक्षण से प्राप्त किया जाये। यह लक्षण विज्ञान का एक ऐसा पक्ष प्रस्तुत करता है जिसे विज्ञानवाद भी सहर्ष स्वीकार करता है क्योंकि निरीक्षण और परीक्षण जिसे निरीक्षण की ही पुनरीक्षण अथवा बहुविधीक्षण रूप कहा जा सकता है- दोनों ही विज्ञप्तिस्वरूप ही माने जा सकते हैं। किन्तु इस लक्षण के साथ ही वैज्ञानिकों की एक अन्य धारणा भी रही है और वह यह कि निरीक्षण एवं परीक्षण सिद्ध ज्ञान अपौरुषेय एवं बाह्यर्थिक वस्तुनिष्ठ तथ्य है। ज्ञानरूपी कल्पना अथवा विज्ञप्तिमात्र नहीं। यह मान्यता बीसवीं शताब्दी के आरम्भ तक निर्वाधरूप से मानी जाती रही और अब भी कुछ एक वैज्ञानिकों का इसके प्रतिमोह है जबकि विज्ञान के विकास ने ही इस मान्यता को गलत जैसा सिद्ध कर दिया है। इसी मान्यता के अनुरूप ही सर्वप्रथम विज्ञान भौतिकवाद का समर्थन करता हुआ लगा और सबसे अधिक विकास भौतिकी एवं रसायन विज्ञान में ही हुआ। जड़ पदार्थों की सत्ता सिद्ध मानी गई और उसके आलम्बन स्वरूप लगभग 12 भूततत्वों की संसार के मूल द्रव्यों के रूप में कल्पना की गई। जीवन और चेतना को जड़ तत्वों से ही उत्पन्न माना गया और द्रव्यमान को ऊर्जा से अलग किन्तु उसका आधार माना गया। जीव-विज्ञान में भी उन्हीं प्रक्रियाओं की सत्ता मानी गई जिनका सम्बन्ध वाह्य गोचर शरीरविज्ञान से जोड़ा जा सकता था और चेतना का आधार दिमाग एवं स्नायुव्यवस्था की गतिविधि को माना गया। मनोविज्ञान का प्रथम स्वरूप भी या तो ज्ञान, भावना, क्रिया की आन्तर्निरीक्षण द्वारा उपलब्ध संगिति में देखा गया या उसे एकदम छोड़ जैसा दिया गया। मन और शरीर, द्रव्यमान और ऊर्जा, जीव और निर्जीव आदि में न पाटे जा सकने वाले भेद माने, यहां तक कि ऊर्जा के विभिन्न रूपों जैसे मैकेनीकल, मक्नातीसी, विद्युत ऊर्जा, ऊष्णता, प्रकाश-ऊर्जा आदि को भी अलग अलग मानकर इस संसार का कुछ ऐसा अनेकात्मक रूप प्रस्तुत किया जो विज्ञप्ति मात्रता से एकदम विरोध में लगता है।

परन्तु बीसवीं सदी के लगभग आरम्भ से ही जो कुछ वैज्ञानिक विकास हुआ है उससे स्थिति एकदम बदल गई है। अधिक विस्तार न करते हुए, यदि कुछ एक वैज्ञानिक चिंतन के विकास के आयामों का उल्लेख मात्र करना हो तो वे हैं:-

मैक्सवैल द्वारा सभी प्रकार की ऊर्जा को एक ही प्रकार का सिद्ध करना; डालटन द्वारा अनिरीक्षित किन्तु मान्य भूत द्रव्यों के आणविक स्वरूप के और आगे विभाजन की संभावना का उद्घोष किया जाना; सर जे. जे. थॉमसन द्वारा कैथोड किरणों के स्वरूप की जांच ले सभी आणविक द्रव्यों के मूल में स्थित इलैक्ट्रोन नामी विद्युतकण अथवा तरंग का उद्घाटित किया जाना; वैज्ञानिक चिन्तकों द्वारा यह स्वीकार किया जाना कि इलैक्ट्रोन जो कि विद्युत का नैगेटिव चार्ज है और जिसे सूक्ष्मातिसूक्ष्म कण अथवा तरंग दोनों ही रूपों में देखा अथवा परखा जा सकता है, परीक्षण में वही एक मात्र भूत द्रव्यों का विज्ञप्ति आधार है- उसके अतिरिक्त भी परुटो ननियुट्रोन आदि माने तो सही किन्तु उनकी सत्ता कल्पित मानी गई; आइनस्टाइन के सापेक्षता नियम ने ऐसा सिद्ध किया है कि काल एवं दिक् की अपेक्षा काल-दिक् को प्रवाह और उनमें स्थित वस्तुओं को वस्तुएं नहीं वरन् घटनाएं माना जाये; जगदीश चन्द्र वसु ने मानव एवं पशु पक्षी की भांति

ही वनस्पति (पेड़ पौधों) को भी सजीव एवं सचेतन सिद्ध किया, मनोविज्ञान को जहां एक ओर व्यवहारवाद द्वारा शरीरविज्ञान के अधिक निकट लाया गया वहां सिगमंड फ्रायड सरीखे विचारकों ने मन की गहराइयों का विस्तार अचेतन एवं अवचेतन मन की कल्पनाओं द्वारा किया।

स्वाभाविक ही है कि वैज्ञानिक चिन्तन पर विज्ञान के इन सभी विकास आयामों का प्रभाव पड़ता है। कुछ वैज्ञानिक तो जैसे यदि नाम गिनने हों तो सर आर्थर इडिंगटन एवं जैम्सजोनस तो अपने आपको विज्ञानवादी घोषित ही करने लगे हैं किन्तु यह बात तो अब निबीध रूप से कही जा सकती है कि आज का विज्ञान भौतिकवाद का पोषक न होकर विज्ञप्ति मात्राता की ओर ही बढ़ा है तथा विज्ञानवाद में प्रयुक्त एवं वैज्ञानिक चिन्तन के मूल में स्थित विज्ञान शब्द का यदि अर्थ नितान्त एक नहीं तो उनके भेद भी कोई मूलभूत नहीं।

* लेख तिब्बती उच्च शिक्षा संस्थान सारनाथ (वाराणसी) में हुई 'दार्शनिक चिन्तन के विकास में विज्ञानवाद का योगदान' विषय पर गोष्ठी में प्रस्तुत किया गया था।

48

संस्कृत में बौद्ध वाङ्मय

शान्तिभिक्षु शास्त्री

बौद्धों में संस्कृत का प्रवेश

परंपरा के अनुसार तथागत ने अपने प्रवचन अपने समय में सर्वसाधारण की बोल-चाल की भाषा में किये थे। वह भाषा आज पालि-भाषा कहलाती है तथा उसके वैयाकरणों ने उसे मागधी कहा है। पर बौद्ध धर्म के प्रसार के साथ उस स्थानीय मागधी से काम न चला। पहले मागधी अपना स्वरूप खो बैठी और वह एक प्रकार की खिचड़ी भाषा में स्थविरवादियों का त्रिपिटक और उसकी अर्थ कथाएं अर्थात् व्याख्याएं पाई जाती हैं तथा उनकी परंपरा श्रीलंका, बर्मा तथा स्याम में सुरक्षित हैं। दूसरी ओर मागधी ने अपना स्वरूप फिर खोना आरंभ किया पर एक नवीन ढंग से, उसने पदों की रचना बहुत-कुछ प्राकृत के ढंग की रखी पर पदों के अंग को जहाँ तक संभव था संस्कृत-सम कर दिया। यह भाषा आज बौद्ध संकर-संस्कृत भाषा (बुद्धिष्ट हाइब्रिड संस्कृत) कहलाती है। अमेरिका के स्वर्गीय प्रो. फ्रांकलिन् एड्जेर्टन महोदय ने इस भाषा का बड़े ही मनोयोग से अध्ययन किया था तथा इस भाषा का एक कोष तथा व्याकरण ग्रन्थ सम्पन्न किया था। ये दोनों ग्रंथ आज इस भाषा तथा इसके अन्तर्गत साहित्य के स्वाध्याय के महत्वपूर्ण साधन हैं। इस भाषा में निर्मित साहित्य के अनेक ग्रन्थ आज भी अपने मूल रूप में मिल गये हैं। (देखिये परिशिष्ट 1) ये सब ग्रन्थ आज परंपरा के अनुसार बुद्धवचन हैं। पर बौद्धों के बीच एक और परिवर्तन हुआ। उन्होंने बुद्धवचनों का मनन करके जिन काव्यों और शास्त्रों का निर्माण किया उनकी भाषा उन्होंने वैसी रखी जैसी कि ब्राह्मण शास्त्रकर्ता रखते थे। इस प्रयोजन के लिए उन्होंने पाणिनीय संप्रदाय के ग्रंथों का भी अध्ययन किया तथा भाषावृत्ति, रूपावतार, काशिका एवं पंजिका के रूप में शब्द शास्त्र के अध्ययन में सराहनीय योगदान दिया। अमरकोष के रूप में संस्कृत के अध्ययन की पद्धति को सरल बनाया। इस अमरकोष का पूर्व समुद्र से पश्चिम समुद्र तक की तथा मेरु से कन्याकुमारी तक की पंडित मंडली ने बड़ा स्वागत किया तथा पठन-पाठन में स्थान दिया। इस ग्रन्थ का यह अपूर्व सत्कार किसी-किसी को इसलिए सहन नहीं हुआ कि इसमें बुद्धवन्दना के साथ-साथ स्वर्गवर्ग के आरंभ में बुद्ध तथा शाक्यमुनि के पर्याय पढ़े गए हैं। वैयाकरण-सिद्धान्तकौमुदी के प्रवर्तक श्री भट्टोजिदीक्षित के विद्वान् पुत्र तथा अमरकोष की व्याख्या की महिमा से पांडित्यपदवी को प्राप्त श्री भानुजिदीक्षित ने अपनी असहिष्णुता प्रकट करते हुए लिखा है- 'वेदविरुद्धार्थानुष्ठातत्वाद् जिनशाक्यौ नरकवर्गे वक्तुमुचितौ' अर्थात् जिन और शाक्य का पाठ नरक वर्ग में करना चाहिए क्योंकि वे जिन बातों का आचरण करते थे वे वेदविरुद्ध थीं। इस निन्दा से ग्रन्थ के महत्व

एवं बुद्ध की महिमा पर कोई भी अन्यथा-प्रभाव पड़नेवाला नहीं रहा है। काव्यों के टीकाकारों ने तो नियम करके अमरकोष को ही सर्वदा उद्धृत किया है। उन्होंने दूसरे कोषों के उद्धरण तभी दिए हैं, जब उन्हें अपेक्षित सामग्री अमरकोष में नहीं मिल पाई है।

बौद्ध आचार्यों एवं विद्वानों द्वारा शुद्ध संस्कृत पर डाली गई अपनी छाप

बौद्धों में संस्कृत के प्रवेश हो जाने पर बुद्ध-वचन के रूप में प्रमाण माने जाने वाले ग्रन्थों में गाथाएं सामान्यतया संकर-संस्कृत में ही रहीं पर गद्य प्रायः शुद्ध संस्कृत में रहा। इसका अपवाद महावस्तु नामक ग्रन्थ है जिसमें गद्य भी संकर-संस्कृत में हैं। बौद्ध आगम का यह भाषा संबंधी रूप, जब बौद्ध आचार्यों और विद्वानों ने स्वयं काव्यशास्त्र के निर्माण का मनोयोग से प्रयत्न किया, तब बदल गया। गद्य तथा पद्य की भाषा शिष्ट-संमत हो गई और उस पर पाणिनीय संप्रदाय की छाप लग गई। फलस्वरूप बहुत से काव्य-शास्त्र के ग्रन्थों का प्रादुर्भाव हुआ (देखिए परिशिष्ट 2)।

इस शिष्ट-संमत भाषा में भी कितने ऐसे बौद्ध प्रयोग बच रहे जिनका श्रौत-स्मार्त परंपरा के विद्वानों में प्रचलन न था। यहां दो-चार शब्दों की बानगी देख लेनी होगी। बैठने, खड़े होने, चलने तथा सोने के लिए बौद्धों में प्रचलित शब्द ईर्यापथ है। यह शब्द बौद्धों के प्रभाव से साधारण लोगों में भी किसी समय प्रचलित हो गया था। इसीलिए अमरसिंह ने चर्या शब्द की व्याख्या में ईर्यापथ शब्द का प्रयोग करते हुए कहा है- चर्या त्वीर्यापथे स्थितिः अर्थात् ईर्यापथ में स्थिर रहना चर्या है। कुहना शब्द की व्याख्या में अमरसिंह ने फिर इसी शब्द का प्रयोग करते हुए कहा है- कुहना लोभान्मिथ्येर्यापथकल्पना अर्थात् लोभ से झूठ-मूठ के ईर्यापथ का करना कुहना है। पर ईर्यापथ का जो बौद्ध-संमत संकेतित अर्थ है वह चिरकाल तक श्रौत-स्मार्त विद्वानों की परंपरा में स्मृत न रहा अथवा दूसरे शब्द में यह कहिए की संकेतित अर्थ उन्हें सर्वथा भूल गया। विस्मरण के दिनों में ही एक टीकाकार ने अमरकोष के प्रथमोद्धृत वाक्य की व्याख्यायों की-ईर्यापथे योगमार्गे स्थितिः चर्या स्यात् (माहेश्वरीटीका) अर्थात् ईर्यापथ योगमार्ग है, उसमें स्थिर होना चर्या है। चलने-फिरने, उठने-बैठने, एवं सोने--लेटने के शिष्ट ढंग का वाचक शब्द जो ईर्यापथ कहलाता है, तथा जिसका संकेतित अर्थ बौद्ध शिष्ट मंडल में आज भी अभिज्ञात है वह अबौद्ध विद्वन्मंडली के लिए रहस्य की वस्तु रहा है, तभी उसकी व्याख्या योगमार्ग शब्द से की गई है।

ईर्यापथ शब्द जैसे शब्द बहुत हैं। उनका ज्ञान न तो पाणिनीय व्याकरण से संभव है और न उनका पता शुद्ध संस्कृत के प्रतिपादक अमरकोष जैसे कोषों से ही चल पाता है। अमरसिंह बौद्ध विद्वान् थे। उन्होंने जैसे बुद्ध के पर्याय संगृहीत कर लिए हैं तथा शाक्यमुनि की नाममाला को अपने कोष में स्थान दे दिया है उसी प्रकार कुछ अन्य दो चार सामान्य बौद्ध शब्दों को भी अंकित कर लिया। पर विशिष्ट बौद्ध शब्द बहुत हैं। उनमें अधिकांश महाव्युत्पत्ति नामक बौद्ध कोष में संगृहीत हैं। इन शब्दों की अपनी विचित्रता है तथा अपने संकेतित अर्थ हैं। यहां इनकी चर्चा छेड़ी नहीं जा सकती, पर बौद्ध संस्कृत भाषा में ऐसे शब्दों का महत्वपूर्ण

स्थान है। दिग्दर्शन के लिए एक शब्द पर यहां और निगाह डाल लेनी होगी। वह शब्द है चित्तप्रशठता। मुझे भय है कि श्रोता कहीं इस शब्द के भीतर किसी के चित्त की बहुत अधिक मात्रा में शठता न समझने लगें। त्रिंशिका विज्ञप्तिमात्रतासिद्धि के भाषा में आचार्य स्थिरमति ने इसका यों विवरण दिया है- अप्रयत्नेन समाहितचेतसो यथायोगं समस्यैव या प्रवृत्तिः सा चित्तप्रशठता अर्थात् किसी आलंबन में एकाग्र हुए एवं समता-भाव से ही युक्त चित्त का उचित-युक्ति-पूर्वक बिना यत्न के ही जो प्रवृत्त होते रहना है वह चित्तप्रशठता है। इस व्याख्या पर ध्यान जाते ही यह स्पष्ट हो जाता है कि चित्तप्रशठता शब्द के अन्तर्गत जो शठ शब्द है। वह अमरकोष में संकेतित निकृतस्त्वनृजुः शठः (निकृत, अनृजु तथा शठ पर्याय शब्द हैं।) सर्वथा नहीं है। निश्चय ही यह शठ कोई प्राकृत शब्द है, जिसके मूल को खोजना विद्वानों का कार्य है और स्थिरमति की व्याख्या इतना इंगित कर ही देती है कि वह शब्द शांति अथवा समता का वाचक होना चाहिए। मैं इस विषय में केवल इतना ही कहना चाहता हूँ कि संस्कृत भाषा में जो शमथ शब्द कदाचित् वही रूप बदल कर शठ न बन गया हो। पालि में यह शब्द समथ है। थकार प्राकृत में ठकार होते देखा जाता है। अतः किसी प्राकृत में समठ ध्वनि भी रही होगी। समठ का सँठ बनना उच्चारण के लाघव के कारण संभव है। अनुनासिक सँ अक्षर का निरनुनासिक स रह जाना बोलने वालों की असमर्थता के कारण संभव है। इस प्रकार प्राकृत शब्द चित्तपसठता बना होगा। उसी प्राकृत शब्द को संस्कृत के ध्वनिमय साँचे में ढाल कर शास्त्रकारों ने चित्तप्रशठता बना लिया होगा। जो भी हो, शाठ्यभाव से हीन बौद्ध शास्त्रचर्या के समय हमें चित्तप्रशठता शब्द का संकेतित अर्थ मन में रखना ही होगा।

बौद्ध शास्त्रों की भाषा के शुद्ध संस्कृत होते हुए भी उसमें आने वाले चित्तप्रशठता जैसे शब्द श्रौत-स्मार्त संप्रदाय के विद्वानों के कानों में पहले भी खटकते थे और आज भी शायद खटकने ही लगेंगे यदि वे बौद्ध शास्त्रों की आलोचना एवं विवेचना करेंगे। सब दर्शनों से अभिज्ञ वाचस्पति मिश्र ने बौद्ध संस्कृत भाषा के भीतर इस प्रकार के प्रयोगों को देखकर कहा था - ग्रन्थतस्तावत् पश्यना-तिष्ठना-मिद्ध-पोषधाद्यसाधुपदप्रयोगः (भामती, ब्रह्मसूत्र 2.2.32 पर) अर्थात् बौद्धों की ग्रन्थ (रचना) में असाधु (व्याकरणशास्त्रविरोधी) पदों का प्रयोग होता है, यथा पश्यना, तिष्ठना, मिद्ध, पोषध इत्यादि जो भी हो, यहाँ इस बात पर कोई संदेह नहीं है कि बौद्धों की शुद्ध संस्कृत भाषा के भीतर भी अनेक विलक्षण शब्द ऐसे प्रयुक्त होते हैं। जिनकी पाणिनीय व्याकरण से सिद्धि नहीं हो सकती। उनके लिए प्राकृत व्याकरण की शरण लेनी पड़ती है। इसके अतिरिक्त इस प्रकार के विलक्षण शब्दों का अपना पारिभाषिक अर्थ होता है जो उनके संस्कृत रूपो में संकेतित नहीं है। विपश्यना प्रज्ञोत्पादक तत्वज्ञान है, उसका अभिप्राय दर्शन शब्द से प्रकट नहीं होता है। पौषध विशेष-व्रत का वाचक शब्द है उसमें उपवसथ शब्द प्रसिद्ध नहीं है मिद्ध तंद्रालस्यवाचक शब्द है तथा तिष्ठना (विशेषण तिष्ठन्तिक) शरीर की जीवितावस्था में संकेतित शब्द है। इन दोनों शब्दों में धातुएं मिह् तथा एया हैं। मिद्ध के समान शुद्ध संस्कृत रूप, त-प्रत्ययान्त मीढ बनता है, पर वह मूत्रवाचक है तथा

अन-प्रत्ययान्त तिष्ठना जैसे स्थान शब्द बनता है, पर वह तिष्ठना का अभिप्राय प्रकट करने में असमर्थ है। यही कुछ कारण पूर्वयुग में अवश्य रहे होंगे जिनके कारण शास्त्रों में इन शब्दों को पड़ा रहने दिया गया था। अस्तु कहने का अभिप्राय यही है कि बौद्धों ने जब शुद्ध संस्कृत में भी लिखा तब भी उनकी संस्कृत में कुछ ऐसे विलक्षण शब्द बीच-बीच में आ ही गए हैं, जिनका पाणिनीय संप्रदाय से मेल नहीं बैठ पाता अध्येताओं तथा अनुशीलन-कर्ताओं को बौद्ध संस्कृत-भाषा की इस विशेषता को ऐतिहासिक दृष्टि से देख कर अपनी गंभीरता को बनाए रखना होगा।

बौद्ध संस्कृत वाङ्मय की भावधारा

बौद्ध संस्कृत वाङ्मय बहुत विशाल था उसके एक महत्वपूर्ण अंश का चीनी भाषा में प्रथम शताब्दी से दसवीं शताब्दी में अनुवाद हुआ था एवं भोट भाषा में सातवीं शताब्दी से बारहवीं शताब्दी के बीच बहुत से विश्वसनीय भाषान्तर किया गया था (देखिये परिशिष्ट 3) दसवीं शताब्दी के बाद यह वाङ्मय कोरिया तथा जापान में बौद्ध धर्म के प्रसार के साथ पहुँचा मध्य एशिया में इस वाङ्मय का प्रथम शताब्दी से पहले ही प्रवेश हो चुका था और फिर उसकी व्याप्ति बढ़ती ही गई थी। मंगोलिया में यह वाङ्मय भोट देश से गया तथा भोट त्रिपिटक के समान ही उसका त्रिपिटक है।

मूल संस्कृत में इस वाङ्मय का एक अंश नेपाल से इस युग में सुलभ हो सका है तथा यूरोपियन विद्वानों ने पूर्वी तुर्किस्तान से अनेक खंडित कृतियों का उद्धार किया है। कितने ही ग्रंथ गिलगिट से भी प्राप्त हुए हैं तथा अनेकों ग्रंथों का भोट एवं चीन भाषाओं से फिर उद्धार किया है। (देखिये परिशिष्ट 3) इस समय हमारे स्वाध्याय के आधारभूत ग्रंथ पचास से कुछ अधिक हैं (देखिए परिशिष्ट 1 तथा 2) इनकी सहायता से हम इस वाङ्मय की भावधारा जान सकते हैं।

बौद्ध वाङ्मय मात्र सब प्रकार की संकीर्णताओं से रहित है। इसमें कहीं भी जातिगत उच्च-नीच भाव को स्थान नहीं है। वर्णभेद या रंगभेद को इसमें कहीं प्रश्रय नहीं दिया गया है। इसमें समूचे विश्व को एक अखंड राष्ट्र बनाने की प्रेरणा है। आवाह एवं विवाह में यह परंपरागत रूढ़ियों का समर्थक नहीं है। सब प्रकार से शान्ति का यह समर्थक है। हिंसाभाव के उपशम का ही इसमें पूर्ण विधान पाया जाता है। यह वाङ्मय में मनुष्य को उसके क्षुद्र स्वार्थों से ऊपर उठाने के लिए निरन्तर उपदेश देता है। मनुष्य के भीतर जो कुछ हीन है, जो कुछ क्षुद्र है, जो कुछ नीच है उसको ही इस वाङ्मय में मार या शैतान कह कर फटकारा गया है तथा पूर्णतया मार को जीतने का आदर्श ही इस वाङ्मय का आदर्श है। मनुष्य अपनी सब प्रकार की कलुष-भावनाओं को धो डाले, वह एक अधूरा मनुष्य न रहे, वह एक परिपूर्ण मनुष्य बन जाए यही इस वाङ्मय की प्रेरणा है।

मनुष्य के भीतर छिपा हुआ मार आगम एवं काव्यशास्त्रों के बहाने कहीं कलुषता न फैलाने लगे, इसलिए इस वाङ्मय के अवगाहन करने के लिए इस बात की ओर संकेत है कि जो वाङ्मय अर्थवत्

हो अर्थात् प्रयोजन वाला हो, जिसमें धर्म-भावना के पद विद्यमान हों, जो तीनों धातुओं अर्थात् तीनों लोकों के मालिन्य को धो डालने वाला हो, जिसमें शांति की ही अनुशंसा दिखाई गई हो, वही वाङ्मय आर्ष वाङ्मय है, बुद्धवचन है। इससे जो विपरीत हो वह अनार्ष वाङ्मय है, वह बुद्धवचन नहीं है-

यदर्थवद्धर्मपदोपसंहितं त्रिधातुसंक्लेशनिबर्हणं वचः।

भवेच्च यच्छान्त्यनुशंसदर्शकं तदुक्तमार्षं विपरीतमन्यथा।।

(बोधिचर्यावतार-पञ्जिका, लुइस् दे ला वाले पुसां का संस्करण, पृ. 432)

इस प्रकार के लक्षण द्वारा बुद्धवचन को एक व्यापक रूप में देखने का यत्न किया गया है। जो बातें बुद्ध के शिष्यों तथा दूसरे साधु पुरुषों ने कहीं, या कह रहे हैं, या कहेंगे, उन सबको शब्दतः न सही पर अर्थतः बुद्धवचन ही माना जाएगा, यदि उनमें मानवों की कलुषता के प्रक्षालन की प्रेरणा है। इस दृष्टि से हम सब यदि ऐसी वाणी बोलें जो क्षुद्र स्वार्थो से ऊपर उठकर मानव-जाति के लिए उदात्तता एवं शांति का संदेश देने वाली हो तो यह कहना ही होगा कि वह हमारी जिह्वा से निकलती हुई भी वस्तुतः तथागत की ही वाणी है। इसी दृष्टि से आचार्य शांतिदेव ने अपनी वाणी को अर्थार्ष अर्थात् अर्थतः बुद्धवचन कहा था। कहते हैं कि ये आचार्य नालन्दा में एक कुटी बना कर रहते थे। अत्यन्त शांत होने के कारण इनका नाम शान्तिदेव था। अत्यन्त शांत एवं सरल होने के कारण छात्र इन्हें बिलकुल बुद्धू समझते थे। इन नटखट छात्रों ने एक दिन धर्मदेशनामंडप में इन्हें प्रवचन-पीठ पर बिठा दिया। उन्होंने सोचा था कि ये प्रवचन तो कर न पाएंगे फिर इन्हें खूब बनाया जाएगा। पर आसन पर बैठकर आचार्य शांतिदेव ने श्रोताओं से जिज्ञासा की -किम् आर्षं पठामि, अर्थार्षं वा, अर्थात् ऋषिवचन (बुद्धवचन पढ़ूँ अथवा अर्थतः ऋषिवचन पढ़ूँ)। यह सूनते ही सब लोग चकित हुए और बोले कि हम लोग आर्ष (बुद्धवचन) तो बहुत सुन चुके हैं, आप अर्थार्ष (अर्थातः बुद्धवचन) सुनाइए। इस पर इन्होंने अपने ग्रंथ बोधिचर्यावतार का पाठ किया। इस ग्रंथ ने श्रोताओं को बहुत प्रभावित किया और आज भी बौद्धधर्म के उदात्त रूप को समझने में यह ग्रंथ अद्वितीय साधन हैं।

बुद्धवचन की उदात्त भावना के कारण उसे एकान्त रूप में सुभाषित कहा गया है। महाराज अशोक ने इस बात को एक शिला पर यों खुदवा दिया है- भगवता बुधेन भासिते सवे से सुभासितेवा (भगवता बुद्धेन भाषितं सर्वं तत् सुभाषितमेव), अर्थात् भगवान बुद्ध का (जो भी) भाषित है वह संपूर्ण ही सुभाषित है। यह शिलालेख राजस्थान के जयपुर-मंडल के एक पहाड़ी प्रदेश के भाबरू स्थान में है। इस लेख का वक्तव्य ऐतिहासिक है और उसका अपना महत्व है पर बौद्धाचार्य केवल इतने से ही संतुष्ट न थे। उन्होंने बुद्धवचन को बहुत व्यापक रूप में देखने का यत्न किया था और घोषणा की थी कि ''यत् किंचित् सुभाषितं तत्सर्वं बुद्धभाषितम् (बोधिचर्यावतापंजिका, पुसां का संस्करण, पृ. 433), जो कुछ सुभाषित है वह सब बुद्धभाषित है।

सुभाषित की दृष्टि से, लोकशांति एवं लोकहित की दृष्टि से बौद्ध-वाङ्मय का स्वाध्याय आज होना चाहिए। ऐतिहासिक दृष्टि से इसका महत्व है ही। समूचे बौद्ध वाङ्मय के भीतर संस्कृत बौद्ध वाङ्मय की अपनी विशेषता है। उसमें बहुत कुछ ऐसे तत्व हैं जिनको हम केवल पालि के अध्ययन से नहीं जान सकते। भारत की उत्तरी सीमाओं को पार कर मध्य एशिया, चीन, कोरिया, जापान में जो बौद्ध वाङ्मय पहुंचा था, वह संस्कृत का बौद्ध वाङ्मय था। इस विशाल भू भाग में भारतीय संस्कृति बौद्ध धर्म एवं दर्शन के साथ बौद्ध संस्कृत वाङ्मय के द्वारा पहुंची थी और उस वाङ्मय के भाषान्तर आज भी वहाँ पाए जाते हैं। पालि वाङ्मय दार्शनिक दृष्टि से दरिद्र है। महायान की उदात्त धार्मिक धारा का पालि में पता ही नहीं है। जातकों में तो आख्यानों के बहाने उस बोधिसत्त्व-साधना की साहित्यिक झलक भर पाई जाती है। मंत्रयान एवं सहज-साधना का ज्ञान बिना संस्कृत बौद्ध वाङ्मय के नहीं हो सकता। ये सब महत्वपूर्ण कारण है जिनको दृष्टि में रखकर संस्कृत बौद्ध वाङ्मय पर शोध का कार्य होना चाहिए, जो ग्रंथ सामग्री सुलभ हो चुकी है, उसका मनन एवं चिंतन होना चाहिए।

बौद्ध संस्कृत वाङ्मय संबंधी शोध के प्रधान क्षेत्र

आज तक जो संस्कृत में बौद्ध वाङ्मय उपलब्ध हो चुका है, उसकी अब तक पूरी व्याख्या नहीं हो पाई है, व्याख्या के लिए कुछ श्रम करना होगा। जो ग्रन्थ अब तक उपलब्ध हुए हैं। उनके संपादकों ने जैसा हो सका है ग्रंथों को प्रसिद्ध कर दिया है। संपादक निश्चय ही व्याख्याकार नहीं हैं। पर संपादकों की असावधानी ग्रंथ का अभिप्राय समझने में बहुत सी बाधाएं खड़ी कर देती है। यहां उदाहरण के लिए डॉ. पी. एल. वैद्य के ललितविस्तर के पृष्ठ 116 पर आई गाथा के पाठ की ओर श्रोताओं का ध्यान आकृष्ट करना चाहता हूँ। गाथा यों है-

सुकुल सुगुणधर परि द्रुमि वसतो

क्षयगतु न च त्यजि कृतु स्मरि पुरिमम्,

मरुपति प्रमुदितु तव गुण स्मरतो

श्रियकरि द्रुमवरि यथरिव पुरिमा।

डॉ. एस. लेफमन् के संस्करण में पाठ कुछ भिन्न है। वहां पृष्ठ 167 पर यह गाथा आई है पर पहले पाद के आठ अक्षर वहां तीन पदों में विभक्त हैं। पहला पद है सकु, दूसरा पद है लसु, तथा तीसरा पद है गुणधर। वैद्य महोदय के पाठ में पहले पाद के आठ अक्षर केवल दो पदों में विभक्त हैं। पहला पद है सुकुल तथा दूसरा पद है सुगुणधर। पदों की भिन्नता के कारण किस पाठ के अनुसार गाथा की व्याख्या की जाए यह एक प्रश्न है।

वैद्य महोदय के पाठ के अनुसार गाथा का अर्थ यों होगा - अच्छे कुल के, अच्छे गुणवाले (तुम) पहले पेड़ पर रहते हुए क्षीण हो गए पर कृतज्ञता का स्मरण करते हुए (तुमने उस पेड़ को) नहीं छोड़ा, मरुपति (अर्थात् इन्द्र) तुम्हारे गुणों को स्मरण करते हुए बहुत प्रसन्न हुए। (और उस) श्रेष्ठ वृक्ष को पहले के समान ही श्रीयुक्त कर दिया। लेफमन् महोदय के अनुसार गाथा का अर्थ यों होगा - गुणवाले, अनलस शुक (तुम) पहले पेड़ पर रहते हुए क्षीण हो गए पर कृतज्ञता का स्मरण करते हुए (तुमने उस पेड़ को) नहीं छोड़ा। मरुपति (अर्थात् इन्द्र) तुम्हारे गुणों को स्मरण करते हुए बहुत प्रसन्न हुए (और उस) श्रेष्ठ वृक्ष को पहले के समान ही श्रीयुक्त कर दिया।

दोनों अनुवादों में सभी कुछ समान है। पर वैद्य के पाठ के अनुसार गाथा के प्रधान नायक शुक का कहीं पता नहीं है। मूल में सुकु-शब्द जो शुकः के लिए था, वह पद-विभाजन की असावधानी के कारण परवर्ती पद के लकार से मिलकर सुकुल बन गया। इस सुकुल में से मैं सुकु अर्थात् शुकः को कभी न पहचान पाता यदि लेफमन् महोदय के पाठ के कारण मुझे वैद्य महोदय के पाठ पर संदेह न हो गया होता। संदेह के कारण मुझे भोट-अनुवाद खोजना पड़ा और वहां मुझे शुक का प्रति शब्द नेचो मिल गया। यह निश्चय हो जाने पर कि यहां मूल पद सुकु वस्तुतः शुकः के लिए था, मैंने समान संदर्भ में खोज निकाले जो मुझे जातकपालि चूल्लसुक तथा महासुक्क जातक में मिले। इन दोनों जातकों में शुक तथा शक्र का संवाद हैं और शक्र द्वारा सूखे वृक्ष को हरा-भरा करने का उल्लेख हैं।

उपलब्ध बौद्ध संस्कृत वाङ्मय की व्याख्या करते समय व्याख्याकारों को दो प्रकार की और भी सावधानी बरतने की अपेक्षा है। पहली सावधानी प्रयोगों की सूक्ष्मता को समझने की है तथा दूसरी सावधानी बौद्ध परम्परा से सुपरिचित होने की है। यदि ये दो प्रकार की सावधानियां न बरती गई तो ग्रन्थ का पाठ ठीक होते हुए भी व्याख्याकार अपनी व्याख्या के द्वारा भ्रम ही फैलाएगा, वह अपनी व्याख्या से किसी प्रकार का ज्ञान की वृद्धि न कर सकेगा, इतना ही नहीं, यदि कहीं कोई भ्रान्त स्थल होगा तो वह उक्त दो सावधानियों के अभाव में उसका शोधन भी न कर सकेगा। इन तीनों बातों को मैं यहाँ उदाहरण द्वारा स्पष्ट करना अपना कर्तव्य समझता हूँ।

महाकवि अश्वघोष संस्कृत भाषा के प्रयोग में बहुत निपुण थे। उन्होंने एक श्लोक में अव्-धातु के लोट्लकार के मध्यमपुरुष एक वचन के अव पद का प्रयोग किया है। यह अव पद उस श्लोक में नौ बार प्रयुक्त हुआ है तथा प्रत्येक बार उसका अर्थ भिन्न-भिन्न है। धातु पाठ में अव्-धातु के उन्नीस अर्थ दिए हुए हैं। फिर भी मगध देश के एक संस्कृत पंडित सूर्यनारायण चौधरी ने अपने बुद्धचरित के अनुवाद में सब जगह अब पद का अर्थ रक्षा कीजिए करके अव्-धातु को एकमात्र रक्षार्थक मान लिया है (देखिये बुद्धचरित, हिन्दी अनुवाद, प्रथम संस्करण, संस्कृतभवन, पूर्णिया से प्रकाशित)। अव्-धातु का धातुपाठ में यों विवरण है- अव रक्षण-गति-कान्ति-प्रीति तृप्त्य्-अवगम-प्रवेश-श्रवण-स्वाम्यर्थ-याचन-क्रिया-इच्छा-दीप्त्य्-

अवाप्त्य्-आलिंगन-हिंसा-अदान-भाग-वृद्धिषु, अर्थात् अव-धातु रक्षण आदि (उन्नीस) अर्थों में प्रयुक्त होता है। अब बुद्धचरित के ग्यारहवें सर्ग के सप्ततितम श्लोक का श्रवण कीजिए, जिसमें अव्-धातु का नौ अर्थों में प्रयोग हुआ है। श्लोक में तथागत के द्वारा राजा बिम्बिसार को आशीर्वाद है। नौ वाक्यों वाला वह श्लोक यों है-

अवेन्द्रवद्, दिव्य शश्वदर्कवद्, गुणैरव, श्रेय इहाव, गामव,

अवायुर्, आर्यैरव सत्सुतान्, अव श्रियश्च, राजन्नव धर्ममात्मनः,

(1) अवेन्द्रवत्। इस वाक्य में अव्-धातु का प्रयोग तृप्त्यर्थ में हुआ है।
वाक्यार्थ है- इन्द्र की भांति तृप्ति रहो।

(2) दिव्य शश्वदर्कयत्। इस वाक्य में अव्-धातु का प्रयोग दीप्त्यर्थ में हुआ है। वाक्यार्थ है-आकाशस्थ सूर्य के समान सर्वदा प्रकाशमान रहो।

(3) गुणैरव। इस वाक्य में अव्-धातु का प्रयोग वृद्धयर्थ में हुआ है।
वाक्यार्थ है- गुणों से बढ़ते रहो।

(4) श्रेय इहाव। इस वाक्य में अव्-धातु का प्रयोग अवगम अर्थात् बोधन के अर्थ में हुआ है। वाक्यार्थ है- श्रेय अर्थात् कल्याण का अवबोधन करो।

(5) गामव इस वाक्य में अव्-धातु का प्रयोग स्वाम्यर्थ में हुआ है।
वाक्यार्थ है- पृथिवी के प्रभु बने रहो।

(6) अवायुः। इस वाक्य में अव्-धातु का प्रयोग अवाप्त्यर्थ में हुआ है।
वाक्यार्थ है- आयु-लाभ करो अर्थात् दीर्घजीवन प्राप्त करो।

(7) आर्यैरव सुत्सुतान्। इस वाक्य में अव्-धातु का प्रयोग रक्षणार्थ में हुआ है। वाक्यार्थ है - आर्यों के साथ सपूतों की रक्षा करो।

(8) अब श्रियश्च। इस वाक्य में अव्-धातु का प्रयोग आलिंगनार्थ में हुआ है। वाक्यार्थ है-श्रियों का आलंगिन करो।

(9) राजन्नव धर्ममात्मनः। इस वाक्य में अव्-धातु का प्रयोग क्रियार्थ में हुआ है वाक्यार्थ है- हे महाराज, अपने धर्म अर्थात् कर्तव्य कर्म को करो।

इस उदाहरण से स्पष्ट है कि व्याख्याकार यदि ग्रंथ के प्रयोगों की सूक्ष्मता को समझने में सावधानी नहीं बरतता तो वह निश्चय ही अपनी व्याख्या द्वारा यथार्थ एवं तथ्य प्रस्तुत नहीं कर सकता।

परंपरा की जानकारी के अभाव में भी बौद्ध संस्कृत वाङ्मय की व्याख्या केवल व्याकरण के ज्ञान के बल पर नहीं हो सकती। दर्शन पढ़ाते-पढ़ाते समय छात्रों को वैभाषिक पद का अर्थ यों समझाया जाता है- बाह्येषु गन्धादिष्वान्तरेषु रूपादिस्कन्धेषु सत्स्वपि तत्रानास्थामुत्पादयितुं सर्वं शून्यमिति प्राथमिकान् अचकथद् भगवान द्विवतीयांस्तु विज्ञानमात्र ग्रहाविष्टान् विज्ञानमेवैकं सदिति। तृतीयान् उभयं सत्य-मित्यास्थितान् विज्ञेयमनुमेयम् इति सेयं विरुद्धा भाषेति वर्ण्यन्तः (केचन बौद्धाः) वैभाषिकाख्यया ख्याताः (माधवाचार्य का सर्वदर्शनसंग्रहस्थ वाक्य) अर्थात् कितने ही बौद्ध वैभाषिक नाम से प्रसिद्ध हुए क्योंकि उनके अनुसार भगवान ने (विशेष अधिकारियों की दृष्टि से) विरुद्ध भाषा अर्थात् परस्पर विरुद्ध सिद्धांतों का उपदेश दिया है। प्रारंभिक शिष्यों को उन्होंने सर्व-शून्यता की शिक्षा इसलिए दी कि वे गन्ध आदि बाह्य तथा रूपादि अभ्यन्तर स्कन्धों के प्रति विरक्त हो सकें यद्यपि ये सब सत् हैं। दूसरों को उन्होंने एक मात्र विज्ञान ही सत् है। ऐसी शिक्षा दी क्योंकि उनकी विज्ञानमात्रता में बड़ा हठीला आग्रह था। (और इसके बिना उन्हें विराग-मार्ग पर लाना संभव न था)। तीसरे प्रकार के शिष्यों को उन्होंने यह शिक्षा दी कि विज्ञेय पदार्थ अनुमेय हैं, प्रत्यक्ष नहीं है। यह शिक्षा के लिए दी कि ये लोग दोनों ही भीतरी तथा बाहरी पदार्थों की सत्यता पर विश्वास करते थे। (इस विश्वास को डिगाने के लिए ऐसा करना आवश्यक था।)

वैभाषिक-पद की इस व्याख्या को सुनकर प्रत्येक बौद्ध परंपरा का जानकार रो देगा। इतना भयंकर अंधकार, इतना भयंकर अज्ञान, वह भी एक बड़े माने हुए विद्वान् के भीतर, बौद्ध-परंपरा के अभिज्ञ को पता है कि कनिष्क के काल में ज्ञान-प्रस्थानशास्त्र (शान्तिनिकेतन से अंशतः प्रकाशित) पर बौद्ध विद्वानों ने एक टीका लिखी थी, जिसका नाम विभाषा था। यह विभाषा अपने चीनी अनुवाद में आज भी सुरक्षित है। इस विभाषा के मानने वाले विद्वद्वृन्द एवं संप्रदाय का नाम वैभाभिक है।

परंपरा के न जानने के कारण, विरुद्धा भाषेति वर्णयन्तः इति वैभाषिकाः, अर्थात् विरुद्ध भाषा है (तथागत की) इस बात की वर्णन करने वाले बौद्ध वैभाषिक कहलाते हैं। यह माधवाचार्य ने कह डाला है, उन्हें यदि विभाषा टीका का कुछ भी पता होता तो वे ऐसा न लिखते। किंच इस प्रामादिक लेख के शोधन की ओर कोई भी संकेत करना असंभव हो जाता यदि फिर से बौद्ध परम्परा का ज्ञान इस युग में न हो गया होता।

संस्कृत बौद्ध वाङ्मय के कुछ अमर रत्न

बौद्ध संस्कृत वाङ्मय की व्याख्या सावधानी से हो सके तो इस विषय में शोध का क्षेत्र प्रशस्त हो सकता है। कुछ कार्य हुआ है। महाकवि अश्वघोष के बुद्धचरित और सौन्दरनन्द हिन्दी में अनूदित हो चुके हैं। महाकवि आर्यशूर की जातकमाला भी अनूदित होकर प्रचार पा चुकी है। इन तीनों कृतियों के लिए बिहार के पं. सूर्यनारायण चौधरी धन्यवादार्ह हैं। संस्कृत बौद्ध वाङ्मय के काव्य ग्रन्थ जो अब तक अनूदित नहीं हो पाए हैं। वे छोटे-छांटे स्तोत्र आदि हैं। काव्यमय शास्त्रग्रन्थ बोधिचर्यावतार बुद्धजयन्ती के अवसर पर लखनऊ के बुद्ध-विहार (रिसालदार-पार्क) से प्रकाशित होकर प्रचलित हो गया है। यह ग्रंथ शिक्षासमुच्चय

के साथ महायान विनय का परिपूर्ण ज्ञान कराने में समर्थ है तथा इसका नवम परिच्छेद बौद्ध दार्शनिक धारा का शून्यवाद का बहुत ही उत्तम स्वरूप प्रस्तुत करता है।

शुद्ध शास्त्रग्रन्थों पर काम बहुत कुछ करना अवशिष्ट है। आचार्य वसुबन्धु का अभिधर्मकोश एक आकार-ग्रन्थ है। यह जायसवाल इंस्टीट्यूट पटना से प्रकाशित तो हो गया है पर इस पर कार्य कुछ नहीं हुआ। इसके संपादक उड़ीसा के विद्वान् श्री प्रहलाद प्रधान ने इस पर भूमिका तक नहीं लिखीं है।[1] स्वर्गीय राहुल सांकृत्यायन के प्रयत्न से[2] कई तर्कशास्त्र के महत्वपूर्ण ग्रन्थ, जिनके रचयिता आचार्य धर्मकीर्ति रहे हैं, पटना से प्रकाश में आ गये है। पर इन पर कोई भी शोध कार्य नहीं हुआ है। इन ग्रन्थों के आधार पर अनेक शोध-प्रबन्ध लिखे जा सकते है। तथा उन पर विश्वविद्यालयों से डाक्टर पदवी का सम्मान प्राप्त किया जा सकता है। आचार्य धर्मकीर्ति के ग्रन्थों में प्रमाणवार्तिक विशाल आकर-ग्रन्थ है। ग्रन्थ कठिन है पर इसकी टीकाएं प्राप्त हो चुकी हैं और अब स्वाध्याय सम्भव है। अभिधर्मकोश तथा प्रमाणवार्तिक दोनों ही बहुत महत्वपूर्ण ग्रंथों में हैं। मैंने भोट विद्वानों से सुना है कि कोश तथा वार्तिक के अध्ययन में भोट विद्यार्थियों को कई वर्ष लगाने पड़ते हैं। इनके स्वाध्याय एवं प्रवचन का पूर्ण सामर्थ्य यदि कुछ युवा विद्वानों में हो सके तो अन्य बौद्ध शास्त्रों के अध्ययन में कठिनता नहीं होगी।

भारत में किसी समय बौद्धसिद्धांतों की जानकारी के लिए अभिधर्मकोश बहुत प्रचलित ग्रंथ था। महाकवि बाणभट्ट ने इसका उल्लेख करते हुए हर्षचरित में यो लिखा है- (श्रीहर्षः) शुकैरपि शाक्यशासनकुशलैः कोशं समुपदिशद्भिः उपास्यमानं सर्वशास्त्राक्षर- परमाणुभिरिव निर्मितं दिवाकरमित्रमद्राक्षीत् (हर्षचरित्, निर्णय सागर संस्करण 1946, पृ. 237) अर्थात् श्रीहर्ष ने दिवाकरमित्र को देखा, जान पड़ता था कि वे सब शास्त्राक्षरों के परमाणुओं से ही मानो बने हों, उनकी उपासना शुकगण भी करते थे, जो बुद्ध--सिद्धांत में निपुण थे और कोश का उपदेश देते थे। यहाँ कोश शब्द पर टिप्पणी करते हुए शंकरकवि ने लिखा है- कोशों बौद्ध सिद्धांतों वसुबन्धुकृतः, अर्थात् बौद्धसिद्धांत का प्रतिपादक वसुबन्धु द्वारा विरचित कोश (अभिधर्मकोश) है। यह कोश अभी-अभी सुलभ हो सका है तथा इसका स्वाध्याय तर्क को छोड़कर अन्य सभी बौद्ध तत्वों पर प्रकाश डालने वाला है। वार्तिक (प्रमाणवार्तिक) की उपलब्धि भी सर्वथा नई है। स्वाध्याय तथा प्रवचन के क्षेत्र में इनकी प्रतिष्ठा हुए बिना इनके सब तत्व प्रकाश में नहीं आएंगे। अपेक्षाकृत नवीन आचार्य शान्तरक्षित के तत्वसंग्रह के द्वारा सभी दार्शनिक सिद्धांतों का एक ओर बोध हो जाता है तथा दूसरी ओर बौद्ध समालोचनात्मक दृष्टिकोण भी प्रकट हो जाता है। यह ग्रन्थ एक प्रकार का तर्क-जाल है। इसी से मिलता-जुलता पुराने आचार्य नागार्जुन का माध्यमिक शास्त्र है, जिसमें शून्यवाद की स्थापना के निमित्त सभी अशून्यवादी पक्षों की बड़ी तटस्थता के साथ आलोचना की गई है। इन चार प्रधान-प्रधान शास्त्रग्रन्थों के साथ आचार्य मैत्रेयनाथ के अभिसमयालंकार को भी संयुक्त करना बहुत अपेक्षित है। बौद्ध संस्कृत वाङ्मय में प्रज्ञापारमिता नामक महायान सूत्र है। इन सूत्रों में बौद्ध साधना तथा दार्शनिक चिन्ताओं का जो स्वरूप है,

वही सुव्यवस्थित शास्त्र रूप में अभिसमयालंकार में है। यह अभिसमयालंकार ग्रन्थ सूत्रों के समान संक्षिप्त एवं क्लिष्ट है। बहुत श्रम तथा बहुत समय लगाने के बाद ही इस पर पूरा अधिकार हो पाता है। दार्शनिकता तथा साधना का यह उच्च कोटि का ग्रन्थ है। शून्यवाद का यह रत्न है। इन पाँच ग्रन्थों के सम्यक् स्वाध्याय के बिना बौद्ध तत्त्ववाद का सांगोपांग निरूपण होना संभव नहीं है। पर इन पांच ग्रन्थों के स्वाध्याय का वही अधिकारी हो सकता है, जिसने तथागत के जीवन के दिव्य एवं ऐतिहासिक स्वरूप को ललितविस्तर आदि ग्रन्थों की सहायता से ठीक-ठीक समझ लिया है, बौद्ध तत्त्व-वाद के प्रवेशक प्रकरणों का जिसने स्वाध्याय कर लिया है अर्थात् शालिस्तम्बसूत्र की सहायता से जिसने प्रतीत्यसमुत्पाद का मनन कर लिया है, पंचस्कंधप्रकरण की सहायता से जिसने एकात्मवाद, कारकात्मवाद एवं वेदकात्मवाद को धर्मविचय के द्वारा स्कंधात्मक रूप में देख लिया है, न्यायप्रवेश एवं वेदकात्मवाद को धर्मविचय के द्वारा स्कंधात्मक रूप में देख लिया है, न्यायप्रवेश एवं न्यायबिन्दु की सहायता से जिसने बौद्ध दर्शन के तार्किक आधार को जान लिया है, त्रिंशिका एवं विंशिका प्रकरणों की सहायता से जिसने विज्ञप्तिमात्रता के स्वरूप को समझ लिया है, तथा शून्यता एवं तथता के अर्थों को शास्त्रवचनों से जिसने ठीक-ठीक जान लिया है- कहने का अभिप्राय यह है कि बौद्ध धर्म के अभीष्ट ज्ञान के बिना आकर-शास्त्रों में प्रवेश करने का यत्न अत्यन्त बुद्धिपीडन के अतिरिक्त और कुछ नहीं है। पर जिसे बौद्ध धर्म का अभीष्ट ज्ञान है, उसे आकरग्रन्थों में सुगमता से प्रवेश प्राप्त हो सकता है तथा वह ज्यों-ज्यों उनका अध्ययन करेगा त्यों-त्यों वे उसके विनोद के साधन बन जाएंगे।

काव्य एवं शास्त्र ग्रन्थों का नाम मात्र से संकीर्तन करने में व्यस्त रहने के कारण आगम की ओर मैंने अब तक संकेत भी नहीं किया है। आगम ग्रन्थ अनेक हैं। उनमें नाना प्रकार के तत्ववाद, साधनाएं तथा दर्शनिक तत्व हैं। सबसे महत्वपूर्ण विषय उनमें बुद्ध का द्विविध स्वरूप है। उनमें एक ओर तथागत महामानव एवं महापुरुष दिखाई पड़ते हैं। वे इतिहास की एक विभूति जान पड़ते हैं। उनका लुम्बिनी में जन्म, कपिलवस्तु में पालन-पोषण एवं विवाह, महाभिनिष्क्रमण, दुष्कर तपश्चरण, बोधिलाभ, धर्मचक्रप्रवर्तन, संघप्रतिष्ठापन, शिक्षापदों का निर्माण, तत्वप्रवचन एवं अन्ततः महापरिनिर्वाण सभी कुछ ऐतिहासिक जान पड़ता ही नहीं, वस्तुतः है भी। हम सब जानते हैं कि तथागत का आयुःपरिमाण कुल अस्सी वर्ष का था पर सद्धर्मपुंडरीक में घोषणा है- चिराभिसंबुद्धोऽपरिमितायुष्प्रमाणस्तथागतः सदास्थितः अर्थात् तथागत चिरअभिसंबुद्ध हैं, अपरिमित आयु वाले हैं। नित्यस्थित है। यह आगम-घोषणा ऐतिहासिक नहीं है। पर बुद्ध के उपासक जो ध्यान के बल से सब ओर तथागत का दर्शन करते रहते हैं। उन्हें इस ऐतिहासिक विरोध से सरोकार ही क्या ? उनके लिए बुद्ध केवल भौतिक काय के नहीं है, जो उत्पन्न होकर चले गए और अब फिर प्राप्त न हो सकेंगे। बौद्ध उपासकों के अनुसार तथागत का स्वाभाविक काय परिशुद्ध धर्मों का प्रकृतिरूप है, परिशुद्ध धर्म जिनकी हम मन से कल्पना नहीं कर पाते, उनका पूर्णरूप तथागत का धर्मकाय है। तथागत

के विषय में उनके रूप-रंग की, उनके शारीरिक लक्षणों एवं अनुव्यंजनों की कल्पना से ओत-प्रोत जो काय है, वह तथागत का संभोगकाय है। जो कर्म धर्मकाय का है, वही संभोगकाय का है पर धर्मकाय अरूपी है, संभोगकाय रूपवान् है। धर्मकाय अपुरुषविध है। संभोगकाय पुरुषविध है। धर्मकाय निराकार है, संभोगकाय साकार है। धर्मकाय अव्यक्त है। संभोगकाय व्यक्त है। इस व्यक्त संभोगकाय का दर्शन हम जिन शाक्यमुनि आदि बुद्धों में करते हैं, वह उपास्य बुद्ध नहीं। उपास्य बुद्ध चतुष्कायात्मक हैं पर ऐतिहासिक बुद्ध का काय केवल एक है और वह भी पार्थिव। इस प्रकार के नाना रहस्यों की सामग्री आगम ग्रन्थों में है। शास्त्रों में वही से सब कुछ लेकर युक्तिपूर्वक निरूपण किया गया है। पर आगम वचनों में जो-जो रत्न भरे पड़े हैं, उनके खोजने में श्रम करना होगा।

बुद्ध की उपासना एक निर्मल कर्म मार्ग है। शील के द्वारा, समाधि के द्वारा तथा प्रज्ञा के द्वारा इस मार्ग पर चलना होता है। साधकों में जो केवल अपनी मुक्ति के अभिलाषी हैं वे निर्जनता का आश्रय ले लेते हैं। अपने क्लेशों का शोधन करके वे अर्हत् हो जाते हैं। जिन्हें केवल अपनी ही मुक्ति में स्पृहा नहीं है वे भी इसी मार्ग पर चलते हैं पर निर्जनता का आश्रय नहीं लेते। लोक में रहकर परोपकार एवं साधना में लगे रहते हैं। स्वाध्याय एवं प्रवचन के द्वारा धर्म की निर्मल ज्योति को जागते रहते हैं। ये सब साधक बोधिसत्व एवं बोधिसत्वकल्प हैं। इन्हीं के उत्साह से पुराने युग में बुद्ध का धर्म आधी दुनिया में फैल गया था।

साधना के बहाने जो मंत्र-मंत्र साधनाएं बौद्ध धर्म में आईं, वे बाह्य वस्तु थीं। उन्होंने अपने को बौद्ध रंग में रंगने का यत्न तो बहुत किया पर वे पूर्णतया बौद्ध धर्म की अन्तरंग वस्तु नहीं बन पाईं। आज हिन्दू तंत्र एवं बौद्ध तंत्र दोनों ही अत्यन्त मूर्छितावस्था में हैं। इनका जागरण शायद ही हो सके पर कुछ स्वाध्याय एवं शोध कार्य हो सकता है। सहजसाधना की भी मूर्छितावस्था तन्त्र-साधना जैसी है पर इस शताब्दी में सहजयानी सिद्धों की वाणियों की भाषा की दृष्टि से कुछ अध्ययन हुआ है। अपने संपादित बौद्धचर्यागीतिकोष में मैंने इस अध्ययन को भाषा की ओर से मोड़कर उसके रहस्यवाद के स्वाध्याय की ओर प्रवृत्त किया है पर उन वाणियों की भाषा की ओर ही विद्वानों का ममत्व अधिक है। इन वाणियों की संस्कृत टीकाओं तथा सदृश शास्त्रों की सहायता से बहुत अधिक बौद्ध रहस्यवादी प्रवृत्तियों पर प्रकाश पड़ सकता है।

उपसंहार

संस्कृत में बौद्ध वाङ्मय की वर्तमान उपलब्धि लगभग एक शती के भीतर किए गए प्राच्य एवं पाश्चात्य विद्वानों के श्रम का फल है। यहाँ मैंने स्वाध्याय एवं शोध की दिशा में जो संकेत किए हैं, उनका महत्व सार्वदेशिक है, पर इस (इस प्रान्त के लेखक का तात्पर्य हिमाचल प्रदेश से है।) प्रान्त के लिए उनका महत्त्व बहुत अधिक हैं। इस प्रान्त के एक अंचल में बौद्ध जनता रह रही है। वह अब भारतीय नेताओं के यत्न से जग उठी है। उनके द्वारा आचरित धर्म का मूल संस्कृत में है, उनके पाठ में आए मंत्र

संस्कृत में हैं। पर उनमें संस्कृतज्ञ नहीं से है। आशा है उनमें इस वाङ्मय के प्रति उत्कंठा जगेगी और वे सब लोग जिनमें इस वाङ्मय के समझने एवं समझाने में सामर्थ्य है, आगे आएंगे, सरकार का तथा समर्थ लोगों का भी यहां बड़ा उत्तरदायित्व है क्योंकि इस प्रकार के कार्य अर्थसापेक्ष होते हैं-सर्वारंभास्तंडुलप्रस्थमूलाः।

1. बौद्ध संकरसंस्कृत भाषा के ग्रन्थ

(इनमें जो ग्रन्थ 2500वीं बुद्धजयन्ती के उपलक्ष्य में मिथिलाविद्यापीठ, दरभंगा से प्रकाशित हुए हैं, उनके आगे कोष्ठक में 'मि' संकेत कर दिया गया है। अन्य संकेतों के लिए देखिये परिशिष्ट 2)।

(क) सर्वास्तिवाद त्रिपिटक के उपलब्ध अंश : विनयपिटक की खंडित सामग्री-1 मूलसर्वास्तिवादविनय (गिलगिट मैन्युस्क्रिप्ट, काश्मीर से प्राप्त)। 2. मूलसर्वास्तिवाद प्रातिमोक्षसूत्र। 3. कर्मवाचना। 4. (अ) सर्वास्तिवादभिक्षुप्रातिमोक्षविनयविभंग (इ) कर्मविभंग कर्मविभंगोपदेश (उ) सूत्रपिटक की खंडित सामग्री। 5. महापरिनिर्वाण सूत्र 6. चतुष्परिषत्सूत्र। 7. महावदान सूत्र। 8. दशोत्तरसूत्र, अभिधर्म पिटक की खंडित सामग्री-अभिधर्म कोश की व्याख्या स्फुटार्था में अभिधर्म के साथ प्रकरणों के उद्धरण पाए जाते हैं। उनके नाम ये हैं- 1 ज्ञान प्रस्थानशास्त्र, 2. संगीतिपर्यायपादशास्त्र, 3. प्रकरणपादशास्त्र, 4. विज्ञानकायपादशास्त्र, 5. धातुकायपादशास्त्र, 6. धर्मस्कन्धशास्त्र, 7. प्रज्ञप्तिशास्त्र, ये सातों शास्त्र-ग्रन्थ हैं, साक्षाद् बुद्धवचन नहीं।

(ख) महासांघिक त्रिपिटक के उपलब्ध ग्रंथ : 9 प्रातिमोक्ष सूत्र, 10 महावस्तु (मि)।

(ग) अन्य हीनयान-ग्रन्थः 11 अवदानशतक (मि)। 12 दिव्यावदान (मि)।

(घ) महायान के नौ आकर ग्रन्थ : 13-21 अष्टसहस्रिका प्रज्ञापारमिता, सद्धर्मपुंडरीक, ललितविस्तर, लंकावतार, (सुवर्णप्रभास), गंडव्यूह, तथागतगुह्यक, समाधिराज, दशभूमिकसूत्र। ये नौ ग्रन्थ नेपाल के बौद्धों में अत्यन्त प्रसिद्ध हैं। इनमें सात 2500 वीं बुद्धजयन्ती के उपलक्ष में मिथिलाविद्यापीठ दरभंगा से प्रकाशित हो चुके हैं और सुलभ हैं। इन आकर-ग्रन्थों को छोड़कर कितने ही छोटे-छोटे सूत्र बहुत प्रचलित रहे हैं। उनमें वज्रच्छेदिका प्रज्ञापारमिता (मि), राष्ट्रपालपरिपृच्छा (मि), सुखावतीव्यूह (मि) और शालिस्तंबसूत्र (मि) प्रधान हैं।

(ङ) तन्त्र तथा सहजसाधना के कुछ ग्रंथ : 22 मंजुश्रीमूलकल्प (गणपतिशास्त्री द्वारा केरल से 1920, 1922 में दो जिल्दों में प्रकाशित)। 23 गुह्यसमाज (गा), 24 साधनमाला (गा)। उक्त सभी चौबीस ग्रन्थ आर्षग्रन्थ अथवा बुद्ध-वचन माने जाते हैं। 25 सिद्धवचनों की संस्कृत टीकाएं। मूल सिद्धवचन अपभ्रंश भाषा में है। बंगाली विद्वान् उस भाषा को पुरानी बांगला, उत्कल देश के विद्वान् उसे पुरानी उड़िया तथा विशाल हिन्दी भाषा-मंडल के विद्वान् उसे पुरानी हिन्दी कहते हैं। इस भाषा में सिद्धाचार्यों ने गीतियां तथा दोहे लिखे हैं। चर्यागीतिकोश तथा दोहाकोश के नाम से ये ग्रंथ प्रसिद्ध हो चुके हैं। इन आचार्यों तथा इनका अनुसरण करने वाले विद्वानों से संकर-संस्कृत भाषा का अनुगमन किया तथा शुद्ध संस्कृत की जान-बूझ कर उपेक्षा

की है। द्रष्टव्य चर्यागीतिकोष, शांतिनिकेतन 1956 (भूमिका पृष्ठ XXXXII)।

2. बौद्धाचार्यों द्वारा लिखित शुद्ध संस्कृत भाषा के ग्रंथ

(बि=बिहार-उड़ीसा अथवा बिहार रिसर्च सोसाइटी पटना की पत्रिका में प्रकाशित। शा=विश्वभारती शान्तिनिकेतन से प्रकाशित। गा=गायकवाड़ ओरियंटलसीरिज, बड़ोदा से प्रकाशित। जा=जायसवाल इंस्टीट्यूट, पटना से प्रकाशित)

बुद्धजीवनपरक काव्य ग्रन्थ - 1 बुद्धचरित, महाकवि-अश्वघोष-विरचित। 2. पद्यचूड़ामणि, बुद्धघोषाचार्य-विरचित। श्रावकयानपरक काव्य ग्रन्थ- 3. सौन्दरनन्द, महा-कवि-अश्वघोष-विरचित। महायानपरक काव्यमय ग्रन्थ - 4 बोधिचर्यावतार, आचार्य शान्तिदेव-विरचित (मि)। बोधिसत्वजातकपरक गद्य-पद्यमय काव्य ग्रन्थ - 5 जातकमाला, महाकवि-आर्यशूर-विरचित (मि)। स्तोत्रमय काव्य ग्रन्थ-6 चतु:स्तव, आचार्य नागार्जुन-विरचित। 7 अध्यर्धशतक, आचार्य मातृचेट-विरचित (बि)। वैभाषिकदर्शनपरक शास्त्र-ग्रन्थ- 8 अभिधर्मकोश, आचार्य वसुबन्धु-विरचित (जा)। 9 अभिधर्मामृत, आचार्य-घोषक-विरचित (शा)। सौत्रान्तिकदर्शनपरक शास्त्र-ग्रन्थ 10 सत्यसिद्धिशास्त्र चीनी भाषा में उपलब्ध ग्रन्थ का शांतिनिकेतन के अय्यास्वामी शास्त्री ने संस्कृत भाषा में उल्था किया है। (शीघ्र ही प्रकाशित होगा)। योगाचारविज्ञानवादिदर्शनपरक शास्त्रग्रन्थ - 11 पंचस्कन्धप्रकरण, आचार्य-वसुबन्धु-विरचित (श्रीलंका से मुद्रित एवं प्रकाशित) 12 त्रिंशिका विज्ञप्तिमात्रतासिद्धि, आचार्य-वसुबन्धु-विरचित। 13 विंशिका विज्ञप्ति-मात्रतासिद्धि-आचार्य-वसुबन्धु- विरचित। 14 अभिधर्मसमुच्चय, आचार्य-असंग-विरचित (शा)। 15 सूत्रालंकार, आचार्य-असंग विरचित। योगाचार तथा माध्यमिक दोनों संप्रदायों का एक प्रियग्रन्थ- 16 अभिसमयालंकार, आचार्य-मैत्रेयनाथ-विरचित, आलोक टीका सहित (गा, मि)। माध्यमिकशून्यवादिदर्शनपरक शास्त्र-ग्रन्थ-17 मध्यमककारिका, आचार्य-नागार्जुन-विरचित (मि)। 18 विग्रहव्यावर्तिनी, आचार्य-नागार्जुन विरचित (बि.) तर्कपरक शास्त्र-ग्रन्थ 19 न्यायप्रवेश (ग)। 20 न्यायबिन्दु, आचार्य-धर्मकीर्ति-विरचित (रायल एशियाटिक सोसाइटी कलकत्ता से प्रकाशित)।21 वादन्याय, आचार्य-धर्मकीर्ति-विरचित (बि)। 22 प्रमाणवार्तिक, आचार्य-धर्मकीति-विरचित (बि)। 23 तत्वसंग्रह, आचार्य-शान्तरक्षित-विरचित (गा)। विनयाचारपरक शास्त्र-ग्रन्थ- 24 विनयसूत्र (यह ग्रन्थ भारतीय विद्याभवन, बंबई से शीघ्र प्रकाशित होने वाला है)। 25 शिक्षासमुच्चय, आचार्य शान्तिदेवविरचित (मि)।

3. संस्कृत बौद्ध वाङ्मय सम्बन्धी सूचनाएं

1. प्रो. माउरिस विन्टरनित्स के लिखे भारतीय वाङ्मय के इतिहास के द्वितीय खंड में इस वाङ्मय संबंधी अनेक सूचनाएं दी हैं। उनका वह ग्रन्थ (ए हिस्ट्री ऑफ इंडियन् लिटरेचर) 1933 में कलकत्ता विश्वविद्यालय से प्रकाशित हुआ था। तब से चालीस वर्ष और बीत चुके हैं। बहुत सी नई सामग्री इस क्षेत्र में आ गई हैं। कुछ की सूचना मैंने परिशिष्ट 1 और 2 में दी है।

2. आर्य-शालिस्तम्बसूत्र अडयार लाइब्रेरी 1950 में शांतिनिकेतन के अय्यास्वामी शास्त्री ने एक

परिशिष्ट में बौद्ध संस्कृत वाङ्मय संबंधी कितनी सूचनाओं को एक स्थान में एकत्रित कर दिया है।

3. बौद्ध संस्कृत वाङ्मय का जो भाषान्तरण चीनभाषा तथा भोटभाषा में हुए हैं, उनकी प्रायः पूर्ण जानकारी दो सूची-कोषों से हो जाती है। इनमें एक सूची-कोष बुनिउ नान्‌जिओ का है (ए कैटालाग् ऑफ चाइनीज ट्रांसलेशन ऑफ बुद्धिष्ट त्रिपिटक, ओक्सफोर्ड, 1833)। दूसरा कितने ही लोगों ने मिलकर बनाया है पर उनमें प्रमुख हाकुजुउइ हैं (ए कंप्लीट कैटालोग् ऑफ दि टिबेटन बुद्धिष्ट कैनन्स, टोहोकु इम्पीरियल यूनिवर्सिटी, जापान, 1394), इन सूची-कोषों से पता चलता है कि भाषान्तरित ग्रंथों के मूल संस्कृत ग्रन्थ कई सौ थे।

टिप्पणियां

1. प्रोफेसर प्रहलाद प्रधान द्वारा संपादित अभिधर्मकोष के द्वितीय संस्करण में भूमिका दी गई है।
2. महापंडित राहुल सांकृत्यायन तिब्बत से ही बहुत बड़ी संख्या में पांडुलिपियां लाये थे। जायसवाल इंस्टीट्यूट में संगृहीत इन पांडुलिपियों को कई विद्वानों ने संपादित की है, इन पंक्तियों के लेखक डॉ. संघसेन सिंह ने श्रीघनाचारसंग्रह टीका को संपादित किया है।